CHOICES

CREATING HAPPINESS
BY BREAKING FREE
FROM YOUR PAST

ANDREA J. MOSES, M.S.W.

CHOICES – CREATING HAPPINESS BY BREAKING FREE
FROM YOUR PAST

Canadian Cataloguing In Publication Data

Moses, Andrea J.
Choices: creating happiness by breaking free from your past

Includes bibliographical references.
ISBN 0-9694227-2-5

1. Self-actualization (Psychology). 2. Happiness.
I. Title

BF637.S4M67 1994 158.1 C94-932318-7

First Printing

Note To Readers

This publication is designed to provide powerful and impactful
information concerning how personal happiness can be created.
This publication is not prescribing psychological treatment.
Please be advised that you must use your own judgement when
using the information and the exercises described herein. The
author and the publisher assume no responsibility for your
actions.

To Thine Own Self Be True,
And It Must Follow,
As The Night The Day,
Thou Canst Not Then Be False
To Any Man.

— **William Shakespeare**

CONTENTS

INTRODUCTION

The gift of life comes with free will. You are free to choose how you want to live your life, how you want to spend your time, with whom you want to spend it, the activities you engage in. Sounds like a good deal, doesn't it? Then why don't you feel happy and joyful most of the time? Why does free will seem like such an illusion? Why, even though you have choices on paper, in reality, there never really seems to be very many options to choose from?

The answer lies in the nature of our emotional needs—the unresolved needs that we carry within our selves from the past. Our past will often hold us at gunpoint, and although we can freely choose to have a few drinks at a party in order to have some fun, in reality, we may be trying desperately to forget the lonely feelings that lurk inside. We may think we enjoy the power and excitement of a demanding and prosperous career, but in reality, we find our selves living on a treadmill of exhaustion whereby getting off seems more life-threatening than staying on. We may think we have found the perfect mate who is giving us the love we had never received as a child, but in reality, we are making daily compromises which are undermining our internal base of security.

Yes, as adults, we all have "choices" and free will, but because of the damage caused by our parents' parenting of us, we are not free at all. Most of us will end up making preprogrammed choices in order to fill the glaring holes in our lives caused by inadequate parenting. On the outside, it may appear that we are living a great life, exciting, and full of options, but in reality, our choices become one dimensional, and our emotions end up controlling us.

In *Choices – Creating Happpiness By Breaking Free From Your Past*, the reality of how you ended up in your current box will be explained to you. Your past has more power over you than you may ever have dreamed possible. Although your past may seem long gone and forgotten, it's with you every breathing moment of your life, controlling your choices and your actions. The truth is, as an adult, you are probably living your life on automatic pilot: the decisions and choices that you're making are the result of the emotional needs that were not met for you by your parents. You are likely spending your life trying to make up for what you didn't receive, and in so doing, you become driven to repeat certain patterns, or make choices which are destructive to your ultimate wellbeing and long-term happiness.

What is this compulsion about? It's about feeling driven to find an instant way to feel complete, loveable, loved and valued. If you were walking down the street one night alone, and a gang of punks brandishing knives started to run after you, chances are you would run for safety. In a self-preservation mode, you would likely not turn around and engage the gang leader in conversation in order to uncover why the gang was feeling so hostile. You would likely not set up a dialogue to convince the gang members that harming you was not going to solve any of their problems. No, you would run for your life. The immediate and best solution would be to ensure your survival.

Well, all of us are running from something from the past: deep grief at not having been loved or having been emotionally abandoned as a child, uncontrollable rage at having been verbally or physically abused, a deep fear that we were unsafe or that we couldn't survive without the love we were receiving, a strong feeling of shame at how we had to compromise our integrity in order to survive.

What we are running from are the emotions we can't face, what really happened to us as dependent children, and the pain that these emotions bring up for us. In the same way that we would run from the gang with the knives, so too we run from the emotional pain we find too unbearable to look at.

On a practical level, when we run away from a situation or a feeling, we must run toward another. Emotionally, what we run toward is a feeling of safety, a feeling of wholeness, completeness, security and internal peace—in a nutshell, feeling good. And so our internal compulsion to make preprogrammed choices will be based on how best and how quickly we believe we can get to feeling good.

As an adult, you are free to choose many ways to feel good. You can choose a substance (alcohol, drugs, cigarettes, coffee, food) which can numb out and override your body's ability to let you know what you are really feeling. You can choose an activity (career-related work, sex, exercise, shopping, travelling or gambling) which can temporarily make you feel powerful and important, and help you forget your own rage, self-hatred, feelings of worthlessness, and nagging self-doubts. You can choose to connect up with a romantic partner, and hope that contact with this person will help you feel secure and take away your feelings of loneliness. You can try freeing your self from your own internal rage by blaming or criticizing your lover, spouse, children, employees or co-workers.

Now, while the choices you are making appear as though you are exercising your free will, in fact, you are not. You are totally controlled by them. For the only way that you can push down the pain, and feel complete and whole is to reach for your instant solution. In this way, if you are work-dependent, you are not free to create a balanced life, because time away from your work would cause you to lose out on the recognition and the challenge, as well as the time demands that would make self-reflection possible. If you are dependent on your spouse or lover for your emotional security, you aren't able to feel secure and strong on your own, because no matter how much you accomplish in your own right, you'll never lose those worthless feelings that are lurking inside of you. If you're dependent on alcohol, coffee, drugs, cigarettes, or food, you can't stay away from your substance for too long, because your unconscious emotional pain will start surfacing, along with the accompanying feelings of discomfort and uneasiness. If you are the type of person who needs to blame or criticize other people in order to feel that you're okay, you won't be able to stop this pattern, because if your anger isn't transferred out, you'll start feeling uneasy and uncomfortable.

And so, while on the surface it may appear that you do have choices, in reality, you will tend to operate on automatic pilot with your choices being preprogrammed for you. You cannot stop your compulsion to run from your emotional pain and to run toward an instant way to feel good, in the same way that a dog cannot stop salivating when he sees a nice juicy steak. Once the pattern of reaching for an instant solution to feel better has been programmed into your brain through repetition and reinforcement, you will become a slave to your program. Goodbye free will. Goodbye choices.

The purpose of *Choices – Creating Happiness By Breaking Free From Your Past* is to give you choices, to enable you to understand how the unreleased emotions from your past have ended up controlling you, and what you can do to create a very happy life.

What you will discover in *Choices* is that you are in fact creating your own reality. Although, right at this moment, it may seem impossible to you that you are creating a life of sadness, loneliness, illness, poverty, powerlessness, conflict, you are in fact doing so—unconsciously. None of you would consciously choose unhappiness, but unconsciously your actions, beliefs, perceptions and feelings are causing you to create an unhappy life. None of you would consciously choose to struggle, but unconsciously your actions, beliefs, perceptions and feelings are causing you to create a life of struggle.

In that you are unconsciously (beyond your awareness) creating the circumstances in your life that currently exist, you have the option to become conscious of what you are doing, why you are doing it, and what you can do to create happiness.

Choices is divided into five sections. In Section I, Revisiting Your Past With 20/20 Vision, you will become consciously aware of why you are feeling so much emotional pain, and why you often feel so incomplete, so unloved, so unappreciated, so ashamed of your self, so terrified for your survival, so angry at the slightest provocation. In Section II, How Your Past Will Come Back To Haunt You, you will become consciously aware of how you have developed your emotional patterns and why making changes is so difficult. In Section III, You Can Run, But You Just Can't Hide, you will become consciously aware of how your past is repeating itself in your present life, and what you need to face in order to free your self forever. In Section IV, Breaking Free From Your Past, you will become consciously aware of what actions you can take to make real changes in your life—how to free your self from your enslavement to past patterns. It will involve some practical work which will allow you to take the bandaid off your wounds, clean them up, and allow them to heal. In Section V, Creating Happiness, you will discover how you can start exercising your free will, and how you can make the choices that will allow you to create a very happy life.

Choices – Creating Happiness By Breaking Free From Your Past is all about freeing you up to take control of your own life, to make your life work for you. *Choices* will offer you the opportunity to create the life you really want—a life full of love, people, opportunity, prosperity, fun, ease and happiness. In *Choices*, you will become consciously aware of the deficits from your past which are interfering with your present happiness, and what you can do to free your self to create the happiness you desire. You do have choices. Choose happiness!

I

REVISITING YOUR PAST
WITH 20/20 VISION

1 | A CONFLICT OF INTERESTS

As an infant, you were born totally helpless. You needed external care for a great many years, and without it, you would not have physically survived. Aside from your requirements for food, shelter, clothing, and physical protection, you also had important emotional needs: the need for love and affection, physical stroking, validation, recognition and the like. It's through the meeting of your physical and emotional needs that you were able to both stay alive and develop feelings of self-worth.

Because you were totally dependent on your parents for your survival, your parents would have appeared as god-like beings, omnipotent in nature. In perceiving that your parents were all-powerful, you would naturally have assumed that the manner in which they were treating you was based on a true assessment of your worth, rather than on the type of people your parents actually were. This means that if you were neglected, abused, overcontrolled, exposed to harsh words, harsh actions, and/or disinterest, you would have experienced this unkind treatment as a negative judgement about your adequacy and worth as a human being.

What you most likely didn't know at the time, and still may not know, is that how your parents treated you had <u>nothing</u> to do with your own worth; it had <u>everything</u> to do with their level of self-worth and their ability to give you love. However, because a gap existed between your needs, and your parents' ability to meet your needs, you may have falsely concluded that you weren't worth loving, and that you were inadequate in some way.

If anyone was inadequate, it was your parents who were inadequate in their job of parenting. Tragically, if your parents were inadequate in their role as parents, it was because as people, they were emotionally empty themselves, having experienced deficits in the fulfilment of their basic needs from their parents. The fact of the matter was, a conflict of interests existed between your extensive needs, as a totally dependent child, and your parents' ability to meet your needs. Because the parenting that you were exposed to will have had such a vital impact on your own feelings of self-worth, it's essential to understand this conflict of interests in greater depth.

THE NATURE OF YOUR NEEDS

LOVE AND PHYSICAL AFFECTION

You wanted to be loved. You wanted to feel that you were really cared about. You wanted physical proof of this caring, and you interpreted touch and hugging as indications of the affection you desired. You wanted to feel that you were very important to your parents—that they would be there for you, and that they would do anything for you.

As an infant, you were born egocentric. The world revolved around you. Your desire to fill your narcissistic needs was far from being indulgent. It was necessary for your survival. Being total dependent on outside caretakers to literally survive, you had to have a mechanism which would be on the lookout for your wellbeing. And so your egocentricity and narcissism (the desire to have all of your needs met as you felt them) were the tools you were born with to protect your interests, and thus your physical survival.

The need for physical contact and affection from outside caretakers was necessary for you to feel safe and secure in the outside world. Don't forget, you had just spent nine months in a very warm cosy environment—your mother's womb. You were surrounded by a physical closeness and warmth. When you were born, or in other words, came out of the womb to face the world, suddenly you entered a very large cold space. Physical contact was essential to make you feel secure, loved and protected.

LOTS OF ATTENTION

To prove to your self that your mom and dad loved you, you

wanted lots of attention. You wanted them to be there for you whenever you weren't sleeping. As a helpless infant, born unable to care for your self, you needed your parents to do everything for you—change your diapers, feed you, bathe you, dress you, play with you, teach you about the world, hug you and love you. As a helpless infant, your parents would have appeared to have been the only game in town; you needed them to ensure your survival.

LOTS OF PATIENCE AND ENCOURAGEMENT

You had to learn how to do everything: how to sit up; how to crawl; how to walk; how to dress; how to tie your shoes; how to feed your self; how to talk; how to read; how to write; how to ride a bicycle; how to judge situations; how to protect your self; how to interact with other people. You were born with the potential to master these tasks, but it was a process to learn them. At birth, you did not come out of the womb, jump on your bicycle and ride around the block.

Teaching you to master these skills required lots of patience and encouragement. Not one of us learned to walk in an hour. It was a process of gaining more muscular control and stability, combined with your parents' being there, holding out their arms and encouraging you to try. Thus, you needed them to put in their time with you; you needed them to tell you how well you were doing. Learning any new skill is a frustrating process because it doesn't happen in a minute. Because you were born with the desire for immediate gratification, not mastering a new skill would have seemed irritating. But with enthusiasm and encouragement from your all important mom and dad, you would have felt that whatever progress you had made on the road to mastery was just fine.

RECOGNITION – VALIDATION – CONFIRMATION

When you were an infant, you believed that you were the centre of the universe. You believed that your reality was everyone else's reality. If you pulled a blanket over your head, you believed that no one else could see you because you couldn't see them. As you grew and your cognitive processes developed, you came to realize that you weren't the centre of the universe. You had brothers and sisters who were competing for your mom's and dad's attention. They wanted what you wanted. Your parents were involved in activities that didn't allow them to be with you every minute: your mom had to cook meals and go food shopping; your mom liked to talk on the phone; your mom/dad would have left the house every day to go to work.

Because there was an increasing amount of time that your mom and dad didn't spend with you, it was most important for you to be reassured that your mom and dad loved you, cared about you, and delighted in being with you. You wanted confirmation that you were both valuable and important to them. You wanted them to feel glad that you were born, that your existence had enhanced their lives. You wanted to feel wanted.

CARING AND SUPPORT

As an infant, caring was shown to you by your parents' meeting your physical needs, being there for you and loving you. As you grew, caring was also shown through having your parents listen to you express your thoughts and feelings, and to take your side. You needed an ally. During your growing up process, many things would have happened which would have both hurt your feelings and confused you. You would have wondered why your big brother was so mean to you, why he hit you, why your mom left you alone to play by your self, why your dad did not spend much time with you, why your little friend did not want to share his toys with you.

As a growing child, you wanted an ally: someone who would take your side when you felt rejected; someone who would understand your hurt feelings and comfort you, telling you not to worry because your mom and dad loved you. You didn't want to be alone with your feelings. You wanted someone to listen to how you felt. You wanted someone to reassure you that you were still okay.

THE FREE EXPRESSION OF YOUR FEELINGS

The desire to express your feelings was as natural to you as the desire to eat, sleep and move around. As a human being, you came equipped with primary feelings: the feeling of anger, the feeling of fear, the feeling of sadness, and the feeling of happiness. You wanted to be able to share your feelings with your mom and dad: your anger, when you felt unhappy with the way you were being treated; your sadness, when you felt that your parents didn't love and value you; your fear, when you were concerned that maybe they wouldn't be there to protect you; your happiness, when you felt excited about being alive. Expressing your feelings would have enabled you to communicate to your parents what it felt like to be you—to let them know how *you* saw the world. As a totally dependent child, you were looking to your parents for comfort and support. By expressing your feelings, you wanted to let your parents know that you wanted them to consider your inner self.

THE FREE EXPRESSION OF YOUR NEEDS

You were born egocentric and narcissistic. You expected your needs to be met because you had grown used to all of your needs being met in the womb—you were fed, you were kept warm and you felt secure. Born into the world, you used your crying as a way to alert your parents as to your needs. Later on, you used speech as a way to express your needs. Being totally dependent on your caretakers, if your needs were not anticipated and met, you wanted to let your parents know what you wanted.

As you grew, you learned that you were not the centre of your parents' universe. Your parents did not sit around waiting for you to express your desires—they had other demands on their time and attention. But your job, as a growing infant, toddler and preschooler, was to make sure that your needs were being met. You were a full time job to your self. Until you were able to meet your own needs, you had to rely on your parents to do so. This meant letting them know what you wanted.

YOU STILL HAVE THESE NEEDS

What you needed and wanted as a newborn, infant, toddler, preschooler, growing child, young adult and adult, you still need and want today. Obviously the dependency on your parental figures has diminished as you learned the skills of self-reliance. As an adult, you will look to many people—spouse, friends, children, work associates, business professionals—as well as your self to meet your needs and requirements. But by virtue of the fact that you are a human being, the satisfaction of all of these needs and wants is essential to your feeling secure and happy in the world.

THE EXPULSION FROM THE GARDEN OF EDEN

As a newborn and infant, you had all of these needs: the need for love and physical affection, the need for lots of attention, the need for lots of patience and encouragement, the need for recognition, validation and confirmation that you were important, the need for caring and support, the need to freely express your feelings, and the need to assert your desires. If you had had all of these needs met during the time you spent with your parents, you would certainly be a happy camper today: you would feel secure; you would love your self; you would give freely and you would receive great abundance from the universe—lots of financial prosperity, lots of friends and lots of support. You would receive these things, because you would be emotionally self-sufficient; by being whole and complete within your self, you would attract great abundance.

But as you know, you didn't get all of your needs met. If it's any consolation, infants and growing children rarely get all of their needs met. In this next section, you'll learn why this is so.

WHY YOUR PARENTS COULDN'T MEET ALL OF YOUR NEEDS

1. YOU CAN'T GIVE AWAY WHAT YOU DON'T HAVE

If I were to ask you to loan me one million dollars to buy a certain property, you would probably say that you didn't have that kind of money, and that you probably never would have it in your lifetime. Assuming for the moment that you would be inclined to loan me this money if you had it, if I asked you again for the million dollars, your answer would probably remain the same—that you didn't have a million dollars, and that you never would have it. Your advice would probably be that if I wanted to buy this property, I would have to look elsewhere for the cash.

In this scenario we are talking about money. In our birth families, we are talking about love. Many of our parents had no love to give. They didn't get the love they needed from their parents (your grandparents). They didn't get their all important needs met, in the same way that you didn't get your all important needs met. As a result, there was probably an empty hole where there should have been a pool of love. To use the money analogy, your parents were probably emotionally bankrupt by the time you came along.

It's extremely difficult to both understand and accept that your parents may not have had any love to give. You needed love. You wanted love. And in being born naturally egocentric and narcissistic, you expected to receive love. There was no way for you to know that your parents were empty cups, and that they too were looking for love from their parents. There was no way for you to know what your parents' childhoods were like— what they didn't get, what they wanted, what they secretly grieved for and what they longed for. You weren't there.

As a newborn, all you knew is what you wanted and what you didn't get. When you didn't get the amount of love you needed, you falsely concluded that your parents had the capacity to love, touch, comfort you and be there for you, but that they chose not to give you these things. Sadly, your wanting love from your parents was not going to give them the capacity to treat you in a loving manner, in the same way that your wanting to borrow a million dollars is not going to enable a moneylender to come up with the money. You can't give away what you don't have!

2. GIVING LOVE IS PERCEIVED AS A LOSS

We have all met people who do not give compliments. No matter how attractive you may look, no matter how well you were able to carry out the impossible, your counterpart will act totally matter of fact about you and your successes. The reason for this is that giving a compliment is perceived as a loss. This person's internal thinking will go something like this: "If I give you a positive (love), I will have less positives (love) for my self. I need to keep all the positives for my self because I don't have very many, not having received very many." This lack of being able to give clearly indicates that this person received very little love and recognition from his parents; feeling empty inside, he can't afford to give any positives away.

The scarcity of recognition, enthusiasm for your successes, encouragement, and excitement for all the little things you were learning to do, as you grew in the world, can usually be explained by understanding perceived loss. Most of us, including our parents, did receive a little love. Except in cases of severe neglect or abuse, most of us did receive some good stuff—some touching, love, and delight in our existence. Little babies are very cute. Until the excitement might have worn off, and the work of providing care had set in, most of our parents would have been thrilled about the wonders of our creation and birth. Even if our parents weren't crazy about us, our grandparents probably would have been. And so all of us, including our parents, probably would have received some love. But because the needs of an infant are so extensive, and because what both we and they received was probably the equivalent of a couple of gallons of water in an ocean, the received love had to be conserved, hence it couldn't be given away.

3. GIVING LOVE IS NOT AN OPTION

Many of you, unfortunately, had abusive parents. Rather than receiving love, you got the reverse: you were traumatized by physical abuse; you were traumatized by sexual abuse; you were belittled; you were made to feel small and unimportant. In the next chapters you will learn why parents abuse their children. For now, suffice it to say that if your parents were abusive, it's because they were abused, physically and/or emotionally.

What your parents were trying to do, in treating you like a punching bag or an object of their immediate gratification, was to discharge their own tension. Inside, they were feeling worthless, unloved and inadequate. Not wanting to face these feelings, they attempted to release them in any way that they could. As a helpless infant and child, totally dependent on your parents for both your physical and emotional care, you were a great target, an easy victim. In having been abused and not valued themselves, your parents not only may not have had any love to give, they may have had a whole lot of rage to get rid of. If you were abused, you were the unfortunate recipient of the deficits in your parents' upbringing.

4. BEING TUNED OUT

The fact of the matter is this: It's not that your parents didn't love you; it's that satisfying their own needs may have overshadowed the amount they had to give in order to satisfy your needs. If what you needed to be filled up emotionally was equivalent to an entire pie, and your parents only had half a pie to start with, and they had to feed themselves too, to stay alive, you can imagine that you might have ended up with a sliver instead of a pie. By default, you would have been left starving for love, attention, recognition, validation, support and encouragement. Because your parents most likely treated you the way they were treated (this dynamic will be elaborated in Chapter Five), you can safely assume that they were emotionally starving too, having been left with a sliver instead of a pie.

Being emotionally hungry themselves, they would have been preoccupied with how they were going to meet their own needs. Who was going to love them? Who was going to be there for them? Who was going to make them feel secure? Who was going to be proud of their accomplishments? Since they had only themselves to rely on, they may have created sources of satisfaction such as drugs, alcohol, food, gambling, making money and being adulated by the public in order to meet their own needs. These substances or activities would then have taken up a lot of the time and interest that would have theoretically gone to you. And so, in being driven to take care of their own needs first, your needs would have been put on the back burner.

5. PHYSICAL UNAVAILABILITY

As an infant and young child, it would have been difficult for you to understand that your mom and dad were physically unable to meet your needs all of the time, even if they had wanted to. Your dad/mom had to go to work to earn the money to financially support your family. This meant that they would have been gone for many hours in the day. There were activities that had to be carried out in order to keep the household running smoothly—food shopping, cooking, cleaning, washing clothes, ironing—and all these activities would have taken time away from you. Most of you would have had siblings who would have come either before and/or after you. It would certainly have been most annoying and hurtful that your mom and dad would have wanted to replace you with a baby brother or sister who would have stolen your attention.

Some of you would have had siblings who were sick, handicapped or who were behavioural problems at home or at school. Dealing and coping with these glaring problems may have taken most of your parents' time, attention and energy. Even if your parents were capable of being saints, there are only so many hours in the day, and only so much that one person is able to give. If you were the good helpful kid, you may have ended up getting very little of what you needed.

Aside from what you missed due to the limitations of time and human energy, your parents may literally not have been there for you due to a life-threatening physical illness. Some of you may have experienced the loss of a parent due to a premature death. Some of you may have lost a parent due to the abandonment of your family, a hostile separation or a divorce. Some of you may have had a severely mentally ill parent who was there in body, but not in mind. As an adult, you may intellectually understand that it was impossible for your parents to be there for you and to meet your needs, even if they did have the best of intentions. Unfortunately, you only go through childhood once. And a loss is a loss, no matter what the explanation for the loss is. You still had your emotional needs; you still looked to your parents to meet them.

THE DAMAGE THAT WAS DONE

There are very few of you who would have had parents who deliberately set out to damage you; in all likelihood, the damaging parenting you received would have happened by default. Your emotional needs: your need for love and physical affection, your need for lots of attention, your need for lots of patience and encouragement, your need for recognition, validation, and confirmation that you were important, your need for caring and support, your need to express your feelings and assert your desires, were simply not adequately met.

Most of you will have had parents who were unable to fulfil your needs. The reasons? Some of them had no love to give; some perceived giving love as a loss; some needed to dump their rage and sense of powerlessness outside themselves; some were so preoccupied with their own need satisfaction that they just couldn't consider your needs; some literally didn't have the physical capacity to give.

The unfortunate consequence of the way you were treated was the decision you would have been forced to reach that survival meant abandoning your true emotional self. In Chapter Two, Only The Tough Will Survive, you will find out why this had to have happened.

2 | ONLY THE TOUGH WILL SURVIVE

Many of you want to forget your childhood and growing up years for good reason: you were dependent on outside forces, your parents, to meet your needs. If you weren't happy with your treatment, you didn't have anyone to complain to. If you wanted more from your parents than they were able to provide, too bad for you. You were powerless to change anything. You had no place to go, and you had years ahead of you whereby your family life would have been the only game in town.

You needed your parents to survive, both emotionally and physically. Because your parents clearly had the power, you, as a dependent child, would have been forced to compromise your need satisfaction in order to survive. It is through these compromises that you would have been forced to abandon your inner self. It is through these compromises that you will have lost your ability to be happy.

THE UNMAKING OF A WONDERCHILD

You were born knowing your own value—you were a human being who was a work of art. You had just survived a nine-month growth period, moving from being a fertilized egg to a very solid vibrant baby boy or girl. You knew your own worth: you were a miracle of creation. Coming into the world knowing your own value, you naturally expected your caretakers, in the form of your mom and dad, to also think well of you. You expected that they would value you, love you, take very good care of you and all of your emotional and physical needs. Nothing but the best for you!

But the realities of living on this earth would have set in shortly after you were born. Taking care of you was a totally demanding, often draining, all-consuming job. Changing your diapers, preparing your food, feeding you, bathing you, and comforting your tears was a twenty-four-hour-a-day job. And this was aside from meeting your emotional needs of making you feel loved, important, valued and cherished. Caring for you required constant giving by people who probably didn't have a whole lot to give.

And so after the novelty and excitement of your birth had worn off, your mom may have stopped coming in to find out what was wrong, as soon as you would have started crying. And maybe after awhile, your mom may have decided to stop coming in altogether. Whether she was trying to discipline you, or because she simply did not have the energy, she may even have started to ignore your tears. What would you have concluded, as a newborn and infant, when your cries for attention were not answered?...Your parents didn't love you; you weren't important; you had no value.

Then of course there were the direct care issues. What would you have concluded, when as a toddler, preschooler, and growing child, your parents would not have had the patience as you learned to crawl, walk, tie your shoes, dress your self, read, write, and ride a bicycle? What would you have concluded when they would have screamed at you: "What's the matter with you?" "Gee, you're stupid." "You sure are a slow learner." "What a dummy." "Your brother learned this in a day." "What do you have for brains?" "Smarten up." What would you have concluded when they would have punished you or would have started beating you for having spilt your milk or broken a vase? What would you have concluded when they would have started beating you or swearing at you for no particular reason?...Your parents didn't love you; you weren't important to them; you had no value to them; they hated you; you were inconvenient to them; they wished you had never been born.

Living with parents who neglected you, ignored you or abused you, you would logically have concluded that there must have been something wrong with you, that you were bad, or that you were defective. This would naturally have caused you to lose the good opinion you had of your self at birth, coming into the world.

Let's not forget, as well, the impact of being the scapegoated child—the one who was labelled "the bad kid," "a behaviour problem in school," "a whiner," "the instigator," "the tattle-taler," "ugly," "dumb," "slow," "the problem-causer." It certainly would have been difficult to conclude anything from these labels except that you were bad news, and that you were lucky that your parents even agreed to continue to care for you.

Other insults to your feelings of self-worth would have occurred if you would have had a brother or sister who was clearly favoured. The favoured sibling would have been treated like a prince or princess, whereas you may have been earmarked to Cinderella/Cinderfella-type status. If you were a rejected child, you would naturally have concluded that there must have been something wrong with you for your parents to have treated you so poorly, and that you were obviously defective.

It was your day-to-day treatment that would have caused you to lose your good opinion of your self. You did not have the luxury that beauty contest contestants have of being evaluated by ten objective judges; you had two very subjective judges, your mother and your father. Their opinions meant everything. And their negative opinions, combined with your interpretation of their negativity would prove to be most destructive to your self-esteem.

THE DAMAGE CAUSED BY A NEGLECTING PARENT

A neglecting parent is one who is consumed by her/his emotional problems. For this parent, surviving day to day is difficult enough; dealing with the needs and demands of a growing infant and toddler is almost impossible. A neglecting parent will likely have a major problem: alcohol or drug addiction, a compulsive addiction such as gambling or workaholism, an emotionally draining problem such as an unhappy marriage, an alcoholic or drug-addicted spouse, an abusive relationship or a demanding parent. This parent may be physically ill and thus unavailable, or mentally ill, and although present in body, is certainly not present in mind. Neglecting parents are often holding a great deal of grief and sadness for the love that they had never received; unconsciously, they are often searching throughout their lives for a parent to love them. Although physically in the parent role, they would probably have preferred to trade places with their child, wishing to have a second chance at being loved.

There are a range of behaviours that can describe the neglecting parent. Some neglecting parents may totally ignore their child's basic physical needs, and will literally not provide regular feedings, change diapers or bathe their child until it becomes a necessity. Some may take care of the physical needs, but not the emotional ones. This type of parent will ignore a child's cries, leaving a child screaming in the crib, rather than go in to see what the matter is. As the child is growing up, this parent will ignore the child's sadness and struggles; s/he won't bother finding out how the child is feeling, but rather, will expect the child to take care of her/his own emotional needs.

A neglecting parent, because s/he lives in denial, will often encourage her/his child to deny reality. For example, it's often the case that a child who is being sexually abused will try to tell this type of parent about the abuse. It's not uncommon for a neglecting parent to respond, "That's impossible. You're lying. Daddy/mommy wouldn't do such a thing to you. Don't ever tell me such things again."

In another entirely different scenario, a neglecting parent may hand over the responsibility to parent the other children, cook, and/or clean the house. This parent is so overwhelmed with just surviving that s/he isn't capable of living up to the responsibilities of being a parent. It's not uncommon for the oldest child to literally become the "mother," bathing, diapering, feeding, putting to bed, comforting, babysitting, and instructing her/his younger brothers and sisters.

The damage caused by a neglecting parent is often greater than the damage caused by an abusive parent, the reason being that because of the absence of an overt assault, you, as a child, may not have realized that you were being ill-treated. If you were expected to take on parental responsibilities, you would have concluded that you had little instrinsic worth, but rather, you had to do things for others in order to be accepted.

If your physical and/or emotional needs were ignored, you would have concluded that the lack of interest shown towards you was due to some inherent defect—that if you were more attractive, perfect, loveable, or if there wasn't something wrong with you, you would have received more attention. The impact of this parenting is much like that of a poisonous gas—it cannot be seen, but the effects are deadly.

Rhonda came into therapy with a life that was devoid of any joy. At age 31, she had a good job working as a scientist in a lab. Although she enjoyed her work, she hated the fact that she was constantly being undermined by her boss. Although her job was secure, she didn't feel her efforts were being valued or appreciated. Her personal life was a mess; she had few close friends; it had been years since she had been involved in an intimate relationship.

Rhonda had no insight into why her life wasn't working. She was a real doer and would try anything to get her life going – workshops, self-help books, social activities. The problem was, Rhonda didn't know that underneath the surface she was feeling depressed, grieving for the love she hadn't received as a child. Her mother, Sarah, was a neglecting parent. To the outside world, her mother appeared strong, capable and personable. But at home, Sarah would withdraw into her own shell, preoccupied with her own loneliness and unsatisfactory marriage. Because her mother ignored her, Rhonda assumed that she, herself, was defective; a deep feeling of worthlessness resulted within.

THE DAMAGE CAUSED BY AN ABUSIVE PARENT

An abusive parent is one who dumps her/his rage, fears, feelings of sadness, powerlessness and inadequacy onto the victimized child. This can be done through verbal, physical or sexual assaults. Verbally, this parent will humiliate and tear down the child's self-worth by pointing out the child's flaws, the child's imperfections, and the mistakes that were made. This parent may tease her/his child in public, bringing up incidents that should have remained private matters. This parent will blame the child for anything that goes wrong. Physically, this parent will beat her/his child for any wrongdoings, mistakes made, or simply because the child is within easy access. Sexually, this parent will use her/his child as an object of gratification.

An abusive parent will rarely take responsibility for, or ownership of, her/his own feelings; rather s/he will rationalize her/his actions by saying that the child needs to be disciplined, needs to learn what life is about, needs to be punished, or that these assaults won't do any harm to the child. The tragic fact of the matter is, an abusive parent is so deeply consumed with her/his own pain, desperation, worthlessness, inadequacy, and powerlessness that s/he's truly unaware (unconscious) of her/his own cruelty.

An abusive parent is frightening to an infant and growing child. Through loud condemning words, physical assaults and sexual affronts, an abusive parent will terrify a child into unquestioning obedience. The message s/he will give is: "Do as I tell you." "You have no rights." "I'm the boss here." "You had better listen to me or else." The "or else" will appear terrifying.

If you had an abusive parent, basic life and death survival would have become a daily issue for you. Even if your abuse had been intermittent, you would naturally have feared for the next round. You would have been truly powerless to protect your self; this lack of control over your own safety would have been experienced as an excruciating trauma. If you had been exposed to extreme abuse, you would have had to emotionally shut down, and literally stop feeling, in order to survive. If you were degraded and humiliated verbally, your conclusions about your self would have been that you were both worthless and inadequate.

David was the first born to Simon, age 23 and Linda, age 22. Simon had insisted on having a child right away and Linda had reluctantly agreed. Although Simon wanted a child, he also wanted his child to be the perfect, achieving child that he was never able to be. Because Simon had always felt inadequate, he needed David to make up for his own perceived deficits. And so, despite the fact that David had always tried to do his best, his best was never good enough; Simon would always put him down. If David were to strike out at a baseball game, Simon would have told him that it was his fault that his team had lost. If his report card had a "B" grading, why hadn't he received an "A"? David's efforts were always ignored, and his defects were constantly brought out for intricate scrutiny. Often in his screaming rages, Simon would lose his composure all together and beat David for his poor performance.

David received similar beatings from his mother, Linda. Linda was not a very happy mother. At age 22, she didn't want to have a child. She felt she was only a child herself, and that now she was saddled down with a lifetime of responsibility. She hated her husband for having forced her to have the baby. She had realized that she had made a mistake in marrying Simon. The fact was, her marriage held no joy for her. She would have liked to have left Simon, but she didn't believe she could have made it on her own. And so all her fears, all her loneliness, and all her hatred that had nothing to do with innocent David got placed on him. Linda used to beat David when he cried, when he spilt his milk, and when he asked her for something as simple as reading him a story.

The result of this double-whammy of abuse? At 18, David became extremely depressed. He just didn't feel like getting out of bed in the morning. He didn't feel like making an effort in school. He continued to function, but he was dead inside. He ended up in therapy because his life had become dead-end. David, like Rhonda, had no idea why he was feeling so low. He hadn't put any importance on the fact that his parents had treated him abusively; rather, he believed that he was inadequate as a human being—a failure in both his mother's and father's eyes.

THE DAMAGE CAUSED BY AN OVERINVOLVED PARENT

An overinvolved parent, on the surface, appears very loving and caring. S/he makes the child the centre of the universe. S/he freely and lovingly gives every ounce of time and energy to meet the child's needs. So far so good. Unfortunately, an overinvolved parent is not motivated to do this because of what is good for the child. S/he's motivated by what's good for her/himself.

An overinvolved parent is very emotionally needy. There's a huge hole of emptiness lurking inside; never having been adequately loved, the overinvolved parent always feels alone and lonely. When her/his child is in the infancy and toddler stage, an overinvolved parent will look like a hero, being the perfect loving and giving parent. As time goes on, the needs of the growing child for independence will conflict with this parent's needs, because an overinvolved parent cannot tolerate separation and loss.

If you had an overinvolved parent, do not underestimate the damage that was done to you. An overinvolved parent would have taken your freedom to be your self away from you. This parent would have been threatened by your thinking independently and wanting to create your own life; any separation would have been perceived as a loss. Out of feelings of loyalty or guilt, it may have been easier for you not to be independent, not to feel your own feelings, but rather, to live as an extension of your parent, sharing the same thoughts, feelings and perceptions. Out of touch with your own feelings, you would not have learned very much from the feedback from the outside world. This would lead you to get "stuck" in life.

Stacy was a very attractive woman. At age 40, she was financially secure. She had a beautiful home and a promising career as a television producer. She had a large circle of friends, and to the outside world, she appeared to have a great life. For Stacy, however, her life was a disaster. What she really wanted was a husband and children, and her biological clock had just about run out. As well, there was no sign of a relationship in the wings.

Stacy's problem was her inability to form intimate relationships with men. Because of her attractive looks, she was able to get an endless number of dates. But her personality turned men off. Stacy was narcissistic, totally preoccupied with satisfying her own needs. She was raised by an overinvolved mother who had made her the centre of the universe. She was the only girl, so she got loads of attention. Stacy had become so used to family members focusing all of their interest on her that she expected the men she dated to want to cater to her in the same way; they didn't, and she remained alone.

Stacy never stopped to consider that maybe she might be doing something wrong. Because her mother constantly remained sympathetic about her "bad luck" with men, telling Stacy that the man in question wasn't good enough for her anyway, Stacy was encouraged to avoid looking at the part she played in the demise of her relationships. So in fact, her mother's overinvolvement was ruining Stacy's life.

THE IMPACT OF THE PARENTING YOU RECEIVED

What happened to you, as a child, when you were not valued? What happened to you when you were not loved? What happened to you when you were made to feel worthless? What happened to you when you were frightened that your very survival was in danger? What happened to you when you felt that your parents needed you to take care of them?...What happened was that you didn't feel free to be your self; you didn't believe it was safe to be your self.

You needed your parents to do many things for you. Born with the instinctual will to survive, you had the brain-power to assess what you needed to do to get both your physical and emotional needs met. If your parents weren't able to give you what you needed, if your parents didn't appear to like who you were, if your parents appeared capable of hurting you physically, you would most likely have thought it wise to stop being your natural spontaneous self, expressing your feelings as you felt them, and to start adapting and adjusting your self to ensure your survival. It was in this adjustment process that you would have had to stop feeling your natural feelings of anger, sadness, fear and shame,[1] and pretend that the treatment you were receiving didn't bother you.

To understand how this could have happened, let's go back to what you would have felt, but not have been able to express, as a result of the treatment you were receiving.

NEGLECTFUL AND/OR ABUSIVE PARENTS WOULD HAVE CAUSED YOU TO FEEL:

SHAME MIXED WITH FEAR

"If they don't like me, there must be something wrong with me. I must be defective. If I were different in some way, perfect, more loveable, had some feature that I don't have, they would certainly love me, want to be with me, encourage me, listen to me, play with me, be with me, show delight when they are around me, or they would give to me in the same way that they give to my sister/brother. I had better do everything to try to please them because if I don't make my self useful, they will want to get rid of me—I obviously have no value to them. Hopefully they will keep me if I don't cause any problems and I try to be helpful."

"I need to hide my defectiveness. If I stand out too much, and ask for what I want, someone might notice that I'm unacceptable. Then mom and dad would want to get rid of me. The safest way for me to live is to try to keep everyone happy. In this way, no one need discover just how defective I am."

---

[1]Psychotherapists tend to view anger/rage, sadness and fear as the three primary emotions that we must get in touch with in order to become one with our inner selves. Many psychotherapists view "shame" as a key emotion that must also be resolved. I would agree that "shame" is an essential emotion to resolve, and it is for this reason that "shame" will be included as a primary emotion.

Excellent references on "shame" include: John Bradshaw, Healing The Shame That Binds You (Deerfield Beach, FL: Health Communications Inc.,1988) and Dr. Charles L. Whitfield, Healing The Child Within (Deerfield Beach, FL: Health Communications Inc., 1989).

NEGLECTFUL PARENTS WOULD HAVE CAUSED YOU TO FEEL:

FEAR *Peur*

"My life is in danger. They don't want me. They don't like it when I'm around. When they aren't screaming at me, they ignore me. It was a mistake that I was born. If they had the chance, I'm sure they would get rid of me. If mom and dad separate, I bet neither of them would want to take me. Then I would die."

SADNESS *tristesse*

"I feel so sad that mom and dad don't love me. I love them. I want to be close to them. I thought I was so loveable. And yet they don't love me. They don't want to hold me. They aren't thrilled when they see me. They don't want to play with me. They don't want me. I don't understand why they always ignore me. And it hurts me so much. Mom doesn't even care when I cry. She doesn't want to listen to my stories. Dad doesn't want to help me learn to read. He never spends time with me. They just don't care about me."

"They never take my side when there's a fight with .... (sibling). They always say it's my fault. And it makes me so sad. They wanted .... (sibling), but they didn't want me. What is the point of living? They don't love me. They don't care about me. They would probably have been happier if I hadn't been born. Then I wouldn't be a problem to them."

ANGER

"This is unacceptable. I don't like the treatment I'm receiving. I don't like being ignored. I don't like the fact that you cater to my brother while you ignore me. I don't like the fact that you don't play with me and that you're always busy with your activities. I don't like the fact, mom, that your friends are more important than me. I don't like the fact, dad, that your work is more important than me and that you are never home."

"I don't like the burden you're imposing on me. I don't want to be a parent to my brothers and sisters. Parenting is your job, not mine. It's not my role in life to bail you out. I have my own life to lead, and I resent doing your job."

ABUSIVE PARENTS WOULD HAVE CAUSED YOU TO FEEL:

FEAR: IN RESPONSE TO PHYSICAL ABUSE

"Dad hates me. When he gets angry and starts hitting me, I'm sure he's going to kill me. He just won't stop, no matter what I do. And I never do anything serious anyway. Sometimes all I have to do is look at him the wrong way and he'll start beating me. I have nowhere to run to protect my self when he's on a rampage. He's going to kill me, I know it. Mom can't stop him. And I have no one to tell. I'm so frightened. I could die any time."

FEAR: IN RESPONSE TO SEXUAL ABUSE

"If I don't do what dad wants, he's going to kill me. He said he would. I can't tell mom what he's doing to me. He'll kill me if I do. And he's so rough with me. He hurts me. I'm afraid he'll crush me. I just can't stand it."

"If I don't do what Dad wants, he won't love me any more. I want him to love me so much. No one loves me but him."

"If I don't do what mom wants, she'll tell dad that I'm a bad boy. Dad will stop loving me because he thinks that I'm a good boy."

SADNESS

"I don't understand why they don't love me. I try so hard to be good. I do everything I'm told. I want them to love me so much. And they don't. Dad hates me. He thinks I'm detestable, that I'm not fit to live. I try so hard to please him. I just don't understand it. It makes me so sad. I love him so much."

ANGER: IN RESPONSE TO PHYSICAL/VERBAL ABUSE

"I don't like the way you scream at me. I don't like it when you hit mom. It makes me afraid. I don't like it when you come home drunk and start throwing things. I hate it when you hit me. I hate it when you tell me that I'm no good. Who do you think you are, telling me that I'm no good?"

"Who do you think you are passing any judgement on me? You're a rotten piece of xy##!! You're an inadequate human being and an incompetent parent. You're not doing your job. You're both pathetic, and I wish you weren't my mother/father. I won't tolerate this treatment from you any longer. Now, this is what I want..."

ANGER: IN RESPONSE TO SEXUAL ABUSE

"You should be arrested. You should be sent to jail. Attacking me—an innocent victim. You know I have nowhere to run. You know you terrify me and I'm scared for my life. You're a weak, inadequate human being and you're disgusting. I wish I could send you to prison."

OVERINVOLVED PARENTS WOULD HAVE CAUSED YOU TO FEEL:

SHAME *Honte*

"I guess I'm not very smart. I made a mistake the last time I tried to do that on my own. I had better just listen to what mom tells me to do so that I won't make any more mistakes."

FEAR *Peur*

"If I tell mom that I want to go play with my friends, she'll be angry that I want to leave her. Maybe she won't be there when I come back. The last time I left her, she ignored me when I came back. I need mom to love me. I'm afraid to make her angry at me in case she stops loving me."

✱ SADNESS *listen*

"Mom doesn't really love me. She doesn't really care about me. She only loves me when I do what she wants me to do / when I follow her instructions / when I keep her company / when I get a good report card / when I get a special prize in school / when her friends tell her how pretty/handsome I am. She doesn't really care about me—just me."

ANGER *Colère*

"I don't like being trapped here with you. I have my own life. I love you and I want you to love me, but I also want to be with other kids. I don't want to have to worry about what you're doing and whether you're happy when I'm away with my friends. I want you to take care of your self. I'm not your parent. ✕ I'm not here to take care of you. You are here to take care of me. This is your job. My job is to grow up and become self-sufficient."

"I hate it when you talk about how sad you are, and how empty your life is. I can't fix your life. Only you can do that. You're wanting me to take care of you. You just want to take the easy way out. You want to turn me into your parent, and I refuse to accept the role. Grow up and become your own parent. I'm not your parent, I'm your child. Get that straight—your child. Needing me to be your full time project is your problem not mine. Get a life!"

excellent rôle de la mère

THE LOSS OF YOUR INNER SELF

To keep your self physically safe and to ensure that you would have received as much love and caring as was available, the best course of action would have been to bury your true emotions. You didn't imagine what was going on around you. You would have accurately assessed the danger you were in, and you responded accordingly.

Unfortunately, in the process of burying your feelings in order to survive, you would have lost contact with your basic emotions, and your inner self. In place of your inner self, you would have created a pretend self, a pseudo-self who looked just like you, but who in fact was not you. It was a puppet of your self, and it operated on automatic pilot. This pseudo-self could live in your body, but would not feel the pain of sadness and shame, the fear that your life might be in danger, and the rage at the poor treatment you were receiving.

Your pseudo-self would not have to face the truth as you lived it: your parents did emotionally abandon you; they didn't care how you felt; your happiness wasn't their priority; your parents would always put your needs second to theirs. If you were sexually or physically abused, or severely neglected, having a pseudo-self would have helped you deny your most horrific reality: you were being sacrificed; you were nothing more than an object of gratification; you had no intrinsic worth to your parents; no one was protecting you; you were abandoned. If you hadn't looked after your own interests, if you hadn't come up with a practical way to cope with the traumas you were being exposed to, you would have died.

Getting rid of your inner self was a good plan at the time. It kept you alive, and you're here to tell the tale. However, you will have paid a huge price to survive—the loss of your personal happiness. There's an expression, "For what it cost me to be free, I might have bought an anchor." The truth of the matter is, by deciding not to feel your true emotions and thus, by abandoning your inner self, you will have lost the ability to exercise your free will, and the power to create happiness and prosperity. In Section II, How Your Past Will Come Back To Haunt You, you'll find out why this is so.

II

HOW YOUR PAST WILL COME
BACK TO HAUNT YOU

3 | YOUR EMOTIONAL OPERATING SYSTEM

Leaving home. You probably thought the day would never arrive. You would finally be free of demands, safe from abuse, and able to meet your own needs. You would no longer have to negotiate for the privilege of staying out late or staying out overnight, buying a special addition to your wardrobe, smoking cigarettes, drinking alcohol and experimenting with drugs. You could do exactly what you wanted, when you wanted. The world would be your oyster.

The best part of being an adult and living on your own would be your ability to meet your own needs: your need for love and physical affection, your need for attention, your need for support and encouragement, your need for recognition and validation, and your need to express your feelings and assert your needs. You now had within your reach a whole world of people to rely on; you no longer had to rely on your parents for your need satisfaction. As well, you had access to substances (food, drugs, alcohol) and activities (work, sex, personal interests) which would add the spice to your life.

There would be only one thing that would interfere with your ability to create a happy life for your self—your backlog of buried emotions. Remember, many of the emotional needs of your inner self had never been adequately met. You had a whole lot of unmet emotional needs that you had to wait to fulfil, and a whole lot of feelings that you were not able to safely release when you were living with your parents. To understand the magnitude of what you had to store up, just think: On average, eighteen years is spent with your parents; that is 6,570 days and 105,120 waking hours. From birth to age 5, when your parents were the main contact you had with the outside world, you were exposed to 1,825 days and 21,900 hours of waking time with them. 21,900 hours is a lot of time to be sitting on your true feelings, without the luxury of expressing them, releasing them, and having the opportunity to satisfy them.

And so as an adult, you will naturally want a way to both correct the emotional deficits from your past and fulfil your present emotional needs. The solution: Your Emotional Operating System—a personally designed system of dependencies which will enable you to meet all of your emotional needs, both past and present. Let's begin by looking at what you want from your Operating System.

THE FUNCTION OF YOUR EMOTIONAL OPERATING SYSTEM

1. PUSH DOWN THE EMOTIONS YOU DON'T WANT TO FEEL: RAGE—SADNESS—FEAR—SHAME

In the previous chapter you saw how it may not have been either practical or realistic to express your true feelings to your parents. As a dependent child, asking for what you wanted wouldn't have made your parents any more capable of giving you what you wanted; if anything, it would have made them see you as ungrateful. In this way, you may have ended up with less.

You no longer need your parents for your physical survival. However, the emotions you would have felt in relation to them, in your childhood, are still with you, whether within your conscious awareness, or outside of this awareness, locked in your unconscious mind.

Emotions, if unexpressed, will stay with you and be as real as they were when you were just a toddler. And so unless these emotions were released at some point in your life, you will still feel them: anger/rage for the disrespectful treatment you were forced to accept; deep grief for not having been valued, appreciated, or loved; fear for not having been able to protect your self from physical assaults, sexual assaults, or verbal abuse; terror at feeling that your mom/dad had the power to kill you; shame for the inadequate person you secretly believe you are.

These feelings are painful, and as an adult, you will most likely prefer to deny their existence rather than face them head-on. Why is denial more attractive than facing the truth? Because expressing your anger toward your offending parent could lead to a loss of love, rejection, emotional abandonment; feeling your sadness will make you feel helpless, vulnerable, powerless, hopeless; feeling your shame will make you feel worthless, inadequate, defective; feeling your fear will make you feel powerless, dependent, helpless. Objectively speaking, feeling these emotions will certainly appear to interfere with your ability to create a happy, fulfilling, dynamic life. And so, denial will appear to be your best option.

In that you will want to deny your true feelings, the next problem is how to do it. Two of the most immediate ways you might choose to deny your true feelings are through a substance—alcohol, drugs, food, nicotine, caffeine—which can both instantly improve your mood and help you forget your unpleasant feelings, or through an activity—work, sex, physical exercise, gambling, housework, shopping—which can help you forget what is really bothering you and provide you with some immediate gratification. What you will be looking for is an instant result. Worrying about the long-term implications of becoming dependent on either a substance or an activity will not be your foremost concern.

2. PROVIDE INSTANT PLEASURE—FUN—HAPPY FEELINGS

We can all use as many of these feelings as possible. We live in fast-paced times where instant gratification has become the norm. Because feeling wonderful was probably not a familiar experience when you were living with your parents, you will now want to make up for the deprivation you experienced. By being able to give your self instant pleasure, you can create the illusion that you are in control of your life.

3. MAKE YOU FEEL LOVED—SECURE—VALUED

If you were neglected, abused, treated as an object of gratification, or overcontrolled, your inner self will not have been filled up with the love, attention, interest, affection, validation, recognition that is essential in making every one of us feel emotionally whole, secure and worthwhile as human beings. By default, you will have been made to feel empty, incomplete, worthless and unloveable. It is natural that you will both want to feel like an important, loveable, worthwhile, valuable person, and that you will feel an urgency about accomplishing these goals. In this regard, your dependency items will appear like manna from heaven to you.

4. GIVE YOU CONFIDENCE—MAKE YOU FEEL POWERFUL

Feeling in control of your life is an essential need. You are the resource, and if you don't believe in your ability to make things happen, living life will prove to be a struggle. If you were neglected, you would not have been taught to problem solve and learn constructive ways to advance your own interests. If you were physically or sexually abused, you would have been the victim of your parents' rage; you would have been powerless to stop the abuse because you would have had no one to turn to and nowhere to go.

These feelings of powerlessness will remain with you. If you were verbally abused, the negative messages of being "no good," "dumb," "stupid," "incompetent" will still be with you today. To offset your sense of powerlessness, you will need a quick way to feel powerful.

HOW YOU CHOOSE YOUR EMOTIONAL OPERATING SYSTEM

How you choose your Operating System is largely based on what system your parents established to deal with their emotions. Children learn by example. We learned by what we saw our parents do, not by what they told us was right. The advice that many parents often used, "Don't do as I do, do as I say," were words that would have fallen on deaf ears—children learn by example.

And why not learn by example? You wanted results, not trial and error. And so, if you saw your dad reach for a bottle of beer or a scotch when he came home from work, you would have started reaching for the same, as soon as you would have had the chance. The alcohol seemed to make him feel good, so why not you? Maybe your mom gorged herself on chocolate cake when she was feeling sad. She would have seemed more relaxed and happy after a binge, so if it worked for her, why not for you? Maybe your mom got very busy with church groups and this seemed to make her happy. Or maybe she spent long hours away from home shopping, and somehow her mood was always better when she returned home with her purchases. Maybe your dad spent most of his time at work. You probably believed that what he was doing was very important, and so you made the decision, as a child, that you wanted to do such important things when you would grow up.

This is not to say that you didn't use your own imagination in terms of what you grew to depend on to meet your emotional needs. You may have chosen a system based on what you saw your peers do, choosing gambling, promiscuous sex, or drugs as your emotional outlet; you may have found your own system, perhaps choosing a substance such as food, because food is associated with love, festivities and nurturing; you may have chosen to keep super busy by working a few jobs simultaneously, or by taking extra courses in university so that you wouldn't have any available time to think about your feelings.

In terms of your Emotional Operating System, in relation to people, you will either have copied your parents' behaviour, or you will have remained the victim of such behaviour in your adult life. For example, if your mom/dad verbally humiliated you, pointing out your flaws, making you feel like a worm, telling you that you would never amount to anything in life, criticizing you for being incompetent, embarrassing you for your shyness, judging you for your failures, blaming you for situations over which you had little control, you would have had a choice: you could either have modeled that same behaviour by becoming abusive to others, attempting to transfer onto other people the shame and anger that had been dumped onto you, or you could have remained a true victim of that abuse, by accepting it as a judgement on your worth; having been made to feel inadequate, you will continue to accept abuse, believing it to be an accurate judgement on who you.

YOUR EMOTIONAL OPERATING SYSTEM IN ACTION

In order to manage our emotions and to make our lives as enjoyable as possible, most of use will rely on a variety of dependencies. These include dependencies on substances, activities, people, victims and our selves.

SUBSTANCE-DEPENDENT

Alcohol—Illegal Drugs—Prescription Drugs—Food—Caffeine—Nicotine

WHY YOU CHOOSE THIS SYSTEM

Access to these substances is usually within your immediate control (except for illegal drugs which might prove to be increasingly costly or difficult to obtain). You don't have to ask another person to meet your needs—you can meet them on your own (except for illegal drugs, prescription drugs when your need becomes excessive, or in the latter stages of alcohol dependency). The substance does the job quickly, and usually works effectively in pushing down feelings. The chosen substance will artificially elevate your mood, provide feelings of security, and make you feel in control of your life.

Over time, of course, you will become a slave to the very substance that had once done your bidding. Because the ingestion is physical, your body will demand more and more of the substance to accomplish the same result. Over time, obtaining and ingesting the substance will turn into a full time occupation.

TYPES OF SUBSTANCE DEPENDENCIES

A. MAIN

You cannot function without the regular intake of your chosen pleasure. Because intake of your substance is essential for keeping you both functioning and feeling good, most of your attention is directed at both obtaining and ingesting the substance at regular intervals.

B. BACKUP

This is a secondary dependency. You are more dependent on another activity or behaviour to stabilize your emotions. This dependency is a supplement to your key dependency.

ACTIVITY-DEPENDENT

Gambling—Sex—Religion—A Cause—Hobby—Reading—Sports—Work—Career Advancement—Money—Pursuit Of

Power—Collecting—Shopping—Children—Housework—
Travelling

WHY YOU CHOOSE THIS SYSTEM

The value of an activity addiction is that it doesn't "appear" to
be a dependency at all. Although it fulfils the requirements of a
dependency system, meeting your need to repress your emotions, provide you with pleasure, make you feel secure and powerful, you can fool your self into believing that you aren't
running away from your feelings. In small doses, any and all of
these activities (except for gambling) are usually components of
a satisfying, fulfilling life, and even if they aren't fulfilling, they
are necessary (shopping, housework, work).

The problem with these activities is the amount of time
you spend in doing them. I know a professional working woman
named Reena who jogs five miles in the morning before work,
swims half a mile at a local pool at lunch, and then goes to an
aerobics class after work. Is Reena running away from herself or
what? I think she is, but she would say she likes being fit.

The work ethic has taken over and it's not uncommon for
executives and entrepreneurs to go into the office for 7 a.m. and
leave at 9 p.m.—a fourteen-hour day. In our society, it's easy to
say that this amount of work is required to get ahead, but is it
really?

TYPES OF ACTIVITY DEPENDENCIES

A. MAIN

Most of your time is spent involved in the activity. As long as
you are engaged in the activity or some variation on the theme,
you are able to feel both happy and secure. The activity keeps
your mind occupied and ensures that you will have little or no
time to think about the emotions that are driving you to run
away from your self and your emotional pain.

B. BACKUP

This is a secondary dependency. You are more dependent on
another dependency or behaviour to stabilize your emotions.
This dependency is a supplement to your key dependency.

Chart 1 - YOUR EMOTIONAL OPERATING SYSTEM

SUBSTANCE-DEPENDENT

Alcohol—Drugs—Prescription Drugs—Food—Caffeine—Nicotine

A. MAIN
You are organized around it. Regular intake is required to regulate your feelings and your mood.

B. BACKUP
To get through stressful times or for instant gratification.

ACTIVITY-DEPENDENT

Work—Money—Success—Power—Gambling—Sex—Religion—A Cause—Hobby—Sports—Housework—Children—Shopping—Travelling

A. MAIN
You are organized around it. Great amounts of time is spent in the activity or in the pursuit of your goal.

B. BACKUP
Backup dependency to get through stressful times or for instant gratification.

PEOPLE-DEPENDENT

A. DEMANDING
You want people to fill in your emotional holes—to make up for the damage that was done to you. You are very controlling, demanding and urgent. You see people in terms of, "What can you do for me?"

B. COMPLIANT
You need people to validate your self-worth, especially in intimate relationships. You are desperate for acceptance and validation. These needs result from being either neglected or abused. You are looking for a nurturing partner to fill in the holes caused by parental damage. You cling to others. You treat others better than you treat your self. You accept abuse as the price you must pay for love and support.

VICTIM-DEPENDENT

Verbal—Physical—Sexual Abuse

A. DUMP SYNDROME
You are constantly feeling enraged, ashamed, hurt, afraid, power-less and inadequate. You regularly use easy targets—your vic-tims—to discharge your emotions. You are so enraged at what was done to you that your attitude is, "You are going to pay for what was done to me."

B. TRIGGER SYNDROME
Your desire to abuse is set off by people and events. An unpleas-ant event will trigger feelings of powerlessness, shame, anger, hurt and fear. You will then seek to discharge your emotions through verbal criticism, blame or violence. You do not take responsibility for your emotions—your target is usually blamed.

SELF-DEPENDENT

You withdraw into your self for survival. You believe that people cannot be trusted and that you must be self-sufficient to survive. You are emotionally isolated. You do not feel connected to peo-ple. On the outside you may appear aloof, confident, strong, suc-cessful, and self-sufficient. Despite your success, you find giving very difficult, if not impossible.

BEING WHOLE

You rely on your self to meet your own emotional needs. You are able to love your self because your painful emotions from the past have been released. You know your own worth and value, and you truly delight in being you. You respect others, appreci-ate others, and are able to give freely. You take full responsibility for everything that happens to you.

PEOPLE-DEPENDENT

WHY YOU CHOOSE THIS SYSTEM

From a logical point of view it makes sense that if it were a person (your parent) who was not able to give you what you needed, it should be a person who should fulfil those needs in adult life. As a people-dependent person you will look to another person to fill in the glaring holes left by your abusive, neglecting or overinvolved parents.

TYPES OF PEOPLE DEPENDENCY

A. DEMANDING

The constant experience of being ignored, humiliated, frightened, devalued, treated as an object, as the result of having had abusive, neglecting or overinvolved parents, would have prevented you from going through the normal developmental growth stages. This means you would have become stuck in the narcissistic stage, whereby as an infant and young toddler, you would have expected your parents to meet all of your needs. In normal healthy development, the child naturally wants to move away from this parental dependency and become self-sufficient. Because of the parenting you received, your need for love, recognition and validation would not have been met. As a people-dependent person, you will have put these needs on hold until the day when you would find an unconditionally loving parent substitute to fill you up. The intensity of your unmet needs is often mammoth.

Many of you may have ended up in this category for entirely different reasons. If you had overinvolved parents, you may not have learned to become self-sufficient, either on a practical or on an emotional level. Because your parents would have done everything for you (out of their own self-interests), what you would have become used to is being serviced. Taking the initiative, which is something that adults need to do to get ahead, would have been foreign to you. Thus, you would need a parent substitute to do for you what your parents used to do.

As a demanding people-dependent person, you give orders for other people to fulfil. You want other people to do all the things that your parents were not able to do for you: love you, be kind to you, agree with you, appreciate you, give to you, listen to you, be there for you unconditionally and take your side. Being consumed with your own pain, you give people jobs to do. You want people to be your private advisor, therapist, entertainer, money-lender, check-payer, or message-runner in the hope that the support of others will make you feel whole. Very often, even though you can do the task or function very well on your own, you want someone else to do it for you; in being served, you feel special and important.

Although you may not consciously realize this, as a demanding people-dependent person, you only care about your own need satisfaction. You are only interested in your own happiness, not in the happiness of the people you are ordering about. Being in a great deal of emotional pain, you are desperately trying to feel better, and you use other people to accomplish this goal.

When I was working as a family therapist, I was saddened by the emotional demands that I saw so many mothers make on their young children. In one situation, this adorable six-year-old boy had taken on the "husband" role vis-a-vis his mom. His mom had had a difficult day at work, and he was trying to both comfort her and problem solve with her. This mom had zero awareness that there was anything wrong with turning her son into an intimate partner. She was so emotionally needy that she had never stopped to consider her son's emotional needs.

Children rarely can say "no" to becoming a replacement parent. Children don't have the freedom; but adults do. The problem in being people-dependent is that you may often end up alone, simply because your friends, your spouse or your lovers will get fed up with playing out your assigned roles. Over time, they will see you as controlling, demanding and selfish; they will come to view you as a person looking for an obedient slave, not a real feeling person who has needs too.

Dawn was a vivacious 39 year old woman, mother of two beautiful children, ages 9 and 7. She had been married for ten years to Charles, a very successful lawyer. I met Dawn and Charles prior to their ultimate separation. They had come in to see me for marriage counselling. Unfortunately, they had waited too long, and the damage was too severe to be repaired.

This is what happened. Dawn was a considerate and thoughtful woman. The problem was, she had severe emotional deficits from her childhood, and was desperate for a man to make her feel secure and loved. She found her dream man in her husband, Charles. Charles was a great guy, very giving and generous. However, because he had a low opinion of himself, he had found his emotional security in doing things for others: by creating roles for himself, he would always feel needed. And so in his relationship with Dawn, he would volunteer to run messages, do the grocery shopping and fix things around the house. Dawn, because she had been so deprived in her childhood, just ate up all that was offered her. It wasn't that she was lazy; it was just that she enjoyed being taken care of.

If Dawn wasn't so emotionally needy herself, she would have twigged onto the fact that Charles was doing more than his fair share: He worked full time—she worked part time. Yet Charles did most of the household tasks. What Dawn didn't know is that Charles didn't want to give so much; he felt he had to give in order to be accepted. But what he really wanted was someone who would look out for him and his interests. Because he was too afraid to ask (asking would have been a dangerous thing to do with his parents), he was hoping that Dawn would eventually notice his unmet needs and do something about them. Because Dawn was emotionally blind due to her own neediness, she didn't.

What did Charles end up doing to take charge of this situation? He ended up having an affair with Susan, one of his clients. Susan was a dynamic, attractive career woman who was prepared to do for Charles what Dawn was unable to do: give to him. As an executive in the advertising industry, Susan had a busy work-related social calender, and Charles was invited to join her. For the first time, Charles was able to sit back and be cared for.

By the time the couple had come in for marriage counselling, the affair had certainly blossomed. Charles did agree to end the affair and try counselling with an open mind. During the time the couple came for sessions, Dawn made a 100% effort to be more giving. Because she was basically a nice person, giving wasn't difficult for her. Unfortunately, too much water had passed under the bridge; the ten year marriage couldn't hold a candle to the glamorous lifestyle that Charles had started to enjoy. The result was that the couple ended up separating.

As a demanding people-dependent person, you may not be demanding in any situation other than in a primary intimate relationship. In many situations, you may play the role of the giver, the money-lender, the supportive friend, the advisor, or the message-runner. However, because it is in intimate relationships that the deficits from your past will surface, your emotional neediness can bring out a different behaviour in you. In an intimate relationship, you will then look to your partner to be for you what your parents were not able to be. Your neediness will then prevent you from seeing that you are not functioning as an adult, in a give-and-take relationship, but rather as a dependent child, wanting your parent substitute to do everything for you. This imbalanced relationship may eventually lose its appeal to your partner, and often you will end up alone.

If you had overinvolved parents who chose to meet your every need, you will likely expect to continue to give orders the way you had done in your childhood. You may often get away with outrageous behaviour simply because people with low self-esteem will be happy to serve you.

Giving other people jobs to do can backfire, as in Stacy's situation, when her source of obedient slaves dried up. It also doesn't work well in situations where you have to take the initiative in order to create new opportunities. If all you have learned how to do is find parent replacements to take care of your needs, and you cannot find the bodies to do the job for you, you may end up very lonely, stuck on a dead-end street.

B. COMPLIANT

When you are a compliant people-dependent person, you are leaving your self wide open to be abused, or to be taken advantage of in a major way. You need other people to validate you, and to make you feel loved, important, and worthwhile, the way an alcoholic needs his alcohol, a gambler needs the race track, and a workaholic needs his work. As destructive as substance-dependent or activity-dependent behaviour is, at least the addict is in control of her/his own destruction. With compliant dependency, you give another person the power to both hurt and destroy you. In order to get what you need from others, you will pay with your self-respect; you will compromise your integrity; you will lend money to a gambler; you will buy alcohol for an alcoholic; you will have sex with a man or woman who belittles you and devalues your worth. All because you believe you need to rely upon a person outside your self to survive.

If you were neglected, emotionally abandoned, rejected or devalued, you will probably not think very much of your self; rather, you'll think the reverse: you'll feel ashamed of who you are; you'll believe that you're defective; you won't believe that you have much to offer anyone; you'll believe that you have to do something to make the special people in your life want to be with you; you'll believe you have little intrinsic worth.

It's for these reasons that you will either willingly take on roles that other people want you to fulfil, or you will create permanent roles in exchange for other people's "friendship." These roles include being the entertainer, the money-lender, the check-payer, the advisor, the therapist, the supportive friend, the other man/woman, the order-taker, the baby-sitter. Taking on roles will make you feel secure. Because you are "doing" something for someone else, you believe this significant person won't want to get rid of you. You won't often say "no," because you believe if you aren't agreeable, your friends, spouse or co-workers will have no use for you and will want to reject you.

Often as a compliant person, you give in the hope of getting something back. You think: "Maybe if I'm supportive and giving to Jill/Jack, hopefully s/he will be there when I need her/him." Unfortunately, the Jills and the Jacks of the world rarely will be. Because you have developed the pattern of always giving, people will usually take advantage of the one-way taking relationship that you've provided them.

Compliant people live a dog's life. Think about it. A dog is a wonderful friend to have because he's always there for you. He's joyous when he sees you, and when you don't have time for him, he usually will wait patiently without demanding too much. His joy in life is to spend time with you. He will always respond to you happily, even if you have shouted at him five minutes before. He doesn't sulk in response to his poor treatment, and he's amazingly responsive when the time is right. When you demand little of your friends and lovers and give everything to them, aren't you behaving a little like a dog?

VICTIM-DEPENDENT (ABUSE)

Verbal—Physical—Sexual Abuse

WHY YOU CHOOSE THIS SYSTEM

As a victim-dependent, your goal is to dump your feelings of rage, shame, fear and sadness onto another person. By doing so, you are able to temporarily relieve your self of your pent-up feelings from the past which are making you feel uncomfortable. During the time of the discharge, you are able to feel powerful and in control. At that moment, you are temporarily able to rid your self of your shame, rage, fear, sadness and powerlessness. At that moment, you are able to make your victim feel as inadequate, as frightened, as ashamed and as worthless as you do.

As a victim-dependent, you will not take responsibility for your own feelings. Rather, you will transfer the responsibility for your feelings onto your victims—your spouse, your lover, your children, your employees—anyone who is powerless in relation to you is a perfect target. These people will tend to accept your abuse (verbal, physical, sexual) because they are frightened of you, because they believe that accepting abuse is the price they have to pay to get their needs met, and because you have convinced them that they deserve to be abused.

How do you transfer the responsibility for your feelings? You will focus on the faults, limitations and weaknesses of the people who are emotionally dependent upon you. Therefore it's not, "I had a bad day at work," but, "You didn't clean the house today." It's not, "I really don't know how to handle this situation," but, "Look at the mess you got us into." It's not, "Your success at work makes me doubt my own abilities," but, "That promotion you got is no big deal. You were just the next in line." It's not, "Your failing that course reminds me of how inadequate I feel about my own dead-end career," but, "You are really stupid. You'll never amount to anything in life."

The tragedy in being a victim-dependent person is that, in all likelihood, you are totally unaware of how cruel you are being to your victims. Your own emotional pain, along with your deep feelings of inadequacy, emptiness, powerlessness and worthlessness are literally preventing you from realizing that you are being abusive. You will not see your self as an abuser; rather, you will feel that you have been hard done by, and that you have the "right" to make other people pay for what was done to you.

TYPES OF VICTIM DEPENDENCY

A. DUMP SYNDROME

You are constantly feeling angry, ashamed, hurt, afraid, sad, powerless and inadequate. Anyone who crosses your path, at the point in time when you are feeling overwhelmed by your rage and your buried emotions, will become your victim. Situations of rape and physical assaults directed at strangers would be examples of the "dump syndrome." Sexual and physical abuse would be examples of the "dump syndrome" played out with family members. In the case of sexual abuse, a routine of abuse will be established based on easy access to the child, and will usually occur when the other parent is either out of the house (at work, shopping) or is physically incapacitated (bedridden, sleeping).

B. TRIGGER SYNDROME

You are constantly feeling angry, ashamed, hurt, afraid, powerless, inadequate and sad. However, in that your self-image is not one of an abuser, you will tend to act abusively in situations where you can justify your rage and your need to make another person feel as inadequate, as frightened, as ashamed, and as worthless as you do.

Thus, your anger will be "triggered" by an event or incident that will vary in degree of seriousness. The greater your need is to unload your emotions, the more insignificant the event or incident will be. For some of you, your lover saying something that you find "stupid," your spouse asking you to take her/him out to dinner, your child asking a "silly question" will spark a torrent of anger in you that will lead you to verbally humiliate, shout at, criticize, bully, frighten or physically assault your unsuspecting victim. For others of you, the incident needs to be fairly major, such as your child being kicked out of school, your child being caught for shoplifting, your spouse losing her/his job; because these types of incidents will have serious consequences for you, you may be thrown seriously off balance.

The key to understanding "trigger" abuse is to realize that your goal is to get another person to accept responsibility for your feelings. In having a logical reason to blame your victim for your anger, you don't need to take responsibility for, or ownership of, your own feelings of rage, anger, worthlessness, powerlessness, emptiness, sadness, inadequacy, fear and shame. You can now really let loose and shout at, criticize, berate, humiliate, and/or bully your spouse, lover, child, employee; because this person has "done wrong," s/he will believe that s/he deserves your abusive treatment.

SELF-DEPENDENT

As a self-dependent, you turn to your self to meet your needs; however, it's not from a position of strength, confidence or self-love. Rather, you withdraw into your self out of desperation. Because you were abused, neglected or overcontrolled by your parents, you no longer trust people. Your life experience has taught you that if you rely on others, you will get hurt. And so you have learned to meet your own needs. On the outside, you may appear strong and self-sufficient. You should be since you've been taking care of your self for quite some time. Your outside image usually fools people: you often appear intimating and aloof to others, when in reality, all you're trying to do is get through the day.

The problem in being self-dependent is that you're actually emotionally isolated from people. Even though you may be in a permanent relationship or marriage, have children and lots of friends, you feel basically alone. Deep down you don't feel that anyone really loves you. People might love you for the things you do for them, but they don't really love you, your inner self. You tend to mask your emptiness with your self-sufficiency.

Single adults are often self-dependent. Having no one but themselves to depend on, they appear strong and confident to the outside world. Not having spouses or children to take up their time, all their money and leisure hours go to making themselves happy. Although on the outside this may look grand, on the inside, life can be very lonely.

Tina is a lawyer, age 42. She had been married in her early twenties for five years, but is happy to be free of her unpleasant ex-husband. She makes a good living, and enjoys spending the money she makes. She fills in her leisure time very easily, going to aerobics classes, having dinner with her friends, and attending the theatre. She travels twice a year, shares a cottage in the summer and a ski chalet in the winter.

Tina gives, and gives, and gives to herself. She's happy that she can meet her own needs, and that financially, she's able to able to enjoy the best. But often, she finds that her life is meaningless. All she's really doing is filling in her time with "glamorous activities." She feels she's going through the motions of living the good life, but in her heart, it all seems quite empty.

Tina grew up in a family where both parents indulged their own pleasures at the expense of their children's emotional needs. From her family experience, Tina concluded that the purpose of life was to give to oneself—not other people. "Arriving" in life meant having the money to indulge one's every wish. She "arrived" by her parents' definition, but inside, her inner self was feeling very lonely. Selfish indulgence did not bring her happiness.

BEING WHOLE

The purpose of *Choices – Creating Happiness By Breaking Free From Your Past* is to help you become an emotionally whole person who is able to love your self. Being whole does not mean that you need to turn into a hermit, or that you need to feel guilty when you want to have a little fun, in whatever way you choose to enjoy your life. Rather, it means that you'll be able to make choices based on what you want to do, rather than on what you need to do to survive—you will no longer be driven by your emotions. You'll be free from all the negative messages and experiences that were programmed into you. Your life will be your own, and you'll be able to treat your self as the magnificent human being you are.

As an emotionally complete person, you will know your own value, and you will only trade equal value. As an emotionally whole person, you will truly be able to love your self. You will see your self as a source of love, and it will become your pleasure to give love to others. Bringing happiness into your life requires that you free your self from your past, and become whole within your self. *Choices* will show you how to do this.

YOUR EMOTIONS ARE THE SAME

In setting up your Emotional Operating System, you probably thought that you would be free of your past forever. As an adult, you have the power to meet both your past and present needs for love, recognition, validation, security, and to bring happiness in your life. Unfortunately, your past will not disappear. The emotions that you would have preferred to avoid will come back to haunt you. Substance dependency will wreck havoc on your life physically, emotionally and financially; being compelled to engage in any activity, for an excessive amount of time, will cause an imbalance in your life which ultimately will bring you unhappiness; being dependent on people will only contribute to your already low self-worth; victim dependency will make you feel deeply ashamed; self-dependency will reinforce your feelings of isolation and loneliness. The very feelings that you were attempting to avoid, through your Emotional Operating System, are the very same feelings that your dependencies will bring on with increased intensity: rage, fear, sadness and shame.

Your Emotional Operating System will give you clues as to the emotional needs you wish to meet. By paying attention to how you have set up your Operating System, you can begin to access the feelings of your inner self.

BECOMING CONSCIOUS OF YOUR EMOTIONAL OPERATING SYSTEM

Becoming conscious of your Emotional Operating System is more difficult than it may first appear. To begin with, your dependency patterns are well-entrenched. Although you certainly know how you like to spend your time, what truly excites you, the habits you want to kick, you may not realize how substance-dependent, activity-dependent, people-dependent, victim-dependent and self-dependent you really are. You may not realize that every time you feel angry, sad, frightened, ashamed, hurt, scared, worthless, inadequate, powerless, empty, unloved, desperate, you reach for your dependency item.

The reason you may not realize this is because you literally are operating on automatic pilot. In the same way that you don't have to think about how to start your car (it comes quite naturally), you don't have to, for example, think about how to handle your feelings of uneasiness. Over time, you have reached for your dependency item so often that it has become a habit, beyond your conscious awareness. And the best part of this "habit" is that it works. Even though your dependency item will ultimately hurt you, in the short term, it does the job.

Then there is your self-image to consider. The fact of the matter is, admitting to your dependencies will be most unflattering. What person would willing admit that s/he dumps her/his rage on weak, vulnerable people? What person would willingly admit that s/he is prepared to accept abuse in exchange for "love"? What person would willingly admit that s/he can't live without her/his dependency item?

To start unravelling the nature of your dependencies, start making the connection between your dependency item and what you are <u>really</u> feeling. For example, when you catch your self criticizing your spouse, be honest about the secret feelings about which you may be ashamed. What is <u>really</u> bothering you? When you find that you are heaping your plate with seconds, even though you are on a diet, think about what is <u>really</u> bothering you. The answers you will come up with may not be pretty, but they will reflect your true inner self.

Discovering your true inner self is a process. Your Emotional Operating System will provide you with some valuable information about the emotions you would prefer not to face.

4 | YOUR EMOTIONAL OPERATING STYLE

Your Emotional Operating System will explain the choices you will make to compensate for what you didn't get in your past, as well as what you will do to make your life meaningful. Your Emotional Operating Style will explain how you will present your self to people in order to get your needs met, as well as how you will interpret people's actions and the events in your life. There are four basic Emotional Operating Styles: anger-based, sadness-based needy, sadness-based strong/distant and love-based.

How can you recognize an anger-based person? An anger-based person will express her/his anger freely, not worry about the consequences of an emotional outburst, will always be ready to defend her/his position and will fight for her/his rights at any given moment. An anger-based person will not worry if her/his counterpart is happy. Her/his main concern will be that Number One is happy.

A sadness-based needy person will present in a somewhat opposite fashion. A sadness-based needy person will rarely express her/his unhappiness or dissatisfaction, will always worry about the consequence of an emotional outburst, will rarely speak out to defend her/his position, and will rarely fight for her/his rights. A sadness-based needy person will always worry about whether her/his counterpart is happy, and will usually be more concerned with her/his counterpart's happiness than her/his own.

A sadness-based strong/distant person will appear quite similar to the sadness-based needy person. However, the underlying reasons for the behaviour are quite different. While a needy person will not express her/his unhappiness for fear of rejection, a strong/distant will not express her/his true feelings for fear of exposing her/his inadequacy. Because a strong/distant's self-esteem is based on appearing strong, s/he will avoid expressing dissatisfaction, and will avoid fighting for her/his rights and defending her/his position.

How can you recognize a love-based person? A love-based person operates from a base of inner strength, confidence and power. Everything that s/he says and does emanates from a strong feeling of instrinsic self-worth and self-love, along with the belief in her/his own right to be happy. A love-based person will seek to satisfy her/his own needs, but will do so from desire, never from feelings of emptiness, and never at the expense of another person's happiness. A love-based person is able to give freely, without feeling depleted in the process, because s/he is emotionally whole.

Let's now review the dynamics of each of these Operating Styles, in order for you to determine which one best describes you.

WHEN YOU ARE ANGER-BASED

At some point in your early childhood, you would have made an assessment about your parents' motivation, ability and interest in giving you the love and affection you desired. If your parents were abusive, neglectful or overinvolved, at some point you would have concluded that they were not going to meet your emotional needs. This would have made you very angry, and rightly so.

Your very justifiable anger would have moved you into a survival mode of operation. Since it was clear that your parents were not going to care for you in the way you wanted to be cared for, you would have come to the conclusion that the only person who could be trusted to meet your needs was you. While it would have been very scary for you, as a young child, to give up your emotional reliance on your parents to look after your best interests, you had no choice but to do so—you had to survive.

Operating from a survival mode, every interaction with your parents, as well as other people, would have become a symbolic life and death struggle. Operating from this survival mode, the last thing you would have done was to admit that you were feeling vulnerable (sad and lonely), afraid (you didn't have the resources to survive), and inadequate (you weren't as good as you pretended to be). Surviving would have meant that you couldn't even think about, let alone feel, the emotions that would have interfered with your ability to survive.

Your anger would then have become your means of survival. You would have learned how to take care of your own interests and to fight for what you wanted. Because you had to stand alone, in order to protect your interests, you would have developed the internal resources to achieve your goals and to get what you wanted. In this process, you will have become both experienced at, and comfortable in, fighting for your rights. Because you will have had so much practice in fighting for your self, you will have learned how to win.

If you are an anger-based person, it is essential for you to realize how your current Operating Style is keeping you a prisoner of your past. Looking at Chart 2, realize that the unconscious reasons for your anger are based on your rage at having been forced to accept disrespectful treatment from your parent/s, your rage at having been unable to stop your parent's verbal criticism, humiliation of you, physical or sexual abuse, your rage at having had your freedom taken away from you, your rage at not having been loved and your rage at having been abandoned. (You were forced to rely on your own resources when what you really wanted was to be loved.)

Because you will not have been able to fully express and release your anger toward your offending parent/s during your childhood, you will bring this same anger into your adult life. Every interaction with a significant person in your adult life will then become a symbolic battle between your self and your mom/ dad. Who is right and who is wrong? Who is going to gain the upper hand? Who is going to grovel? Who has the power? Who is going to win? On an unconscious level, each time you "win," you will feel powerful, believing that you have achieved retribution for your childhood treatment. But the problem for you is that "winning" is only a temporary victory. When your "victory" has worn off, your unreleased rage from your past will resurface.

As an anger-based person, you will have become locked into a pattern of denial—denial of your shame, your fear and your sadness. You had no choice but to deny these emotions—you had to survive. Admitting weakness, even to your self, would have undermined your own emotional strength and ability to survive.

Chart 2 – YOUR EMOTIONAL OPERATING STYLE

ANGER-BASED

Conscious Mind

- You Have A Fight Mentality
- You Are In A Survival Mode
- You Are Self-Reliant

Unconscious Mind

ANGER

- You Are Enraged At Having Been Forced To Accept Disrespectful Treatment
- You Are Enraged At Not Having Been Loved
- You Feel Betrayed/You Don't Trust

SADNESS

- You Will Never Show Your Vulnerability

FEAR

- Triumph Or Be Destroyed
- Win Or Lose All

SHAME

- You Deny Your Feelings of Inadequacy/Worthlessness

SADNESS-BASED NEEDY

Conscious Mind

- You Are Desperate To Be Loved, Recognized, Validated
- You Feel Powerless

Unconscious Mind

REPRESSED ANGER

- Shame – You Feel Worthless
- Fear – You Will Be Killed If You Disobey
- Sadness – You Can't Risk Abandonment

SADNESS

- You Are Grief-Stricken At Not Having Been Loved
- Being Loved Is Your Primary Reason For Living

FEAR

- Obey Or Be Harmed
- Conflict is Dangerous

SHAME

- You Feel Worthless
- You Believe You Deserved To Be Abused/Neglected/Controlled
- You Believe You Have Nothing Of Value To Offer

SADNESS-BASED STRONG/DISTANT

Conscious Mind

- You Are Self-Reliant
- You Believe You Must Hide Your Own Needs
- You Believe You Must Appear Strong

Unconscious Mind

REPRESSED ANGER

- Shame – Your Worth Is Based On Fulfilling Others' Needs
- Fear – You Will Lose Your Self-Respect If You Self-Disclose
- Sadness – You'll Never Be Loved For Being You

SADNESS

- You Feel Sad, Empty, Lonely For Having Received Conditional Love
- You Believe You Must Fulfil Roles In Order To Be Loved

FEAR

- You Believe Your Inadequacies Must Never Be Discovered

SHAME

- You Believe You Are Inadequate
- You Believe You Must Hide Your True Self

LOVED-BASED

- You Love Your Self, You Know Your Own Worth
- You Have Resolved Your Past Emotional Issues
- You Feel Powerful, You Feel Emotionally Whole
- You Assert Your Needs With Confidence

Why would you have felt shame? After all, you would have become very good at standing up for your self and defending your self against attacks on your worth. To the outside world, and even to your self, you would have put on a very convincing act that you were confident. Unfortunately, even though you may have been able to fight off your mom/dad's verbal criticisms, humiliations, and judgements on your worth, the negative messages that you were exposed to would have shaped the way you see your self today. You were not immune to the harm that the verbal, physical or sexual abuse would have caused you. Even though you may have defended your self like a trooper, a part of you would have believed the negative judgements about your self to be true. Even though you may have fought against your horrible treatment, your inner self would have believed that you deserved it and that in fact, you were worthless.

Emotions that cannot be integrated into our daily lives are pushed down beyond our conscious awareness. Thus, consciously feeling ashamed and fighting back would not have worked well together, because your shame would have undermined your feelings of self-confidence and your ability to "win" each battle. So your shame would have had to be placed out of your conscious awareness, into your unconscious mind.

In the same way, your sadness would have had to be pushed out of your conscious awareness. All children want to be loved. It would been very hurtful that your parents were not giving you the love you wanted. But feeling your sadness would have caused you to doubt your own ability to fight back. You would have had no choice but to push your sad feelings out of the way.

Getting rid of your fear would have been a necessity as well. As a small child, or even as a growing adolescent, standing up to your parent/s would have appeared frightening. You certainly didn't have the resources you do as an adult. You naturally would have worried about your ability to survive without your parents' support. Even if you didn't fight back openly, inside your mind, you would have been "doing battle." To win your battles, you would have had to pretend that your parents' abusive, neglecting or intrusive treatment didn't bother you; you would have had to pretend that you weren't afraid.

Anger is a protective emotion. Feeling your anger and expressing it will ensure that no one will ever take advantage of you. Being in touch with your anger, you will never allow another person to hurt you or your interests (and rightly so). The problem however, when you are anger-based, is that your anger will end up controlling your life. If you're afraid to look beyond your anger, realize that you are a slave to your anger.

Anger is a powerful emotion (energy), and it must be discharged. If you look at your Emotional Operating System, you will realize that your anger is both driving you and controlling your life. In order to discharge your anger, you will need to become dependent on a substance (drugs, alcohol, food, cigarettes), an activity (work, physical exercise, sex, gambling, shopping, anything that keeps you super busy), people, or victims as a way to push down your anger. Being controlled by your dependency item will turn you into a slave, for you will no longer be free to make choices concerning how you will spend your time, and what you will do with your time—getting rid of your anger will become a full time occupation.

YOUR ROMANTIC RELATIONSHIPS

The need to get rid of your anger will prevent you from enjoying an intimate loving relationship. The reason? If you have never discharged your anger at the source (your parents), you will turn your intimate relationships into a battleground. Winning a fight will be far more important to you than becoming close and loving because your self-esteem will be on the line. Moreover, you won't be inclined to get close to your intimate partner because you will perceive opening up emotionally to your partner as being both dangerous and self-destructive. Whether you openly drive your intimate partners away through verbal or physical abuse, or whether you stay away to preserve your own identity, your unresolved anger will prevent intimacy from occurring.

As an anger-based person, you will find giving to your partner (understanding her/his needs and issues, making sure that s/he is happy) to be extremely difficult. Because you have so much stored-up resentment for the way you were treated as a child, most of your energy will be directed at discharging your own powerful feelings. Because you are consumed with your own needs, you will have neither the energy nor the inclination to focus on your partner's needs. This again will prevent intimacy from occurring.

The sad part in being an anger-based person is that your own actions are contributing to your need to remain angry. Just like every other human being, you want love, you want closeness, you want kindness, you want caring. In using your anger to protect your self, you will be driving those people who want to love you away from you—in other words, it is difficult to hug a cactus. In a self-fulfilling way, you will be building on the feelings of resentment that you have brought with you from your childhood: intimate partners can't be trusted; they will betray you in the end; there is no one you can count on but you; exposing your vulnerability will hurt you.

YOUR CAREER SUCCESS

The ability to express your anger easily will work well in some career-related situations, and will seriously hurt you in others. If you are exceptionally talented (in sports, making money, music, the arts, politics, science), very wealthy, very physically attractive, very powerful, your tendency to get easily enraged and/or verbally abusive to others will be tolerated. If you have achieved great success in your career, your anger may even add to your aura.

If you are in sales or in the business world, your anger may work to your advantage, allowing you to "win through intimidation." I know of one superstar salesperson who channels his uncontrollable rage by partnering with his clients against the "bad guys" out there who are trying to take advantage of them. Being anger-based can also be of value when you are entrepreneurial in nature. Because you are naturally egocentric and you refuse to be defeated, you will often be successful at bringing your own internal vision into reality.

On the other hand, being anger-based can seriously harm your ability to do well in your career. As a child, survival would have meant believing that your way was the right way. Now, as an adult, you will be more concerned about expressing your ideas than in, for example, listening to your customers express their concerns or needs, or in asking your customers for their opinions. While the skill-building courses you may attend will teach you about the importance of good listening, your emotions will tell you otherwise. Your lack of true interest in your customers' needs will be picked up on an unconscious level and will ultimately hurt you. (The same can be said for your inability to listen to the directives of upper management and the needs of your employees. Many a promising career has been ruined by poor people skills.)

Being anger-based will cut down as well on your ability to resolve conflict. Because you will be caught up in defending your own point of view, you will have an extremely difficult time looking at a situation from your counterpart's perspective. This will cause you to become entrenched in a "black or white" position, preventing you from creating win/win solutions in shades of grey. Your need to be right will also prevent you from identifying how you are contributing to the problems in your life and what you can do differently to achieve your goals.

YOUR HAPPINESS

If you are anger-based, you will look far happier to other people than you will actually feel. The reason? Your various dependencies—alcohol, drugs, gambling, sex, work, money, power, sports, self—along with your expressive, outgoing personality will fool people into believing that you are having a lot of fun and that you have a great deal of self-confidence. You may even fool yourself sometimes. But deep down you will know that your anger is driving you and that you are not free to say no to your dependencies.

As an anger-based person, you are not able to relax on your own because your unconscious rage is continuously boiling up inside of you, wanting to get out. Without the help of an external dependency item, you will truly feel like you are jumping out of your skin. Because anger is such a powerful emotional, it literally does become a full-time job to keep it buried. In being controlled by your anger, you will be prevented from creating a relaxed, happy, joyful life.

WHEN YOU ARE SADNESS-BASED

When you are sadness-based, you will be carrying unreleased feelings of grief and powerlessness within you: grief in that you weren't love, valued, appreciated, recognized or cared about in the way that was important to you; powerlessness in that no matter how hard you tried to be the perfect kid, you were not able to get more of the emotional goodies you so desired.

In that expressing your feelings and asserting your needs

would have neither changed your parents' ability, nor their desire to put your need satisfaction before their own, you would have concluded that your best option was to accept the few crumbs of affection you were receiving, rather than risk losing the little love that was so important to you. If you were physically or sexually abused, you would have been so terrified for your very survival that asking for what you wanted would have appeared dangerous. In either case, you would have perceived that your best option was to wait and hope that your needs would have eventually be noticed and satisfied.

Underlying your feelings of powerlessness and grief is a deep feeling of shame. As a dependent child, you would have believed that your parents didn't truly care about you because you were either defective or inadequate. This would have made you feel ashamed—you would have believed that it was your own inadequacy that was causing your parents to neglect, abuse or become overinvolved with you.

Another key emotion that will feed into your sadness-based personality is your unconscious fear. Believing your self to be powerless, your emotional response to your parents' abusive, neglectful or controlling treatment would have been fear. You would have believed that disobeying, fighting back, refusing to comply, or complaining about your treatment would have lead to abandonment. Because in your eyes, abandonment would have meant death, obedience would have appeared to be your only option. Survival would have meant compliance.

If you are sadness-based, the emotion you will have the most trouble getting in touch with is your anger. To a sadness-based person, anger is an extremely dangerous emotion, because as a child, expressing your anger would have appeared self-destructive. For some of you, the expression of your anger would have made you feel afraid—you would have risked losing whatever love, affection and goodwill you were receiving. (Your fear would have been that your parents would have retaliated by withdrawing their love from you. This loss of love would have intensified the feelings of abandonment you were already experiencing.) For some of you, expressing your anger would have caused you to feel deeply ashamed—you would have been revealing your own inadequacy in that you were wanting love. In this regard, revealing your true feelings would have caused you to lose the little self-worth you were trying desperately to maintain. (By pretending that your parents' treatment of you didn't bother you, you would have been trying to win the battle for your self-respect.) For those of you who have been sexually or physically abused, you would have believed that you would literally have been killed if you had spoken out or had tried to defend your self.

On a practical level, if your parents were neglecting, abusive, or overinvolved, expressing your anger would not have appeared to make good sense. The fact was, you would have accurately assessed that your parents were incapable of considering either your true interests or your needs. Expressing your feelings would neither have made them more capable, nor more interested in doing anything differently to make you happy— your happiness was not their priority. (The reason for this is that they were consumed by their own emptiness, their own rage, their own sadness, their own fear, their own shame; emotionally surviving for them would have meant putting your needs and feelings second to their own.)

And so, in all likelihood, you would have found that expressing your needs would have caused you to get less of your needs met (retaliation), made you feel more inadequate (it was because you were defective that your mom and dad were not meeting your needs), or less powerful (in revealing your need to be loved, you would be showing your vulnerability). Thus, pushing your anger down beyond your conscious awareness would have appeared to be both the safest and wisest thing to do. Sadly, in pushing down your own feelings, you would have concluded that there was something wrong with you, rather than concluding that there was something wrong with the ability of your parents to give you the love you deserved.

In being sadness-based, you will either have become sadness-based needy, whereby you will look to significant others to fill in the deficits resulting from your abusive, neglecting or overinvolved parenting, or sadness-based strong/distant, whereby you will have overcompensated for your emotional deficits by becoming undemanding and self-reliant, taking on the role of the caretaker. It is possible as well that you will have combined both styles—needy and strong/distant into your way of operating. It's not uncommon for a "needy" person to operate as a "strong/distant" person in the work environment or with other "needy" people, while living out the "needy" style with an intimate parter. Let's now look at these two styles in more detail.

SADNESS-BASED NEEDY

Having been made to feel worthless, you would have concluded that you did not have the capability to create a happy life for your self. Feeling powerless, you would thought that it was in your best interests to find other people who would be able to do for you what you couldn't do for your self: love you, care about you, make you feel important, provide you with the practical supports you needed to create a functional life.

In being sadness-based needy, you will be stuck in the past, looking outward, waiting to be loved and cared for by your parents or a parent substitute. As an infant and dependent child, you were made to feel so powerless—powerless to be noticed, recognized, valued, acknowledged, loved—that you didn't believe you had the ability to do anything but wait. What were you waiting for? What are you waiting for?...Someone to love you, make you feel whole, make you feel secure, make you feel important, provide you with a comfortable lifestyle.

This is not to say that you have never made the effort to improve your life, or that you don't try different ways to create the life you want. In that you will have developed some resourcefulness, you may initiate many opportunities which can potentially be successful. Unfortunately, because of your underlying feelings of powerlessness and worthlessness, you will usually find that success will elude you, no matter how hard you may work; alternatively, if you are in fact successful, your emotional discomfort with success will often cause you to destroy what you have achieved.

YOUR ROMANTIC RELATIONSHIPS

In being consumed by your own emptiness, you will feel a sense of urgency in relation to your romantic partners. You will tend to see your partner as a way out of your emotional pain, and as an opportunity to correct the emotional deficits from your childhood. Feeling desperate to feel worthwhile, you will want your partner to love you, make you feel complete, valuable and important.

Unfortunately, your intense need will drain the life out of

your romantic partner. In not being able to see beyond your own need, you won't realize that what you want is more than any one person can give you. Even if your romantic partner tries to give "love" to you, s/he will never be able to give you enough love to fill up your emptiness. No matter how promising a relationship looks in the beginning, over time it will end up deteriorating. (This will be explained in more detail in Chapter Six, Anchors For Life.)

YOUR CAREER SUCCESS

Being sadness-based needy will tend to limit your career success. The reason? Receiving external validation and recognition will tend to be more important to you than a large paycheck, career advancement or career status. In that you were made to feel both inadequate and powerless when living with your parents, you will usually find great satisfaction in both mastering a trade, skill or profession and in being recognized by your colleagues. In finding some emotional security in your career, you will often stay in a situation that may not offer you a great future.

YOUR HAPPINESS

You will perceive happiness as an illusion—what you will tend to find is that there will never be enough love to fill you up. No matter how promising a new relationship or a new opportunity seems in the beginning, over time you will feel let down. This is because there is a deep hole of emptiness within you, resulting from your parents not having been able to give you the love and recognition you so desired. To create happiness, to fill your life with love and prosperity, you must learn to fill your own self up, and give to your self all those emotional goodies you are seeking from the signficant people in your life.

SADNESS-BASED STRONG/DISTANT

You ended up creating a veneer of strength because you believed it was in your best interests to do so. In being self-sufficient and undemanding, your hope would have been that by pleasing your mom and dad, you would have been able to increase the amount of love and attention you were receiving. In this way, you would have been rewarded with the emotional goodies you wanted. Even though you may have been getting some recognition for performing your assigned role (being a caretaker, being a parent to your siblings, being the perfect child), you would have felt that the recognition was conditional on you fulfilling the required role—you were not being recognized for being you.

Understandably, you would have been afraid to let on that you wanted to be loved outside your assigned role for fear that by being demanding, you would have lost out on the love you were receiving. As well, in that you would have believed that you were inadequate in your own right (you were not acknowledged for who you were, but rather for the role you were fulfilling), you would have been afraid to expose your own needs by asking for more recognition. This would have made you feel inadequate, thus humiliating you and causing you to lose your self-esteem. As an adult, your strongest desires will be to hide your perceived inadequacies, to "appear" strong, to pretend that you are perfect and that don't have needs.

YOUR ROMANTIC RELATIONSHIPS

In being strong/distant, realize that your veneer of self-sufficiency and distance is preventing you from enjoying true intimacy with your partner. For even though, as a human being, you crave closeness and true sharing, you will tend not to reveal your inner thoughts and feelings. The reason? Underlying your need to appear strong is your fear. You're afraid that if you expose your own desire to be loved, you will be hurt and betrayed the way your parents both hurt you, and betrayed your trust. You're afraid that if you reveal your vulnerable feelings, you will lose your power. If your parents tore down your self-esteem through abuse, neglect or overinvolvement, you would have chosen to pretend that how you were being treated didn't bother you; not showing your vulnerability would have enabled you to preserve your own identity and self-worth.

And so in your romantic relationships, your Operating Style will be similar to that of the anger-based person: revealing your true emotions will appear to be self-destructive. Thus, you will keep your emotional distance. Although you secretly crave closeness and love, you will rarely feel that it is safe enough to reveal your true feelings to your romantic partner.

In being strong/distant, you will feel obligated to pretend—

pretend you are happy, pretend that your partner's behaviour doesn't bother you, pretend that you don't have your own painful problems. In keeping up a public image of strength, you will naturally feel very alone and lonely. In needing to keep up appearances, you will keep the people who could both love and emotionally support you far away from you; your own actions will prevent you from receiving love.

YOUR CAREER SUCCESS

In being strong/distant, you will usually be very competent at whatever you undertake. This is because you are used to being in the caretaker role, and you are used to being responsible. However, because you appear so strong and self-sufficient, you may often lose out on receiving the recognition and acknowledgement you desire. In that people will see you as being strong and self-sufficient, they will not tend to think about the fact that you have needs too.

In being strong, and overly responsible, you may end up doing more than your fair share of the work because you will automatically jump in and take control. In that you don't readily express your feelings and needs for fear of revealing your own inadequacy (you have needs too), you may choose to do more than your fair share of the work, rather than voice your complaints.

YOUR HAPPINESS

Because being strong is an integral part of your identity, you will rarely let down your guard and reveal who you really are. You fear that self-disclosure will cause you to lose the esteem of your counterparts. When you do take the chance and reveal who you are and what you want, you'll usually find that your romantic partner/s, family members, work associates, friends will be unable to fulfil your needs because they are empty themselves— they are looking to you to fill them up. More often than not, they will see you as a parent replacement: in the same way that a child does not perceive his parent as having needs, neither will your counterparts.

The fact is, as a strong/distant, you will have resigned your self to your reality: the significant people in your life will not meet your needs. You will tend to see these people in the same way as you, in all likelihood, saw your parents: weak, needy, troubled, empty, demanding, irresponsible, child-like, selfish, inconsiderate, and/or totally preoccupied with their own satisfaction and happiness. You will believe that if you want your relationships to work, you will have to be the one who is strong, giving, supportive, compassionate, understanding and caring.

And you are right. In the same way that if you would have asked your parents for more love, consideration and attention, they wouldn't have been able to give you what you wanted, so too, if you would ask the significant people in your life to give you more, in all likelihood, they wouldn't be able to oblige your request. Why? Because you can't get blood out of a stone; you can't expect an empty cup to fill you up; you can't expect a person who is preoccupied with her/his own emotional survival to think about your happiness and what is good for you (unless s/he perceives that your happiness will enhance her/his own happiness). In other words, you will have accurately assessed the limitations of your counterparts' emotional capabilities.

What you must come to realize, as a strong/distant person, is that you have created your own reality. Not all people are like your parents; not all people are weak, needy, troubled, empty, demanding, irresponsible, child-like, selfish, inconsiderate, and/ or totally preoccupied with their own satisfaction and happiness. You are attracting these people into your life because you are prepared to fulfil the role demands that both needy and anger-based people desire, and because you are as emotionally needy as the people you attract. (This will be explained in greater detail in Chapter Six, Anchors For Life, and Chapter Seven, The Law Of Attraction.)

Realize that you can create a new reality, a life where you will experience real love and happiness, a life where your needs will be considered as important as those of your counterparts. For this to happen, you must learn to love your self. *Choices* will show you how you can do this.

SPECIAL NOTE

If you identify with two of these three Operating Styles (anger-based, needy, strong/distant), it means that you have both a primary and a subordinate Operating Style. Your primary style will most completely reflect your belief about how you can best meet your needs; your secondary style (subordinate style) will provide you with an alternative way to handle those social situations where your primary style won't be of value to you. For example, while as an anger-based person, you will quite freely express your anger when it suits you, you may not feel comfortable expressing your anger to an offending parent, a controlling boss, or to a new romantic partner; you may not feel inclined to express your anger to a supportive friend, a helpful work associate or a caring child. In these situations, your subordinate style will be that of the strong/distant person. If you are a sadness-based needy person, with your neediness revealing itself in your intimate relationships, you might find that you feel obligated to take on the role of the strong/distant with your needy friends and family members, and in the work environment. If you are a strong/distant, you will choose to appear strong, calm and in control at all time. However, when your back is up against the wall, your subordinate style will be that of an anger-based person; as a strong/distant, you will avoid showing your need, and thus you would never present as being needy.

When deciding which Emotional Operating Style/s best describes/describe you, realize that your style will be based on how you believe you will best meet your needs: anger-based people believe in fighting and demanding; sadness-based needy people believe in pleasing; sadness-based strong/distant people believe in presenting a front of strength and in hiding personal inadequacy. Realize as well that although the external presentation of all three styles is completely different, the unresolved emotional issues are similar.

WHEN YOU ARE LOVE-BASED

When you are love-based, it means that you are operating from a position of self-love—you are emotionally whole, and you genuinely delight in being you. Your motivation to succeed and to love others comes from an inner sense of confidence, belief in your self, and self-love. You go for what you want because you find challenges fun, exciting, and stimulating; you don't need to prove anything to anyone. You express your feelings and assert your needs spontaneously and honestly. You believe in win/win relationships. You choose to become intimate because you love your self and you want to share your love with a special person. You don't need your partner to do anything for you except to be the person s/he wants to be; you don't need your partner to complete you because you are emotionally complete within your self. Giving love is a pleasure and love flows through you. (You will learn how to create a love-base in Chapter Twelve, and how to operate from a love-base in Chapter Fourteen.)

THE CONNECTION BETWEEN YOUR EMOTIONAL OPERATING STYLE AND YOUR EMOTIONAL OPERATING SYSTEM

If you are anger-based, sadness-based needy or sadness-based strong/distant person, you will use your Emotional Operating System to fill in the gaps in your life, as outlined in Chapter Three. All of you will rely on specific dependencies to make your self feel emotionally whole. To speak in generalities, all of you can become substance-dependent, activity-dependent and self-dependent, as a main or as a backup dependency.

In terms of people dependency, if you are anger-based, you will be demanding, but never compliant; if you are sadness-based strong/distant, you will be compliant, but never demanding; if you are sadness-based needy, you will be compliant. As a sadness-based needy person, you can also be demanding, but you will tend to do so indirectly, in a "poor-me" sort of way.

In terms of victim dependency, if you are anger-based, you will usually, but not always, have victim dependency in your Emotional Operating System. Being anger-based, you will often discharge your intense feelings of rage by dumping on a person weaker than your self. If this is the case, you will use verbal abuse—criticism, humiliation, intimidation—physical abuse or sexual abuse to accomplish your goal. (Abuse is any behaviour where you do not treat another person with both respect and consideration, granting her/him the same right that you desire to be both happy and satisfied.) If you are sadness-based needy, you will not be victim-dependent; rather, you are most often the victim, and are readily abused by your anger-based counterparts. If you are sadness-based strong/distant, you will rarely be abusive because you choose to avoid revealing your true emotions.

If you are love-based, you will be emotionally whole. This means that you will not rely on any substance, activity, or person to make you feel powerful, valuable, worthwhile, loveable, important or special. You will know your own worth because you truly love your self. Whatever you choose to do and whomever you choose to spend time with come from your desire for pleasure and to be the person you are. You never feel empty because you are filled up with your own love. You give freely and perceive giving as a pleasure. You take full responsibility for everything that happens to you in your life.

SPECIAL NOTE

When working with both your Emotional Operating Style and Your Emotional Operating System, realize that the purpose of these systems of categorization is to help you understand your current patterns. You ended up developing the patterns you did in order to survive—survive your life as a dependent child. *Choices* will help you break free from the hold that your past has over you. The first step is to become consciously aware of how your past is impacting every minute of your adult life.

5 | IS THE WITCH OF THE WEST A GOOD ROLE MODEL?

If you were to choose an ideal mother, it likely wouldn't be the Witch Of The West. You remember her, that evil woman who was giving Dorothy and her friends a hard time in the classic story, The Wizard Of Oz; she was mean, and did everything in her power to destroy Dorothy and prevent her from returning to Kansas. You likely wouldn't want to choose Snow White's stepmother, the woman who looked in the mirror wanting to find out if she was the fairest of them all; when she found out that Snow White was the winner of that contest, she felt compelled to destroy Snow White. While we're on the subject of who you wouldn't want as a mother, the evil fairy who arranged to have Sleeping Beauty prick her finger and die, simply because she hadn't been invited to the birth celebration, probably wouldn't be on your list either.

Now imagine these scenarios. Scenario One: You're five years old and you have come home crying because a bully has pushed you down. You go to your mother for comfort. She's on phone when you come in. Even though your clothes are torn and you have dirt on your face, she tells you to stop crying and to go to your room. When she gets off the phone, she screams at you for having torn your clothes.

Scenario Two: There was a major incident at school. You're eight years old and someone in the class has stolen money from the teacher's purse. The child who probably did it calls out and says that you're the thief, that he had seen you do it. You are innocent and you tell the teacher so. However, you're fearful that if you tell the teacher who the thief really is, he'll beat you up. So you remain silent, and the teacher punishes you. When you go home to tell your parents the truth, they don't believe you; they believe your teacher.

Scenario Three: You're eleven years old. You're working on building a model airplane, and you're having a great time. Your mother comes in and says that your eight-year-old brother is having trouble with his homework. She wants you to help him with it. You complain that you're busy with your airplane. She responds by telling you that how your brother does in school is more important than your plane set, and to go help him right now.

If you had the choice, you probably wouldn't want to choose an evil witch as your mother. Somehow she doesn't fit the role of the unconditionally loving parent. Nor would you want to choose any of the three mothers just described in the above scenarios. Yet the fact is, in all likelihood, the way these fictional mothers would treat you, as their child, is almost identical to the way you are treating your self right now.

YOUR INTERNALIZED PARENT

The greatest tragedy of life is that the way your parents have treated you, as a growing infant and child, is most likely the way that you will end up treating both your self and your own children. You are the product, the end result of your parents' parenting of you, in the same way that your parents are the end results of the parenting they received from their parents. In other words, if your grandparents were your parents, you would most likely have ended up with the same emotional difficulties and problems that you are experiencing today.

The reason for this bold statement is the fact that you can't give what you didn't get. If your parents were not attentive to you, were not warm and supportive, it means that they didn't receive these warm cuddlies from their parents. Not having been made to feel valued, loved, and important, they didn't know how to make you, their child, feel these things; nor would they have been inclined to do so if they had perceived giving as a loss. As well, because of their own emotional deficits, they would have stored up a backlog of their own sadness, shame, fear and rage. These painful feelings would have caused them to neglect you (they would have been preoccupied with their own hurt), abuse you (they would have wanted to rid themselves of their own shame and rage), or become overinvolved with you (they would have wanted to fill up their own emptiness).

The hardest thing for any of us to admit is that we have turned out "just like" our parents. If we're in touch with our own feelings, we would most likely feel some anger toward our parents for not having loved us the way we wanted to be loved. To then admit that we are "just like" them is certainly distasteful.

Tania, age 43, hated her mother. Tania's mother, Lorraine, had been a cold distant parent. To the outside world, Lorraine appeared to be a good parent. She had kept Tania clean, well-fed and well-dressed. She had always made sure that Tania was responsible about doing her homework. Lorraine was reliable and consistent. She used to make great birthday parties for Tania, and as a homemaker, rarely left her Tania with babysitters.

On the affective level however, Lorraine left much to be desired. She wasn't able to hug Tania. She used to give her what looked like a hug, but Tania had always felt her to be stiff and uncaring. Lorraine believed in making her children strong and independent, so she would usually leave Tania crying in her crib in order to toughen her up.

What kind of parent did Tania turn out to be?—one just like her mother. She had two beautiful children, a boy and a girl. As a parent, she felt that teaching good discipline was the most important thing she could do. On one occasion at a family cookout, her five-year-old daughter, Victoria, not having gone outside to check the weather, said she did not want to wear her sweater. The weather suddenly turned cooler, and when little Victoria went outside, she found that she was cold. She asked Tania for her sweater, but was refused it because she had already said she hadn't wanted it. While the adults at the table were free to put on extra clothing, Tania wasn't given this privilege because she had already made her decision; she was not allowed to change her mind.

Does Tania think herself to be like Lorraine? Of course not. She hates her mother, and on a conscious level, Lorraine is the last women on earth she would choose as a role model. Yet it's from her mother that she learned to parent—parent herself and parent her own children. And the fact is, the way Tania treats her daughter is identical to the way she treats herself.

MORE ABOUT YOUR INTERNALIZED PARENT

Tania parented her daughter, Victoria, in the same way that

her mother had parented her. That's what she saw, and that's what she did. As humans, we learn by example. We copied our parents' behaviour because to us, as dependent helpless children, our parents were Number One. We wanted to be just like them.

As children, our parents were god-like. We were dependent on them to take care of us, protect us, and make sure we would have food, shelter and clothing. And they could do so many things we couldn't do: earn a living, solve complicated problems, go to fancy parties, drive a car, make things and handle endless numbers of difficult situations. They were so big and so powerful. As children, all we wanted was to be just like them.

Because we saw our parents as god-like, few of us would have ever believed that our parents were <u>incapable</u> of controlling their own emotions—their fear, shame, sadness and rage—and taking responsibility for their actions. Few of us would have ever believed that our parents did not have the capacity to be kind, loving and considerate. Few of us would have ever believed that it was our parents' feelings of powerlessness, emptiness and despair that drove them to mistreat, abuse, humiliate and ignore their own flesh and blood. <u>Rather, because our parents appeared god-like, most of us would have believed that the way we were being treated was based on our own lack of intrinsic worth, not on our parents' emotional incapacities. In believing that our parents were correct in treating us badly, we would have begun to treat our selves in the same negative way.</u>

HOW ARE YOU TREATING YOUR SELF?

Not very well! In reading the three scenarios, you may have thought, "I would never be that mean and cruel to my child. I would never be that unfeeling to my own inner self." The fact is, you are often that cruel. At various times, in various circumstances, you'll ignore the cries of your inner self who is seeking comfort; you won't take your own side; you'll take care of other people's needs before your own. You won't do these things, however, because you're masochistic. You'll do these things because you're trying to ensure that your needs will be met, and often, it may appear that the quickest way to get your needs met is to deny your inner self.

YOU IGNORE YOUR INNER SELF

I recently saw a program on television focusing on the tragic lives of children suffering from cancer. One story was about Tim, a nine-year-old boy who was suffering from a rare form of cancer. Tim had bouts of chemotherapy and frequently had to be hospitalized. As a result of his treatments he became physically frail, having little weight on him. And yet, when speaking to the interviewer about what his life was like for him, he said it was hard for him, but it was even harder on his mother, and that he was worried about her. Tim was dying of cancer, and he was worried about his mother's wellbeing!

What is the reason that Tim would think more about his mother's feelings than his own? Self-interest. Tim needed his mom to take care of him. If she would falter under her grief and fear, she wouldn't be there for him (literally), and he would surely die, sooner than later. Taking care of his mom was more important than taking care of himself directly, because if his mom's needs were met, his needs would also be met. So in fact, taking care of his mom would be the same as taking care of himself.

In this case we are talking about a sick child. But the same pattern will exist in all families. As a child, you needed your parents to take care of you—to ensure your physical survival. If your parents appeared troubled, lonely or unhappy, you would have done your best to take care of them. By bolstering up their resources, your hope would have been that they would have been more capable of loving you and paying attention to your needs. And so as a child, even though you had your own fears, your own sadness, your own feelings of anger and shame, you would have, in all likelihood, been more concerned about your parents' feelings than your own.

YOU DO NOT TAKE YOUR OWN SIDE

If you had developed the habit of making your parents' needs and feelings your priority, you would have started valuing your own self less and less: your feelings were not as important as their feelings; your happiness was not as important as their happiness. After all, if your parents were happy, they would have been more likely to give to you and to make you happy. Thus, what you would have done, as a dependent child, was the equivalent of giving a person ten dollars out of your own savings and then allowing that person to "treat" you to a movie and a snack; it was your money, but the other person got the credit.

In learning that there was a benefit in focusing on satisfying your parents' needs (indirectly, your needs would be better met), you would have begun to look outward, as opposed to inward, for your need satisfaction; you would have begun to think it was more important for your mom and dad to be happy than it was for you to be happy. In this process, you would have begun to believe that your point of view wasn't as important as your parent's point of view. In this process, you would have begun to devalue your own worth.

Michael had been out of work for some time. He had been an advertising executive for many years but when his agency was bought out, he was one of the bodies to be let go. Because of the glut of advertising executives on the market, he was having a difficult time getting offered a permanent position. Then he had a stroke of luck. Through a contact, he was able to arrange an interview at a new advertising agency that was growing rapidly. He was interviewed by Miranda, the owner and president. Miranda told Michael that they were bidding on a project and if they got it, she would want him to come on board and work with them. She said in the meantime, she would like him to learn about their office and style. She said that her vice president of new projects, Neil, could use some help, and that if Michael found it acceptable, she wanted him to report to work on Monday.

Michael was thrilled with the opportunity. He thought his problems were over. Unfortunately, Neil wasn't pleased. Neil was an empire builder, and saw Michael's coming in as a threat. He was furious that Miranda would not even have consulted him on the "hiring" of Michael, and so when Michael came in on Monday morning, the situation turned ugly. Michael had thought he was going to start working, but Neil treated the meeting as a rake-over-the-coals type of interview. He challenged Michael; he questioned his capacity to offer anything to the company.

How did Michael deal with the turn of events? He froze. He was shocked. He was horrified. He felt hurt. Here he was, invited to come in by the company president, and instead of being greeted with appreciation, he was attacked. He wasn't prepared for what happened. While the healthy natural response would have been to clarify the situation, to explain to Neil (or to remind him) that he had been invited to work at the agency on the request of Miranda, that he wasn't there to be interviewed, but he was willing to discuss Neil's feelings about his being there, Michael got up and left, saying that he obviously wasn't wanted. As hard as it is to believe, he never called Miranda back to give her hell. He allowed himself to be written off without so much as a peep.

Why? Because Michael had never learned to take his own side. By what had happened, he had realized that Miranda had not informed Neil of his arrival. He felt that Miranda had made a mistake in "hiring" him under these circumstances, and that the best way to correct the situation would be to disappear. He didn't fight for himself; he let Neil win; he didn't take his own side. (Michael is a sadness-based strong/distant.)

YOU TAKE CARE OF OTHER'S NEEDS BEFORE YOUR OWN

If you believe (out of your own self-interest) that making other people happy will ensure that your needs will be met, you will usually choose to satisfy the needs of others before your own.

Wanda always found herself trapped into putting the needs of others before her own. Being in therapy, she was making an effort to be good to herself. Because one of the things she loved to do was to take an entire day and immerse herself in a good book, she planned out that the following Sunday, she would do just that. Everything was all set, and then the phone rang. It was Bonnie, her closest friend, and Bonnie was in need. Bonnie's husband has been on a drinking rampage the night before, and he had started to throw things. The house was a mess. Bonnie was distraught. The kids were screaming. Could Wanda help her out?

Under normal circumstances Wanda would have had to say no. She had her own kids to take care of. But because she has planned this special day for herself, she had made arrangements for their care. Technically, she had the time. And then she rationalized: Which was more important, indulging herself by reading a book, or offering support to her traumatized friend? Wanda couldn't say "no" to Bonnie, and so she went off to help her out.

In reality, Wanda didn't know how to say "yes" to herself. She was not important enough in her own eyes. When her friend Bonnie called, asking her for help, Wanda felt sucked into Bonnie's world. She felt sucked into Bonnie's urgency and neediness, and she didn't feel that saying "no" was an option. But the fact of the matter was, Bonnie was always in need. Bonnie was a taker and a user. She looked to Wanda to be her full time therapist, and Wanda didn't know how not to oblige her. She had grown so used to putting her own needs second to those of her parents, her husband, her children, her friends, that when it came time to choose, she never chose herself. (Wanda is a sadness-based strong/distant.)

SPECIAL NOTE

The pattern of taking care of your parents' needs before your own most completely describes the emotional dynamics of the sadness-based person. If you are anger-based, your reality may have been the reverse. As an anger-based person, you would have realized that your parents were not going to meet your needs. Because you wanted to have your needs met (and rightly so), you may have decided that the only way you were going to get <u>any</u> attention was to act out. If this was the case, you would have been extremely demanding, being very vocal about what you wanted, getting your self into trouble all the time, doing the exact opposite of what your parents wanted you to do—in short, making your parents' lives miserable.

Your goal in being difficult was to get your needs met, just as the goal for the sadness-based person was to get her/his needs met. The difference between the styles is simply this: anger-based people try to get their needs met directly; sadness-based people try to get their needs met indirectly, by bolstering up an external source of need satisfaction. Unfortunately, neither style would have changed your parents' capacity to give you what you deserved—love, affection, kindness, attention, consideration; neither style would have changed your parents' capacity to treat you as the very special and most wonderful person you were and are.

HOW ARE YOU TREATING YOUR SELF?

The fastest way to find out how you are treating your self is to do this exercise:

1. Make a list of all the people who are important to you, all the people you love, and all the people you hate: your mom, your dad, your siblings, your spouse, your children, your friends, your boss, your co-workers.

2. Next to each name, write out why you like them, and why you don't like them.

3. If you haven't already done so, translate your likes and dislikes into what this means for you. For example, if you say your mother is "opinionated," how this might affect you is that she is always giving you advice, and telling you what to do, disregarding your age, your opinions and your feelings. Larry's list looked like this:

Mother

Disinterested in me; she wants to hear about what's going on in my life so that she can tell me how I should fix things. She hates my wife and keeps telling me I shouldn't have married her.

Father

Not very interested in me at all. He likes to talk about football and how his teams are doing, but he doesn't show an interest in my career. He expects me to be sympathetic to his aches and pains. He expects me to feel sorry for him because his life hasn't worked out the way he wanted it to.

Nancy (Wife)

She's very reliable, pretty, smart, a great cook and a hard worker. I like the fact that I can really count on her. On the negative side, I find her too demanding. Although she has the resources, she doesn't solve her problems on her own. She turns to me to support her in everything: dealing with her family, dealing with her boss, dealing with the kids. Her endless personal problems drag me down. I feel I have to take care of her needs before my own, because she can't seem to function without my support. I resent her for taking so much time away from me.

Carl (Older Brother)

He doesn't respect me. I don't make as much money as he does, and he is always reminding me that I have a long way to go. He puts me down every chance he gets. He makes me feel inadequate.

Alex (Male Friend)

He was great when I was single. He used to be there for me, and
we had fun chumming around. Now that I'm married, it seems
like our relationship is a one-way street. He wants me to do
things for him—invite him to dinner, fix him up with women—
but he isn't there for me. When I try to bring up my problems, he
just changes the subject, saying that I don't have any problems,
that I have a gorgeous wife and a nice life.

Boss

A real slave-driver. No praise coming from him. No appreciation. Nothing is good enough for him. And if it is, I am rewarded
with more work. He takes so much out of me.

4. Now face up to it. Everything you don't like about how someone else is treating you, you are doing to your self—that is,
   you are doing to your inner self. Let's review what each person
   in Larry's life tells him about himself:

Mother

Because his mother shows little interest in how Larry is feeling
about his own life, Larry will have learned to be disinterested in
his own feelings, especially his key emotions: sadness, rage, fear
and shame. Ignoring his inner feelings, he will most likely try to
fix his life externally, not internally. His mother's criticalness of
Nancy suggests that he will have learned how to be critical from
her; thus he will be hard on himself for any decision he has
made that has not worked out. His mother's negativity about
Nancy reflects his own doubts about her.

Father

Larry experienced disinterest in himself from both his mother
and his father—a double-whammy. Thus, from his father as
well, he will have learned not to be interested in his own feelings. In addition, he would not have been given much help from
his father in how to problem solve. Even now, although his
career advancement is of concern, he probably has few ideas as
to how to get it moving. Rather than trying to figure out what he

could do to improve his situation, Larry will likely get stuck in self-condemnation for his inadequacy at not having advanced quickly enough.

Larry was programmed to put the needs of his father before his own. Despite the fact that Larry's father never gave him very much love or support, he now expects Larry to be very caring and giving. From this Larry can learn that he will likely repeat this pattern with significant others, treating others as Number One, with himself taking the Number Two spot.

Nancy (Wife)

The main problem that Larry finds with Nancy is that she takes up a lot of his time. Her needs are more important than his own. Well, we know where he must have learned that! However, what it suggests for his own life is that he's not paying attention to his inner self and his own needs; he's putting other people's needs before the attention he must pay to himself. He wasn't made to feel important by his parents, and so he doesn't put much importance on his own feelings and needs; he puts others before himself.

Carl (Older Brother)

Carl's lack of respect for Larry reflects the fact that Larry doesn't respect himself. Again, Larry was not made to feel important and valued in his growing up years, and so he doesn't value himself as a growing and evolving human being. The inadequacy Larry feels reflects the shame and inadequacy he felt in not having been good enough to his parents. By his parents' not having paid much attention to him, Larry had to have concluded that there was something wrong with him. It's no wonder that his career is not going well.

Alex (Male Friend)

Larry has a pattern—he's constantly being used by others. His friend is no exception. Larry is supposed to give, while his friend takes, without feeling obligated to give anything back. Again, this shows that Larry is not paying attention to his inner self and his own need for love, recognition and validation. Not considering himself to be as important as others, he again allows himself to end up in the Number Two position.

Boss

Is it surprising that Larry has a slave-driver as a boss? His boss fits right into his program: I am Number Two. Please take advantage of me. Again, Larry is not focusing on his own value, worth and importance; he's putting himself second.

WHY PEOPLE'S TREATMENT OF YOU IS SO REVEALING

It's a question of toleration. You will never allow another person to treat you any worse than you are treating your self. In looking at Larry's situation, Larry allows his mother to criticize his wife, Nancy. Although he doesn't like it when she does so, he tolerates it, because deep down inside, he has the same doubts about Nancy. If he felt great about Nancy, he would simply tell his mother that he loves his wife, that she is the best thing that has ever happened to him, and that he wants her (his mother) to say nice things about Nancy. A clear message coming from a clear feeling of certainty.

In most other situations, Larry allows other people to take the Number One position. He puts others' needs before his own. Why? Because he has grown used to doing so. He pushes down his own inner self's need to feel important, valued, appreciated and loved. He pushes down his own inner self's need to express his own feelings and to assert what he wants.

If Larry were connected with his true inner feelings, he wouldn't tolerate being Number Two; he just wouldn't stand for it. He is Number One, and he intends to live that way. When Alex attempts to take and not give, Larry would make it known that he's not playing ball by those rules—he has needs too, and he expects reciprocation. When Nancy comes to him with her incessant demands, he would tell her that he has problems too, and that he would like some time and attention. He would also tell Nancy that she needs to find other supports, and that he can't be all things to her. He might suggest, in a supportive way, that she work with a therapist to help her overcome her unresolved pain from the past. To his father, Larry would say he wants a two-way relationship and some interest shown in his own problems and needs.

Larry's brother, Carl, would respect Larry if Larry respected himself. In order for this to happen, Larry has to start taking his own side. He has to understand that his life has gotten stuck because he was neither valued, nor made to feel important. Being criticized rather than supported, he has grown used to being Number Two. To respect himself, Larry has to start paying attention to his own needs, and to start treating himself as the important person he is. When Larry starts showing respect for his inner self, and the wonderful person he is, Larry's problems with his boss will clear up as well. Often it's not necessary to say anything to anyone—the way we treat our selves will communicate clearly to others the way we expect to be treated.

SPECIAL NOTE

It was just explained that people will never treat you any worse than you are treating your inner self, simply because you wouldn't tolerate it. It is possible, however, for people to treat you better than you are treating your inner self, or better than you are treating them.

The reason? People will treat you in the way it <u>appears</u> that you are treating your self. And so if you <u>appear</u> to be enjoying your self through the use of your dependency item—drugs, alcohol, sex, gambling, an extended work day, exercise, shopping, being super busy—it will appear that you are being good to your self. People will match the way you appear to be treating your self. Even though indulging in a dependency item is the means you may use to avoid facing your own pain, to an outsider, it will appear that you're having fun, and that you like your self. Thus, people will treat you well because they will fall for the illusion that you are treating your self well.

In the same way, if it appears that you have a "right" to treat other people poorly (you are smarter, more powerful, more wealthy, more knowledgeable, more skilful, more creative, more confident, more angry), or if you use intimidation or bullying tactics to assert your own desires, the people with whom you are interacting will accept your abuse, your criticism, your judgement on their worth. Believing you to be better than themselves, the people you abuse will treat you in an appeasing manner, rather than in the same abusive way you are treating them.

A KEY TO YOUR BELIEF SYSTEM

How people are treating you will also reveal the nature of your belief system. Your beliefs about your self are often beyond your conscious awareness because as a dependent child, you may have chosen to block out the negative messages that had made you feel ashamed, and the negative treatment that had made you feel worthless. And so on a conscious level, you may have forgotten that you were called "dumb," or "no good," or that you would never amount to anything. On a conscious level, you may never have realized that being ignored, abused, humiliated or criticized would have caused you to feel worthless in adult life.

Whatever belief you hold to be true, you will live out. A belief that you may have had imprinted into you, as a child, is that you were responsible for your parents' wellbeing and happiness. This may have occurred for a number of different reasons. You may had been sickly as a child, and it was only through your mom/dad's constant time, effort and vigilance that you are alive today. Your parent would then have taken on the role of saviour and in your gratitude, you would have felt obligated to "give back" by constant servitude.

The same scenario may have been played out in relation to a school-related problem. Again, it may have only been because your parent went to bat for you, fighting your cause, that you were able to succeed academically. In this case gratitude from youth may have turned into servitude in adult life. In a completely different scenario, you may have had a parent who was physically ill, suicidal, addicted to drugs or alcohol, or very lonely and needy, and her/his needs and lack of taking personal responsibility for her/his own happiness would have been placed on your shoulders. For whatever reason, you may have been expected to become the caretaker, being obligated to assume the role of your parent's parent.

If you were made to believe that you were responsible for providing care, and for keeping your parents happy, you will continue to live out this belief as an adult.

As a child, Norm had a life-threatening illness. Coming from a family of four children, Norm saw the strain that the constant care of him was putting on his mother. Keeping him alive meant frequent trips to the doctor, crisis admissions to the hospital, and around-the-clock attention when he was bedridden.

Unfortunately for Norm, his mother was not a happy woman. Because she was "sacrificing" her life for Norm, she saw in Norm a convenient target to dump her own misery. Thus she would complain to him about how difficult it was to take care of him. She would complain to him about how empty her life was, and how horrible her marriage was. Norm, being dependent on his mother for his survival, felt he had no option but to become his mother's confidant and target of blame.

In his adult life, Norm found himself in the permanent role of taking responsibility for other people's happiness. He always found himself getting sucked into the role of building up a friend's ego. In his marriage, he allowed himself to be dumped on by his wife, accepting the blame for her unhappiness: it was his fault that their finances were poor; it was his fault that she was in a bad mood; it was his fault that the relationship was not going smoothly.

As an adult, Norm is living out his belief that he is responsible for the happiness of other people. His actions reflect this belief: he defers to other people's authority; he puts his needs and interests second to other people more "important" than himself; he accepts less than respectful treatment; he allows himself to be criticized; he allows himself to be blamed; he allows himself to be screamed at; he feels it's his job to keep the peace. (Norm is a sadness-based strong/distant.)

In examining your life, if you find that people are taking you for granted, are critical of you, are expecting you to keep them happy, look closely at your beliefs. If you believe that you're responsible for a significant other's happiness, you will act in ways that will give this person a clear message concerning this very belief. How will you show this? If there's an argument, you'll be the first to give in; you'll be the one to compromise your interests. If arrangements become difficult, you'll be the one who will go out of your way to make the situation work out. If there's a stalemate, you'll be the one to apologize first. In short, you will act as the glue to keep the relationship on an even keel.

This pattern of being responsible for another person's happi-

ness will repeat itself in all your key relationships. So be aware
that you are in fact creating your own reality by being subservient to others. By observing how people are treating you, you
can discover your internal beliefs that are acting as a blueprint
for all of your behaviour.

WHO WOULD HAVE BELIEVED IT?

For those of you who have always believed that your past
has little to do with your present life, the information in this
chapter will certainly appear strange. However, if you examine
your present relationships (those that are important to you), you
will find marked similarities between your present and your
past. The reason? You will treat your inner self the way your parents treated you, and you will allow other people to treat you as
you treat your inner self. Thus, you will replicate the relationship you had with your parents in all your significant relationships. In the next chapter, Anchors For Life, you will discover
exactly how this replication will occur with your intimate partners.

6 | ANCHORS FOR LIFE

The desire to mate is instinctive. It's human nature to want to share who you are with a special partner. You want to give your love, and you want to receive love back. You want to be intimate. You want to break your personal isolation by inviting a special person into your life: someone whom you can trust; someone who will be kind and caring; someone who will appreciate your worth; someone who will love you. As a human being, you are looking for that unconditionally loving parent— the parent you didn't have, but the parent who you, as a child, always dreamed about—someone who would understand you; someone who would think you were wonderful just because you're you; someone who you wouldn't have to serve, cater to, please or do things for, because s/he wouldn't want anything from you except that you would be happy.

And now, as an adult, you are free to find that special person. In the same way that you can reach for your favourite alcoholic beverage and expect that you'll get a little buzz and warm positive feelings, so too you are free to search for that special person who will treat you the way you wanted to be treated as an infant and child. Unfortunately, in the same way that your Emotional Operating System will ultimately backfire, so too will your choice of mates. Let's now find out why that is.

HOW APPEARANCES DECEIVE

In an intimate relationship, the <u>illusion</u> does exist that your partner will take away your emotional pain; the <u>illusion</u> does exist that your partner will make up for the deficits from your past; the <u>illusion</u> does exist that your partner will be consistently kind and loving toward you; the <u>illusion</u> does exist that your partner will show you the same intense interest and admiration two years down the line that s/he will show you on the first date; the <u>illusion</u> does exist that your partner truly "understands" you and will be everything you need her/him to be.

The truth of the matter is, first impressions are deceiving, and so too are the personality traits and the hidden problems of the men/women to whom you are attracted. It's all a question of time and familiarity. Until you get to know a person:

• going out for a few drinks after work is fun; living with an alcoholic isn't.

• having a few lines of cocaine at a party is racy; living with a cocaine addict isn't.

• going to the race track is a new adventure; living with a gambler isn't.

• going to Los Vegas for the weekend is "living in the fast lane"; living with a gambler isn't.

• having wild erotic exotic sex is fun in the beginning; living with a sex addict isn't.

• finding a high-powered millionaire may appear like a dream come true; living with a compulsive workaholic isn't.

• finding a dynamic man/woman who has an exciting career, a six-figure income, a full social calendar, and all the important possessions money can buy may appear wonderful; having your plans cancelled repeatedly because of her/his urgent meetings isn't.

• finding an attractive woman who "dresses to kill" may be a feather is your cap in the beginning; living with a shopaholic isn't.

• finding a divorced man who loves his children may appear to be a sign of a capacity to give love to you; spending every waking moment with his kids isn't.

- finding an attractive man/woman who turns heads may make you feel important and special; living with a self-indulgent narcissist doesn't.

- finding someone who wants to devote every waking hour to you may appear to be a dream come true; living with a controlling personality isn't.

Appearances can be deceptive. Because of your unmet needs and your emotional cravings from the past, you will often deny those personality traits that don't quite fit your ideal image of your perfect partner.

BEWARE DENIAL

There's a familiar expression, "You see what you want to see and you believe what you want to believe." The signs of the type of person you are dealing with are usually visible by the second date. Whether you want to admit that they exist is another story.

Sally had a difficult time finding men she liked to spend time with. At age 29, she was attractive and was employed at a small accounting firm. But she never seemed to have the right kind of relationship. She got stuck in the cycle of finding "nice" guys who bored her or "snakes" who treated her badly. And then she met Richard. Richard was a lawyer who was successful, charming and very attractive to her. Sally felt that she had found her soulmate.

Richard was everything to her. He was tender, loving and caring. Because Sally had come from a very abusive background, she craved positive attention and affection. And so she took, and took, and took while Richard gave, and gave, and gave. What Sally didn't know, until the relationship was on the wane, was that Richard resented giving; he gave because he felt he "had to" give in order to be accepted and loved; yet everything he gave, he resented. The fact was, he had wanted Sally to give to him, but he was not able to ask for what he wanted; so he gave in the hope that Sally would give back the support and caring that he craved. Sally, however, was not capable of giving. Because of her excessive neediness, she only wanted to take, and she believed she had carte blanche to do so.

What happened over time was that Richard started to abuse Sally verbally, and later physically. His own rage, at not having had his own needs fulfilled, started to build. At first he dumped on Sally verbally, by criticizing her weight, her personality, her friends and her career prospects. Later the verbal abuse escalated and moved into threats on her physical safety. It was at this point that Sally parted company with Richard.

Sally was in a state of shock at what had happened to her wonderful relationship with Richard. Everything was so perfect—perfect that is, if you want to wear a blindfold. The truth was, Richard had many of the characteristics of an abuser. Friends of Sally who had met Richard found him to be most unpleasant. He was very controlling; he always had to have his own way; he interrupted conversations; he usually had a disparaging comment to make about the waiters who served him, the people he worked with and whoever else was in his vision. An emotionally uninvolved observer would not have voted him Mr. America. Richard met Sally's needs, and so she chose not to see the obvious. (Sally is sadness-based needy. Richard is anger-based.)

WHY DENIAL IS SO DEADLY

The rule of thumb is this:

1. The more unmet needs you have from the past, the more you will deny signs of your partner's true nature and character.

2. The more you believe you don't have the resources to meet your own needs, or the more you believe you need your partner to complete you, love you, make you feel whole and secure, the more you will deny those behaviours of your partner which are disrespectful, or which will undermine your integrity.

3. The worse you treat your self (see Chapter Five), the greater the amount of abuse you will tolerate. In this case the abuse you receive will seem so familiar that it won't even appear unacceptable.

What you might deny, in order to maintain loving feelings toward your partner, includes the following realities: your partner may not truly value, respect and appreciate you; your happiness may not be a priority to your partner; your partner does not have the emotional capacity to consider your needs; your partner is preoccupied with her/his own rage from the past, and sees you as a dumping ground for her/his unreleased anger; your partner is preoccupied with her/his own sadness from the past, and sees you as a way out of her/his loneliness; your relationship has no future; your relationship is destructive for you.

If you match up with a partner where you have to deny your self and your perceptions in order to preserve your relationship, you will ensure that your inner self and your true feelings will never surface. Your dependency on your partner will leave no room for you to be your self; there will be no room to risk rejection. Ironically, the more that you aren't able to be your self, the more you will need your partner to take care of you. In other words, you will both create and magnify your own need.

WHO IS YOUR PERFECT MATCH?

Because you will have most likely blocked out the pain of your experiences as an abused, neglected or overcontrolled child, as an adult, you will remain unaware of the feelings you have blocked out. In this way, you will not be aware of your feelings of shame, sadness, rage and fear that are now stored in your unconscious mind.

Your lack of conscious awareness of your true feelings doesn't mean that these same feelings don't control you. Rather, it is these painful feelings of which you are largely unaware that will directly influence your choice in romantic partners.

The often times inconvenient reality is that you will always be attracted to your perfect match. A romantic partner will mirror your emotional profile, and will match the same degree of pain that you are unconsciously feeling, the same degree of denial of unresolved painful emotions, the same unreleased emotions (anger, sadness, fear, shame), the same unresolved emotional issues (trust, abandonment, betrayal, respect, self-love, self-worth).

Although your unconscious emotions will be the same, the Emotional Operating Style of your partner and your self will either be the same or complementary. If you are anger-based, please refer to Chart 3 for a summary of the Emotional Matching that will occur in your romantic relationships; if you are sadness-based needy, please refer to Chart 4; if you are sadness-based strong/distant, please refer to Chart 5. If you are love-based, or if you are striving to become love-based, please refer to Chapters Twelve, Creating A Love-Base.

In looking at these charts, what you will immediately

notice is that there is no mention of the dynamics of a match with a love-based person. This is because love-based people will only match up with love-based people. The reasons for this will be explained in Chapter Twelve.

WHEN YOU ARE ANGER-BASED

When you are anger-based, you will tend to get angry easily, you will not be afraid to show your anger, you will believe you have to fight for your rights, you will believe that showing your vulnerability is a dangerous thing to do, and you will believe that putting on a strong front to the world is the only way to survive.

YOUR EXACT MATCH: ANGER-BASED TO ANGER-BASED

As an anger-based person, you might choose a partner who presents to the world exactly as you do. Your anger-based partner, being just like you, will feel comfortable jumping into a fight to ensure that her/his needs are being met. Being just like you, arguing and determining who's right and who's wrong will be very important.

If this is the case, your relationship is likely to be loaded with conflict. Every incident that takes place will become a battleground for who is right and who is wrong. "Winning" an argument will be far more important than developing a close and intimate relationship. While you will respect your partner for being as strong as you, you will often find your relationship to be stressful and not very loving. Often, it will appear like "work" to maintain.

YOUR COMPLEMENTARY MATCH:
ANGER-BASED TO SADNESS-BASED NEEDY

On the other hand, as an anger-based person, you might choose to avoid someone who is just like you, but rather, seek out your complement, a sadness-based needy person who is compliant, passive, loving, giving and kind. Because your sadness-based needy partner is desperate to be loved, s/he will want to keep the peace. This partner will not engage in battles with you, but rather, will want to maintain harmony at any price, even though her/his self-esteem is the price of harmony. Thus, being with a sadness-based needy partner will appear safe to you, and this safety will very often attract you.

As well, there will be a part of you that envies your needy partner's ability to show vulnerability. When you're anger-based, you must always be ready to do battle. And this means never showing vulnerability. While your fight mentality does work for you, this mode of operation will keep you in a constant state of tension. Although you'll never risk letting down your guard, a part of you wishes you could just let go, and show who you really are. Being with a sadness-based needy partner will enable you to "act out" your sadness, fear and shame without your being obligated to do so in the real world.

The problem for you, in being with a sadness-based needy partner, is that you will feel an emotional distance because you will perceive your partner as being weak, and not at the same level as you—s/he will not have developed the self-sufficiency that you have had to develop in order to survive. Your needy partner will want you to take care of her/him. This neediness will drain you, and over time, your partner will often lose her/his appeal.

PSEUDO-COMPLEMENTARY:
ANGER-BASED TO SADNESS-BASED STRONG/DISTANT

As an anger-based person, you may perceive a sadness-based strong/distant person as being your perfect match. In that a strong/distant person will be masking deep feelings of inadequacy, s/he will not want to reveal her/his true feelings about being criticized, not being considered, being made less of a priority than other matters of importance in your life.

S/he will tolerate your need to vent your anger and will tend to be both understanding and supportive of your emotional needs. Because a strong/distant person needs to appear self-sufficient, s/he won't drain you in the way that a sadness-based needy person would.

The problem you will have with a strong/distant partner is that you will tend to feel an emotional distance between your partner and your self. Remember, your strong/distant partner will have the same desire as you have to appear strong and to not reveal inner feelings. In that it is impossible for two emotionally distant people to become intimate, over time, your relationship

Chart 3 – ANGER-BASED MATCHING

COMPLEMENTARY

TO SADNESS-BASED NEEDY

REPRESSED ANGER

- Shame – S/he Feels Worthless
- Fear – Obey Or Be Harmed
- Sadness – S/he'll Do Anything For Love

SADNESS

- Grief-Stricken At Not Having Been Loved
- Desperate To Be Loved, Validated, Recognized
- S/he Feels Powerless

FEAR

- Obey Or Be Harmed
- Conflict Is Dangerous

SHAME

- S/he Feels Worthless
- S/he Believes S/he Deserved To Be Abused/Neglected/Controlled
- S/he Will Accept Abuse In Exchange For Love

ANGER

- S/he Has A Fight Mentality
- S/he Is Self-Reliant
- S/he Is Enraged At Past Disrespectful Treatment
- S/he Feels Betrayed/Doesn't Trust

ANGER-BASED

ANGER

- You Have A Fight Mentality
- You Are Self-Reliant
- You Are Enraged At Past Disrespectful Treatment
- You Feel Betrayed/Don't Trust

SADNESS

- You'll Never Show Your Vulnerability

FEAR

- Triumph Or Be Destroyed
- Win Or Lose All

SHAME

- You Deny Your Feelings Of Inadequacy/Worthlessness

EXACT – TO ANGER-BASED

SADNESS

- S/he'll Never Show You Her/His Vulnerability

FEAR

- Triumph Or Be Destroyed
- Win Or Lose All

SHAME

- S/he Denies Feelings Of Inadequacy/Worthlessness

PSEUDO-COMPLEMENTARY

TO STRONG/DISTANT

REPRESSED ANGER

- Shame – Her/His Worth Is Based On What S/he Does For Others
- Fear – S/he Will Lose Self-Respect By Self-Disclosure
- Sadness – S/he'll Never Be Loved For Being Her/His True Self

SADNESS

- S/he'll Never Be Loved For True Self
- S/he Must Fulfil Roles To Be Loved

FEAR

- Her/His Inadequacies Must Never Be Discovered

SHAME

- S/he Feels Inadequate
- S/he Must Hide Her/His True Self

Chart 4 – SADNESS-BASED NEEDY MATCHING

COMPLEMENTARY

TO ANGER-BASED

ANGER

- S/he Has A Fight Mentality
- S/he Is Self-Reliant
- S/he Is Enraged At Past Disrespectful Treatment
- S/he Feels Betrayed/Doesn't Trust

SADNESS

- S/he'll Never Show You Her/His Vulnerability

FEAR

- Triumph Or Be Destroyed
- Win Or Lose All

SHAME

- S/he Denies Feelings Of Inadequacy/Worthlessness

SADNESS-BASED NEEDY

REPRESSED ANGER

- Shame – You Feel Worthless
- Fear – Obey Or Be Harmed
- Sadness – You'll Do Anything For Love

SADNESS

- You Are Grief-Stricken At Not Having Been Loved
- You Are Desperate To Be Loved, Validated, Recognized
- You Feel Powerless

FEAR

- Obey Or Be Harmed
- Conflict Is Dangerous

SHAME

- You Feel Worthless
- You Believe You Deserved To Be Abused/Neglected/Controlled
- You Will Accept Abuse In Exchange For Love

EXACT COMPLEMENTARY

TO STRONG/DISTANT

REPRESSED ANGER

- Shame – Her/His Worth Is Based On What S/he Does For Others
- Fear – S/he Will Lose Self-Respect By Self-Disclosure
- Sadness – S/he'll Never Be Loved For Being Her/His True Self

SADNESS

- S/he'll Never Be Loved For True Self
- S/he Must Fulfil Roles To Be Loved

FEAR

- Her/His Inadequacies Must Never Be Discovered

SHAME

- S/he Feels Inadequate
- S/he Must Hide Her/His True Self

EXACT EXACT – TO SADNESS-BASED NEEDY

SADNESS

- Grief-Stricken At Not Having Been Loved
- Desperate To Be Loved, Validated, Recognized
- S/he Feels Powerless

FEAR

- Obey Or Be Harmed
- Conflict Is Dangerous

REPRESSED ANGER

- Shame – S/he Is Worthless
- Fear – Obey Or Be Harmed
- Sadness – S/he'll Do Anything For Love

SHAME

- S/he Feels Worthless
- S/he Believes S/he Deserved To Be Abused/Neglected/Controlled
- S/he Will Accept Abuse In Exchange For Love

Chart 5 – SADNESS-BASED STRONG/DISTANT MATCHING

EXACT COMPLEMENTARY

SADNESS-BASED NEEDY

REPRESSED ANGER

- Shame – S/he Is Worthless
- Fear – Obey Or Be Harmed
- Sadness – S/he'll Do Anything For Love

SADNESS

- Grief-Stricken At Not Having Been Loved
- Desperate To Be Loved, Validated, Recognized
- S/he Feels Powerless

FEAR

- Obey Or Be Harmed
- Conflict Is Dangerous

SHAME

- S/he Feels Worthless
- S/he Believes S/he Deserved To Be Abused/Neglected/Controlled
- S/he Will Accept Abuse In Exchange For Love

STRONG/DISTANT

REPRESSED ANGER

- Shame – Your Worth Is Based On What You Do For Others
- Fear – You Will Lose Your Self-Respect By Self-Disclosure
- Sadness – You'll Never Be Loved For Being Your True Self

SADNESS

- You'll Never Be Loved For Being Your Self
- You Must Fulfil Roles To Be Loved

FEAR

- Your Inadequacies Must Never Be Discovered

SHAME

- You Feel Inadequate
- You Must Hide Your True Self

PSEUDO-COMPLEMENTARY

TO ANGER-BASED

ANGER

- S/he Has A Fight Mentality
- S/he Is Self-Reliant
- S/he Is Enraged At Past Disrespectful Treatment
- S/he Feels Betrayed/Doesn't Trust

SADNESS

- S/he'll Never Show You Her/His Vulnerability

FEAR

- Triumph Or Be Destroyed
- Win Or Lose All

SHAME

- S/he Denies Feelings Of Inadequacy/Worthlessness

EXACT EXACT – TO STRONG/DISTANT

REPRESSED ANGER

- Shame – Her/His Worth Is Based On What S/he Does For Others
- Fear – S/he Will Lose Self-Respect By Self-Disclosure
- Sadness – S/he'll Never Be Loved For Being Her/His True Self

SADNESS

- S/he'll Never Be Loved For True Self
- S/he Must Fulfil Roles To Be Loved

FEAR

- Her/His Inadequacies Must Never Be Discovered

SHAME

- S/he Feels Inadequate
- S/he Must Hide Her/His True Self

may become empty. Over time, it may appear as though you are simply going through the motions.

WHEN YOU ARE SADNESS-BASED

As a sadness-based person, you will tend to feel lonely, empty and unloved. If you are sadness-based needy, you will make finding love your reason for living. If you are sadness-based strong/distant, you will want love in the same way that every human being wants love, but because your greatest need is to preserve a veneer of strength, you will keep your emotional distance when you find love.

As a sadness-based person, you may choose to match up with your Exact Match, another sadness-based person. Your Exact Match will either be a person who is seeking a partner to fill up her/his emptiness (sadness-based needy), or a person who feels most comfortable in being emotionally distant (sadness-based strong/distant). It will be your Exact Exact match if both you and your partner want the same thing—either to be filled up or to preserve distance; it will be your Exact Complementary Match if you desire to be filled up, while your partner desires to preserve her/his distance or vice versa.

EXACT EXACT MATCH: STRONG/DISTANT TO STRONG/DISTANT

If you are seeking a partner who feels most comfortable in being emotionally distant, and you feel most comfortable in being emotionally distant, you will rarely enjoy true intimacy. You won't tend to reveal your vulnerable feelings—your desire to be loved, cared for, recognized, appreciated, considered, understood—and neither will your partner. In that both of you will find it more important to preserve your veneer of confidence and self-sufficiency, rather than risk being hurt, betrayed, disappointed and made to feel inadequate, your lack of closeness will often cause your relationship to feel both empty and unsatisfying.

EXACT COMPLEMENTARY MATCH: STRONG/DISTANT TO NEEDY

If you are seeking a partner who wants to be filled up, while you, on the other hand, feel most comfortable in being emotionally distant, you will find that your partner will eventually drain you. You will find that her/his demands and needs are bottom-less: there will always be a new problem or issue to replace those that have been resolved. In addition, there will always be a sense of urgency about your being obligated to solve a problem or fulfil a request. (It's your responsibility to make your partner feel better). No matter how much you give, it will never be enough. And what you did for your partner yesterday will be quickly forgotten as you tackle today's issues. ("I really need your help.")

Needless to say, your personal issues will rarely if ever be addressed. This is because your partner will perceive you as being a parent replacement; s/he will not realize that you have needs too. Because it's important for you to mask your own per-ceived inadequacy, you will rarely let on that you have your own issues to address. And so, while your needy partner will allow you to preserve your veneer of strength (this will enable you to feel safe), you will naturally feel very lonely and empty. Over time, your freedom may often appear more desirable than the sex, caring and personal contact you enjoyed through your rela-tionship.

EXACT EXACT MATCH / EXACT COMPLEMENTARY MATCH: NEEDY TO NEEDY / NEEDY TO STRONG/DISTANT

If you are seeking a partner to fill up your emptiness, to fill you up with love, and make your feel emotionally whole, complete, important and worthwhile, realize that while in the short term, your partner may initially satisfy your needs, in the long term, your feelings of emptiness will return. Over the long term, you will find that your partner will either be unable or unwilling to give you the love you need, and even if s/he does try, there will never be enough love to fill you up. What will usually happen over time is that either you will drain your partner's resources, or s/he will drain yours. What you'll end up finding is that two empty cups cannot fill each other up.

What you will find specifically if you are matching up with a strong/distant partner is that you will experience the same feelings of "longing for love" that you used to feel in relation to your parents. Why? Because your partner will tend to keep her/his emotional distance. Your partner literally will not have the capacity to be intimate because s/he will have cut off her/his vulnerable feelings in order to preserve both her/his self-esteem and identity. A strong/distant person does not want to become "too close" because closeness feels dangerous. Although your partner may appear warm and loving, s/he will rarely be able to respond to you in the way that you desire. (Many strong/distant people substitute sex for true intimacy. While they are able to express their need for affection and closeness through sexual contact, they are unable to reveal their true feelings through their words and actions outside of the bedroom.)

YOUR COMPLEMENTARY MATCH: NEEDY TO ANGER-BASED

As a sadness-based needy person, you may choose to match up with your complementary match—an anger-based person. This is the classic abuser/victim relationship, with you unfortunately being the victim. Why is an anger-based person your complementary emotional match? Because you are angry too. You have the same degree of anger. The difference is, your partner's anger is out on the table while yours is buried beyond your conscious recognition and recall.

As a sadness-based needy person, you crave love and harmony. Being loved is what you live for. Because you will not be perceived as being a great threat to your anger-based partner, you will receive some "love" (conditional attention and affection) intermittently. But there's a price to be paid for this "love": you must compromise your integrity and self-respect; you must accept abuse; you must accept criticism; you must have your flaws magnified; you must take the blame for things that have nothing to do with you; you must do everything in your power to keep your partner happy.

What you're really doing is acting as a dumping ground for your partner's anger, fear, shame and sadness. In all likelihood, you won't recognize this because your own unconscious shame and fear from your past will prevent you from valuing your own worth. Because you have a low opinion of your self, you'll believe that your partner is "better" than you: more intelligent, more knowledgeable, more wealthy, more worldly, more street-smart, more experienced, more creative, more capable, more successful; because s/he's "better" than you, you'll believe that your partner has the right to judge you; you'll believe that you have to do things for your partner, or change aspects of your personality in order to be acceptable and accepted.

There's another reason why you are attracted to an anger-based partner: s/he makes you feel safe. The emotion of anger is a survival emotion, with your feelings of anger alerting you to protect your interests. As a dependent child, feeling and expressing your anger would have appeared self-destructive: it would have caused you to risk losing the love you had. If you were physically or sexually abused, you may have been frightened into believing that you would literally have been killed if you had expressed your anger.

In either situation, as a sadness-based needy adult, you will have lost your ability to both feel and express your anger. Thus, you will have lost your ability to protect your self and your interests. And so you will be very attracted to an anger-based person, a person who clearly knows how to express anger, a person who clearly knows how to protect her/his interests. What you really want is the ability to express your own anger, to protect your own interests, and to really let loose and not have to pretend that you're happy when you're not.

Unfortunately, your attraction will be lethal to you. Your attraction will ultimately destroy you. This is because the anger that is so attractive to you will be used against you. You will become the victim of your partner's rage. Rather than achieving your goal of becoming stronger and more powerful, you will begin to feel more inadequate and worthless than ever before. Your weakened self-image will increase your neediness and dependence on your partner. On an emotional level, you will be going backwards.

If you are a sadness-based needy person, realize that there's only one way to match up with your ideal partner, and that is to release your backlog of denied emotions: your grief at having been abandoned; your shame at having been made to feel contaminated, worthless and/or inadequate; your fear in that you still believe that if you say "no," your life will be in danger; your rage at having been treated as an object of gratification, and/or as a dumping ground for your mom/dad's rage; your rage at having been stripped of your rights to protect your own interests; your rage at having been neglected and betrayed. As well, you must realize this: <u>The only person who can truly protect your own interests is you. If you pass that responsibility onto your partner, you will end up remaining a victim forever.</u>

PSEUDO-COMPLEMENTARY MATCH: STRONG/DISTANT TO ANGER-BASED

As a strong/distant person you will tend to perceive an anger-based person much as you perceive a sadness-based needy person. Even though the anger-based person's Operating Style is polar opposite to that of the needy person, on a practical level, they are the same—they are both takers, they both demand a great deal of time, understanding, and patience.

As a strong/distant person, you want to hide your inner self, and so you will tolerate your anger-based partner's need to vent her/his anger, rather than express your dissatisfaction with such behaviour. You will tend to accommodate your anger-based partner's need to make her/his personal interests a priority. You will accept your anger-based partner's narcissism and self-preoccupation. You will be understanding of the reasons why your anger-based partner behaves in the way s/he does.

Over time, you will find your relationship with your anger-based partner to be both draining and empty. Over time, you will find that while your anger-based partner is very good at taking, s/he is not very good at giving. Over time, the emotional appeal of your anger-based partner's dynamic personality will often wane.

EMOTIONAL MATCHING IN ACTION

SADNESS-BASED STRONG/DISTANT TO ANGER-BASED

Shame is the emotion that you'll feel when you don't value your own worth. If your parents didn't make you feel important and special, if they became overinvolved with you, or if you were verbally, sexually or physically abused, you won't value who you are. Rather, you'll feel that you aren't good enough as you are and that there's something wrong with you. If you were abused, you will likely feel that it was your fault that you were abused; you will believe that you were "bad," or that you deserved the abuse you received.

As an adult, you will most likely try to hide your low self-worth; in believing you're defective, you certainly don't want anyone else to find this out. One way to hide low self-esteem is to choose a romantic partner who "appears" to have high self-worth. In the following example, notice that while the Operating Styles of the partners are different, the underlying emotion of denied shame is the same.

Greg was a self-made millionaire. He had built up his business from scratch, and his hard work had paid off. Although he should have been proud of himself for his business acumen, his financial success had not changed the way he felt about himself. He still felt inadequate. In his childhood, Greg's mother had been very controlling and overinvolved with his life. She was always trying to "help" him out. Although her intrusive parenting had not interfered with his business success, the damage she had done clearly showed up in his romantic life.

To compensate for his belief that he was "lesser-than," Greg always made sure he was romantically involved with a "head-turning" women. Mercedes was no exception. Coming from South Africa, her family had enjoyed prosperity and an easy existence. Moving to Canada, she took up the profession she knew best: spending wealthy men's money. She met Greg at a gala reception and they soon moved in together. It was a great relationship. Greg gave, and Mercedes took. Mercedes had no concern for either Greg's business stressors or his personal issues. She was only concerned about his ability to keep giving her the money she needed to feed her habit—making herself beautiful.

Greg and Mercedes were very similar: they both were secretly ashamed of who they respectively were. Mercedes was shopping dependent. She did not value her own "inner self"; rather, she needed an attractive "outer self" to make herself feel worthwhile. Greg too didn't value himself. He believed he needed an attractive exterior, in the form of a beautiful woman, to indicate to other people that he was a "man," and that he had some value.

Sadly, Greg paid an enormous price to hide his own shame. For the price was his own integrity. In order to feel worthwhile (by having Mercedes by his side), he had to accept being used; he had to play the role of personal banker to a women who had no interest in his emotional wellbeing. Ironically, by denying his own inner self, Greg reinforced his own feelings of worthlessness.

SADNESS-BASED NEEDY TO ANGER-BASED

Ellen was both neglected and abused. Being the last child in a line of six children, she was clearly an accident. Her mother had never let her forget this. Ellen was constantly being reminded that if it wasn't for her, her mother would have left her father. As a result of these constant reminders of her accidental birth, Ellen had secretly wished that she had never been born. When her mother was not abusing her, she was ignoring her. Most of the time she acted like Ellen was not even there. She focused her attention on Ellen's next oldest sister, the apple of her mother's eye. Ellen's father was a passive man, and tended to keep much to himself.

Understandably, Ellen was in desperate need for love, attention, validation and support. She had never received the caring that she had so desired. What kept her going during her very painful growing up years was the hope that she would find her true love who would fill in all the holes in her soul that her unpleasant childhood had created.

Because of her extreme need and desire to fill in her own emptiness, Ellen deliberately sought out men who appeared to be strong and self-reliant (men who appeared to be able to give her what she needed). The men with whom she ended up getting involved, however, were anger-based men who had a great deal of rage to discharge. They appeared confident because they were dependent on either substances, activities or victims to discharge their enormous amounts of rage, and to muster up feelings of self-worth. Ellen, on the other hand, felt weak, because she was dependent on her man to make her feel good about herself. Although in reality, her romantic partners were as sad, as ashamed, as afraid and as angry as she was, their Operating Styles fooled her. She saw her partners as being strong and confident, while she saw herself as being both weak and inadequate.

Perceiving that she had no intrinsic worth, Ellen believed she had to pay a price to receive the love she desired. In one relationship with a race-track fanatic named Ed, Ellen agreed to lend Ed money to make up for the peaks and valleys that occurred as a result of his gambling addiction. She didn't do this voluntarily however. Ed pressured her into doing so by emotionally withdrawing, becoming nasty, and criticizing her for being cheap and not "loving him as he loved her." Ellen believed she had to keep Ed happy, or else she would lose him. Because she couldn't risk losing the relationship that was giving her a reason to live, she compromised her integrity to keep Ed by her side.

ANGER-BASED TO ANGER-BASED

Stan was a really likeable guy. At age 45, he was married to Arlene, an attractive career woman. Stan and Arlene had a perfect marriage, that is, on the outside. The reason everyone thought that they had such a great marriage was because they both worked on creating a phoney appearance of happiness. What really was going on was another story.

Stan had had an overinvolved mother. Out of concern that he wouldn't become successful, his mother constantly gave him direction as to how to live. Her helpful advice had always felt like abuse to Stan, because nothing he could do was right. If he had received a "B" in school, his mother wanted to work with him so that he would get an "A." Stan was afraid of his mother because she had a viperous tongue. He saw how she had decimated his father, and he didn't want the same slurs directed his way; so he sat on his anger and stewed.

Arlene had come from a home where she had been verbally abused by her father. Arlene was a pretty girl. Around the time of puberty, her father, feeling dissatisfied with his own marital relationship, had started to feel sexually attracted to her. Feeling ashamed of himself for having been attracted to his own daughter, he had mountains of shame to get rid of, and he did so by insulting and verbally attacking Arlene. Over time, Arlene had learned to fight back, and she regularly became entrenched in huge screaming matches with her father.

What Stan and Arlene had in common was that they were both made to feel inadequate during their growing up years; they both came into the marriage with an equal feeling of worthlessness and a bottomless pit of rage that had never been discharged. The result? Rip-roaring battles. Arguments about everything. They both became experts at dissecting each other's weaknesses. If one of them dished out an abuse, the other one would hurl one back, faster than the speed of light.

Needless to say, the marriage was not a happy one. Nor did it last very long. The attraction that they had both felt toward one another got lost during the daily battles. Both Stan and Arlene saw their respective partner as the "bad guy," not realizing that their buried emotions from the past were the real source of the problem.

THE OPERATING STYLE THAT ATTRACTS YOU

The expression, "Opposites Attract," refers to the fact that you will often be attracted to a personality style, a lifestyle or a quality that you do not possess or have access to. In that we, as human beings, will often take the path of least resistance, many of us hold the belief that the fastest way to get what we want is to associate with a romantic partner who has what we want. Thus, either through osmosis or proximity, we will enjoy the desired goal as quickly as possible.

In considering what "Opposites Attract" means, realize again that your inner emotions are not opposite—they are exactly the same—as the previous section has outlined. What is opposite is what you do with your emotions in the outside world. Thus, one person who feels deeply ashamed can attempt to develop self-worth by becoming a millionaire; another person can attempt to feel better about himself by helping the poor and dispossessed. One person who is angry can "win through intimidation," and become very successful in business; another person can repress that anger and become an obedient worker who is ultimately betrayed by his employer.

In terms of the nature of your attractions, you will be attracted to a person who is either the same as you, both inside (emotionally) and outside (how s/he presents to the world), or the same as you on the inside (emotionally) but who "appears" different or opposite to your self in the outside world. The categories of what you will be attracted to include:

A. PERSONALITY QUALITIES OR ATTRIBUTES

genuineness, sincerity, honesty, openess, warmth, giving nature, reliability, loyalty, stability, vulnerability, compliancy, kindness, confidence, relaxed manner, intelligence, appearance of being successful, aggressiveness, energetic nature, enthusiastic, fun-loving, happy

B. ABILITY TO EXPRESS EMOTIONS

happiness, joy, anger, sadness, vulnerability, shame, fear

C. ACTUAL POSSESSIONS OR SKILLS

money, material wealth, ownership of property, lifestyle, friends, knowledge, ability to fix things, resourcefulness, self-reliant, creativity, knowledge

D. THE FAMILIAR

unpleasant familiar feelings: feeling trapped, feeling vulnerable, feeling helpless, feeling angry, feeling controlled, feeling ashamed, feeling worthless, feeling frightened, feeling terrified, feeling lonely, feeling sad, "longing for love"

pleasant familiar feelings: feeling happy, feeling accepted, feeling respected, feeling appreciated, feeling valued, feeling loved, having fun, feeling wonderful

WHEN AN "OPPOSITE" OPERATING STYLE ATTRACTS YOU

If your partner possess qualities that you don't possess, realize that you are attracted to the parts of your self that you have not as yet developed. For example, if you are shy, but are attracted to a person who is dynamic and outgoing, realize that you would like to be that way also. The reason you may not have developed the outgoing personality style was due to a fear you had, when you were dependent upon your parents, that being outgoing was dangerous to your ultimate security and happiness. Whether being outgoing would have prevented you from receiving love or attention, would have enraged your parents, or would have made you feel too visible and exposed, you would have decided that the best way to get your needs met and to ensure your survival was to keep a low profile.

Although the danger is now over, and you can now become the person you want to be, your personality style has become well-entrenched. You now think of your self as a quiet, shy person who is incapable of being outgoing, self-confident, dynamic, personable, entertaining and interesting to others. And so rather than realizing that you can develop those dormant parts of your self, you think it's impossible—that it's just not you.

In the following chapters you will learn exactly how you can break free from your past and become the person you want to be. For now, realize that whatever you are attracted to in your romantic partner, you do want for your self. (If you possess the trait to which you are attracted, you are already on the right track.) Although you may believe that the fastest way to get what you want is to associate with the person who has it, realize that the only way you can ensure that you'll have what you want forever is to develop it within your self. That way it can never be taken away from you, you'll never be dependent on anyone outside your self to give you what you want, and thus, you'll never have to compromise your integrity in order to get your needs met.

ANCHORS FOR LIFE

Whether consciously or unconsciously, every one of us has dreamed of finding a romantic partner who would have the qualities of an unconditionally loving parent—a person who would make up for the emotional wrongs that we have experienced as children, a person who would take away our pain.

Why is it then that the relationships we have with our spouses and our lovers will turn out to be just like those we had with our parents? Why is it that if we felt lonely and unloved as children, we will end up feeling the same way with our romantic partners? Why is it that if we felt angry at our parents for not having loved us, or for having betrayed our trust, we will end up feeling the same way toward our partners?

We will end up repeating the past with our romantic partners because we will recreate the past through playing out our unresolved emotions. Let's look at what happens when you bring your feelings of inadequacy from childhood into your romantic relationships.

If you are anger-based, you will fight your unconscious feelings of inadequacy by attempting to prove that you are worthwhile. To build your self up, you will unconsciously try to tear your partner down by attacking her/his worth. If your partner is anger-based, s/he will likely respond by attacking your worth. Suddenly, your loving relationship will have turned into an ongoing battle to preserve your self-esteem. If your partner is sadness-based needy, s/he may accept your abuse without a struggle; however, by abusing your partner, you will feel deeply ashamed of your self for both hurting the person you love and being unable to control your own anger. By abusing your partner, you will reinforce your own unconscious feelings of inadequacy. If your partner is strong/distant, her/his veneer of calmness and strength will tend to make you feel inadequate by comparison.

If you are sadness-based needy and your partner is anger-based, after the initial "in love" phase is over, your partner will likely begin to treat you disrespectfully. Because you will believe you cannot live without your partner's love, you will accept her/his criticisms, judgement on your worth, and/or inconsiderate treatment in the same way that you did as a child; you will accept abuse in exchange for love, just as you did as a child. (This will reinforce your own unconscious feelings of inadequacy.)

If you are sadness-based needy and your partner is sadness-based needy, or sadness-based strong/distant, s/he will likely try to fill you up with the love you so desire. But no matter how kind and giving your partner will be in the beginning, over time, your bottomless pit of need will drain her/him. Because you don't value your self, you will always want more than any one person can provide. Your excessive neediness and dependency on a person outside your self will reinforce your own feelings of inadequacy.

If you are sadness-based strong/distant, you will feel obligated to fulfil your partner's role requirements in order to ensure her/his "love." To keep your partner happy, you will feel obligated to push down your own conflicting needs. In order to mask your own perceived inadequacy, you will choose not to express your own feelings. In that you perceive your partner's love to be conditional on you pleasing her/him, you will continue to feel the same inadequacy (lack of intrinsic worth) that you did when living with your parents.

No matter how wonderful your romantic relationship is in the beginning, it will become a repeat of your past unless you free your self from your past unresolved emotions: your anger, sadness, shame and fear. If you do so, you will be able to create a warm, loving, supportive relationship that will enhance your life. If you do not, you will find that your intimate partner, once seen as your soulmate, will now turn out to be your anchor, keeping you firmly grounded in your past.

III

YOU CAN RUN, BUT
YOU JUST CAN'T HIDE

7 | THE LAW OF ATTRACTION

The Law of Attraction states that we act as magnets to pull people and occurrences into our lives. Circumstances don't just "happen." We bring them to our selves. The Law of Attraction is a spiritual law in the sense that there is no scientific proof of it; we only know of its existence through observation.

The Law of Attraction is of great use in explaining why our lives may not be working as well as we would wish. It explains why, even though we may make great efforts to succeed, initiating a lot of contacts in business, going to a lot of parties, we still do not have prosperous, exciting lives. It explains why, in the area of intimate relationships, we will repeatedly end up finding the wrong people. A modern day expression is most apropos: "Same shit, different day."

The Law of Attraction is not foreign to any of us. Whenever an event occurs that is amazingly strange, we will usually put it down to coincidence. "Coincidence" is defined in Webster's New World Dictionary as an accidental and remarkable occurrence of events or ideas at the same time, suggesting but lacking a casual relationship. The question is, "Is the relationship a 'by chance' occurrence, or are there some magnetic forces, that we cannot see, bringing about the result?"

The word "synchronicity" comes from the Greek: syn – together and chronos – time. The word "synchro" (as defined by Webster's New World Dictionary) describes an electrical system consisting of a generator and one or more motorlike devices connected electrically so that, upon receipt of a signal from the generator, the rotors of the synchronous motors always assume positions identical with that of the generator rotor. There are physical reasons that explain the operation of synchro. The questions are, "Do our lives work in the same way?" "Do we in fact send out signals that people in the world receive and respond to?"

WHAT ARE THE ODDS?

We all have our stories that defy the law of averages. One of mine happened on a ski vacation, several years ago, at Blackcombe Mountain in British Columbia. One evening, I had spent a few hours talking with a man I had met in a local bar. His parting comments to me were quite disrespectful. Although I did react to his comments at the time, I hoped that I would be able to see him again, in order to have the last word.

In the meantime, it's now the next day, and it's snowing furiously. I'm standing in the singles ski line in the midst of hundreds of skiers, waiting to ride the four-seater chair up the mountain. For anyone who has not skied at Blackcombe Mountain, the waiting line for the chair is a fast-moving maze where the doubles line and the singles line merge just prior to boarding the chair. Many thousands of skiers are taken up the mountain daily through this state-of-the-art system.

And now for my "coincidence." Not only did I see this man again, my line connected up with his thirty seconds before we both ended up on the same chairlift going up the mountain. He couldn't have avoided me, even if he had tried. Because we were both like pellets on an assembly line, we had to come together at that moment. He, of course, was not happy to see me; he was embarrassed about his behaviour. And you can be sure he wasn't happy to see me the next two times we bumped into each other "by chance" at the summit restaurant. The third time he saw me, he gave up. I must have appeared to him as a sign from above that he had done something wrong, and that he must be punished. Seeing me, combined with a snowstorm made him decide to pack it in at one o'clock and hope that the next day would be a better one for himself.

I would call what had happened here synchronicity. We were both drawn together for different reasons: he to me so that I could get my emotional retribution; me to him to remind him that he had to be accountable for his actions, because the past could come back to haunt him.

LOOKING AT THE EVIDENCE

On another occasion where I experienced synchronicity, I was attending a meeting. I wasn't certain that I wanted to attend, but in the end, I bit the bullet and went. Three incidents occured shortly after I walked in that confirmed I had made the right decision. The first was that the meeting chairperson called me by name. I didn't expect to know anyone at this meeting, and no one knew I was attending. I was shocked since I didn't know him. It turned out that he remembered me from a sailing club we had both been members of, more than ten year before. The second incident that appeared strange was that this same man asked me if a certain woman had given me the details about the meeting. Again I was shocked, because the name he had mentioned, being a fairly uncommon name, was actually the name of a friend of mine who wouldn't have had any information about this meeting. It turned out that the woman he was referring to "just happened" to have the same name as my friend. The third incident that was uncanny was that the carpet in the room was identical to the one I had in my bedroom, when I was a teenager living with my parents. It was a most unusual rug in that it was a bright orange shag rug. The rug was special to me in that I was allowed to choose it, bright colour and all. I had never seen a rug of that colour, in the texture, outside of my own home.

In my interpretation, these three incidents did not happen by chance. They somehow got pulled in together by my magnet. They told me that I was in the right place at the right time.

WOULD YOU BELIEVE?

Laura, a New York resident, had had her purse stolen by a fellow patron at a posh restaurant. The theft was done so skilfully that Laura had commented to the women who had stolen her purse that she had a beautiful purse, not realizing that the purse she was admiring was her own.

In any case, the thief decided to make use of Laura's chequebook, by cashing a cheque made out to herself. She went to Laura's bank to carry out this transaction. Guess who the bank teller was at Laura's bank?...Laura's sister.

Unfortunately, the thief was not apprehended at this time.

For when Laura's sister (the teller) realized that this woman was an imposter, she then tried to stall in order to figure out what to do next. Sensing that something was wrong, the thief then made her escape, unapprehended.

OUR UNCONSCIOUS MAGNETS

Nathan had the problem of not being treated with respect at work. As a real estate agent, it was important that his colleagues would show him professional courtesy and that they would back him up in front of his clients. Despite the fact that Nathan would always try to conduct himself in a totally professional manner, he would often run into situations where his co-workers would undermine him. The following is one incident out of Nathan's life.

Nathan's boss, Barry, whom Nathan was reporting to, had developed a reputation for being a whiz at selling high-end properties. Nathan was thrilled that he would have the chance to work under Barry, because he would have the opportunity to make sizable commissions on the properties that he would sell. Being a hard worker, Nathan found some exclusive properties that had been on the market for some time; he believed he could move them with a new marketing approach. He did the initial footwork of meeting with the listing agent to arrange to co-broker the properties. Everything would have been fine if Nathan was able to sign the deal on his own. But Barry had to be present, and Barry wanted to undermine him.

In front of the agent/client, Barry directly contradicted what Nathan had told him about the terms of business: Barry offered a 5% commission structure, even though moments before, Nathan had told the agent that it would be 6%; Barry told the agent that he didn't have to sign the listings right away, even though Nathan had specifically requested that he do so. At a later date, Nathan insisted that the signed listings be faxed to his office, prior to his having to make the three-hour trip to the town where the properties were located; Barry contradicted him by saying it wasn't necessary.

Despite all of these disasters, Nathan had earned the respect of the agent and the vendors involved. One of the vendors made a special point of telling him that she had agreed to his involvement because she was so impressed with his professionalism.

And so what do you think happened after the big pow-wow with all the necessary players? Barry decided that he didn't want Nathan on the listings at all, and that he wanted to give them over to another agent, one with whom he had felt a greater compatibility. The next day, Barry went into the office of the company owner and lied, telling the owner that the vendor had complained about Nathan, and that the vendor didn't want Nathan on the listing. The company owner believed Barry; Nathan had no option but to resign.

Was this incident a chance occurrence in Nathan's life? Unfortunately not. This scenario surfaced in various ways, in many totally different circumstances. Despite the fact that Nathan worked hard and did his best, people didn't seem to treat him with respect. Why not? Because Nathan believed that he was worthless. As a dependent child, Nathan had been both physically and verbally abused by his mother. He was made to feel that he was defective, as if something were wrong with him. His "I Am Worthless" magnet was very powerful. Even though his outside behaviour was professional, his internal belief that he was "no good" was somehow picked up; he was treated according to how his true emotional self felt about Nathan. His conscientious efforts to conduct himself professionally were almost irrelevant.

THE INTIMATE PARTNERS WE ATTRACT INTO OUR LIVES

In Chapter Five, you learned that people will treat you in the way that you are treating your self. For example, if you turn your self into a doormat, your actions will invite someone to step on you. We don't need to use the Law of Attraction to explain the obvious. But we may need the Law of Attraction to explain how in our romantic relationships, we will usually end up finding partners who independently share the same emotional profiles as we do, and that even though our Operating Styles may look different on the outside, on the inside, our unresolved emotional issues are the same.

Sylvia was a strong, reliable, giving person. She was good at her job and was always helpful to people in need. When it came to romantic partners, Sylvia was attracted to handsome, successful men. She was particularly attracted to these type of men, because they appeared to be so emotionally strong and in control of their lives. Sylvia had come from a family where her father was very anxious and needy. She had hated the way he had relied on her for advice and emotional support, and she wanted to be sure, in her romantic relationships, to get as far away from this personality type as possible.

Sylvia, herself, lived a "double life." On the outside, she was strong and giving. On the inside, she was scared, anxious and unsure of herself. Because her ailing father was quite needy and emotionally demanding, wanting sympathy and support for all his physical aches and his psychic pain, Sylvia had directed all her attention to him, hoping in this way that she would receive the love she craved. Because she had to take on the parent role, her own emotional needs had been ignored and neglected. And so, despite the fact that on the outside she appeared strong, on the inside, she was a scared little girl, wondering who was going to take care of her. (Sylvia's primary Operating Style is sadness-based needy; her subordinate style is strong/distant.)

Who did Sylvia attract into her life?...Men who had a "double life." One of them was Victor, a strong rugged man; the type of man who would photograph well as the cowboy in a Marlborough cigarette advertisement. Victor was a successful photographer. He was making a good living at his trade, but legitimate business was a bit dull for him. Victor liked to live on the wild side. And so despite the fact that he did not need the money, Victor set up a number of illegal money-making schemes on the side.(Victor's primary style is anger-based; his subordinate style is strong/distant.)

And then there was Wally. Sylvia was attracted to Wally because he was such a kind, supportive and considerate person. If she had a problem, Wally would always be there for her. But Wally, too, had a "double life." What did he do for a living?...Rip people off. For ten years, Wally had been involved in boiler room scams which involved a preplanned con routine. Wally would be the "opener" using the promise of quick wealth to entice desperate people to invest their hard-earned savings. Because the stocks sold were all held by the selling company, their prices could be manipulated. Wally's company would then make sure that the client's stock went up, after which a closer would go in for the kill, encouraging the client to invest more in this guaranteed money-making opportunity. Later on, Wally got tired of this con and moved into the home repair business, selling vastly overpriced home renovation projects to retired pensioners living in outlying areas. (Wally's primary style is anger-based; his subordinate style is strong/distant.)

And then there was Ryan. Ryan was a doctor who had a very successful practice. People liked Ryan because he was extremely kind, caring and concerned. He did everything in his power to be there for his patients. Sylvia liked him too, for similar reasons. But Ryan had another side to him, almost having a "double" personality. For when it came to the sexual area, Ryan was totally disinterested in Sylvia's feelings: he insisted on being satisfied on demand. He wasn't concerned that Sylvia might not have been inclined to make love. "No" was not acceptable to him. His personality totally changed when the opportunity for sex presented itself. (Ryan's primary style is strong/distant; his subordinate style is anger-based.)

The similarities in these three circumstances are remarkable. Sylvia, living a "double life," attracted men who paralleled her existence. Whether Sylvia chose to stay with these men or leave them is irrelevant. The fact is, she somehow magnetically attracted men with the same level of denial of their true emotional selves—people just like her who believed they needed to live a "double life" to survive.

THE PATTERN WILL REPEAT

What happens if you don't want to take notice of who and what you attract into your life? What happens if you don't believe in the Law of Attraction? It's quite simple. If you don't pay attention to the messages you are receiving on a daily basis, you will find your self living out a variation on the same theme until the day you die.

The fact is, you are the magnet. You can only attract to your self people who are just like you, who have the same emotional profile as you, and people who will treat you in the same way that you are treating your inner self. And so for example, if you attract abusive people, people who frighten you, bully you, intimidate you, criticize you, judge you, humiliate you, ignore your needs, you can be sure of the following: this person was treated that way by her/his parent/s; this person treats her/his inner self in this same unkind way; you were treated in this same unkind way by your parent/s; you treat your inner self in this same unkind way; you have within your self unresolved/denied feelings of fear, vulnerability, helplessness, powerlessness and worthlessness.

Please understand, I'm not saying that you're an "abuser," or that you abuse other people. But I am saying that you abuse your inner self, and that you have within your self unresolved feelings of fear, vulnerability, helplessness, powerlessness and worthlessness. And, I can guarantee that if you attract abusers (an abuser is any person who does not treat you with total respect, consideration and interest in your happiness), you are not kind to your inner self; you regularly compromise your integrity to get your needs met; you put other people's need satisfaction before your own; you do not consider that your happiness is as important as your counterpart's happiness.

Admitting that we abuse our selves, we compromise our integrity in order to survive, we believe we are worthless, we deceive our selves, we lie to our selves is not easy. The truth is often most unflattering, but it is the truth, and it is empowering. By admitting the truth and facing it, we can then empower our selves to stop repeating old patterns and start creating a life where we can choose happiness.

Because our internal magnets are usually beyond our own conscious awareness, Chart 6, Your Activated Magnets, will provide you with a clear guideline as to your unresolved/denied emotional issues. It will also explain why your life may be filled with people who are not enhancing your happiness.

To summarize Chart 6: If you have within your self unresolved/denied feelings of worthlessness, shame, fear, vulnerability, helplessness, powerlessness, you will have the following activated magnets: I Abuse My Self, I Compromise My Integrity, I Am Worthless, I Am Powerless. With these activated magnets, you will attract abusers and narcissists. (Narcissists are people who are totally preoccupied with their own need satisfaction, and who operate as though they are royalty while everyone around them is unpaid help.)

If you have within your self unresolved/denied feelings of being betrayed: your trust was betrayed by your parents in that your own unique self was sacrificed to meet your parents' needs, your basic safety was not protected, your own integrity was either compromised or violated, you were not respected, you

Chart 6 – YOUR ACTIVATED MAGNETS

If You Have Within Your Self Unresolved/Denied Feelings Of:	YOUR MAGNET	YOU WILL ATTRACT
Worthlessness	I Accept Abuse	Abusers
Shame	I Compromise My Integrity	Narcissists
Fear		
Vulnerability	I Am Worthless	
Powerlessness	I Am Powerless	
Helplessness		
Being Betrayed	I Deceive My Self	Deceivers
Your Trust Was Betrayed: You Were Sacrificed You Were Not Protected	I Deny The Truth	Liars
You Were Used Your Integrity Was Violated	I Betray My Self	Betrayers
Low Self-Worth	I Have To Please	Users
Not Feeling Good Enough	I Am Not Good Enough	Irresponsible People
		Demanding People

If You Know Your Own Worth	I Love My Self	Kind, Loving, Giving,
If You Delight In Being You	I Am Loveable	Warm, Generous People
If You Believe It's Your Right To Be Happy		

were not granted any rights, you were not allowed to express your feelings and assert your needs, you were made to feel terrified for your very survival, your best interests and happiness were irrelevant to your parents, you will have the following activated magnets: <u>I Deceive My Self</u>, <u>I Deny The Truth</u>, <u>I Betray My Self</u>. With these activated magnets, you will attract deceivers, liars and betrayers—people who will con you into believing they are trustworthy, people who will have no moral problem in deceiving, lying, betraying, and denying your value as a human being worthy of total respect. These type of people are so enraged at what was done to them (how they were treated by their parents) that they feel it is their right to dump their pain and misery onto any convenient target.

If you have within your self unresolved/denied feelings of low self-worth and not feeling good enough, you will have the following activated magnets: <u>I Have To Please</u> and <u>I Am Not Good Enough</u>. With these activated magnets, you will attract users, irresponsible people and demanding people.

On a positive note, if you know your own worth, if you delight in being you, if you believe it is your absolute right to be happy, you will have the following activated magnets: <u>I Love My Self</u> and <u>I Am Loveable</u>. With these activated magnets, you will attract kind, loving, giving, warm, considerate, generous people—people who will respect you, love you, admire you, give to you, and enjoy your company.

This information about the Law of Attraction and magnets may be hard to digest initially, because the truth is often both painful and unflattering. But facing the truth is the first step to freeing your self from the prison of your past. In Chapter Eleven, Releasing Your Emotions, you will learn what you can do to free your self from your negative programming. So don't despair and read on.

8 | READING YOUR EMOTIONS LIKE A BOOK

If you realized just how much you were revealing about your self by the way you react to the people and events in your daily life, you would likely be a lot more careful about how you choose to present your self to the world. What we are talking about here is the Iceberg Theory of Emotions. In the same way that when you see a beautiful iceberg floating serenely in the cold Arctic waters, you know that there is a mountain of rock-hard ice supporting the tip that surfaces above the water line, so too when you witness a person either getting strongly emotional about an incident, or not emotional at all when the situation warrants it, you know that there is an Iceberg of Denied Emotions underneath the surface.

Emotions are an energy that want to move out of the body. Releasing your emotions is a good thing—it's healthy and natural. What you need to look at though is what makes you get emotional. To one person, being cut off by a truck when driving his car can trigger profound rage; to another it's a meaningless event in the day. To one salesperson, being rejected by a prospective customer in a cold call situation is meaningless, with each customer being considered part of the numbers game; to another salesperson, this rejection triggers feelings of discouragement, inadequacy, and a feeling of "why bother?" To one business person, losing a deal is part of the game; to another, the disappointment triggers feelings of discouragement and results in months of unproductive activity.

To one person, the death of a spouse is the end of the world with her/his own death following shortly afterward; to another, the death is an end of a chapter of one's life, to be followed by a new beginning. To one person, a romantic partner ending a relationship is cause for months, if not years of suffering and deep grief; to another, it's a sign that it's time to move on and create a relationship that is happier and more satisfying. To one person, being "dumped" by a marital partner causes uncontrollable rage to surface; to another, this situation is interpreted as a statement that the partner did not value her/his worth, so why waste time with a person who is not prepared to openly discuss and work through differences?

Your reaction to an event, and to how you perceive you are being treated is the direct result of the experiences you had as a child, and the underlying emotions that you have stored up from the past. If you are anger-based, you will usually flair up with anger at the slightest provocation. If you are sadness-based, your tendency will be to both not react, and pretend to be happy, even though you're not. Let's now look at some everyday situations and discover the buried emotions that your emotional responses will reveal.

WHEN YOU ARE ANGER-BASED

Let's say you become very angry at a parking attendant because he has taken another patron's cash before yours, even though you were there first. While this situation might be considered by some as annoying, in the grand scheme of things, it's no big deal. It is a big deal though if you were ignored as a child, treated disrespectfully, humiliated or abused. The small incident then becomes a "trigger" to stronger emotions that lie in your unconscious mind. The fuming feeling that starts taking over is in fact being fuelled by your unreleased rage from your past. On an unconscious level, you are being reminded of the way you used to feel when you were being treated disrespectfully by your mom/dad.

The anger or rage that surfaces is really the Tip of the Iceberg of Denied Anger that should have been expressed to the parent who ignored or humiliated you when you were a child. As you learned in Chapter Two, it was most likely not very safe to express your anger to a parent who could have withheld love if s/he had so desired, or a parent who would have retaliated by treating you worse than s/he would have done previously.

The parking attendant example is obviously not of the same emotional significance as the ending of a marriage or a romantic relationship. It's natural to feel the full range of emotions in the face of a great loss: emotions of sadness/grief, anger/rage, shame at not feeling good enough, and fear caused by the uncertainty—can you really make it alone, both emotionally and financially?

The emotional acceptance of a significant life change does take time, and it's reasonable to expect that you will feel a full range of emotions for a period of time. The real issue is the intensity of the emotions you feel. The clue is this: If your rage is uncontrollable, all consuming, murderous, and although you really aren't planning to murder your partner, the thought has crossed your mind more than once, you know you have moved into denied rage from the past.

Please understand that it's important to both feel and express your emotions. But when you find that your emotions are controlling you, and that you cannot seem to move beyond your strong feelings, your past has come back to haunt you. At this point it's easy to deny the importance of the past, and focus on your present circumstances. After all, you do have good reason to feel the way you do. Your partner did do outrageous things to you, and objectively speaking, does deserve your wrath. The past is long gone and quite frankly, you don't even remember ever having felt so angry or enraged at your mom/dad.

Keep in mind that the reason you may not remember ever having been that enraged at the way you were being treated is because at the time, it may have appeared too dangerous for you to feel and express your true feelings. Although you may have wanted to hurt your parent in the same way that s/he was hurting you, it wouldn't have been in your best interests to act out your feelings. To keep on surviving, the best option may have been to ignore your angry feelings.

Although forgetting about your anger may have helped you survive your childhood, it does not erase the fact that you felt angry. The same anger is sitting within you now, and is leaking out into your present life. If you find your self easily provoked by the way people are treating you, realize that you are facing an Iceberg of Denied Anger, Rage, Sadness, Shame and Fear.

WHEN YOU ARE SADNESS-BASED

We've been talking about how your outward reaction will

Chart 7 – ICEBERGS OF DENIED EMOTIONS

ANGER-BASED

- Small Incident Enrages
- Significant People Trigger Enormous Rage

Conscious Mind

Unconscious Mind

- Rage At Having Been Forced To Accept Disrespectful Treatment: Abuse, Neglect, Overinvolvement
- Rage At Not Having Been Loved

SADNESS-BASED STRONG/DISTANT

- Will Fulfil Role Demands
- Will Accept Own Needs Being Ignored

Conscious Mind

Unconscious Mind

- Strong Need To Hide Own Inadequacy
- Feelings Of Obligation In Making Others Happy
- Sadness At Having Been Given Conditional Love

SADNESS-BASED NEEDY

- Disrespect Is Tolerated
- Abuse Is Tolerated
- Lack Of Consideration Is Tolerated

Conscious Mind

Unconscious Mind

- Terror
- Powerlessness
- Fear Of Being Harmed
- Feelings Of Worthlessness
- I Deserved The Abuse
- Grief At Not Having Been Loved
- Desperate To Be Loved
- Longing For Love

SADNESS-BASED NEEDY

- Rejection Triggers Grief, Feelings Of Worthlessness, Powerlessness, Helplessness

Conscious Mind

Unconscious Mind

- Deep Grief At Not Having Been Loved
- Ashamed Of Worthlessness
- Feelings Of Powerlessness In Not Being Able To Create A Happy Life

speak volumes about your unreleased emotions. But the same analysis can be applied as well when you don't react emotionally to situations where you have just cause. If you are sadness-based, you will most likely just let things go. If a person doesn't treat you respectfully, he's having a bad day. If a person doesn't consider your interests, that's just the way the person is. If a person is critical of you, you begin to doubt your own adequacy.

Not reacting when you have just cause indicates that your Iceberg of Denied Emotions relates to your buried anger, fear, sadness and shame. If you accept less than respectful treatment, it means that you don't truly value your self. This means that you were not valued or treated with due respect. As an adult, you will allow people to treat you as you are treating your inner self. If you accept being abused, ignored, not considered, not valued, you can safely conclude that you were either abused, physically, sexually or verbally, or that you were neglected. You would have learned, early in life, that it was neither safe, nor in your best interests to reveal what was on your mind. So you would have learned to stop expressing your natural, spontaneous feelings.

There are two key scenarios which would have contributed to your not wanting to express your true feelings. If you are sadness-based needy, in all likelihood, your mom and dad were treating you abusively, neglectfully, or in an overcontrolling manner. Their treatment of you would have caused you to feel ashamed of your self: you would have believed that your inadequacy was the reason for their poor treatment (there was something wrong with you). Your thinking would have been, if you were okay, your parents would have treated you well. Since your mom and dad were treating you badly, there must have been a defect in you. And so in fact, you deserved this bad treatment. In carrying this negative belief within you, in situations where you are being criticized, blamed or condemned, you will feel that your abuser is accurate in her/his assessment of you. Thus you will <u>accept</u> the negative treatment.

Poor treatment may also trigger the emotion of terror. Although you may not consciously be aware of it, being shouted at, or being humiliated may arouse in you the feelings that your life is in danger, that you will be killed if you step out of line, or that you are powerless to protect your self. Although in the present day none of these beliefs may be realistic, the emotions you feel are very real. Alternatively, you may feel terrified because you believe your very security and happiness is dependent on the happiness of your abuser. When your counterpart is not happy, you may feel that your security is in danger as well. Both these emotional responses will cause you to clam up rather than assert your rights and take charge of the situation. If you find your self not speaking up at such moments, your past is taking hold of you.

Poor treatment may also trigger feelings of grief in you. As you are listening to another person condemn you, you may be thinking, "All I want is for you to love me. Why don't you love me? I would do anything for you to love me. I would do anything to please you." And so instead of telling your abuser that s/he's inappropriate, that her/his comments are unacceptable, and that you want an apology, you accept the garbage that is dished out, and you pray silently that s/he will stop abusing you, and start loving you again. If you feel sad rather than angry at such a moment, you know your past is taking hold of you.

If you are sadness-based strong/distant, in all likelihood, your parents either gave you a role to fulfil or expected you to be the perfect, compliant, undemanding child. In either case, you would have concluded that you had little intrinsic worth, but rather, your acceptability was based on either your job performance or your ability to be "perfect." In being made to feel inadequate, you would have become highly self-critical. Being criticized or being humiliated will trigger your own self-critical nature. Thus you will silently tolerate criticism from other people.

As a sadness-based strong/distant, you will tend to tolerate being taken advantage of or being used. Because your identity and self-worth is based on <u>appearing</u> strong, you will never want to reveal your true feelings. In your mind, revealing your feelings will be showing up your own inadequacy. Revealing your feelings would force you to admit that you have needs too. Since your need fulfilment in childhood was based on not drawing attention to your needs, but rather, in fulfilling your parents' needs, you will perceive the expression of your needs as being self-destructive. As an adult, you will prefer to accept inconsiderate treatment rather than reveal that you aren't happy with the way you are being treated.

WHEN YOU ARE LOVE-BASED

If your present-day emotional reactions are a trigger to past denied emotions, what happens when you release your past emotions as outlined in *Choices*, and are able to create a love-base? Does this mean you will no longer ever feel anger, fear, shame or sadness?

Yes and no. Yes, you will have access to your anger, fear and sadness. If it so moves you, you will both feel and express them. But you certainly won't feel these emotions as often, or with the same intensity that you do now. You will experience your emotions as clues to alert you to your true feelings, and to help you identify practical paths to add to your happiness. If you are angry, you will express your feelings to the appropriate person at the time, and work out a solution that will address your interests; if you are afraid, you will identify your concern, and take a positive action to protect your position; if you are sad, you will want to identify both the loss you are feeling, and the ways you can fill your self up.

Concerning the emotion of shame, when you release the backlog of emotions from your past, you will come to love your self. From a position of self-love, shame is not an emotion that you will feel. If there's an area where you believe you fall short, then you will see this as an opportunity for growth and learning. You will not judge your self as being inadequate. Shame is a negative emotion that should be released and cleared permanently.

THERE'S NOTHING WRONG WITH ME

The best part of clearing out your buried emotions from your past is that you will rarely get triggered by other people's actions. Instead of getting hooked in, wanting to defend your self when a person criticizes you, you will think, "There's nothing wrong with me, but there sure is something troubling my counterpart." You might then ask her/him what is bothering her/him, or whether s/he is feeling hurt, angry about something else, or worried.

In being cleared of your past emotions, you will become aware that people most often attack others when they are feeling afraid (the best defence is an offence), when they are feeling inadequate, or when what they really want is love and support.

You will realize, when your counterpart reacts to you in a negative way, that s/he is being triggered by you (reminded of the way s/he used to feel with her/his parents: trapped, angry, sad, hurt, afraid, ashamed, powerless, worthless).

When you have established your own base of self-worth, you won't interpret what your counterpart does as a personal affront, but rather, you'll see it as a desperate move on her/his part to feel whole, valued, important, secure, loved, worthwhile. This is not to say that you shouldn't express your feelings about the way you are being treated. (Please refer to Chapter Fourteen, Operating From A Love-Base, for guidelines in this area.) But the fact is, when you are cleared of your old emotions, what another person does or does not do, in relation to you, will not change the way you feel about your self.

YOUR EMOTIONAL REACTIONS PROVIDE CLUES

Sigmund Freud must have found that looking for the hidden meaning in his enjoyment of smoking cigars to be too close to home, and so he was quoted as having said, "Sometimes a cigar is only a cigar." The same can be said of analyzing your emotional reactions. Analyzing your emotional responses to people and events might indeed make you feel too transparent. And so rather than looking at the root cause of your emotional reaction, you might want to stay focused on the current reasons for why you are feeling the way you do. In so doing, you might choose to ignore the past.

Why dig up your past? Because your present-day reactions are simply a trigger to the past events and feelings that you have never resolved. Your present reactions are the Tip of the Iceberg. If you find your self becoming angry over insignificant matters, if you find your self becoming consumed by your rage or grief, if you find your self feeling inadequate, if you find your self accepting disrespectful treatment, if you find your self lacking the energy required to take the actions necessary to turn your life around, or if you find your self being afraid to take risks, facing your past will free you up to live a fully conscious life—a life where you can make decisions about how you wish to respond to the people and events in your world, a life where you can choose to become the person you really want to be.

9 | YOUR BODY IS TALKING BUT ARE YOU LISTENING?

W e were all raised to believe in the power of medical science. We were all taught to think of dis-ease as something that "happens" to us because of both our genetic heritage and the contagious germs and viruses to which we are exposed. Not to minimize the importance of our genetic heritage and the existence of germs, there's a great body of "unscientific" evidence that provides us with some very interesting explanations about why some people get sick.

One very interesting example of this concerns the life of Michel de Notredame, better known to us as Nostradamus, a French doctor and astrologer (1503-66). Nostradamus is usually known because of his famous predictions; writing in the 16th century, he was able to read the future and describe events that have come to pass hundreds of years after his death. Why his life is of particular interest to me is because Nostradamus started off his career as a medical doctor treating the plague. The plague, or the black death as it was usually called, was an instant killer. Stories were told of the ravages of this disease, and how people who had breathed in the germs of disease-ridden patients would die within a few hours.

Nostradamus did not run away from the plague; rather, he treated it with his own concoction of rose petals and the recommendation of clean air and water. Through his efforts, he was able to cure towns of this deadly disease. And yet, in this entire process, he never became a victim of the disease. Tragically, he wasn't able to save his wife and two children from sudden death; he was left to deal with the pain of losing his loved ones. But amazingly enough, he didn't succumb to the disease. Obviously, he must have developed antibodies to the deadly disease. But the question is, "Why did he, when so many others did not?"—a question that will always remain unanswered.

WHAT YOUR BODY IS TELLING YOU

Your bodily symptoms will provide you with two very important pieces of information: one relates to the unreleased emotions that are brewing within you; the other relates to your body's ability to fight dis-ease.

Concerning your "unreleased" emotions, if you were able to express your emotions directly: your anger through angry words, your sadness through tears, your fear and shame through both admitting what you are afraid and ashamed of, and expressing these emotions in any way that you choose, you would not need your body to contain your repressed emotional energy. If you release your emotions directly, they will just flow out of you. If you push them down, they will turn into a physical pressure that your body will be forced to contain. Imagine trying to stop a volcano by sealing up the top of the mountain. It can't be done! In the same way that lava within a mountain can't be contained, so too your emotions can't be contained; if unreleased, they will erupt through your bodily organs, muscles and tissues.[2]

Concerning your body's ability to fight dis-ease, what you must realize is that in becoming ill, your body is showing you that it is feeling powerless. Since your body is you, this would mean that you are feeling powerless—powerless to end your emotional pain, fill up your own emptiness, create the life you want, make your self happy, bring people and opportunity into your life, bring love into your life, love your self. Your body's powerlessness in fighting dis-ease will be directly related to your feelings of powerlessness in controlling your own life, as the following story will illustrate.

YOU MAKE ME SICK

People can appear to make you sick—literally. Marie's

---

[2]An excellent reference outlining the connection between bodily symptoms and emotions is by Louise L. Hay, You Can Heal Your Life (Santa Monica, CA: Hay House, 1987).

health was a good example. Marie had been living with her boy-friend, Ned, for two years. She wanted to get married, he didn't. Ned just didn't feel ready. Marie gave him an ultimatum: marriage within the next year, or the relationship was over. Ned agreed to the marriage in body, but definitely not in spirit.

Shortly after they had set the wedding date, Ned emotionally withdrew. He was there, but he wasn't there. He refused to discuss any details about the wedding reception, and showed little enthusiasm for their future together. Marie hoped that Ned was just nervous, and that it was only a matter of time before he would snap out of his negativity. In the meantime, she tried to act "normal," pretending that his behaviour didn't bother her.

Ned did snap out of it—four months later. Marie hung in there, holding up her phoney image of happiness. She fell apart around the time when Ned started acting like his old familiar self. She didn't know that she had fallen apart though. Instead, she got sick.

Marie was sick for over a year and a half. She got every virus and flu bug that was going around. As soon as she recovered from one illness, she picked up a new one. She spent weeks in bed with each new bout, suffering from fevers and total exhaustion. Her doctors were at a loss as to how to make her well.

On the surface, Marie just kept getting sick over, and over, and over again. In reality, Marie's prolonged illness was a symptom of her unexpressed feelings—her feelings of abandonment, betrayal, sadness, fear and rage—which resulted from Ned's withdrawal of love prior to and shortly after their wedding. She was not able to express her feelings openly because she believed that in doing so, she would lose Ned forever. The powerlessness she felt in her life was reflected by her body's "powerlessness" in fighting the viruses that every one of us is exposed to on a daily basis.

The decline of Marie's health is a classic example of how unresolved emotions can surface through illness. But please be aware of a key concept here: People cannot "make you sick." The only thing another person can do to you, on an emotional level, is trigger emotions that are already sitting within you—unresolved emotions from your past. Marie had never dealt with her feelings of abandonment and betrayal as the result of the parenting she had received. She had never released her shame, her sadness, her fear and her rage. Although she had good reason to feel these emotions again, as the result of what had happened between Ned and herself, her emotions only duplicated those she had experienced in living with her parents.

I CAN'T EXPRESS MY ANGER

Many years ago, I was involved in a romantic relationship with a man who continuously infuriated me. He had a very controlling personality, and had an impossible time making any sort of compromise. Because I was the more flexible of the two of us, I usually was the one who did the compromising.

Although I was angry about this man's lack of flexibility, I didn't consciously feel angry about it. Rather, I ignored those aspects of his personality that I didn't like. My anger did not go away though. It just went underground, and showed itself through physical symptoms. I had bladder infections and eye infections running consecutively for two years, the entire length of the relationship. When I wasn't consumed by the throws of these symptomatic illnesses, I enjoyed the sudden onset of twenty-four hour flus and chills on a regular basis.

Did I have a clue that I was angry? Absolutely not! I made no connection at all between my feelings, which I had totally blocked, and my bodily symptoms. I must confess that I did wonder why I was getting sick so often. Prior to this symptom extravaganza, I had been amazingly illness-free. Except for an annual flu, I was never sick.

How did I handle my new illnesses? I visited medical doctors frequently; I took dose upon dose of antibiotics; I started to swim less, believing the chlorine to be the cause of my eye infections. I certainly did not connect my bodily symptoms to my repressed anger until years later, when I came to understand the physical power of repressed emotions.

YOUR BODY IS YOUR FRIEND

We often treat our bodies as though they were our enemies: they annoy us because of the inconvenience they can cause us; they stop us from having fun; they stop us from completing work projects on time; they slow us down when they run out of energy. We want to run and they want to crawl. And when they say, "No more, I need to rest," they have the gall to shut down altogether!

Your body is not your enemy—it's your friend. It provides you with a surefire indicator of the emotions you're not wanting to face. Your body will physically manifest your true emotional self, the part of you who was never listened to, the part of you who wanted to be noticed, loved and understood. Your body will physically manifest the unreleased emotions that are stored in your unconscious mind. If you want to find out how you are really feeling about anything, you need look no further than your own body.

10 | THE WORLD OF DREAMS

What can our dreams tell us? Dreams provide us with a direct look into our unconscious minds. Through symbolic representation, they tell us what our emotional issues are, what we are feeling, what our concerns are, what we are afraid to look at consciously, what is important to us, and what problems we are trying to resolve. Our dreams connect us to the life of our true emotional selves, and give us clues as to the work we need to do in order to become emotionally whole.

INTRODUCING A SECRET

Wendy had been sexually abused by her father. She had been forced to perform fellatio on him when she was three. This lasted to age five. Then at age eleven, her father started raping her again, this time with intercourse being involved. Wendy had no conscious recall of these events.

In the course of her therapy, Wendy had two dreams which brought her sexual abuse into the open. In the first dream, she was lying in her bedroom with her father fast asleep beside her. She wondered why he was lying there in bed with her. In fright, she jumped out of bed and ran to the bathroom. She noticed, while in the bathroom, that she had sperm coming out of her body.

Her second dream was similar to the first. This time, she was in bed with her father snuggled up behind her, kissing her the way her husband would kiss her. Again, she wondered why her father would kiss her as would a lover.

It would be several years before Wendy was ready to look at the issue of her sexual abuse. Her dreams, however, provided her with a good starting point.

A SYMBOL OF THE TRUTH

Paul, age 50, had an empty feeling within himself that was most noticeable when he was relaxing. He didn't relax very often though, keeping busy by putting in a twelve-hour day at the office, spending time with his wife and kids, and indulging in his passions, golf and skiing. Paul had no idea why he would feel empty, considering the fact that he had such a full life. When being active didn't seem to work for him, he got involved in therapy.

During the course of his therapy, he had a telling dream. He was with his mother, visiting his aging grandmother. As he was driving along the street with his mother, he noticed one of his old ski boots lying on the street. He thought it strange that he would have left his old boot out on the street, so he got out of the car to pick it up. When he looked at it more closely, he noticed that the inner lining of the boot was missing; all that remained was the outer shell.

From this dream, Paul was reminded of the compromises that he had to make in order to get his needs met. Living in a super-strict Catholic home, he was expected to follow instructions and be compliant. Putting up a fuss or being playful and spontaneous was not acceptable. And so he had learned that in order to survive, he would have to "gut his insides," and keep up appearances. The shell of the ski boot was a symbol of what he had done to himself; his insides were gone. His work in therapy would be to reclaim his inner self.

SHOWING YOU YOUR PROGRESS

Sometimes dreams don't reveal as much as they summarize where we are at in our lives. This dream will be analyzed in greater detail showing what can be revealed by analyzing the words that are written down to describe the dream, after the dream is over.

Jay was struggling to both express and release his feelings of rage toward both his mother and father. He knew he was angry, but he had a difficult time connecting up with his feelings. During the time he was in therapy, Jay had a dream that he was standing on a dock, extending into a raging sea. He was standing back, and his only protection was a frame of a window with four panes of glass. The next thing he knew, he was being dragged into the water by the crashing waves; Jay saved himself by grabbing hold of a towel an ex-boss was holding out to him.

The raging sea represented his raging emotions. "Sea" sounds like "see" which would mean what he saw/experienced made him very angry. His only protection was a "wooden frame" consisting of four "panes" of glass. The word "wooden" sounds like "would not"; "panes" is "pain," with "four" representing the four emotions he was working on feeling: anger, sadness, fear and shame. Thus, the frame, or the way he saw his world consisted of four emotions which he would not feel because of his pain.

Being dragged into the water was a good sign in that Jay was being pulled into experiencing his emotions. He perceived that he was able to save himself with the help of another person. He remembered that his boss had put out a towel for him to grab onto, but that he, Jay, had done the work of getting out of the water. Jay believed this ex-boss was in the dream because she was a highly emotional woman, which meant that he, Jay, was saving himself through connecting up with his emotions.

WORKING WITH YOUR DREAMS: SOME SUGGESTIONS

1. Don't be lazy! When you wake up suddenly in the middle of the night, write down your dream. A powerful dream will usually wake you up, for a moment anyway. Because you will likely be feeling tired, you might want to take the easy way out and go back to sleep. Get into the habit of turning on your light and writing out your dream. This means having a pen and pad of paper next to your bed.

   Mornings are another time to easily access your dream material. Because your alarm clock will likely wake you up, you will often be disrupted, right in the middle of your dream. Try to recall your dream immediately upon hearing your alarm or radio. If you make the effort, it will come back.

2. If your dream is very powerful, you will be left with emotional feelings about it. Try to stay with those feelings. Write down your immediate feelings about your dream after you have written out its actual content.

3. Write out your dream as accurately as you can. Once you have your dream written down, you will have a lot of material with which to work. The key to using words, to enhance the information derived from a dream, is to change the context of the words. We dream in symbols, and we can translate these symbols into words; thus a window "pane" can be translated into the emotion of "pain"; "wooden" sounds like "would not" and so forth. By changing the context, you can double the amount of information you can learn from any one dream.

4. Another way to gain insight from dreams is to simply keep reading out what you have written, over and over again. Most dreams are remembered in fragments and/or appear to be a strange menage of disconnected events. Don't worry if in the beginning, they don't make sense. If you keep reading your dream over and over, you will start tuning into what your dream is telling you.

   In your dream, you might have a flash of a childhood event; perhaps you will be left with a fragment of a feeling; perhaps it will be a picture of a childhood article of importance to you; perhaps you will be right smack in the middle of a difficult situation, like climbing a mountain, moving a heavy piece of equipment or running to save your life. After tuning in to your feelings, ask your self the question, "Why?" Why do I feel I have to climb this mountain? Why do I feel this mountain is about to explode? Who am I running away from? What am I hoping to find? If you keep asking your inner self the questions, you will get back from your inner self a lot of interesting answers.

FINDING YOUR INNER SELF

Your dreams will provide clues as to where your true emotional self is hiding. Remember, in order to survive, your inner self had to run away a long time ago. In the same way that Hanzel (from the fairytale Hanzel and Gretel) left a trail of crumbs in order to retrace his steps back home, your dreams can serve as the pathway to finding your inner self, and the emotions you were not able to release during your childhood.

IV

BREAKING FREE
FROM YOUR PAST

11 | RELEASING YOUR EMOTIONS

Why do you need to release your stored-up emotions of anger/ rage, sadness, fear, and shame? If you survived by burying your pain from childhood, why do you need to dig it out now? You may feel you have good reason to forget your past. It has been a lot of years since you were a newborn, infant and toddler, and a lot of water has passed under the bridge. Most likely, you are functioning well as an adult: you can be productive at work, pay the rent, and look good at parties; you can be in a permanent relationship, have children, and create the appearance that you are living a good life; sometimes you can even feel happy. So why go through the pain of releasing those emotions that supposedly belong in your past?

There are three main reasons why it's advisable to release your emotions. These are related to your health, your happiness and your personal freedom. In terms of your health, please consider that although you may have stopped thinking about your painful feelings: your sadness, anger, fear and shame, and although you may have <u>consciously</u> forgotten your unpleasant experiences, your body has not forgotten them. Your aches, pains and illnesses, both serious and minor, indicate that your true emotional self is trapped in your unconscious mind, trying to get out. By denying your true feelings, you are wearing out your body. Remember, a volcano cannot be stopped by sealing off the top; your unexpressed emotions cannot be stopped by your denial of their existence.

In terms of your happiness, if your life isn't working out the way you want it to, if you secretly have a low opinion of your self, believing your self to be worthless, then your internal magnets will continue to attract people and situations which will reflect your own low self-worth. If you don't truly value your self, people will pick up on your own self-doubts. This will then translate into a lack of success in the outside world and a whole lot of struggling, suffering and frustration for you. Despite the fact that you may try very hard to create a prosperous life, somehow it will always seem to elude you.

In terms of your personal freedom, think about your life-style and your Emotional Operating System. Is being controlled by your dependencies enabling you to exercise your free will? Or are you living a life controlled by your need to emotionally survive? Think about your Emotional Operating Style. Is responding to most situations and people from an anger-base or a sadness-base (needy or strong/distant) enabling you to be the person you want to be? Do you have the emotional flexibility to create the life you want? If your own personal freedom is important to you, you will need to release those painful emotions from which you are trying to escape.

EMOTIONAL GLUE

What happens when you release the anger, sadness, fear and shame from your past? You will be able to free your self from the damage of the abuse, the neglect and the overinvolvement that you have experienced as a dependent child. How you feel about your self today is based on the way you were treated by your parents, and your response to their treatment as an infant and growing child. If your parents abused you physically, sexually or verbally, if they ignored your feelings and your needs, if they tried to control your every move, you would have felt ashamed of your defectiveness, deeply grieved that you were not truly loved, angry that you weren't valued, afraid that you wouldn't survive.

Sadly, you wouldn't have been able to share your true feelings with your parents because, by the very fact that you were feelings such things, you knew that your parents would have been neither receptive to hearing about your feelings, nor interested in doing anything differently to give you the comfort and love you wanted. By not having had the opportunity to express your true feelings, you would have held them in and pushed them down. In doing so, you would have "glued down" the offending treatment that had produced these feelings in the first place.

You are who you believe you are. If you believe you are a wonderful, joyous human being who has an unlimited source of creativity and potential for happiness, you will live a happy, full, balanced life. If you believe that you have little intrinsic worth, and that you are defective and inadequate, you will avoid opportunities for financial prosperity, intimacy and true happiness.

Who you believe you are is the result of the way you were treated by your parents, and your emotional response to their treatment. If you don't like your self, then in fact, you don't like the way you were treated. You must reject the impact that their negative treatment has had on you. To do this, you must both feel and express all the emotions that you did not want to feel, and were not able to express in your infancy and childhood. By releasing your painful emotions, you will be letting go of the impact that your parents' negative treatment has had on you.

If you were walking down the street, feeling particularly good because you had just won $10,000 in the lottery, and a passerby on the street told you that you were a worthless piece of garbage, would you stop feeling good, and start feeling like a pathetic human being? Probably not. You would most likely think that this weirdo had a serious problem, but his problem had nothing to do with you. You wouldn't accept his negative treatment. Because you were feeling good, you wouldn't take in his negativity; you would reject it.

In the same way, you can reject your parents' abusive, neglecting and overinvolved treatment of you. You can do this by choosing today to both feel and express the emotions that your inner self had to hold in so many years ago. Why should you choose to reject their negative treatment?...Because the parenting you received had nothing to do with you.

In Chapter One you learned the reasons why your parents were not able to fully meet your needs for love, affection, attention, encouragement, recognition and validation. The reasons for their inability? You can't give away what you don't have; giving love is perceived as a loss; giving love is not an option; being tuned out; physical unavailability. Your parents were operating out of their own sadness, their own anger, their own fear and their own shame. They dumped their pent-up unresolved emotional pain onto you, their innocent child. You were the recipient, and you had no choice but to accept their negative treatment. You needed your parents to take care of you; you needed them to teach you about the world. You had no other frame of reference to learn about your self, except that of your parents.

<u>During your growing up years, you would have had no idea that how your parents were treating you had nothing to do with either you or your worth, but rather, directly reflected on their own feelings of powerlessness, emptiness and desperation.</u> The problem is, your parents' treatment of you will have caused real damage to your own sense of self-worth. Understanding intellectually that your parents didn't intend to harm you, or that they really did love you (in their own limited way) is not going to radically change your ability to be happy, fun-loving, and joyous. To free your self to live the life you desire, you must go through the process of physically discharging the emotions that are now stored in your body and your unconscious mind.

BECOMING AN ACTIVE PARTICIPANT IN YOUR OWN LIFE

Feeling your own emotions is the most liberating experience imaginable: feeling angry when someone doesn't respect your worth, feeling sad when you don't feel loved, feeling afraid when you perceive your life to be in danger, feeling proud when you have accomplished an important goal, feeling happy when you know that your life is working out the way you want it to.

Feeling your feelings will allow you to be your self every minute of the day. Feelings are a life force, and experiencing your feelings should be as natural as breathing in the air. But if you were neglected, abused, emotionally abandoned, or made to feel ashamed, you may have stopped feeling your true feelings.

Jack had a difficult time knowing what he was feeling. He had been verbally abused as a child, being told that he was stupid, lazy, dumb, and that he had no brains. He was often called selfish and good for nothing when he didn't want to do what his parents had asked.

Jack hated his parents for calling him these mean names. He hated them so much that he didn't want them to know just how much they were hurting him. So he started putting on an act that he didn't care. No matter what they said to him, he would pretend that their insults didn't bother him. This especially annoyed his dad, but it didn't stop him from hurling insults his way.

In order to survive, Jack had to stop feeling his feelings. As an adult, he never got angry if someone took advantage of him. He would just say, "That's the way the person is." He would make excuses for everyone, and would always end up doing far more than his share of the work. People loved having Jack around because he was so easy to take advantage of.

Jack was not happy in his life. He felt a general resentment toward people, but he didn't know why. By having numbed out his feelings, in order to survive his childhood, he also numbed out his ability to understand what was happening to him in his life. (Jack is a sadness-based strong/distant.)

Vicki had felt emotionally abandoned by her parents. On the outside, she had a "normal" family life. Her family was financially well-off, and she had enjoyed the basic comforts: nice clothes, summer camp, a university education. Her mother had been a full time homemaker, and had always made sure that the children were fed three good meals a day.

Although Vicki's physical needs had been met, her emotional needs, her need for love, recognition, affection, and validation had never been met. Her father was a workaholic and wasn't home very much. Her mother, although at home, was not there for her on an emotional level. Vicki was expected to fend for herself.

Because her parents didn't seem interested in listening to her talk about herself, and what she was really feeling, she assumed that "there must be something wrong with having feelings." No one else in her family seemed bothered by the lack of emotional connectedness that existed. The only thing she could conclude, without being able to talk about this matter openly, was that feelings were somehow bad. They were a private matter, like going to the toilet. And so she tried her best to ignore her feelings by keeping busy, spending time with her friends, doing her homework, and being helpful around the house.

Vicki succeeded in stopping her primary feelings of anger, sadness, fear and shame. All she was able to feel was anxiety and a feeling of doom. She had no idea why she was feeling anxious. Because she had cut herself off from her natural emotions for so long, she was no longer capable of making the connection between the events in her life and what these events actually meant to her. In therapy, Vicki had to learn to connect the events in her life to her own feeling response to them. She had to teach herself to feel again. (Vicki is a sadness-based strong/distant.)

LET'S STOP BEING PASSIVE

If you have been sexually or physically abused, many of you will have turned into passive adults, adults who do not have the self-confidence or the personal power necessary to create a dynamic life. The reason? As a dependent child, survival would have meant being passive. As a human being, you were born with an instinct to protect your self and to survive. Animals in the wild know instinctively that when they are attacked, they must fight back. But as an infant and child, dependent on your parents to provide you with physical and emotional care, survival might have meant the reverse; survival might have meant not fighting back.

As a tiny child, you would have been no match to a big strong adult. As a tiny child, you would not have been able to defend your self against physical assaults on your body. Survival would have meant accepting the assaults without a struggle. For fighting back likely would have caused your mom/dad to have become even more enraged. In this way, you would have believed that fighting back would have caused you to be killed (literally). And so shutting up and accepting the abuse would have probably been your best survival option.

If you were verbally abused, emotionally neglected, or if you had overinvolved parents who wanted to live your life for you, many of you will have turned into passive adults. By having been made to feel worthless, you would have concluded that you didn't have the ability to achieve your goals and realize your dreams. And so in your adult life, you may not even bother trying to make any major changes.

If your life isn't going the way you would like, and you don't believe you are capable of turning your life around, in effect, you have been programmed to be passive. As a dependent infant and child, being passive was your only way to survive. As an adult, you can now take active control of your own life. To do so, you must get in touch with and release the emotions that are locked inside your unconscious mind: your anger, sadness, fear and shame.

REUNITING WITH YOUR INNER SELF

Getting in touch with your feelings is a process, and the first step is opening up to them. The following fables will be a starting point. These fables are addressed to your inner self and are almost identical, except one is written for little boy selves and one is written for little girl selves.

ARAMIA—THE PRINCESS WHO LOST HER SELF

Baby Aramia was a beautiful child. Her parents, the king and queen, were very excited about her birth, and there were great parties and celebrations in the land. Aramia was thrilled at having been born into such a beautiful world. But her sunny world would soon became cloudy. She had no one to play with. Her mother and father were busy with court affairs. They didn't care that she was feeling lonely and unloved. Her mother was beautiful, but she cared more about her appearance than giving Aramia a hug. Her father was strong and handsome, but he was usually off hunting and handling court matters. Aramia used to cry herself to sleep every night.

One day, her mother found her crying and asked what was wrong. Aramia was so happy that her mother had finally shown some interest in her feelings. And so she told her about her lonely feelings and her worries; she worried that neither she nor her father really loved her or wanted her around.

Her mother listened to her and then said, "Stop being such a silly little girl. The job of a princess is to look pretty and to act happy. It's time for you to grow up and stop being such a baby. If you don't feel happy, just pretend that you are happy. Let's have no more complaining."

Aramia didn't know how she could stop feeling sad, but in time, it sort of happened on its own. Since she didn't feel happy, she decided to pretend to look happy. The more she put on a happy face, the more attention she got from her mother, father and the people at court. So she thought, "It's not so bad to not feel my true feelings. Putting on a happy appearance seems to be getting me a lot more attention than if I were sad."

Over time, however, Aramia lost her ability to feel her feelings. She became lethargic and started to become sickly. All the doctors in the kingdom examined her, but they had no idea what was wrong. Aramia, once a healthy child, began to waste away. No one could stop her deterioration—all the power and money in the kingdom couldn't save her.

One day, in her weakened condition, Aramia fell into a deep sleep. She imagined herself transported to a beautiful sunny land where there was sunshine and flowers and little fairies dancing in the wind. She saw a happy, pretty little girl playing in the grass, jumping and frolicking. Aramia was happy to find a playmate and asked what the little girl's name was. She was told that her name was Aramia.

The little princess said, "But that's my name too. Why do you have my name?"

The happy little girl responded, "I have the same name as you because I am you. I am the part of you that you left behind when you stopped feeling your true feelings. I have been waiting a long time for you to come and find me."

"Will you come home with me?" asked the little princess. "We could have a wonderful life together. You could play with me, you could be my permanent friend, and I will never have to be alone again. I would be so happy if you would come back with me. Please say yes."

The happy little Aramia said, "I would like a friend too, and I would like to be with you also, but I can't come back with you because I live far away. I am only in your mind, not in the physical world where you reside."

"But there must be a way," said the little princess. "There must be a way," she repeated. For once the little princess had found her other self, the part that had been missing, she didn't want to live without her.

"Well there is one way," said her new found friend. "But I don't know if you will be able to do this."

"I'll do anything," said the princess hopefully.

"Well in that case I'll tell you. What you must do to bring me back is for you to cry, and cry, and cry. Cry out all your sadness at being left alone. Cry out all your sadness that no one loves or cares about you. Cry out all your shame that there must be something wrong with you because your parents don't care. Cry out all your fear about who is going to take care of you because there is no one that you can count on. Cry out all your anger that it isn't fair that you aren't being loved and appreciated the way you deserve to be. Cry out all the emotions that you have been holding back, that you haven't been able to feel, and you will create a physical river of tears that will enable me to float back with you, and enter the physical land where you live."

"But I don't know how to cry," said the little princess. "I don't feel like crying, and I don't feel all these feelings your describe: anger, sadness, fear, shame."

"You don't feel them," said the princess's new friend,

"because your feelings have grown rusty. You have to decide what you want to do, but let me assure you that all these feelings are sitting within you, ready to be released, when you give the word."

"I'm afraid," said the little princess. "I'm afraid that if I let them go, something terrible will happen to me. I feel that I will fall into a deep hole, never to return."

"You are already in that hole," said Aramia. "You already know, deep in your heart, that if you don't release your true feelings soon, you will surely die. The reason you are sick now is because you are tired of not being your self, tired of not feeling your own feelings, and tired of putting on an act. Crying me a river is the only way to reunite with me so that you can become the whole Aramia, the princess you really are.

"Now take a few minutes, relax, and just start feeling your feelings. Just let them go. I'll have to say goodbye for now, but I'll be watching you. Remember you are the only person who can bring me back—the only person. It's up to you. I can only reunite with you if you cry me a river and allow me to return to you.

"It's now time for you to return to your life. But remember, if you do what I say, we will reunite, and you'll be happy forever. All you have to do to reunite with the happy part of you is to cry a river and release all the feelings that you have pent up."

The little princess Aramia woke up alone and thought about her dream. She remembered what her new friend, the happy little Aramia, had said about crying out a river. At first she thought she wouldn't be able to do it. So she lay there quietly and just thought and thought. Then she began to feel and feel. And then she began to cry and cry. And she cried and cried for days and days. The king and queen came in to see her and told her to stop crying. They said that crying was not something a little princess should do, and that she must stop crying. But Aramia wouldn't stop. She said that she had a right to feel her own feelings, and that she wanted to be left alone.

Princess Aramia cried for one hundred days. Her tears turned into a river, and the river enabled the lost part of her self, the happy Aramia, to come back into her life. After she had reunited with her lost self, the princess was able to live happily ever after.

ARAMINE—THE PRINCE WHO LOST HIS SELF

Baby Aramine was a beautiful child. His parents, the king and queen, were very excited about his birth, and there were great parties and celebrations in the land. Aramine was thrilled at having been born into such a beautiful world. But his sunny world would soon became cloudy. He had no one to play with. His mother and father were busy with court affairs. They didn't care that he was feeling lonely and unloved. His mother was beautiful but she cared more about her appearance than giving Aramine a hug. His father was strong and handsome, but he was usually off hunting and handling court matters. Aramine used to cry himself to sleep every night.

One day, his mother found him crying and asked what was wrong. Aramine was so happy that his mother had finally shown some interest in his feelings. And so he told her about his lonely feelings, and his worries; he worried that neither she nor his father really loved him or wanted him around.

His mother listened to him, and then responded by saying, "Stop being such a silly little boy. The job of a prince is to look handsome and strong, and to act happy, even if you aren't happy. It's time for you to grow up and stop being such a baby. If you want to be the next king, you must start acting like a little king right now."

Well Aramine didn't know how to stop feeling sad, but in time, it sort of happened on its own. Since he didn't feel happy, he decided to pretend to look happy. The more he put on a happy face, the more attention he got from his mother, father, and the people at court. So he thought, "It's not so bad to not feel my true feelings. Putting on a happy appearance seems to be getting me more attention than if I were sad."

Over time, however, Aramine lost his ability to feel his feelings. He became lethargic, and started to become sickly. All the doctors in the kingdom examined him, but they had no idea what was wrong. Aramine, once a strong, healthy child, began to waste away. No one could stop his deterioration—all the power and money in the kingdom couldn't save him.

One day, in his weakened condition, Aramine fell into a deep sleep. He imagined himself transported to a beautiful sunny land where there was sunshine and flowers and little fairies dancing in the wind. He saw a happy, handsome little boy playing in the grass, jumping and frolicking. Aramine was happy to find a playmate and asked what the little boy's name was. He was told that his name was Aramine.

The little prince said, "But that's my name too. Why do you have my name?"

The happy little boy responded, "I have the same name as you, because I am you. I am the part of you that you left behind when you stopped feeling your true feelings. I've been waiting a long time for you to come and find me."

"Will you come home with me?" asked the little prince. "We could have a wonderful life together. You could play with me, you could be my permanent friend, and I will never have to be alone again. I would be so happy if you would come back with me. Please say yes."

The happy little Aramine said, "I would like a friend too, and I would like to be with you also, but I cannot come back with you because I live far away. I am only in your mind, not in the physical world where you reside."

"But there must be a way," said the little prince. "There must be a way," he repeated. For once the little prince had found his other self, the part that had been missing, he didn't want to live without him.

"Well there is one way," said his new found friend. "But I don't know if you'll be able to do this."

"I'll do anything," said the prince hopefully.

"In that case I'll tell you. What you must do to bring me back with you is for you to cry, and cry, and cry. Cry out all your sadness at being left alone. Cry out all your sadness that no one loves or cares about you. Cry out all your shame that there must be something wrong with you because your parents don't care. Cry out all your fear about who is going to take care of you because there's no one you can count on. Cry out all your anger that it isn't fair that you aren't being loved and appreciated the way you deserve to be. Cry out all the emotions that you have been holding back, that you haven't been able to express, and you will create a physical river of tears that will enable me to float back with you, and enter the physical land where you live."

"But I don't know how to cry," said the little prince, "and besides, princes aren't supposed to cry. I'm going to be the next king, and that means I have to start getting ready for being tough right now." The little prince felt that he had taken control of the situation.

"I figured that you would say that," said his friend. "It's really up to you. You don't have to feel your feelings and let them go. But as I have told you, you will have to do a whole lot of crying if you want me to come back with you. If you want to remain alone, you don't have to do anything differently than you are doing right now."

"Okay," said the prince. "I'll try to cry, but quite honestly, I don't really feel like crying. I don't feel all these feelings you describe—anger, sadness, fear, shame."

"You don't feel them," said the prince's new friend, "because your feelings have grown rusty. Let me assure you that all these feelings are sitting within you, ready to be released, when you give the word."

"I'm afraid," said the little prince. "I'm afraid that if I let them go, something terrible will happen to me. I feel that I'll fall into a deep hole, never to return."

"You are already in that hole," said the other Aramine. "You already know, deep in your heart, that if you don't release your true feelings soon, you will surely die. You know that the reason you are sick now is because you are tired of not being your self, tired of not feeling your own feelings, and tired of putting on an act. Crying me a river is the only way to reunite with me so that you can become the whole Aramine, the little prince you really are.

"Now take a few minutes, relax and just start feeling your feelings. Just let them go. I'll have to say goodbye for now, but I'll be watching you. Remember, you are the only person who can bring me back—the only person. It's up to you. I can only reunite with you if you cry me a river and allow me to return to you.

"It's now time for you to return to your life. Remember, if you do what I say, we will reunite, and you will be happy forever. All you have to do to reunite with the happy part of you is to cry a river and release all the feelings that you have pent up."

The little prince Aramine woke up alone and thought about his dream. He remembered what his new friend, the happy little Aramine, had said about crying out a river. At first he thought that he wouldn't be able to do it. So he lay there quietly and just thought and thought. Then he began to feel and feel. And then he began to cry and cry. And he cried and cried for days and days.

The king and queen came in to see him and told Aramine to stop crying. They said that crying was not something a little prince should do, and that he must stop crying. But Aramine wouldn't stop. He said that he had a right to feel his own feelings, and that he wanted to be left alone.

Prince Aramine cried for one hundred days. And his tears turned into a river, and the river enabled the part of himself that he had lost, the happy Aramine, to come back into his life. After he had reunited with his lost self, the prince was able to live happily ever after.

GETTING IN TOUCH WITH YOUR FEELINGS / EXPRESSING YOUR FEELINGS

It's now time to do the emotional release work that will enable you to reunite with your inner self. The following exercises will start you off in this process. Working with a psychotherapist who encourages you to release your feelings, right in the therapeutic session, will certainly help you in your process.

THE POWER OF LETTER WRITING

The idea here is to get in touch with all your buried emotions: anger/rage, sadness, fear and shame. You will want to get in touch with each of these categories of emotions, and to identify why you felt/feel this way. Why writing letters is so powerful is that the writing process allows for a strong emotional connection to take place between your thoughts and feelings. Writing allows for deep feelings to come up. The goal is to connect up with your feelings. So if you feel like crying, banging the wall, screaming, sobbing, please do so; you're on the right track.

STEP ONE: WRITE OUT LETTERS 1 AND 2

In these first letters, write a separate letter to both your mother and your father. Write it from your present age. In your letter, review how you felt/feel about each parent in each of the following categories, and the reasons for your feelings. Use any of the sentences or ideas that ring true for you, and add your own.

A. ANGER

I hated / I hate you because ....
I despised how you treated me: explain ....
I resented / I resent the way you ....
You have your .... (swear as freely and as much as you want) nerve for treating me the way you did.
You have your .... nerve for not being a parent to me.
You are a .... for abandoning me.
You never acted like a responsible parent. You abused me. You neglected me. You ignored me. You were too busy with your own needs to notice me.
You never let me be me. / You still don't allow me to be me.
You thought for me. You controlled me. You manipulated me. You used me as an object for your own interests. / You still try to control me.
You never loved me. You wanted a child who would impress your friends.
You never cared about me. You only cared about ....
I resent the responsibilities you imposed on me.
I resent that I had to become a parent to my brothers and sisters—that you couldn't cope with them.
It was your decision to have children not mine. I despise you for taking my life away from me.
You took away my childhood and made me an adult at age 3.

B. SADNESS

I was brokenhearted because ....
You hurt me deeply by .... / You still hurt me deeply.
You broke my heart by .... / How you treat me still breaks my heart.
I was so hurt that you loved .... more than me. I am still hurt.
How could you have ignored me the way you did? / How can you ignore me now?
How could you have abandoned me? How can you abandon me now?
I used to cry myself to sleep.
I was so sad when you went out. I thought you didn't care about me.
Why didn't you love me? I loved you. / Why don't you love me now?

I would have done anything for you. I loved you. I still love you. All I wanted from you was that you would love me. But you didn't. You didn't care about me at all. You only cared about .... I didn't want to live without your love. / I still want your love.
I just wanted you to put your arms around me and hug me. I still want your affection.
I wanted you to notice me. Why didn't you notice me? / Why don't you notice me?
Why didn't you care about me? Why didn't you love me? Why don't you love me now? Why aren't you kind to me now? Why don't you think about me now?

C. FEAR

I was / I am afraid of you because ....
I was terrified / I am terrified of you when you ....
I was terrified that you would ....
I was terrified that I would die ....
I was terrified that no one would take care of me ....
I always felt that you would hurt me if I gave away your secret.
I really believed that you would destroy me when you started beating me.
I never felt safe. I never felt protected.
I always felt so exposed.
I always felt that you could come in any time and hurt me.
I felt like you could destroy me any time you wanted.
I felt I had no way to protect my self. You terrified me.

D. SHAME

Your not loving me made me feel like there was/is something wrong with me.
Your not loving me made/makes me feel worthless.
You made/make me ashamed of having feelings.
You made/make me want to hide my true self.
You made/make me have to pretend my entire life.
You made/make me feel defective.
You made/make me feel worthless.
You made me want to die.
I have been so ashamed my entire life—wanting to hide the real me.

I have always thought no one would want me because you didn't want me.

I felt I had to hide my vulnerability. I didn't want anyone to know that I was scared, that I was lonely, that I was sad. I felt ashamed and felt I had to put on an act to be acceptable to others.

You made/make me feel contaminated. You made me feel that I had to be grateful for crumbs because no one would want me as I am.

E. HOW YOU FELT IN GENERAL / HOW YOU FEEL IN GENERAL

I felt so lonely every day of my life. / I still feel lonely.
I felt abandoned. / I still feel abandoned and isolated.
I felt unloved. / I still feel unloved.
I felt unwanted. / I still feel unwanted.
You made/make me feel unloveable.
You made/make me feel like a zero, a nothing, a worm.
I felt like nothing. I still feel like nothing.
I felt there was no point living.
I felt trapped—you gave me no options. I still feel that way.

F. WHAT YOU WANTED FROM EACH PARENT / WHAT YOU WANT FROM EACH PARENT

I wanted you to love me. / I still want you to love me.
I wanted you to value me. / I still want you to value me.
I wanted you to recognize me. / I still want you to recognize me.
I wanted you to care about me. / I still want you to care about me.
I wanted you to think I was important. / I still want you to think I am important.
I wanted you to think I was special. / I still want you to think I am special.
I wanted you to be interested in me, my friends, my school work.
I wanted you to help me with my problems. / I still want your support.
I wanted you to take my side. / I still want you to take my side.
I wanted you to listen to me. / I still want you to listen to me.

G. HOW EACH PARENT DAMAGED YOUR LIFE *

You ruined my life because of the way you treated me.
You taught me that I was worthless and because of you, I choose
people who treat me as badly as you treated me.
Because of you, I treat my self like dirt.
Because of you, I cannot hold down a job.
Because of you I have suffered every day of my life.
Because of you, I serve others rather than take care of my self.
Because of you, I don't treat my self with value.

* Don't be afraid to get really angry at your parents. Your goal
here is to get your feelings out. Getting angry does not mean giving up responsibility for taking charge of your life. It means
acknowledging where the problem originated. You were not the
source of the problem. You were the victim—the helpless victim
of your parents' emotions. Whatever damage was done to you is
now on your shoulders to solve. The purpose of feeling and
releasing your anger is not to have a convenient excuse which
explains why you cannot move forward in your life. The purpose
is to release the stored-up emotions that are preventing you
from being able to enjoy your own life.

David's Letter

Dear Dad,

*I'm writing to tell you how much you have made me suffer
and to let you know what a bastard you were to me. I was your
first born. I know you wanted me. So how could you have
treated me like a dog? You were cruel to me. You abused me.
You tore me to shreds. You always focused on my faults, and
you ignored the good in me. You ignored the wonderful child
that I was. I loved you. I loved you so much. I wanted to be like
you. I tried my best. I did everything you wanted and it wasn't
good enough. You humiliated me at that baseball game. You
know the one—where you blamed me for causing my team to
lose. Boy, were you ever a bastard to me. I had so much promise. And you always found a way to make me feel worthless.
You knocked the very life out of me. I was terrified of you.*

*You made me terrified of you—my own father. When you
started to rage at me, I thought you were going to kill me. So*

unfair. So cruel. I detest you. You destroyed me, and you don't even know it. And now you expect me to take care of you. Now that you are old, you need me to give to you. And I do. That's the amazing thing! I still want your love. I still want you to say that you love me. I still try to please. I still try to deny the hatred I feel toward you in the hope that you'll still love me. I want an apology from you, and I want some recognition for the wrongs you have done me.

David

STEP TWO: WRITE OUT LETTERS 3 AND 4

Now write out responses to your letters from each of your parents <u>acknowledging</u> everything you have just said. A big part of why we deny our feelings (and why our feelings don't even reach our conscious awareness) is because our parents denied what was really going on in our families; they denied that they were treating us poorly. They were so busy with themselves, their own problems and pressures, that they ignored us, our feelings and our needs. Most of the time they didn't even realize that they were doing so!

In letters 3 and 4, write a letter from each of your parents to your self:

a. <u>apologizing</u> for their poor treatment of you.
b. <u>admitting</u> to each wrongdoing.
c. <u>asking your forgiveness</u> on each point.

You might have difficulty writing a letter, written by your abusive, neglecting, or overinvolved mother/father, in which s/he both takes responsibility for what s/he did to you, and asks for your forgiveness. You might say this is totally unrealistic and that s/he would never agree to do that. I agree that in all likelihood, s/he wouldn't do it. But your mother/father isn't writing the letter, you are. The purpose of this letter is to help you, not your parents. Your goal here is to end the denial that has occurred in your family. By getting your mother/father to admit, even if you write the letter, that s/he has treated you poorly, in whatever way s/he has done so, you will be ending the denial in your self. You will be freeing your self from taking responsibility for actions that belonged to your mother/father.

David's Dad's Response:

Dear Son,

I'm writing to ask for your forgiveness. I have wronged you. I admit it, I abused you. I screamed at you. I raged at you. You were a wonderful child. I was so angry for my own failures in life that I dumped them all on you. You were a convenient target. You were an easy target. You had no place to run. I wanted you to be perfect because I felt so flawed. I wanted you to be perfect so that I could show my parents that I was good. But I made you feel small. I made you feel worthless. I made you feel that there was something wrong with you. You tried so hard, and I'm truly ashamed of how I cut you down. At that baseball game when your team lost that day, I blamed you for not being good enough. It was me who wasn't good enough. I wanted to dump my own feelings of worthlessness onto you. I remember your downcast face. I took the very life out of you. I ruined you. You had so much promise, and now you don't want to do anything. I crushed you, a beautiful child. I'm so sorry.

I can tell you sincerely that I want the best for you. I was a lousy, rotten parent to you. I was caught up in my own misery, and I didn't give you the love you deserved. I can't change the past. I admit to the damage, but it's up to you to fix it. I want you to feel good about you. I want you to believe in you. I believe in you. It was me whom I didn't believe in. I know you can achieve your dreams because you're a hard worker and a good person. My best wishes are with you for all that you undertake. I only hope you can make up for the damage I have done.

Love Dad

STEP THREE: PUT THESE LETTERS ON AN AUDIO CASSETTE

Writing out your feelings and getting them acknowledged will help you connect up with what has happened to you in your life. To add to the effectiveness of this technique, record your letters and your parents' responses onto audio cassette. Listen to your cassette at least once a day. Being reminded of your feelings, and hearing your parents' acknowledgement of your feelings will help open you up.

STEP FOUR: KEEP REPEATING THIS PROCESS ON A WEEKLY BASIS

Writing these letters and recording them should not be a one-time event. It should be the start of a process. As you begin connecting up with your emotions, new feelings, memories and dream-like images will come back to you. Something that is an issue today might be resolved in a month's time and in a month's time, a whole new set of issues may come up. So make a commitment to your self to write a series of letters on a weekly basis, and notice how powerful this approach can be in helping you connect up with your feelings.

THE POWER OF THE EXPERIENTIAL CONVERSATION

Lie on a couch, close your eyes, and imagine, through your mind's eye, that your parent is right there in front of you. Talk to you parent about your feelings, this time being <u>the age you were when the event took place</u>. For example, if you were seven years old when your dad was teaching you to ride a bicycle, and at the time, he had made you feel inadequate, be seven years old when you're talking to your dad about your true feelings. Talk to him from a position that you have a right to your feelings and that you're going to let him know just how furious you are about the way he's treating you. Always use the <u>present tense</u>. Try to get in touch with each of your four emotions: anger, sadness, fear and shame. Express your emotions by screaming, kicking, yelling, banging, swearing, crying, sobbing, or in whatever way works best for you. Remember, the purpose of these conversations is to release your emotions, so don't hold back.

THE EXPERIENTIAL CONVERSATION ON TAPE

A variation of this process is to record your conversation with your parent on an audio cassette tape. Imagine that your parent is sitting there in front of you, and this time, from <u>your present</u>

age, proceed to tell it like it is. Express all your thoughts and feelings—everything you always wanted to say, but weren't able to. You are encouraged to get worked up and express your feelings of rage, sadness, fear and shame by screaming, yelling, shouting, swearing, crying or hitting a pillow. Don't be afraid of the feelings that come out of you. These feelings belong to you. Although you may feel uncivilized, or find that you feel out of control, nothing bad will happen. In this process, you are simply discovering who you really are.

Once you complete your conversation, play it back on a regular basis. The value of this is that you will be reminded of your true feelings with no holds barred. When an emotional outburst is not recorded, you might forget that it ever took place. With it on tape, you can stay in contact with your true feelings, and be triggered to remember additional incidents that may have made you very angry, sad, terrified or ashamed. When you get tired of listening to the same recording, it's probaby time to add a new conversation or connect up with a new feeling. Be creative and flexible about how you use this process. Whatever works for you is the right way to go.

THE POWER OF THE INTERNAL DIALOGUE   *TOUJOURS !*

Another way of connecting up with and releasing your feelings is to begin having an internal dialogue. Create a conversation between your inner child self and your adult self. Close your eyes and become that five-year-old child who is scared, hurt, angry and ashamed, and tell the adult you how horrible it is to be dependent on your parents. Tell the adult you how badly you are being treated; how no one is considering either you or your feelings; how you are being ignored; how worthless you feel; how lonely you feel; how abandoned you feel; how sad you feel; how hurt you feel; how enraged you feel; how trapped you feel; how afraid you are to speak up for fear that you will lose the little you have. Tell the adult you, your kind, considerate, loving, understanding adult self just how unbearable your life is for you.

And now be your kind, loving, understanding adult self, and comfort the little five-year-old you. Use the following script as a model for the loving messages you want to give to your inner child self:

"It's truly horrible the way you are being treated. I want to make up for the pain you have been forced to experience. I want to save you from your misery and loneliness. I plan to take care of you from now on. I will always be here for you. I will always listen to your problems. I understand just how bad it is for you. It's not right that you are exposed to such cruel treatment. Your parents are cruel to you. <u>You do not deserve such uncaring parents. You do not deserve such unkind treatment. The treatment you are receiving has nothing to do with your worth.</u> It's not your fault that you are being neglected. It's not your fault that you are being ignored. It's not your fault that you are being abused. Your parents are <u>incapable</u> of treating you according to your true worth. They just don't have any love to give. They are empty themselves. They are loaded with rage, shame, sadness and fear, and they are dumping their pain and misery onto you. You are truly a <u>vic-tim</u> of their pain. They are using you to try to feel better about them-selves. I am so sorry that you are being made to suffer for their feelings of inadequacy.

"I want you to know that I can help free you from your pain. I am here for you. I am here for you always. You have a friend in me. You need never feel alone or lonely again. I am here for you. There's no need to suffer any longer. I want to make up for the pain that you have suffered. I love you completely and unconditionally. I am so happy to be part of you. You are such a wonderful, delightful, joyful, loveable little self. I love you."

The goal here is to unite your little lost self with your adult self. Because of all the feelings that you had to block, your inner child self may have gotten lost. It's time to reconnect with your inner child self. You can become that loving parent to your self that you never had. The fact is, as an adult, you no longer need your birth parents to love and take care of you. You can do that for your self. But your inner child self may not know this. Inside of you, there may still be a five-year-old child who is waiting to be loved. You can become the loving parent to your self that you have always longed for. You can become the best loving parent imaginable by beginning this internal dialogue.

A COMBINATION PROCESS

PART ONE

Lie down, close your eyes, and relax deeply. Take about five minutes to completely relax your body. You can do this by concentrating on each breath, and repeating, "With each breath I am feeling more and more comfortable, more and more relaxed."

When you're fully relaxed, say to your inner self, "There's a part of me that is feeling very unhappy. What exactly am I feeling? Am I feeling sad? hurt? angry? enraged? afraid? ashamed?" Concentrate on what you're feeling. Then ask your self: "When is the first time I felt this way?" "What am I doing?" "Who am I with?" "What is happening around me?"

You will then draw into your conscious mind a scene from your past which was painful to you: perhaps you were being beaten by your father; perhaps you were being humiliated by your mother in front of your friends; perhaps you were sitting at the dinner table and eating in silence, being forced to stop your natural desire to talk cheerfully about your day; perhaps you were feeling furious because you were being forced to babysit when what you really wanted to do was go out with your friends.

Once you bring forward the scene, live it again, but this time, tell your parent what you were not able to say then. Tell your parent how you <u>feel</u> (present tense) about the treatment you are receiving, and what you think about her/him. If you are feeling angry, the following script can be a useful model for you:

"You have no god damn right to treat me the way you do. You have your x#0#! nerve for treating me this way. I detest you. I despise you. You are a disgusting human being, humiliating me this way, running your power trip. You are able to get away with this because I'm powerless to stop you.

"Well, I'm not putting up with this any more. I don't have to take this. You have no right to do this to me, and I won't take it. I refuse to accept your abuse. Do you hear that? I refuse to accept your abuse. So you can #x0#! right off. I won't be your slave any more. I won't be treated this way any more. From now on, I'm protecting my self. I have the power to say NO, and I am saying NO. You will have to answer to me. From now on, I'm going to be treated with respect.

"And I have news for you. I'm not going to let you beat me and I'm not going to let you abuse me because I want your love. You don't love me. You're using me. You're controlling me. You're manipulating me. But you don't love me. Love is kindness. Love is caring. Love is wanting <u>me</u> to be happy. You aren't capable of loving me. You aren't capable of valuing me. You aren't capable of cherishing me. You are a pathetic human being who thinks only of your self. Well I hope you're happy because I'm not going to be your slave any more. Get the x#l#0 out of my life."

PART TWO

Once you have released your feelings, in any way that works for you, you are ready to turn to your adult self for comfort. Be your inner child self again, but this time, tell your kind, loving, understanding adult self how badly you are being treated, how angry you are feeling, how cruel your parent is and so forth. Then be your kind, loving, understanding adult self, and respond kindly to your inner child self, as outlined above in The Internal Dialogue.

RECALLING PAST EVENTS

Unless you become consciously aware of your emotional patterns, you will just keep repeating them until the day you die. Your patterns are well-entrenched, and their origin stems from what happened to you in your childhood. Therfore, the more you can recall about your past life, the greater will be your ability to free your self from your negative patterns.

Every one of us has denied aspects of our past that were too horrifying, too terrifying, too humiliating, too shameful, too hurtful and too infuriating for us to bear. We can recall some of our memories through systematically thinking about our lives. Other memories will be beyond our conscious recall, and are now buried in our unconscious minds. Memories get stored in the unconscious when they are too painful for our conscious minds to face. If you want to access a greater amount of your unconscious material, you will need to work with a psychotherapist who is trained in this area.

In any event, you do have within your conscious access many memories that you'll be able to work with through systematic recall. Most of us, if we give it some thought, can remember a craving we may have had for recognition or appreciation by our moms and dads. Perhaps there was a time when your mom and dad ignored a special effort you had made to please them. Or perhaps there were times when you had to pretend to be happy, when in fact you were enraged inside.

To pull up memories that you can then work to release, think about:

a. Your school years; where you lived; what schools you went to; what teachers you had; who your friends were; the clothes you liked to wear; your favourite toys and possessions; your interests and hobbies; the sports you liked; how you spent your free time.

b. Regular events such as birthday parties, and holidays such as Christmas, Thanksgiving and Easter/Passover.

c. Routines: mealtimes; bathtime; bedtime. What kind of things did you do with your brothers and sisters? Who looked after you when your parents went out? What happened during these times?

d. Parental care: How did they discipline you? Were your parents overinvolved, distant(neglectful) or abusive? What did they do to you that you hated? What did they do that made you angry? sad? afraid? ashamed?

e. Fondest memories

f. Family secrets

g. Family tragedies: deaths, illnesses

i. Your secrets: unacceptable assaults that were committed against you such as sexual and physical abuse. You may have been so ashamed about these horrible experiences that you may have never told anyone about them.

A NOTE ON FAMILY SECRETS

We all tend to deny those parts of our selves that don't quite fit our ideal self-image. In addition, we tend to feel "lesser-than" when we compare our selves to the images that the advertising industry thrusts upon us on a daily basis. What are we constantly exposed to?...Pictures of beautiful people living the good life.

Is sunning on the Riviera or enjoying a Bacardi and rum in the Bahamas the way people live on a daily basis? No, but that's what we all dream about. Because most of us want to live the "good life," what we actually have and how we live our lives pale by comparison. And so we hide our true experiences, and we deny what living our lives is really like for each of us. Instead of being honest, we tell each other, "Everything is just wonderful," because if we don't, we worry we will lose the esteem of our peers.

Believing that other people live grand old lives, and that we don't, forces us to deny—deny who we are, and deny the issues with which we are struggling. Rather than releasing our pent-up emotions, we will often spend our energy pushing them down. In so doing, we will end up suffering from physical and emotional anguish for the rest of our lives.

In this regard, family secrets can prove to be an incredible burden which can truly ruin your life, without you really being aware of their insidious nature. An excellent reference in this area is a book by Harriet Webster, entitled, Family Secrets—How Telling And Not Telling Affect Our Children, Our Relationships And Our Lives.[3] By reading about the strain that family secrets have put on others, you may start feeling more comfortable looking at your own.

One of the most out-of-the-ordinary family secrets that I have ever heard was told to me by Alan, a soft-spoken, gentle psychiatrist from France who was doing a residency rotation in a psychiatric treatment program where I was working. Although Alan had been through years of psychoanalysis, he struck me as being very secretive. He had good reason to be secretive. What he had to live with was the following. During the second world war, his father had joined the French army, leaving Alan and his brother in his mother's care. With her husband now absent, his mother became romantically involved with a man who moved in with Alan's family. Whenever his father would get a leave to return home, his mother's lover would move out. As soon as his father had left to take up his duties, his mother's lover would return. At the end of the war, his father moved back home, and family life continued as though nothing had ever happened.

What a terrible thing to have done to Alan and his brother. They were forced to pretend that this extra-marital relationship had never taken place. The dilemma that Alan was facing was an impossible one. If he relieved himself of the pressure he was

---

[3](Don Mills, Ontario: Addison Wesley, 1991)

under by telling his father the truth, his father might have left his mother. Because Alan would naturally have felt closer to his mother, simply because his father had been away for so long, he would have alienated her totally by this exposure. He would then have been forced to worry about both the loss of love to himself, and the possible abandonment and/or rejection by his mother. Not a great alternative. He kept his silence and suffered the rest of his life by not being able to be open and truly intimate with other people.

FACING YOUR PAST WILL SET YOU FREE

There's no substitute for facing your feelings and releasing them from your gut. We all have absorbed negative messages and beliefs about our selves that are simply not true; they belong to our parents. The only way to free your self from the negative impact of such messages is to both acknowledge and release your painful feelings. Because of your upbringing, you may believe that it's not okay to be honest about your feelings. The truth is the reverse: It's not okay not to be honest about your feelings. Denial leads to physical and emotional pain, along with a life that's devoid of happiness. It's time to start taking care of your interests.

The question that often arises is, "What if my mother/ father is dead? Shouldn't I only think well of her/him because s/ he cannot defend her/himself against my attacks?" To answer this question, ask your self: "Did s/he respect you as a child? Did s/he ever think about the damage that was being done to you? Did s/he ever consider your suffering and torment? Did s/ he ever consider the fact that s/he was depriving you of your right to be happy and to live your own life?" (These same questions are applicable if your mother/father is still alive.)

We all have a job to do, here on earth, and that is to be the person we really are. The only way for this to happen is to free our selves from the unreleased emotions that are dragging us down. You owe it to your self to release your emotions!

12 | CREATING A LOVE-BASE

It's time to start truly valuing your own worth. Once you free your self from your bottled up rage, sadness, fear and shame, you will be ready to work on connecting up with the love within your self, and to become the unconditionally loving parent you never had. When you start truly loving your self, your happiness quotient will increase dramatically.

There's a great misconception about "love," and that is that it must come from outside our selves. Because we were dependent on our parents to be kind, considerate, affectionate, caring, and concerned about our wellbeing, we have grown used to looking outward for these warm fuzzies. As adults, we will then continue to look outward for these signs of "love" from other people, and especially from a lover or spouse. For those of us who have lost our trust in people, we will turn to love substitutes: making money, power, alcohol, drugs, food, sex, or gambling. What we didn't learn is that we <u>can</u> give love to our selves; what we didn't know is that we can create a pool of self-love which can fill our selves up—fill the empty hole created by our parents who were not able to love us completely.

WHAT IF I'M NOT WORTH LOVING?

In order to do the work to create a love-base, you must first believe that you are worth loving. Right now you might believe that you're not worth loving. You may believe that there's something wrong with you: you're defective, inadequate, imperfect, not good enough. Even though you may pretend, when you are with other people, that you are confident and sure of your self, you may secretly believe that you're worthless, and certainly not worth loving.

If you hold the belief that you are inadequate and not worth loving, realize that your self-assessment is based on an incorrect interpretation of the facts. This negative interpretation would have resulted from the way you were being treated by your parents, and your <u>acceptance</u> of their treatment as being justified. If your parents treated you abusively, if they neglected you, ignored you, humiliated you, didn't consider your feelings, or didn't treat you with respect and admiration, you would have concluded that you didn't <u>deserve</u> better treatment. You would have concluded that if you were more acceptable, they would have treated you well, but because you were defective and inadequate, their treatment of you paralleled your true worth. Your logic: If you had more worth, you would have been treated well; because you were not worth much, your parents were correct in treating you poorly.

Now this logic is incorrect. You were not the <u>cause</u> of your parents' poor treatment of you. You were the <u>victim</u> of their poor treatment. The way your parents treated you had <u>nothing</u> to do with your worth. It directly reflected the way they felt about themselves. By treating you neglectfully, abusively, and in a controlling manner, they were dumping their anger, their sadness, their fear and their shame onto you. Any male/female child, in your birth order, with your parents, would have received the same poor treatment. You were just the unlucky child who happened to be there.

You were worthy and deserved to be loved, valued and treated as the precious jewel you were and are. Unfortunately, in that we all create our own reality, you will live out your negative self-beliefs. And so if you believe that you are inadequate, imperfect, defective, and not worth loving, you will act in ways that will bring your belief into reality. Let's look at what happens when you hold the belief that you are not worth loving when you enter into a romantic relationship.

John was extremely successful in business. He was an entrepreneur, and through his hard work and business acumen, he had built up a computer business generating millions of dollars annually. John had a good role model in his father, in that he too was a successful business man. But his father had done great damage to John, continuously and sadistically criticizing him for insignificant matters. John had chosen to block out his rage toward his father by channelling his intense emotions into the creation of a business that would make him feel good about himself.

The problem however was that John was driven by his business. Because of his father's abusive treatment, John had concluded that he was not worth loving; he believed he was defective in some way, and undeserving of kind, loving treatment. And so John was desperate to feel good about himself. The only place he was able to achieve these good feelings was at work where he had total control of his environment, and where he was able to achieve the outward signs of success: money, power and status.

Unfortunately, his desperate need to feel good about himself through total involvement with his business meant that he had nothing to emotionally give to the women with whom he was romantically involved. When he was away from his factory, and was removed from negotiating for supplies and doing deals, he began to feel uneasy and irritable. He would then need to get rid of his tension, and he did so by becoming verbally abusive to his romantic partner. As well, after a fourteen-hour work day, he was exhausted. He didn't have much energy to focus on his partner's day or on what she needed, because he was depleted. Taking care of himself was a full time job.

Understandably, his romantic relationships never lasted. Because John had nothing to give his partners emotionally, and because he both verbally abused them and ignored their needs, in time the women in his life disappeared. Having no awareness that it was his own actions that drove his partners away, John concluded that he was not worth loving—why else would these women have left him? His belief that he was not worth loving in turn fuelled his need to rely on his business success for his self-worth, and ensured that in his next relationship, he would have even less to give.

Rosalie came from a family where she had not received much love. As one of five children, she got lost in the shuffle. She was expected to fend for herself. Her mother was so depleted by a loveless marriage and the demands of her children that she had emotionally withdrawn herself. Although she took care of Rosalie and her siblings from an instrumental point of view, there was little nurturing. Rosalie's father spent long hours at the office and did not see himself as needing to provide anything to the children but the financial necessities of life.

Because Rosalie did not receive warm, tender loving from her parents, she concluded that there must have been something wrong with her. She came to see herself as being truly inadequate and defective as a human being. Although she secretly believed that she was not worth

loving, she rationalized that if a man would love her, she would magically become adequate and worthwhile.

Rosalie needed men to love her in the same way that an alcoholic
needs his alcohol and a drug addict needs his chemicals. Because she
felt inadequate, and not worth loving, she needed a man to make her
feel worthwhile. Unfortunately, this desperate need for a man's positive attention and love drove men away from her. Her intense need to
be loved was perceived as a burden to the men in her life. Although
she did have a number of long-term relationships, including a marriage, in time they all ended. Each time a relationship ended, Rosalie's
belief that she was not worth loving was confirmed.

RE-EVALUATING YOUR BELIEFS

The first step then, in creating a love-base, is to admit that
your conclusions about your self—you're not worth loving, you
don't deserve to be loved, there must be something wrong with
you, you're unloveable—are incorrect. No matter how many
times your outside reality has confirmed that you are "unwor-
thy," as the above situations have outlined, realize that you have
created this reality through your own actions. Remember, John
was not able to create a loving relationship because he was not
able to give to his partners; all his emotional energy was
invested in his business. Over time, his abusive behaviour, combined with his disinterest in his partners' needs drove them
away. Rosalie was not able to create a loving relationship
because she was not able to give to her partners; she was so desperate for their love that she both drained them and drove them
away. (John is anger-based, Rosalie, sadness-based needy.)

And so, if you feel that you are defective, imperfect, lesser-
than, inadequate, not good enough, not worth loving, not
deserving of love, please open your mind to the facts that you
were unaware of as a child:

1. It was your parents' treatment of you that made you think
   badly about your self. If you were ignored, neglected, humiliated, criticized, or abused, you will have concluded that you
   were worthless. Because you were totally dependent on your
   parents for both your physical and emotional care, you would
   have had no choice but to accept their treatment of you as a
   judgement on your worth as a human being. Your parents'

treatment of you had nothing to do with your worth. It had everything to do with the way they felt about themselves and their inability to give love.

2. You were a <u>victim</u> of your parents' parenting of you. You had <u>no choice</u> but to accept their care. You had no place to go. You were stuck with their parenting. Although you will have grown used to the way you were being treated, realize that what you have grown used to is living in a poisonous environment. You adapted to your poisonous environment in order to survive, but the poison is now in your system. It has contaminated your self-image. Realize as well that any male/female child who was placed in your home environment, with your parents, in the birth position you held, would have been equally contaminated.

3. <u>It was not your fault. You did not deserve the treatment you received.</u> You were the object of your parents' anger, fear, sadness and shame, resulting from their unhappy childhoods. The fact that you were neglected or abused meant that your parents were deeply troubled people. They were empty inside, and they were totally consumed with their own emotional survival. They had no love to give, and a whole lot of rage, sadness, fear and shame to get rid of.

4. You are worthy of love and you deserve to be loved. Your loveless past has nothing to do with your love-filled future. You can bring love into your life starting from this moment onward.

WHY DO YOU NEED TO CREATE A LOVE-BASE?

When you believe you are not worth loving, you will bring about this reality through your own actions, as the stories about John and Rosalie illustrate. But in addition, you will attract people who are incapable of loving you because you are incapable of loving you. When you believe that you are inadequate or not worth loving, through the Law of Attraction, you will match up with a partner who feels the same way about her/himself. Remember, your partner will only have the same capacity to give and receive love as you do—you are a mirror image of each other's emotional profiles. John didn't feel worthy of (receiving) love, so he made himself emotionally unavailable. Rosalie didn't feel worthy of (receiving) love, so she grabbed love for fear that it wouldn't be given freely. Neither of these people could give love, or understand the needs of their partner, because they were both empty inside; neither could see beyond their own need to feel worthwhile.

The fact is, if you feel inadequate and worthless inside, you will always match up with a person who feels the same way about her/himself. In the same way that when you look in the mirror, what you will see is a reflection of your outer self, when you look at your romantic partner, what you see will reflect your inner self. Objectively speaking, if you don't love your self, you will always match up with a man or woman who is incapable of loving you, reinforcing your belief that you aren't worth loving.

From a totally selfish perspective, the only way you can get the love you want is for you to love your self first. The only way for you to feel you deserve to be loved is for you to love your self first. For when you love your self, you will be able to match up emotionally with a person who loves her/himself. This person will have love to give you because love exists within. Giving love will then be an exchange, not a depletion. And love will build upon love.

So face reality as it is. You have to learn to create your own base of self-love in order to bring love into your life.

CREATING A LOVE-BASE

What do you need to do to love your self? You must give your self everything you always wanted to receive from an unconditionally loving parent. What are these things?—love, recognition, validation, to be seen as important, to be cherished, encouragement, consideration, kindness, attention, to be listened to, the freedom to express your feelings, the freedom to assert your needs, unconditional acceptance no matter what mistakes you make, being valued for who you are.

If you can't imagine doing all these things for your self, it means that you have not released enough of your pent-up emotions that are keeping you locked in the past. If you were abused, neglected or overcontrolled, you would have falsely assumed that there was something wrong with you, and that you were not worth loving exactly as you were and are.

The way your parents treated you had no reflection on who you were and are; it directly reflected on the way they felt about themselves. By treating you neglectfully, abusively, and in a controlling manner, they were dumping their anger, their sadness, their fear and their shame onto you. You were worthy and deserved to be loved, valued and treated as the gem you were and are today.

BECOMING YOUR OWN LOVING PARENT

Your inner self may not have received very many unconditionally loving messages from your parents. And so, because you will care for your self in the way that your parents cared for you, you will end up treating your self the way your parents treated you: harshly, critically, impatiently, and unkindly; you won't take your own side; you will ignore your true feelings.

There's no need to bring the past into the future. The past was miserable enough living through it once. There's no need to continuously repeat the past until the day you die. But repeat it you will unless you make a conscious commitment to release your pent-up emotions from the past and to love your self. The following exercises will help you on your path to self-love.

BEING YOUR OWN LOVING PARENT

In Chapter Eleven, Releasing Your Emotions, you were first introduced to the technique of creating an internal dialogue. Acting as a loving parent to your inner self is not a one-shot deal—it's something you must do on a regular basis to become emotionally whole within your self.

You can work with the internal dialogue, formally, by recalling incidents from your childhood where you felt particularly angry, sad, ashamed or afraid. Then, close your eyes, and being the age you were when that painful incident occured, tell the adult you how horrible you feel, and how painful your life is for you. Fully describe your feelings. Then, as the adult you, listen to little you, your inner child self, in a compassionate, supportive, kind, understanding way, and reassure little you that you will take that pain away because you understand how horrible it is. Tell little you that you no longer need to suffer; it's time to create a happy, joyous life.

You can also work with the internal dialogue, informally, on an as needed basis, each time you get "triggered." Being "triggered" is when you experience a strong emotional reaction to a person with whom you are interacting. Although the person may arouse in you strong feelings of anger, disgust, rage, fear, longing, shame, the intensity of your reaction is revealing to you your own unresolved feelings from your past. What's actually happening is that the person in your present life is <u>reminding</u> you of the way you used to feel as a dependent child: powerless, dependent, helpless, trapped, humiliated, hurt, unloved, enraged. These past feelings are fuelling the intensity of your reaction in the here and now.

Loving your self means wanting to free your self from your unreleased emotions from the past. Rather than blaming some other person for your present problem, or blocking out your true feelings through your Emotional Operating System, go back to the source of the problem and create an internal dialogue within your self.

When you were a child, totally dependent on your parents for your care, who made you feel this angry? who made you feel this afraid? who made you feel so entrapped? who made you feel that there was no way out? who made you feel that you would lose your identity if you gave in?

Once you connect up with the feelings you felt as a child, be that child, at that age. Close your eyes, and then tell the adult you exactly how you <u>are</u> feeling, always speaking in the <u>present</u> tense. Tell the adult you how enraged you feel, how humiliated you feel, how terrified you feel, how helpless you feel, how entrapped you feel, how desperate you feel. Don't spare any details. Tell the adult you exactly what your mom/dad is doing to you, and how horrible it is for you.

Then be your kind, loving, understanding adult self, and tell little you that you are there for you: you will protect you; you will never need to be alone again; you love you; you want to help you release your pain; you are here to create a happy life together; you are delighted to unite with such a wonderful, joyous, happy little self.

UNITING WITH YOUR INNER SELF

If you have been severely abused, either verbally, physically or sexually, or, if you have been neglected, you will have shut down emotionally. In order to survive, you will have closed your heart to your parent/s. Your thinking would have been, "You can hurt my body, but you can't hurt my spirit." Unfortunately, although you did survive childhood with this strategy, as an adult, your heart may still be closed off to everyone, including your self.

Before anyone else can love you, you must love your self. Therefore you must open your heart up to your own love. The following is a dialogue between your kind, loving parent self and little you. It's suggested that you read this dialogue onto an audio cassette tape, and listen to it repeatedly.

LOVING PARENT SELF

"You are the most beautiful little boy/girl. It's a crime that you were never given real love before today. You were forced to beg for crumbs of love. You were forced to pray that someone would notice you. You were forced to pay with your integrity just to get some attention. You were forced to accept abuse just to get some attention. You were humiliated, you were used, and you had no choice but to accept this disgusting treatment.

"You deserved real love. You were totally worthy of real love. You deserved total delight in your existence. You deserved consideration and respect. You deserved appreciation and recognition for the wonderful little being you were. You didn't get it before, and I want to make it up to you now.

"I love you totally, completely, and unconditionally. I love everything about you. You are the most wonderful person in the world. I adore you. I adore you completely. I delight in your existence. I am so thrilled that you were born.

"I want you to open up your heart to me. I want you to trust me. I know that you had good reason to stop believing in people and to stop trusting people. Your trust was violated. You were betrayed by the people who should have loved you. But that is in the past, and together we can create a happy future.

"I want you to open up your heart to me. (Repeat 5 time.) I love you and I want you to come back. I want you to trust me. I am here for you. I care about you. I want to give you love. I want to show you that you can count on me, that I am reliable, that I am here for you. But you have to open up your heart to me and to trust me. I'm here for you and I want to unite with you. I want us to be one. You can count on me. You can rely on me. Whatever you want, I am here for you. I love you."

INNER CHILD SELF

"I'm so happy that you've come to get me. I've been so lonely and so lost. I wanted you to find me. I wanted you to bring me back. I didn't think anyone cared about me. I didn't think that anyone loved me. But you love me. I know you love me. I know I can count on you. I know you won't let me down. I want to love you. I want to open up my heart to you. I'm afraid though. I'm afraid I'll be hurt again. It's been a long time since I've trusted anyone. I had to stop trusting. My life was in danger. I had to shut down. But I want to be with you now. I want to love you. I want to be one with you. It's such a wonderful feeling to be loved."

FORGIVING YOUR SELF

If you were abused, sexually, verbally or physically, if you were ignored, neglected or emotionally abandoned, if you were controlled or manipulated by your parent/s, it is highly doubtful that as an adult, you will either like your self or accept your self. In all likelihood, you will probably hate your self. The reason? Because your parents didn't "like" you (they did not treat you with love, kindness and understanding), you will have concluded that you weren't very "likeable," the reason being that there was something wrong with you—you were either defective or a "bad" person. If you weren't so inadequate, or if you were not such a "bad" person, they would have liked you, and treated you well. Because they treated you poorly, you would have concluded that there must have been something wrong with you. You would have concluded that you deserved your rotten treatment, and that you just weren't good enough as you were. And so you would have become ashamed of your self.

As an adult, you will then continue to treat your self the way your parents treated you. You will be critical of your self, and judgemental of your accomplishments. You will set standards of perfection for your self. If you don't meet them, you will conclude that your parents were right—you are inadequate.

Every time you remind your self of how you have fallen short of what you want to accomplish in your life, you are judging your self: perhaps you don't believe you have made enough money; perhaps you haven't gone as far up the career ladder as you would have hoped; perhaps you don't have a meaningful relationship; perhaps you don't have enough good friends, or the "right" friends; perhaps you aren't having much fun; perhaps you feel that you are a failure; perhaps you believe you aren't very smart; perhaps you never got that university degree; perhaps you can't lose those extra ten pounds, no matter how hard you diet; perhaps you can't cut out your addiction to alcohol or drugs.

It's time to stop beating your self, and to start forgiving your self. It's time to say, "I forgive my self for not being a millionaire." "I forgive my self for not being part of the 'in crowd.'" "I forgive my self for not having graduated from university." "I forgive my self for not being able to lose those ten pounds." "I forgive my self for starting to smoke again." "I forgive my self for not being chosen for that position." "I forgive my self for this relationship not working out." "I forgive my self for my marriage breaking down."

The issue here is not about happily remaining a drug addict. The issue here is not about giving up hope that your life will take a turn for the better. The issue here is not about blaming your parents for your problems, and feeling sorry for your self until the day you die. No. <u>The issue here is about accepting your current emotional capacity to achieve your goals. The fact is, you are doing the best you can with the emotional capabilities you currently possess.</u>

Wherever you are at in your life, you have come a long way from where you have started. You have survived. Because your unconscious mind will have blocked out traumas from your childhood, you may not consciously realize the horrors you have been through. And so from a conscious perspective, you probably don't see any reason why you aren't able to do more, and accomplish more than your current levels.

As you begin to connect back to your early childhood, and gain access to your buried pain, you will come to realize that there are very good reasons why your life has turned out the way it has, and why, at this point in time, you are unable to achieve your desires. Remember, your outside world will always reflect your inner world. If you don't like your self, if you don't accept your self, if you are ashamed of your self, if you believe you are inadequate, people and circumstance will respond in kind.

In order to create the life you want, and bring happiness into your life, you must begin by forgiving your self for any inadequacy you believe you have. You are perfect as you are. You are good enough exactly as you are. If you don't change one thing in your life, be proud of your self. <u>You're a wonderful human being, and even if you aren't where you want to be right now, you've always done the best of which you were emotionally capable.</u>

It's recommended that you get into the habit of forgiving your self for everything that doesn't work out the way you want it to. Just say, "I forgive my self for not getting that promotion." "I forgive my self for screaming at the kids." "I forgive my self for cheating on my diet." "I forgive my self for losing my cool with the bank manager." Then say, "I'm doing the best I can with my current emotional capabilities. I'm doing the best I know how. I accept my self as I am. I love my self."

Forgiving your self is a truly liberating experience. You might however have a hard time in doing so, believing that you should be able to do better. You may believe that your best is just not good enough. While it is true that in time you will be able to achieve more, realize that right now you are achieving all that you can with the emotional capabilities you currently possess. Realize that it's your buried emotions from your past that are preventing you from being where you want to be, and accomplishing what you want to accomplish.

Telling your self that you're dumb, stupid, no good, a failure, a hopeless case, or that you deserve your misery would be similar to a doctor whipping a patient because he has a broken leg. All the whipping in the world is not going to mend that broken leg; all your self-criticism is not going to develop your emotional capacity to achieve your goals.

Forgive your self for being human. Forgive your self for not being perfect. Forgive your self because you are doing the best you can with your current emotional capabilities. It's time to stop beating your self. It's time to stop feeling ashamed of who you are. It was not your fault that your parents treated you poorly. You didn't deserve such poor treatment. Forgive your self.

For those of you who doubt the value of self-forgiveness, realize this: As long as you condemn your self, you will be preventing your self from achieving your goals. Right now, in all likelihood, so much of your energy is being consumed in self-criticism and self-hatred that you are preventing your self from coming up with the creative answers necessary to achieve what's important to you. As soon as you start taking your own side, as soon as you start forgiving your self, you will be flooded with an energy that will enable you to get to where you want to go. Forgive your self. You are truly doing the best you can.

LETTING GO OF YOUR SELF-HATRED

If your parents didn't treat you with loving kindness, you will have concluded that you weren't worth loving, and that your inadequacy was the cause of their lack of love. You will then have become angry with your self, despising your self for not having been good enough to be loved. This is the origin of self-hatred.

But the origin of your self-hatred may go beyond that. Deep in your unconscious mind, you may hate your self because you believe that you have betrayed your self. You will hold your self responsible for whatever you had to do to survive. And so for example, if you had to accept sexual abuse in order to receive a few crumbs of affection, you will have believed that you "agreed to" the abuse because in fact you wanted it. What you really wanted was genuine love and affection. Sexual abuse was the only way you were able to receive what "appeared" to be love.

Now as an adult, on an unconscious level, you will either hate your self for selling out, or believe that you freely chose to accept that abuse. In either case, you will be so focused on your own self-hatred that you won't see that you didn't have a true choice about whether or not to accept the sexual abuse: you were a victim; you were not responsible for the way your mom/dad treated you; you did not betray your self; you took care of your self; you chose to survive. You did the right thing.

In the same way, you must not hold it against your self that you didn't fight back in situations where you were either being physically abused, or verbally humiliated by your mom/dad. You're not a traitor to your self. You had no choice. Children need love. Caring, attention and affection are as important to a growing child as are food, clothing and shelter. As a child, a lack of love would have appeared like death to you. As a dependent child, you would have thought that if you weren't loved, your parent might not have wanted to continue to care for you. Abandonment would have meant death, and survival would have meant doing whatever you had to do to ensure that your parents would be there to take care of you.

You must forgive your self for whatever you had to do to survive. Why? Because if you were a child who was raised by abusive, neglecting or overinvolved parents, you would have been treated as an emotional slave. Historically, slaves did what they were told because their choices were limited: compliance or death. Although in all likelihood, your parents would not have killed you if you did not comply, as an infant and growing child, it may have appeared that way to you.

And so please accept this important truth: You did not sell out. You did not betray your self. You chose to survive. You are alive and well, and that is the way it should be. Never, never, never be ashamed of what you did to be where you are right now.

You had no choice then—no true choice. You were dependent on the goodwill of your parents to ensure your survival. It's time to start forgiving your self for whatever you had to do to survive. Use the following affirmations to help in this process:

1. I forgive myself for passively accepting abuse. I was forced to beg for crumbs of attention and affection. I was afraid for my own safety. I had no choice.

2. I forgive myself for accepting criticism and humiliation without fighting back. I had no choice.

3. I forgive myself for pushing down my anger when what I really wanted to do was fight back. I had no choice.

4. I did not deserve the cruel, abusive, neglectful, controlling, manipulative treatment that I received. I did not deserve intermittent and conditional attention and interest.

5. I am in no way responsible for the way I was treated. Mom/dad was incapable of treating me with the love and respect I deserved.

6. I deserved love, affection, kindness, consideration, caring, respect, attention and understanding.

7. I deserve to be loved, respected and admired by all the important people in my life.

8. I want to face my anger. I want to face my sadness. I want to face my fears. I want to face my shame. I want to break free from my negative self-beliefs. I want to love my self.

ADMIRING YOUR SELF

It's time to start working on the positives. Once you let go of your self-hatred, you will start seeing your self as the wonderful person you really are. To help the process along, start admiring you. The following exercises will be of value.

PART A

Take the last three romantic relationships you have been in. Even if you have been married for some time, think back to relationships you were in, in your unattached days. Write out what each of these men/women admired about you.

A good way of doing this exercise is to pretend that you are your romantic partner excitedly telling a friend that s/he has just fallen in love with the most wonderful person (you), and then write out the gushing exuberance that will follow. Start with: "I just met the most wonderful person imaginable. You wouldn't believe how special s/he is ...."

After writing these comments out, read them over on a regular basis, until it starts sinking in what a special person you are.

PART B

Imagine that you are at a fund raiser and you are one of the dates that people are bidding on for a charitable cause. Write out a brief biography about your self, why you are the most interesting, enticing, wonderful person to be with. Describe how you have risen out of the adversity of your past. Describe your accomplishments. Describe your interesting life experiences. Describe your special unique perspective on life.

Every one of us is unique. And truly there will never be another person on this earth exactly like each of us. So let's tell the world who we are and as a start, tell your self who you are.

Break the habit of always looking outward and start looking inward. Truly, there are acres of diamonds in your own back yard.

BEING "WOWED" BY YOU

In the same way that we overlook who we are, and our important life accomplishments, so too we tend to overlook our daily and weekly accomplishments. It is through acknowledging our accomplishments, however, that we will provide our selves with the building blocks of self-respect, admiration and self-love. So let's start systematically reviewing what we've done.

PART A

On a daily or weekly basis, write out the things you've done that you are extremely pleased about. These things should address personal accomplishments, and should focus on how, through your own efforts, you have created remarkable results. Now we're not talking about results that would be reported in your local newspaper. We're talking about results that indicate your own personal evolution and growth. If you were able to do something today that you were not able to do yesterday, write it down. If you were able to express your needs in a situation where previously you would have compliantly gone along with authority, write it down. If you were able to stop your self from criticizing your spouse and were able to take responsibility for your own uncomfortable feelings, write it down. If you were able to express your feelings honestly, in any circumstances, write it down. Write down anything that makes you proud of your own personal development.

PART B

In this part, take your accomplishments inside your self. To do this, use focused breathing and visualization during the time you are reviewing each and every one of your accomplishments.

Start by creating a quiet environment, lying down on your bed or sitting quietly on your couch. Start focusing on your breathing and consciously try to deepen your breathing so that you draw air right into the base on your lower abdomen. After about five minutes of this focused breathing, visualize each of your "wow" experiences. Review exactly what happened, what you did, what the reactions were. Feel the feelings of personal pride, success, achievement, excitement and power. Think about what success in this circumstance can mean for your future prosperity. Visualize the next step up. If you're speaking to a group of ten, imagine speaking to a group of one hundred. If you're speaking to your boss about a new creative idea that will increase the company's bottom line, imagine speaking to the president, or speaking at a board meeting. Let your imagination wander. Think big, bigger, biggest.

All the time you are doing this, keep breathing slowly and deliberately. In this way you will be registering into your conscious mind the wonderful person you are.

If this exercise seems artificial and unnatural, it's probably because you've never done it before. In contrast, people who love themselves follow this format regularly, albeit not in a structured way. Because they love themselves, they take delight in reviewing just how good they are. Consider this nursery rhyme:

Little Jack Horner,
Sat in the corner,
Eating his Christmas pie;
He put in his thumb,
And pulled out a plum,
And said, "What a good boy am I!"

Little Jack Horner loves himself! Jack doesn't need anyone to tell him how good he is, because he tells himself he's great all the time. If you were lucky enough to have had attentive, loving parents, you would have received the positive attention and interest that would have made appreciating your self a natural thing to do. If you didn't have such parents, you will have to start this process off by making a deliberate effort to appreciate your own worth.

For those of you who use word processing software on a computer, you know that if you don't press the "save" key, the information you are working with will be lost. In the same way, if you don't consciously register into your inner self how wonderful you are, you will continue to take your self for granted, and not see your self as truly special. So take the time to start being "wowed" by little old you. You are doing remarkable things in your life. Start noticing them.

TAKING RESPONSIBILITY FOR LOVING YOUR SELF

Learning to love our selves is truly hard work. That's why we, as human beings, want to pass off the responsibility for loving our selves onto our spouse, our lovers, our parents, our children, and our friends. How do we pass off our responsibility? We ask these people to demonstrate their love by fulfilling our requests.

Playing this scenario out in an intimate relationship, a woman might tell her partner, "I need you to tell me you love me in order for me to feel loved by you." A man might tell his partner, "If you loved me, you wouldn't expect me to give up my freedom in order to make this relationship work."

In both these scenarios, the woman and the man are placing the responsibility for feeling loved onto their partner. If the woman in this scenario loved herself, she wouldn't need her partner to do anything to "make" her feel loved. She would know that she was loveable, and she would feel loved, appreciated, valued, and wanted because she would hold these feelings within herself. She would not need any external proof to confirm this reality. If the man in this scenario loved himself, he wouldn't need so much space. The reason he's afraid to "give up his freedom" is because he needs his time to try to make himself feel loved and worthwhile through such things as work, male friends and sports activities.

When you give another person a job to do in order to complete your self, there is bound to be resentment and distancing. The fastest way to reduce conflict within an intimate relationship is to work on changing your self, rather than on changing your partner. The work that needs to be done is on creating your own base of self-love.

FILLING THE WELL

Everyone wants love and needs love. Feeling loved is an essential ingredient to feeling secure, happy, content, at peace, in control and that all is right with the world. Since most of us have received less love from our parents than we desired, as adults, we are trying desperately to fill our selves up.

The problem that most of us have is that we want to receive love before we give our love out. Because we are operating from a love deficit, the little love we have within our selves must be conserved. What if we give our love away and it's not returned? Then we will have less love to rely on.

If all you had for a lifetime was $100 worth of love, and you are now down to $16, you aren't going to take many chances about squandering it foolishly. You will want some guarantees in advance that you will be getting it back.

But what if you could manufacture $100 worth of love every day? You could then fill your self up, and still have a lot of love to give out. You wouldn't have to worry about getting it back, because you would know that there's a lot more love where that came from.

The point is, someone has to start the process of giving love. In the same way that money goes to money, so too love goes to love. If you give it out, you'll get it back. On the other hand, if you conserve your own, and approach people and romantic partners begging for a handout, you will likely not get any more than a few cents worth coming your way.

Love can be created from within. Love can be manufactured within your self. What filling the well is all about is being kind to your self; being respectful of your self; admiring your self; taking your own side; caring about your feelings; making sure that you are happy; making sure that your needs are being met; treating your self like a precious jewel.

Filling the well also means saying no to any person who does not value you, and who does not respect your worth. If you are not fully appreciated for the wonderful person you are, you must leave that person behind. Allowing people to remain in your life when they do not value you means that you are still stuck in the past whereby getting some attention was better than getting none. The only way that you can feel great about your self is when you surround your self with people who respect you completely. Being loving to your self means saying "no" to people who are not capable of truly valuing the person you are.

GIVING LOVE

Once you have filled your own self up, you can then give some of your love to the important people in your life. What does giving love mean? It means allowing the special people in your life to live independent lives from you, to get pleasure from aspects of their lives that have nothing to do with you. It means viewing love as sharing what is given freely, not as ownership. It means allowing people to be themselves, without interference from you. It means accepting people as they are, limitations and all. It means giving people the space to be themselves. It means forgiving people their inadequacies, just as you forgive your self for yours.

Giving love means realizing that your family members, your work associates, your friends, your lovers, your spouse are in all likelihood operating from a love-deficit position; chances are, they are truly empty inside. If you are expecting the important people in your life to give you something that is not forthcoming, realize that this is probably happening because they have little to give—either to themselves or to you. Remember, you can't give what you didn't get.

Giving love means not feeling hurt or angry when the people in your life are not as considerate as you would like them to be. When you are able to give love, you will come to realize that most people operate in a survival mode, trying desperately to fill the emptiness they feel inside, trying desperately to feel whole, secure, and happy. Because they are preoccupied (consciously or unconsciously) with their own rage, sadness, fear and shame, they may truly be incapable of considering anyone but themselves.

This does not mean that you should surround your self with people who are consumed with meeting their own needs, or incapable of considering your wellbeing. It simply means that there's no need to get hooked into another person's less than perfect behaviour, when in reality, it has nothing to do with you. Giving love means being compassionate about another person's struggles. Giving love means forgiving others for being human.

The key to giving love is to realize that you must love your self before you can love anyone else. If you love your self first, if you fill your own self up, what you give out will be an overflow. It will not be important to you whether you receive love back because it's in the giving of love where the true pleasure lies; giving love feels good.

HONOURING YOUR SELF

The greatest joy in life is in discovering your own worth. You are a beautiful person, a magnificent jewel who mistakenly believed you were a worthless pebble. You must re-evaluate your opinion of your self and open your mind to who you really are. If you were not valued by your parents, you would have concluded that you had little worth. If you were viewed as an inconvenience, you would have ended up feeling grateful for crumbs of attention and affection. You certainly would not have concluded that you <u>deserved</u> to have it all.

It's time to start turning around this thinking. If you were treated with anything less than total respect for your integrity, and admiration for the wonderful little being you were and are, realize this: <u>The way your parents treated you had nothing to do with your true value; it only reflected their own incapacity to give love.</u>

Unfortunately, your parents' inability to provide the love you deserved has likely caused you real damage: you may no longer value who you are; you now take your self for granted; you are hard on your self; you are critical of your self; you become impatient with your ability to change and to grow; you treat your self the way your parents treated you.

But you have free will. And you can <u>choose</u> to treat your self better than the way your parents treated you. You can <u>choose</u> to treat your self as the jewel you are. You can <u>choose</u> to honour your uniqueness, your efforts to improve your life, your goodness, your kindness and all your wonderful qualities. No one is stopping you from making this choice, the choice to both value and love your self.

As an adult, you have free will, and it's your decision how the rest of your life is going to go. The first step is choosing to break out of the box that you are living in and decide that you want your future to be different than your past. It means deciding that because your parents were <u>incapable</u> of loving and valuing you, it doesn't mean that you are <u>incapable</u> of loving and valuing your self, and honouring your unique contribution to the world in which you live. It's time to start looking with open eyes at who you really are, and realize that you can <u>choose</u> to love your self. And when you love your self, you will then be able to bring love and happiness into your life.

13 | DRAWING FROM YOUR OWN ACCOUNT

Creating a love-base means meeting your own needs for love, recognition and validation. If you don't meet these needs your self, but rather, you rely on other people to meet these needs for you, you will become dependent on them. If you are dependent on other people, you will have to do things for them in exchange for what they do for you. This means you will have to start fulfilling their role requirements and expectations, just as you expect them to fulfil yours. If this sounds familiar, it should be. This scenario is a replication of what you experienced as a dependent child growing up with your mom and dad. Because you were dependent on your parents for both your physical and emotional survival, you may have had to compromise your self-respect in order to get your needs met. Dependency creates compromise—always. And the necessity to compromise means losing the freedom to be your self, and the freedom to say "no."

What you need to do then, in order to be strong, happy and free, is to start doing for your self what you want others to do for you. YOU MUST START DRAWING FROM YOUR OWN ACCOUNT. You have the resources within your self to be very happy. In the previous chapter, you learned what you could do to satisfy your own needs for love, recognition and validation. The purpose of this chapter is to make you aware of just how much you have passed off the responsibility for meeting your basic needs onto significant others, and how you can start empowering your self by looking to your own internal resources to meet your own needs.

WHAT DO YOU WANT FROM OTHERS?

PART ONE

Write out a list of all the people in your life who are important to you. Next to each person's name, write out what you would like from each of them, what you would like them to do for you or how you would want them to be with you:

Mother

Father

Sibling

Sibling

Spouse/Lover

Child

Child

Boss

Co-worker

Friend

Friend

Others

Mark's list looked like this:

Mom

I would like her to show an interest in my work. I would like her to ask about how my business is going rather than getting me to talk about superficial things that don't interest me. I would like to hear her say that she loves me.

Dad
I would like him to show an interest in what's happening with me in my life and not simply talk about superficial things like the football game. I would like him to admit that he was mean to me when I was a kid.

Erin (Sister)

I would like her to admit that I'm right once in awhile. I would like her not to begrudge the good things that happen to me.

Susan (Wife)

I want her to be more considerate of my needs. I would like her to take more initiative. She always leaves it to me to sort out the practical details. I would like her to agree with what I want, without having huge arguments. I feel I have to mortgage my soul to get my own way around her.

Sam (Son)

I would like him to do well in school. I would like him to do his homework without arguments.

Boss

I would like him to help me advance in my career, to give me more responsibility and some opportunities to increase my salary.

Tony (Co-worker)

I would like him to be there for me when I need him. He always expects me to be there for him, but he never has the time when I have the need.

Arnold (Friend)

I would like him to think about what's good for me, rather than expecting me to make him happy all the time.

Matthew (Friend)

I would like him to make the effort to get together with me. He's always so busy with his work, and his family. There never seems to be any time.

PART TWO

LEARN FROM YOUR DESIRES AND PERCEPTIONS

LEARNING ABOUT YOUR UNMET NEEDS

Sharing love and enjoying the company of people who are special to you are wonderful experiences, and certainly contribute to the joys of living. However it's important to be aware of why you want to be with the people in your world. Is it to share your love, or is it to be filled up, validated, recognized, acknowledged, and made to feel important? Is it to give your love, or is it to have the opportunity to discharge your tension and to feel powerful by making another person feel small? What you want from other people will give you important clues as to what initiatives you must take to make your self happy.

LEARNING ABOUT YOUR EMOTIONAL TRIGGERS

Being "triggered" by another person means that you are being reminded of buried emotions of which you are not consciously aware. Because your past unresolved emotional experiences are too painful for you to face, you will have both blocked them out and consciously forgotten about them. These experiences however are still with you and are troubling you on an unconscious level. That is why you will be irritated by certain behaviours of another person, not realizing that you have not resolved these very same issues. And the fact is, you will specifically notice in others the very issues that you are struggling with on an unconscious level.

Let's look at some examples. If you don't like the fact that your counterpart is critical, it means that you're self-critical and most likely are critical of others as well. If you find that your counterpart is "cheap," it means that you either can't spend money, or that you have a difficult time when you do spend money. If you find that your counterpart is selfish and cannot see beyond her/his own need satisfaction, it means that you have the same difficulties as well.

In an entirely different scenario, let's say that your brother is wasting his talents. What you would like him to do is to take some initiative in his life. Now, although your feelings about your brother are quite real, and come from a caring place, they may have less to do with your brother, and more to do with you, for the following reasons:

1. You may feel that you are on the same dead-end street as your brother. However, because the prospect of changing your life may seem too overwhelming, you avoid facing your own situation by focusing on his. (Overinvolved parents do this all the time. Instead of focusing on the mess that their own lives are in, they prefer to straighten out their children's lives.)

2. You may not even <u>realize</u> that it is <u>you</u> who is feeling troubled. If you are cut off from your own feelings or have grown
   used to focusing on other people's needs, you may neither
   have taken the time to examine your own feelings about your
   life, nor have you given any serious thought as to how you
   could improve your <u>own</u> situation.

   Whenever you have a strong emotional reaction to another
   person's situation (or strong opinions about the course of
   action another person should take), examine the similarities
   between her/his situation and yours. You will learn a lot
   about your own buried feelings if you do so.

PART THREE

TAKE RESPONSIBILITY

a. Identify the needs you want this person to meet for you.

b. When applicable, identify how this person's struggles and
   issues remind you of those you have not resolved (your emotional triggers).

c. Identify what you can do to meet this need or resolve this
   issue.

Mother

Father

Sibling

Sibling

Spouse/Lover

Child

Child

Boss

Co-worker

Friend

Friend

Others

Mark had these ideas:

Mom

Unmet needs: recognition, validation, love

Solution: I'm going to tell mom about the work I'm doing, whether I'm asked about it or not. I'm not going to wait until she shows an interest in me. I'm going to assert my needs and share how proud I am about my successes. If she cuts me off and says she isn't interested, I will say that it's important to me to share my progress and that I would like her to listen. I'll ask her if she loves me and if she says yes, I will ask her to tell me so.

Dad

Unmet needs: recognition, validation, acknowledgement

Solution: I'm going to volunteer information about my life and what I'm doing. If he changes the subject, I'm going to say that we both have equal rights to be recognized and valued, and that I'm not prepared to be involved in a one-way relationship any more. I'm going to bring up some of my childhood experiences. I'm going to tell him how much he has hurt me, and how cruel I felt he was to me. I'm going to ask him for an apology.

Erin(Sister)

Unmet needs: recognition, validation

Solution: I'm going to show more of an interest in her life and what she's doing. I'm then going to tell her that I'd like to share with her more about what I'm doing. (I don't want to have a superficial relationship with her any more.) If she shows a resentment toward my successes, I'm going to tell her that I would like her to be happy for me, just the way I would be happy for her. I'm going to have to work on believing that I'm right. I'm asking her to do something for me which I have to do for my self—believe that I'm worthwhile.

Susan (Wife)

Unmet needs: love, recognition, validation
Trigger: I was always expected to take care of my siblings when it was really mom's responsibility.

Solution: I'm going to have to work on being nicer to my self, indulging my self, doing more of what I want so that I don't have to depend on Susan to agree to do what I want. I really am expecting her to do for me what I'm not doing for my self.

Susan's lack of initiative is stressful for me because I feel that if she doesn't take charge, it's my obligation to take care of the problem. I'm taking on the same role of being super-responsible that I did when I was a child. I'm going to have to bring this issue out in the open. I don't want to be the caretaker any more.

Sam (Son)

Unmet need: validation
Trigger: I don't feel 100% about my career. Even though I'm doing well, I still feel that it's not good enough.

Solution: I'm going to leave Sam be. He's a responsible kid. I'm sure that if I leave him alone, he would be responsible. Of course I want him to do well in school, but I don't really think that his marks are the issue. It's my marks that are bothering me. I guess I don't feel worthwhile. I guess I still don't love my self, and I'm equating my worth with my career success. I'm going to start working on loving me for who I am.

Boss

Unmet need: recognition, validation

Solution: I can't believe it! I'm sitting back waiting for him to do something for me. If I want to make more money, I'm going to have to show him that I'm worth it. I'm going to have to take the initiative and show him that I'm a leader.

Tony (Co-worker)

Unmet need: recognition
Trigger: being taken advantage of

Solution: I'm going to assert my needs. I'm going to tell him that our relationship has to be a give and take, and that I expect him to be there for me. If he's not prepared to give me what I give him, I'm going to tell him not to come to me for help any more.

Arnold (Friend)

Unmet need: recognition

Solution: I'm going to tell him that I want to have a two-way relationship. I'm not prepared to give without getting anything in return. I'm going to assert my desires and tell him that we both have to be happy in order for our relationship to work out.

Matthew (Friend)

Unmet need: recognition

Solution: I'm going to take the initiative and invite him over for dinner, or make arrangements with him to go to a ball game. Matthew is a busy person. If I want to see him, I'm going to have to do something about it.

DRAWING FROM YOUR OWN ACCOUNT

Drawing From Your Own Account is empowering. The only way you can be truly free to be happy, to be your self, and to create the life you really want is to become self-sufficient and to meet your own needs. Drawing From Your Own Account means acknowledging that you have the resources within your self to realize all of your dreams. Drawing From Your Own Account means doing for your self what you had previously wanted other people to do for you. Drawing From Your Own Account means asserting your own needs and making it clear to others that you expect to get back what you are giving to them, that you now want to have a two-way equal relationship. Drawing From Your Own Account means identifying why another person irritates you so that you can go inside your self and work on your own emotions. Drawing From Your Own Account means emotionally backing all your own endeavors (believing in your self). Drawing From Your Own Account means being absolutely free to be the person you want to be.

V

CREATING HAPPINESS

14 | OPERATING FROM A LOVE-BASE

It's time for you to change the way you interact with all the people in your life. In the previous chapter you learned how to take the initiative in meeting your own needs vis-a-vis the important people in your life. Now you must learn to do this with every person you encounter in your daily life. If you were abused, neglected or overcontrolled, you will have ended up repressing your true feelings in order to survive. Whether out of fear, or out of feelings of shame, inadequacy or helplessness, you will have thought it wise not to express your self, spontaneously and honestly.

Once you rid your self of your anger, sadness, fear and shame and direct it at the source, your parents, you will start feeling proud of who you are. You will start loving your self. You will delight in your own existence. You will start feeling like the valuable, wonderful person you really are (and always were). You will create a love-base.

Operating from a love-base, you will be ready to present your self to the world in a different way—with pride. No more accepting second best. No more being grateful for crumbs. No more adapting. No more pleasing. No more swallowing your feelings as you pretend to be happy. No more being understanding of your counterpart's feelings and needs while your needs go unattended.

You deserve to be treated with respect and appreciation. You deserve to have it all. In learning to love your self, in creating a love-base, you will be moving away from those Operating Styles, anger-based, sadness-based needy, sadness-based strong distant, which prevented you from being able to express your <u>true</u> emotions, spontaneously, honestly and openly. When you have done the emotional release work that will allow you to love your self, and thus to operate from a love-base, you will want to conduct your self differently with the people in your world. The information you will learn in "Operating From A Love-Base" will help you make this transition.

BE FOREWARNED

There's no question about it—people don't like change! People will not want you to change. In the short term, your friends, your spouse/lover, your co-workers, and your family members will find your changing to be most inconvenient. They will want you to stay just the way you are. Many of you will have compromised your own best interests in order to be accepted by others or to preserve your own self-esteem. In putting your own needs second, you may have "appeared" as the perfect spouse, lover, friend, employee, parent, son/daughter. When you start letting your counterparts know that you have needs too, that you won't be pushed around, that you won't accept not being respected, recognized, appreciated, acknowledged, considered, valued and that you expect your counterparts to be accountable for their actions in relation to you, you may run into some major discontent.

The truth of the matter is this: When you operate from a love-base, many of your current relationships will no longer be satisfying to you and you will no longer be satisfying to your counterparts. In that you can only attract and be attracted to people who are just like you on an emotional level, the bonding between you as a love-based person and your counterparts as anger-based sadness-based needy and sadness-based strong/distant people may very well diminish over time.[4]

Do not despair at these changes! Remember the Law of Attraction. If you operate from a love-base, so will the people you attract. If your internal magnet is one of self-love, you will attract people who love themselves. People who love them-

---

[4]This is not the case when you are a parent. As a parent, when you are able to operate from a love-base, you will dramatically improve the quality of your relationships with your children. Giving love to your children will help open them up emotionally. When you give love to your children, you will be helping them to become love-based as well. When you become love-based, your relationships with your children are guaranteed to improve.

selves rely on themselves; they respect other people; they are considerate; they are kind; they are able to give to others; they find giving a pleasure because they are full of love. And so by loving your self, by operating from a love-base, you will start attracting a whole new range of people, business opportunities and good fortune into your life.

In that developing a love-base is a process, and does take time (the amount of time it takes is equal to the amount of time required to free your self from your past unreleased emotions), you will need some guidelines which will enable you to learn to live as a love-based person. In this regard, the following parameters will prove useful.

OPERATING FROM A LOVE-BASE

1. EXPRESS YOUR FEELINGS

WHAT DOES THIS MEAN?

This means that if you don't like the way you are being treated, say so at the time—not three weeks later. Right then and there. Positive feelings also work best when you share them at the time.

WHY YOU DIDN'T?

There are a number of reasons why you would have chosen not to express your true feelings. These relate to your very legitimate desire to avoid being abandoned. You needed your parents for your physical and emotional survival. If your parents were neglecting you (ignoring your need for love, attention and kindness), treating you in a cruel manner (tearing down your self-esteem, physically assaulting you, sexually abusing you, retaliating by withdrawing their love), if they were consumed with their own sadness, if they made you feel ashamed for wanting love or wanting your needs met, you would have learned not to ask for what you wanted. Asking for what you wanted would have caused you to get less than what you were getting before you had asked. In looking after your own best interests, expressing your feelings would not have appeared as a realistic option.

Rather, keeping silent would have appeared to be your best course of action.

WHY IT'S IMPORTANT?

Although this may be a foreign concept to you right at this moment, realize this: <u>You can choose to expect the people in your life to be accountable to you for their actions in relation to you.</u>

You don't have to accept abuse. You don't have to accept being frightened into compliance. You don't have to accept disrespect. You don't have to accept criticism and judgement on your worth. You don't have to accept being ignored. You don't have to accept not being considered. You don't have to accept "fitting into someone else's life." You don't have to accept that "your happiness isn't as important as your counterpart's happiness."

You can choose to be totally and completely respected, considered, and valued. You deserve to be treated with consideration. Because you may never have been respected, considered and valued, you may not even know what it feels like to be well-treated. Thus you may not expect the important people in your life to treat you well because you don't have a point of positive comparison. (The only comparison you may have is on the negative scale. In this way, you won't allow anyone to treat you any worse than you are treating your self, or any worse than your parents treated you.)

In choosing to expect the people in your life to be accountable to you for their actions in relation to you, realize that you will risk rejection; you will risk "abandonment." Many people in your life may have enjoyed the one-way taking relationship that you have provided for them because of your desire to avoid "abandonment." They may not want to change their ways simply because you are asking them to account for their actions in relation to you.

Standing up for your self and choosing to ask people to be accountable to you for their actions in relation to you is a process, in the same way that becoming love-based is a process. Until you release your feelings of shame, anger, sadness and fear, you will not be able to develop the inner self-worth required to express your true feelings as you feel them. Rather, you will probably feel more comfortable playing it safe and appeasing your counterpart. Don't be too hard on your self if you aren't able to express your feelings freely. In time you will.[5]

HOW TO DO IT?

Whenever possible, start where your counterpart is at: "You don't seem very happy right now," or, "You seem distant." "What's on your mind?" "What's bothering you?" "Why are you not wanting to talk about this?" Follow up whatever response you receive with: "What's really bothering you?" Although you will not want to turn every conversation into a therapy session, reaching for the truth, as opposed to a socially acceptable response, will enable you to create much more honest relationships.

Once you have established what is important to your counterpart, it's now time to express your feelings. Remember, being understanding is not the same as expressing your own feelings. Being understanding (sadness-based strong/distants are too understanding) simply will enable you to open up a discussion as opposed to venting your anger, as anger-based people will do quite naturally. You must express your feelings. You have an equal right to be happy. Even if you understand completely why your counterpart is behaving as s/he is, this doesn't mean that you should push down your own unhappiness as you "try to be understanding and accomodating." You have feelings too, you have needs too. You are an equal player in your relationship; your counterpart must be made aware of your perspective.

To facilitate a discussion rather than elicit a defensive response, make "I" statements:

---

[5]Please note that if you are anger-based, you will not have a difficult time expressing your anger. The problem you will be facing is the reverse: You will too readily express your anger in situations where it is not appropriate. Because of your overload of unreleased rage, you will not be able to distinguish between situations where a person is legitimately not treating you respectfully, and situations where an incident truly has nothing to do with you. By releasing your backlog of rage, you will be able to reduce your need to fight old battles (the battle for your self-esteem that you were fighting with your mom/dad). Keep in mind that as an anger-based person, the feelings you will have most difficulty in expressing will relate to your shame, fear and sadness.

Limiting: "You are a #o/#x> for ignoring my needs."
Opening: "I'm feeling really lonely right now. I don't feel that
         you are concerned about my needs. I don't feel that
         you're respecting me. I don't feel that you are
         acknowledging my perspective."

To facilitate a happy solution rather than getting caught up in
the labelling of blame, talk about a win/win resolution.

Limiting: "I didn't like what you did."
Opening: "It's important for me that communication is clear.
         Can we make it a policy to ...."
Opening: "It's important for me to feel respected / recognized /
         acknowledged. What can we do so that both of our
         needs are met here?"

2. ASSERT YOUR NEEDS

WHAT DOES THIS MEAN?

This means you ask for what you want. You don't cower. You
don't beg. You ask with the full conviction that you expect your
relationship to be win/win and that your happiness is of equal
importance to your counterpart's happiness.

WHY YOU DIDN'T?

In a word—survival. You weren't unaware of what was going on
around you. If you were living with parents who were abusive,
neglectful or overinvolved, asking for what you had wanted
would have certainly been the wrong thing to do: asking would
have made you seem ungrateful; asking would have made you
feel ashamed, for likely your parents would have looked back at
you with blank stares; asking would have caused you to get
fewer emotional goodies than you had before you had asked.

WHY IT'S IMPORTANT?

For the same reason that expressing your feelings is important.
You have the same right to be happy as every other human
being. If you don't assert your needs, then you are choosing to
live as an emotional slave, choosing to service others. ("Slave" is

defined in Webster's New World Dictionary as a human being who is owned as property by, and is absolutely subject to the will of another—a person who is divested of all freedom and personal rights.) If you don't assert your needs, you are voluntarily turning your self into a slave.

Realize this: <u>Our country gives us civil liberties, but only you can give your self emotional liberties. Only you can choose whether you live as a free man or woman, or whether you choose to live as an emotional slave, serving the needs of others.</u> If you are treating other people better than you are treating your self, it's time to make some changes.

HOW TO DO IT?

- "I would like you to ...."
- "I would appreciate it if you would ...."
- "Would you mind doing .... for me."

3. TRADE EQUAL VALUE

WHAT DOES THIS MEAN?

This means that every one of your relationships should be based on equality, mutual respect, free will, and the understanding that your happiness and your counterpart's happiness are of equal importance. This means that whatever you give your counterpart (kindness, consideration, respect, recognition, emotional support), you should expect the equivalent in return and vice versa.

Trading Equal Value means that you don't have to provide counselling, emotional support and understanding, while your counterpart ignores your needs; you don't have to "do favours" for your counterpart, while s/he never has the time or the inclination to oblige your requests; you don't have to make your counterpart's needs a priority while you are Number 10 on her/his list; you don't have to "fit into" your counterpart's life because s/he is busier, has a more demanding work schedule, is more powerful, is more recognized by people in the outside world, or is earning more money than you.

Trading Equal Value means living this truth: <u>Your worth and your counterpart's worth are identical.</u> If you don't believe this is so, you haven't yet come to appreciate just how good you really are.

WHY YOU DIDN'T?

You didn't have a choice in this matter. If your parents ignored your worth, if they were not concerned about your happiness, if they made it appear that you should have been grateful for crumbs of affection and attention, if you were not free to say "no," you would have concluded that you were not very important; you would have concluded that you didn't have much value. In feeling that you had little worth, you would have believed that you were required to do more for significant others, in order for them to accept you, than they were required to do for you.

WHY IT'S IMPORTANT?

In a word: self-respect. Ralph Waldo Emerson, the great American philosopher (1803-1882), said it most eloquently in his essay entitled *Self-Reliance*. "I cannot consent to pay for a privilege where I have intrinsic right. Few and mean as my gifts may be, I actually am, and do not need for my own assurance or the assurance of my fellows any secondary testimony."

In other words, you do have intrinsic worth. You are valuable. You will not realize this, however, if your parents treated you without respect, concern for your happiness, and recognition of your worth. Rather, you will have concluded that you aren't worth as much as significant others, and that you do have to discount your value in order to get your needs met.

HOW TO DO IT?

Always think about the real value that you are offering another person, or the real value s/he is offering you, before you put a price (figurative or literal) on what you are prepared to do for your counterpart.

WHEN YOU ARE ASKED A FAVOUR

"I can do that for you, no problem, on condition that you do .... for me."

The idea here is that you give with an expectation that you will get something in return. In a mutually respectful relationship where there is a give and take, this nail-down technique will not be necessary. But if you are dealing with a taker, you are going to have to start setting the terms.

WHEN YOU ASK A FAVOUR

"I would like to ask you to do .... for me. I would certainly appreciate it and I will owe you one for that. / In return I can do .... for you. Do we have a deal?"

WHEN YOU ARE NEGOTIATING A BUSINESS TRANSACTION

When it comes to talking price, you may believe that you are talking about dollars, but in reality, you are talking about worth or value. In the end, most people will agree to pay for the value that they perceive they are receiving. (This reflects their own self-interests.) If you are the vendor, and you find that you are scrambling to preserve your profit margin, go back to first establishing the value of what you are selling. Once the value is established, you will be much better able to justify your asking price.

In a note of warning, be aware that there are abusive, disrespectful people in the world who do want to get something for nothing, who would like you to sacrifice your self-respect and who would like you to compromise your integrity in order to get their business. These type of people will try to intimidate or bully you into agreeing with their terms. If this is the case, realize: If there's no respect, there's no deal. You are selling value, you're not selling your soul. If you are dealing with a person who refuses to acknowledge your worth, your best bet is to move on.

4. SAY "NO"

WHAT DOES THIS MEAN?

When you are asked to do something that is inconvenient, say "no." Especially say "NO" to takers. Takers are people who never give back. They just ask, and they usually receive. Because these type of people will usually appear very self-confident in their requests, be aware that you might feel obligated to fulfil their requests. You might feel that they are more important than you, and that their happiness is more important than your happiness. In this way, you may not feel that you have the option of saying "no," even though as a free person, you do have this very option.

In an entirely different scenario, realize that you can choose to say "no" in any situation where you are feeling pressured to comply. For example, you don't have to accept implied emotional threats: "This relationship is over if you don't do what I ask you to do," or, "I'm going to cut you off emotionally/financially if you don't please me."

WHY YOU DIDN'T?

As a dependent, helpless child, saying "no" was in all likelihood not an option. It may have been dangerous emotionally. (You would have risked abandonment and the loss of love.) It may have been dangerous physically. If you were being sexually or physically abused, you may have believed that if you didn't comply, you would have been killed. Thus compliance would have appeared to be your only option.

WHY IT'S IMPORTANT?

Your actions define who you are. You're a free person; you're not a slave. A slave is not able to say "no." You can say "no." Saying "no" tells others that you are a free human being who has choices. If you choose to fulfil the request, then you should do so by trading equal value.

If you oblige a request by not asking for anything in return, you are saying through your actions, "Your satisfaction is more important than mine. If you are happy, then hopefully you will remember that I have been considerate of your needs, and hopefully you will be considerate of mine." A familiar cartoon in the comic strips states, "Are you a man, or are you a mouse?" Your actions will answer this question. (If you are sadness-based needy, this scenario should sound familiar.)

HOW TO DO IT?

SCENARIO 1

When a person has an urgent need, and says, "I have a problem that's urgent, do you have a minute?" you know it won't take a minute. It will take more like half an hour. You also know that this person's problems never end. You fix one problem today, and tomorrow another one pops up to take its place; there's a bottomless pit of need. You also know that you'll never get equal time. If you're lucky, you may get 5% of the total amount of time you spend together, talking about your self and your needs.

YOUR RESPONSE

"I'm so sorry that you're feeling troubled right now. It sounds like you're really suffering. But there's something I need to discuss with you, in terms of our relationship, before I can talk with you about your concern.

SCENARIO 2

You're at a party, engaged in an important conversation with a business associate or friend. An acquaintance approaches you, and attempts to interrupt your conversation.

YOUR RESPONSE

"Hi, <u>name</u>, it's good to see you. You've really caught me at a bad time though. I'm right in the middle of a conversation here. We'll be a while finishing this up, so what I'll do is come and look for you when I'm free."

SCENARIO 3

You are in a business relationship. Your counterpart tells you that s/he is not conceding on a certain point and that the deal is off if you don't comply with her/his request (demand). Alternatively, s/he may give you an ultimatum—agree with the terms as stated, right now, or the deal is off.

YOUR RESPONSE

"May I clarify something here. Are you saying that our relationship is over if I don't agree with your request? Are you saying that the only option you are granting me is immediate agreement with your terms?"

If s/he tells you that you do have the option of saying "no" and ending the relationship, discuss the implications of this course of action. "Is that really want you want? Is it really in your best interests to do that? Is that really how you believe you can best achieve your goals?"

If your questions are successful in encouraging your counterpart to rethink her/his position, continue with, "I have to feel satisfied with this agreement too. I have to be happy with this agreement in the same way that you have to be happy with this agreement. What can we do so that both of our needs will be met here?"

If your questions irritate and/or enrage your counterpart, realize that you are being bullied, that your counterpart is totally disinterested in your happiness, that your counterpart's interests are only in being served, and that if you want the relationship to continue, you will have to assume the role of a slave. The choice is yours.

5. CONFRONT DENIAL

WHAT DOES THIS MEAN?

This means, "You calls them as you sees them," an old baseball expression for speaking the truth. People try to suck us into their emotional systems. In your family, your parents may have denied your needs; they may have denied the pained look on your face; they may have ignored you; they may have pretended you weren't there. Even though you may have been silently screaming in pain, they may have acted like nothing was wrong.

As a result of this type of treatment, you will have learned to pretend you weren't seeing what you were seeing; it was probably safer for you that way. This is the reason why you will often doubt your self: You were taught to negate your own perceptions. You may have lived with the equivalent of standing in the pouring rain, and being told that it was actually a nice sunny day. This would have caused you to become confused. So get this straight: Your perceptions were correct; your parents just couldn't tolerate hearing them.

You may also have grown hypersensitive to interpreting what someone else would have wanted you to express, and what they would have preferred you to ignore. But remember this: You have the right to make people accountable for their actions in relation to you. You don't have to accept disrespectful treatment.

You don'thave to accept being ignored. You don't have to "fit into someone else's reality." You don't have to be subservient in order to be both recognized and considered. You have the right to make people accountable for their actions in relation to you.

HOW TO DO IT?

- "I want to discuss what just happened here."
- "I'm feeling really uncomfortable about what just happened here."
- "From your comments/actions, I'm assuming that you are wanting to .... This is different from my understanding of our agreement. I'd like to talk about this."

Be prepared for denial. Many people will find it too threatening to be honest, and/or accountable for their actions in relation to you. These people will deny your perceptions and lie to cover their tracks; they will postpone discussing the issue indefinitely; they will state that they don't want to talk about it and will suggest that the problem will go away on its own.

Don't back down in the face of denial. If your counterpart doesn't want to discuss this matter, keep in mind that you do, so ask, "How can we resolve this situation to our mutual satisfaction?" If your counterpart is not interested in your feelings, perceptions, satisfaction or happiness, realize that you're dealing with a person who neither values nor respects you. Whether you are involved in a business transaction or in an intimate relationship, disinterest in your wellbeing should be a red flag that there's no future. Move on.

6. SURFACE HOSTILITY

WHAT DOES THIS MEAN?

This means that if you sense that your counterpart is unhappy or angry about what is happening between you, talk about it— bring the conflict into the open.

WHY YOU DIDN'T?

As a child, you would have avoided surfacing tension or conflict because you would have believed that it wasn't in your best interests to do so. If you believed that you were responsible for your parents' happiness, surfacing an area of their discontent would have meant that you would have been obligated to do even more to try to make them happy—a win/lose proposition. Thus it would have been in your best interests to pretend not to notice that anything was wrong.

If you were sexually, physically or severely verbally abused, you would have begun to equate conflict with probable death (your own destruction). Because you would have perceived that you had no option but to passively accept the abuse (you had no rights), conflict will continue to terrify you; conflict will trigger your unresolved feelings of powerlessness, helplessness, fear, and vulnerability. Thus you will avoid surfacing conflict.

WHY IT'S IMPORTANT?

If you don't bring the tension or hostility to the surface, you will unconsciously start feeling that you are to blame, and that it's your fault that your counterpart is unhappy. In believing this, you will then feel obligated to appease your counterpart, feeling that it is your responsibility to make her/him happy. In getting emotionally sucked in, you will forget that you have your own perspective on the matter, your feelings count too, you have rights, and your happiness is as important as your counterpart's happiness.

If on the other hand, you address your counterpart's hostility or tension, and table it for discussion, you will enable your self to be an equal player in a win/win relationship. The truth is this: <u>You are not responsible for your counterpart's unhappiness—s/he is. Let your counterpart express her/his concern openly. As a free party, you can then listen, assert your position, and work out a win/win resolution.</u>

HOW TO DO IT?

"You seem bothered about something. What's on your mind?" or, "You obviously don't feel that your needs are being met right now. Would you mind if I ask why that is? Why do you feel angry? What would you like me to do for you?" After you receive an answer, respond with, "Okay, as I understand it .... is important to you. Now .... is important to me. We both want to end up happy, so how can we resolve this?"

7. HANDLING "NO"

When someone says "no" to you, don't back down and walk away. Find out the reason for "no," and seek to resolve the situation in a win/win fashion: "This issue is important to me. How can we find a way to resolve this so that we can both be happy?"

SAYING "YES" TO YOUR SELF

The scenario: A friend asks you to do something for him. The pressure is on. Should you do what he wants and please him, or should you say "no," and please your self? Many of you will have become so conditioned to taking care of someone else's needs that saying "no" will feel risky to you. Your fear: "If I say 'no,' will he still want to be my friend? Will he still like me? Will I still be able to count on him?"

You may get so caught up in the "yes/no" dilemma that you may forget one key component: your self. What about you? What about your satisfaction? What about your happiness? Do you want the job of keeping other people happy until the day you die? Is being an emotional slave part of your job description? Is servicing others what you were born to do? Making other people happy will be your permanent assignment, if you aren't planning to make any changes in the way you operate; it won't be, if you start operating from a love-base, and start saying "yes" to your self. You are a player in this relationship—you have equal rights.

You may have learned in your childhood that it was in your best interests to meet your parents' needs, in order to ensure that they would meet yours. But as an adult, it doesn't work that way. The only way you can ensure that your needs will be met is to take charge of them your self. And that means saying "yes" to your self. When you're in a dilemma about which way you should go with a request, think: "What do I want to do? What's good for me? What would make me happy?" You had better believe that your counterpart is thinking about what's good for her/him.

It's time to start loving your self and taking care of your own interests. It's time to start operating from a love-base and making your own self happy. It's time to start saying "yes" to your self.

15 | HOW AM I DOING SO FAR?

Changing the way you operate is a process, and as a process, it takes time and patience. I can assure you that as soon as you start releasing your pent-up emotions from the past, your life will start improving. You'll start seeing signs that you're being respected more by other people; you'll start seeing signs that you are respecting your self a whole lot more. But realistically, changing your magnets, changing the people you attract into your life will take time, and the amount of time will range anywhere between six months and six years.

Why does real change take so long? In a word, conditioning. You remember Ivan Pavlov, the Russian scientist who is the father of behavioural conditioning? In his famous experiments, he was able to condition dogs to salivate at the sound of a bell. What he did was take the dogs' reflexive response of salivation at the sight of meat, and link that response (salivation) up to a bell by ringing the bell at the same time that the meat was being presented. And so after a series of trials, all Dr. Pavlov had to do was ring the bell, and the dogs would salivate in anticipation of the meat which was to come.

What do these experiments have to do with humans? Human beings are conditioned in the same way that these dogs were conditioned. The abusive, neglectful, or overinvolved parenting that you experienced would have made deep tracks in your brain and your behavioural patterns. For example, if your dad had asked you to do something for him, and you had said "no," and then you were hit or screamed at, and this happened a number of times, you would have then been conditioned to equate saying "no" with being hit or screamed at. You would have been conditioned to believe that you were in danger emotionally (you would have been risking abandonment and the loss of love) and/or physically (if you would have chosen not to comply, you would have been harmed). So you would have learned (become conditioned) to stop saying "no." Even though you will not be hit when you say "no" today (unless you are living with an abusive partner), you may still believe it's a dangerous thing to do.

Another example of conditioning would have been when, as a child, you had gone to you mom, saying that you were feeling lonely. Rather than comforting you, your mom would then have become angry, telling you to stop bothering her with your little problems and to solve them on your own. After this scenario was repeated a few times, you would have learned (become conditioned) that expressing your feelings produces anger in another person and humiliation in your self, and that it wasn't in your best interests to do so.

In short, who you are, and the way you respond to situations has been conditioned or programmed into you. In the same way that a computer operates in certain ways based on the information that has been programmed into it, you will operate in certain ways based on the information that has been programmed into your brain. In emotionally-charged situations, you will continue to operate (respond) as you did when you were a child.

Now let's just review the statistics again. On average, 18 years is spent with your parents—that is 6,570 days and 105,120 waking hours. From birth to age five, when your parents were the main contact in your life, you were exposed to 1,825 days and 21,900 waking hours. That's a lot of hours of conditioning/ programming. When you think how quickly a dog would be conditioned to salivate at the sound of a bell, and a rat conditioned to jump on a treadmill to get rewarded with some cheese, you can imagine how deeply entrenched is your human conditioning/programming. When you wonder why it takes so long, and why it's so difficult to change your behavioural patterns, just think that you're fighting against 105,120 hours of conditioning.

SPEEDING UP THE PROCESS

The length of time it will take for you to create happiness will depend on the degree of damage you have experienced in living with your parents. The rule of thumb is this: The more that you had to emotionally shut down, in order to survive, the longer it will take to reunite with your inner self.

A helpful analogy would be that of being buried under a huge mound of garbage. It's not your garbage. It's your parents' garbage. They were the ones who dumped it on you. Unfortunately, their garbage is now your problem. You are lying there, pinned under it, and you cannot move because of the heavy load. The length of time it will take you for you to stand up and walk around <u>freely</u> is dependent upon the amount of garbage that is piled on top of you. The more garbage there is, the longer it will take to clear it away.

What can you do to speed up the process? You can learn to evaluate what's happening to you in your life, and start working on the issues as they show themselves. Your key indicators will be:

1. Your Emotional Operating System
2. Your Emotional Triggers
3. Who And What You Attract Into Your life
4. How People Are Treating You
5. What You Want From Other People
6. Why You Are Attracted To Your Romantic Partner
7. What Your Body Is Telling You
8. What Your Dreams Are Telling You
9. Do You Operate From A Love-Base?

1. YOUR EMOTIONAL OPERATING SYSTEM

In Chapter Three, your Emotional Operating System was explained in depth. To review, you have in operation an Emotional Operating System to push down the emotions that you find too difficult to face: anger, sadness, fear and shame. In addition, your Operating System will be designed to provide you with pleasure, make you feel secure, worthwhile and powerful.

Your Emotional Operating System is totally revealing because it will explain the nature of your needs. Unless you are already connected with your inner self, in which case you would be whole and complete within your self, you will tend to rely on certain crutches or dependencies to make your life meaningful. These include substance dependencies (alcohol, drugs, food, caffeine, nicotine); activity dependencies (gambling, sex, religion, causes, interests, sports, work, money, power, success, children, shopping, travelling); people dependencies; victim dependencies; self-dependency.

The fastest way to free your self from your past is to cut out your reliance on your dependency item. Remember, you reach for your cigarettes, that piece of chocolate cake, or a beer in order to feel secure. You lose your self in work, in shopping, or in gambling in order not to have to face your inner sadness, anger, shame and fear. You scream at your lover, spouse, child or employees in order to release the rage that is boiling up in you. Cutting off your escape route to feel complete and secure will leave you face to face with those painful feelings.

In order to release your painful feelings—your anger, sadness, fear, shame—you will first have to feel them. Because these unpleasant feelings are often buried deep within your unconscious mind, you may have lost your ability to access them. You may truly not be <u>consciously aware</u> of the extent that your father's criticism enraged you. You may truly not be aware of your deep hurt resulting from the indifference shown to you by your mother. You may truly not be aware that you cannot trust anyone because your mother/father violated your trust. You may truly not be aware that you are so ashamed of who you are, because your parents didn't value you, that you have to bolster your self up with alcohol just to feel like you are a person. You may truly not be aware that you are still so terrified of being harmed by your parent that you will accept abusive treatment rather than risk a confrontation.

TO WORK WITH: YOUR EMOTIONAL OPERATING SYSTEM

To take the lid off your emotions, cut out your dependency item. Stop reaching for a cigarette or a coffee when you start to feel anxious or tense. Cut out your trip to the bar after work. Cut down the time you spend at work. Take a vacation. Don't go to the race track on Sunday. Stop your self when you want to scream at your child or spouse. Don't appease your partner. Don't call that romantic partner who is always on your mind. Say, "no."

I'm not suggesting here that you go cold turkey on ending a dependency. But I am suggesting that you stop long enough to start looking at the feelings you have been trying so desperately to avoid. Use Chapter Eleven, Releasing Your Emotions, as a guide to help you connect up with and release your painful feelings from your past.

2. YOUR EMOTIONAL TRIGGERS

Your past is with you in your present life on a minute-to-minute basis. This is because your past unreleased feelings are lurking there within you, very close to the surface, despite the fact that they are beyond your conscious awareness. Because they are so close to the surface, circumstances in your present life will "trigger" or remind you of your past unreleased feelings.

Thus, if you become enraged at your romantic partner for not loving you, giving to you, caring for you in the way that you desire, your present rage will be "triggered" by your past rage— the rage you felt (consciously or unconsciously) toward your mother/father for not having given you the love you needed. If you become enraged at an employer for having betrayed you by promising you a promotion and then backing down on his word, your present rage will be "triggered" by your past rage—the rage you felt (consciously or unconsciously) toward your mother/ father for having betrayed your love and your trust, and for having forced you into a position of powerlessness. What is actually happening within you, on an unconscious level, is that you are being reminded of the way you used to feel as a dependent child: powerless, helpless, vulnerable, hurt, sad, empty, lonely, enraged, betrayed, terrified, ashamed.

And so, despite the fact that you may have good reason, in your present life, to be angry, sad, afraid or ashamed, realize that it's your past unreleased emotions that are both setting off your current emotional reaction and fuelling the intensity of your response. Realize as well that the intensity of your past unreleased emotions will usually distort your present reality.

The fact is, your past unreleased emotions can be so powerful that they will prevent you from perceiving reality as it is. Rather, they will cause you to interpret the events in your life in the same rigid, limiting manner as you interpreted them as a child. A practical analogy is this: If your past unreleased emotions are the equivalent of your being obligated to wear glasses that have a red lens, then every significant person with whom you interact, and every significant situation you are in will appear to have a red hue.

For example, if you are anger-based, you will be storing a great deal of unreleased rage resulting from the way you were treated by your mom/dad: you will have been humiliated, ridiculed, put down, criticized, ignored, overcontrolled, physically assaulted, or sexually assaulted. <u>In carrying this unreleased rage within you, you will tend to distort the meaning of people's behaviour towards you, often perceiving meaningless actions as deliberate "slights" against you.</u> In perceiving these "slights" as hostile actions, you will feel compelled to do battle with every person who inadvertently "slights" you. Even though your counterpart's behaviour may in all likelihood be harmless, you will interpret her/his actions as an attack on your worth. The "slight" will then "trigger" the deeper rage that lies within you (your Iceberg of Denied Anger). Even if, objectively speaking, you do have good reason to become angry, your anger will become all-consuming and bottomless in nature.

In an entirely different scenario, if you are sadness-based needy, you will be storing deep-seated feelings of powerlessness, sadness, and worthlessness within you, resulting from the way you were treated by your mom/dad: your needs as a child were never recognized, your parents were disinterested in your happiness, your happiness was irrelevant to your parents, you were expected to pretend that the treatment you were receiving was acceptable to you. <u>In carrying deep-seated feelings of powerlessness within you, you will tend to distort both the meaning of people's behaviour toward you and the events in your life, perceiving any significant rejection and any significant circumstance where you were unable to accomplish your goals as being proof that you are both inadequate and powerless to improve your life.</u> Your lack of present success will "trigger" your past unreleased feelings of powerlessness.

The result? Rather than confronting your counterpart who has either rejected you or treated you disrespectfully, or objectively assessing what you can learn from your lack of success, you will feel like giving up (and you may even go into a depression); you will believe that there's no point either asserting your needs or expressing your anger because "no one cares about your happiness anyway"—asserting your needs neither changed your parents' ability to meet your needs, nor their desire to put your need satisfaction before their own, and expressing your anger would have caused you to lose the little love you had.

What you must consider, as an adult, is that your present

does not need to be a repeat of your past if you don't want it to be. For there is a <u>real difference</u> between the present and the past. In the past you had few options to improve your situation, in the present you do. In the past you had limited choices— dying emotionally or physically (due to your dependency on your parents for survival), or accepting the terms your parents dished out.

In the present, as an adult, you are free to both express your feelings and assert your needs in each and every interaction you have with another person. You no longer have to accept abuse. You no longer have to accept disrespectful treatment: being humiliated, ridiculed, criticized, judged. You no longer have to accept having your feelings and needs ignored. You no longer have to accept being used. You no longer have to do what you don't want to do. You no longer have to meet your counterpart's needs while your needs go unattended. You no longer have to please your counterpart in order to get your needs met. You no longer have to pretend you are happy when in fact you're not.

You have options. If you don't feel that you are being respected, you can both express your feelings and assert your needs to the appropriate person. If you don't feel that you are being appreciated, you can both express your feelings and assert your needs to the appropriate person. If you don't feel that you are being acknowledged or recognized, you can both express your feelings and assert your needs to the appropriate person. If you feel you are being pressured into compliance, you can speak out and make sure that the appropriate person is aware of both your perspective and your expectation that your happiness is of equal importance to her/his happiness.

In having options, realize that if your counterpart is not interested in your feelings, your perceptions, your satisfaction or your happiness (once you have made your perspective known), you are dealing with a person who neither values nor respects you. If this is the case, your best option is to move on. Realize that if you do choose to stay, you will be obligated to assume the role of a powerless slave who is dependent on your counterpart to treat you kindly "out of the goodness of her/his heart." <u>The fact is, whether you are involved in a business transaction or in an intimate relationship, disinterest in your wellbeing should be a red flag that you have once again duplicated the servile relationship you had with your mom/dad.</u>

TO WORK WITH: YOUR EMOTIONAL TRIGGERS

Triggers in the present can be a superb way of connecting up with your past unreleased emotions. To work with triggers, realize that your present emotional response to situations will directly parallel the way you felt about your parents, and your life with them during your dependency years. Realize, as well, that because you would have blocked out many of your painful emotions from your childhood, you will literally have forgotten many incidents that would have enraged you, scared you, or made you feel sad or ashamed. And, as outlined in Chapter Two, you may not even have ever allowed your self to feel these emotions at all, because feeling them would have appeared too dangerous.

In that it is impossible to be consciously aware of the painful feelings you have blocked out, you might be inclined to believe that your present situation has nothing to do with your past. But it does. Your emotions are the same. And so when you become enraged at a person in your present life, ask your self, "Who else made me feel this way? Who am I really angry at here?" Then focus your attention on your feelings from your past: your feelings of being powerless, trapped, humiliated, betrayed, enraged. Release your feelings as outlined in Chapter Eleven.

The same analysis of parallel feelings should take place with all your strong emotional reactions (triggers). If you are in a situation which is frightening you, think back to when else in your life you felt frightened. If you do so, you may come to realize that living within you is a five-year-old child who believes that s/he will literally be killed if s/he says "no," a child who believes that conflict equals death. Exploring the source of your strong emotions will free you up to live as you choose—in the present!

3. WHO AND WHAT YOU ATTRACT INTO YOUR LIFE

In Chapter Seven, you first learned about the Law of Attraction. The Law of Attraction is the "unscientific" body of evidence that explains why you keep having the same lousy luck that you do; why no matter how promising a situation looks at the beginning, it usually ends up in the wrong way; why the people and business associates you encounter are never quite "normal"; how even when you're introduced to a whole new group of people at a party, you always end up meeting the most "fucked-up" person there; how your intimate relationships usually end up having similar dynamics, even though the people you started with "appeared" so different. The fact is, you can't run away from your self. Your self will come back to haunt you. It's simply a question of whether you're prepared to look at who and what you're attracting, and attempt to do something about it, or whether you decide to deny that such a law exists, and explain away your unhappy fate as being "bad luck."

What you attract into your life, or in other words, the events that happen to you on a daily basis can give you great insight into the painful situations from your past that you would prefer not to face. And the truth is, these "events" will keep reoccurring until you both pay attention to them, and take the necessary action to release your emotions.

Robert was working on his rage toward his father. He had blocked out of his conscious memory the fact that he had been sexually abused by his father, and now his feelings were surfacing. Around this time, he was backing out of his drive on a snowy, slippery day. Because another parked car was obstructing his view, he didn't see a large car driving down the road, on his side of the street. When he finally saw the moving car, he thought to himself, "He sees me. I know he'll put on his brakes. I know he'll take responsibility." But the other driver either didn't make any effort to stop, or wasn't able to stop on such short notice. Because the other driver had the right of way, he wasn't responsible for the accident and so he got off completely. Robert had to live with his dented car.

Why did this accident happen? Because Robert had it fixed in his mind that the other driver would take the responsibility for stopping; he had fully expected this driver to stop prior to the collision. Even though he may have had a few seconds to move his car back off the road, he didn't do so because he had given over the responsibility for saving the day to this stranger.

Why Robert would have had these expectations, at this particular time, is because he was feeling troubled about why his father had not taken responsibility for stopping his own actions—that is the abuse. In his mind, Robert was wishing that his father would have stopped abusing him, and would have started loving him. From this accident Robert learned that he would have to start taking care of himself. If he didn't take full control over his own life, he would end up suffering.

TO WORK WITH: THE LAW OF ATTRACTION

It's easy and truly amazing! Just make a mental note of what happens in your day. Did good things happen, or was it one disaster after another? If things didn't work out, what was the problem? What do you think this problem is trying to tell you about your inner life and the feelings that you don't want to face? Remember, your outer world will always reflect your inner world. Start paying attention to the clues your life is giving you about what's going on inside.

In working with the Law of Attraction, always keep in mind that You Are The Magnet. For example, if you find that you usually end up in situations where you are "powerless" (your counterpart is disinterested in changing her/his behavior, despite the fact that you have expressed your unhappiness, your prospective business clients don't return your phone calls, your romantic partner "dumps" you without letting you know what s/he is unhappy about), you have an activated I Am Powerless magnet. Because as a dependent child, you were made to feel powerless (your parents were disinterested in satisfying your needs and making you happy, you were ignored, neglected, abused or over-controlled), and you were not allowed to be powerful (asserting your needs would have interfered with your parents' need satisfaction), you will carry these feelings of powerlessness within you into your adult life.

With an activated I Am Powerless magnet, you will attract narcissists (people who are totally preoccupied with their own need satisfaction) and abusers (people who must dump their overload of rage onto a convenient target). The people you attract will be those who have neither the emotional capacity, nor the interest in considering your needs and your right to the same happiness (win/win) that they desire. (This description will probably duplicate the emotional profile of your parents.)

Sadly, in feeling powerless, you will attract people who will keep you in a state of powerlessness. Why? Because no matter how often you express your feelings and assert your needs, narcissists and abusers will not be able to do anything differently to acknowledge your worth; their own need to emotionally survive will prevent them from considering your needs. Thus if you are looking to either a narcissist or an abuser to respect you, recognize you, or acknowledge your worth, you will always remain powerless in relation to them. You cannot get blood out of a stone!

To deactivate your <u>I Am Powerless</u> magnet, you must work on accepting some basic truths:

1. Your parents were emotionally <u>incapable</u> of meeting your need for love, attention, affection, consideration, kindness, and recognition of your true worth. In being consumed with their own pain, their own emptiness, their own powerlessness, their own rage, their own shame, their own fears, they were <u>incapable</u> of putting your need satisfaction before their own.

   Emotional survival for your parents would have meant ignoring your needs as a helpless, vulnerable infant and growing child. Emotional survival would have meant denying your feelings and your needs. Emotional survival would have meant using you as an object of their gratification or as a dumping ground for their rage.

2. In that your parents were emotionally <u>incapable</u> of meeting your needs, the truth is, as a dependent child, you were <u>powerless</u> to change your reality. All your wishing, hoping and trying to be the perfect, compliant child was not going to make your parents any more capable of either being considerate of your needs or giving love to you. You cannot get blood out of a stone!

3. You didn't deserve the disrespectful, inconsiderate, unkind treatment you received. You didn't deserve to be frightened. You didn't deserve to be bullied into compliance. No child deserves abusive, neglectful and controlling treatment. You deserved kind, considerate, loving care. The way your parents treated you had nothing to do with your worth. It totally reflected upon their inability to give love and/or their need to dump their unresolved emotional pain onto a target which wouldn't fight back (you).

4. You have free will and you can choose to create a new reality for your self. Start expecting people to be accountable for their actions in relation to you. You no longer have to accept disrespect, being criticized, being judged, being ignored, being made to fit into your counterpart's plans.

   To create your new reality, start expressing your feelings and asserting your needs whenever you are unhappy. You deserve total respect and consideration. You have the same right to be happy as every other human being. Start letting people know that you have needs too.

5. If your counterpart is disinterested in your happiness (win/win), it means that s/he is emotionally incapable of seeing beyond her/his own needs. Her/his own feelings of rage, shame, sadness, fear, emptiness are preventing her/him from respecting you and recognizing your worth. If this is the case, move on.

6. You create your own reality. In the next section, How People Are Treating You, you will be reminded that people will only treat you in the same way that you are treating your inner self. You have to start respecting your self and appreciating your own worth before you can expect any other person to do so.

You can let people know how you expect to be treated simply by calling them on any behaviour which is not 100% respectful to you. If you tolerate any form of disrespect, you are alerting your counterpart to the fact that you are prepared to compromise your integrity in order to get your needs met.

In order to start feeling powerful and being powerful, you have to treat your self with total respect and recognition of your worth. When you start expressing your feelings and asserting your needs to all the people in your life, you will deactivate your I Am Powerless magnet and you will attract considerate, kind, respectful people into your life.

4. HOW PEOPLE ARE TREATING YOU

In Chapter Five, you first learned about the insights provided by how people are treating you. It's not easy to admit that people will tend to treat you in the same way that your parents treated you, and in the same way that you are treating your inner self. It's particularly difficult to admit this since you will naturally hate it when people are treating you poorly. So to think that the things you hate most about how people are treating you, you are doing to your inner self is certainly a hard pill to swallow. And it's even more unpleasant to accept that most of the things you hated about the way your parents treated you, you are in fact doing to your inner self.

Let's look at this more closely. Let's say that you are being treated in an abusive manner by your spouse/lover. This would suggest that either your mom or dad treated you abusively, and that you are treating your inner self in an abusive manner. Now, if you are a kind, considerate, thoughtful person, you might have a hard time believing that you abuse your inner self. But you are in fact abusing your inner self when you don't love, respect and value your own worth as a human being; when you feel inadequate, imperfect, not good enough; when you push aside your own needs, being satisfied with the Number Two position; when you don't consider that your own inner feelings, needs and happiness are as important as your spouse/lover's feelings, needs, and happiness.

In terms of the way your parents treated you, you might have a hard time believing that your mom or dad were abusive to you. If your parents are elderly and have mellowed out in their old age, if your parents are dead and you have chosen to remember the good times, if either your mom or dad died when you were a young child and you forgot what really happened, if you wanted to be loved so badly by your parent/s that you had to deny how you were really being treated, if your treatment was so traumatic for you that you had to block out the truth in order to survive, you might believe that it's impossible that you could have been abused.

If you are being abused as an adult, and your only childhood memories are happy ones, it suggests that you had/have a strong need to block out your past pain. It is recommended that if you wish to explore your past, you should work with a professional psychotherapist.

The way people are treating you will also provide you with clues as to the beliefs you hold about your self. Your internal beliefs act as a blueprint which explains all of your actions. And so for example, if you allow another person to treat you poorly, you can safely assume that you hold some of these beliefs: you aren't very important; you have little intrinsic worth; your personal happiness is not as important as your counterpart's happiness; your counterpart's issues are more important than your own; you have to do something for your counterpart in order to make her/him want to be with you.

TO WORK WITH: HOW PEOPLE ARE TREATING YOU

There are two ways you can work within this category. One way is to identify what you don't like about the way another person is treating you, and then work on both accepting that your parent/s treated you in this same unkind way, and admitting that you are treating your inner self in this same unkind way. (It goes without saying that you should do the emotional release work as outlined in Chapters Eleven and Twelve.)

For example, if you find that another person is ignoring your feelings, it means that your mom/dad ignored your feelings and that you are ignoring your own inner feelings. If you find that people are lying to you, it means that your mom/dad lied to you and that you are lying to your inner self. If you find people are critical of you, it means that your mom/dad was critical of you and that you are critical of your inner self. If you find that people betray your trust, it means that your mom/dad betrayed your trust and that you are betraying your own trust (you aren't being true to who you really are).

How you feel about the way people are treating you, or even more simply, what irritates you about their personalities will reveal to you how you were treated by your parents during childhood and how you are treating your self as an adult. Instead of being annoyed at the unpleasant people who cross your path, take advantage of what your reactions are telling you about your own past and present life.

The second way to work with this area is to use how people are treating you as a clue in discovering your own self-beliefs. For example, if you find that people are often criticizing you, then the belief you hold about your self is that you are inadequate, and that you deserve to be judged.

Remember though, the way you have come to view your self is the result of the treatment you received as a dependent child, your belief that you deserved this disrespectful, inconsiderate treatment, and your belief that this treatment accurately reflected your true worth. You can free your self from your negative self-beliefs by releasing the feelings—shame, anger, sadness, fear—that are keeping you locked into your past.

5. WHAT YOU WANT FROM OTHER PEOPLE

In Chapter Thirteen, you first learned about the fact that what you want from other people is equivalent to what you aren't giving your self. Remember because of the abusive, neglectful and overinvolved parenting you may have received, many of you will have learned to become very passive about taking the initiative in meeting your own needs. You may have grown passive out of feelings of inadequacy, fear or hopelessness. You may have remained passive, hoping against hope that one day someone would come along to save you from your misery. In either scenario, you will often look to other people to meet your needs.

The only way for you to be happy is to meet your own needs. If you are dependent on other people, you will be forced to compromise your integrity—dependency breeds slavery. Learn to do for your self what you want other people to do for you. And most important of all, do the work involved in loving your self. Rather than looking outward for love, focus on your own ability to both manufacture love, and give love away. By changing your orientation to one of self-love, you won't need other people to do anything for you at all, because you will be filled up with your own love.

TO WORK WITH: WHAT YOU WANT FROM OTHER PEOPLE

Use the exercises outlined in Chapter Twelve, Creating A Love-Base and Chapter Thirteen, Drawing From Your Own Account, in order to develop your capacity to become self-sufficient and emotionally whole.

SPECIAL NOTE

Please don't confuse the necessity of meeting your own needs with your right to be satisfied, happy, respected, acknowledged and valued when you are interacting with other people. While another person should not be expected to do for you what you find too difficult to do for your self—love you, fill up your emptiness, make you feel worthwhile, make you feel important, validate you, take away your pain—you should certainly expect all the people who are important to you to respect your feelings and your needs, and to recognize that your happiness is just as important as their own (win/win).

6. WHY YOU ARE ATTRACTED TO YOUR ROMANTIC PARTNER

Because your romantic partner (spouse/lover) will be one of the key people in your world, you will learn a great deal about what you need to do for your self by working through the exercises as outlined in the previous section. In addition, because your relationship with your romantic partner will most accurately mirror those parts of your self that remain undeveloped, you can discover the areas that you need to develop simply by analyzing the reasons for your attraction.

A great many of us believe that the fastest and best way to get what we want is to become romantically involved with a person who already has what we want; in this way we hope to either magically absorb her/his abilities, or be able to enjoy the end result of these abilities without needing to develop them. If you are one of these people, realize that there are no free lunches. The only way to peacefully enjoy what you want is to develop your own capacity to realize it. This means developing it for your self, within your self.

While it is true, for example, that developing the ability to be powerful will take a lot longer than hooking up with a powerful man or woman, realize than once you develop your own power, you will know that no one can ever take it away from you; you can enjoy that feeling of power for as long as you live. The result is that you won't have to compromise your integrity in order to enjoy the lifestyle that having personal power allows; you won't have to give up your self-respect in exchange for your need satisfaction.

The same dynamic can be applied to any reason that you are attracted to a romantic partner. Perhaps you like being with that person because s/he's fun-loving. You may find that you aren't able to enjoy the same kind of fun on your own. Well, if you aren't able to have great fun on your own, it's likely because you're still holding a great deal of unreleased grief within your inner self. Your grief is preventing you from enjoying your own life. Once you succeed in releasing your grief, you will find that living your life is a whole lot of fun.

For many of you, you will be attracted to your partner because of her/his ability to acknowledge, feel, and express any or all of the emotions that you are not able to access or express: fear, sadness, vulnerability, anger, shame, happiness, and joy. If this is the case, realize this: <u>In the same way that another person cannot consume food on your behalf (you have to take in your own nutrients), or recover from a dis-ease on your behalf, another person's ability to express an emotion is not going to</u>

give you the ability to express and release that emotion. You have to do it for your self. You have to discover why you have been unable to access that emotion, and take the steps required to release it. Use all the exercises in *Choices* to help you in this process.

HOW TO WORK WITH:
WHY YOU ARE ATTRACTED TO YOUR ROMANTIC PARTNER

Why do we hook up with our other half romantically, rather than work to develop those qualities and abilities we admire? Aside from the fact that as human beings, we are often lazy, we may not even consider doing the work because of the beliefs we hold. For example, if you hold the belief that you aren't very smart, or not very resourceful, you won't even make the effort to figure out a strategy for accomplishing your goals. Your lack of belief in your own abilities will prevent you from even trying. One way to break out of your self-limiting way of thinking is to set small goals for your self in areas that you have never previously undertaken. As you try out new activities, you will discover just how capable you really are.

But it may be more complicated than that. You may hold the belief that it isn't necessary to meet your own needs. There may have been a division of roles in your family, and you might believe that what was good enough for your mom and dad is good enough for you. If you hold this belief, realize that dependency on another person will force you to give up something that's important to you in exchange for what you want. If your freedom is important to you, self-sufficiency is the only way to go.

Looking more deeply into your beliefs, you might hold the belief that it isn't wise to become self-sufficient. You might hold the belief that self-sufficiency will lead to loneliness and a loveless life—if you don't want anything from another person, will there be any reason to bond? If you hold this belief, realize that the reverse is true: By becoming emotionally whole and self-sufficient, you will attract people who are emotionally whole and self-sufficient. It's only whole, complete people who are able to give love because they're not preoccupied with meeting their own needs. Because they love themselves, they will have love to give away. And the same goes for you. When you are self-sufficient, you will be freed up to give love to others, to focus on their needs and to be understanding of what's important to them. You'll be able to give love to others, without feeling depleted in the process. By being whole within your self, you will attract loving people, and you'll be able to enjoy more love and more happiness than you ever imagined possible.

Some of you may feel guilty about the idea of meeting your own needs. If you grew up in a family where your parents lead you to believe that you were responsible for their happiness, or where you felt it was in your best interests to keep your parents happy (if you bolstered them up, they would be more able to meet your needs), you would have been labelled "selfish," or you would have labelled your self "selfish" for thinking about your self, and what you wanted. Because need satisfaction is essential to personal happiness, you may have rationalized that while it isn't okay to think about your self and what you want, it is okay for another person to think about you and to meet your needs. After all, he or she is volunteering!

If you hold the belief that it's wrong to think about what you want and to "selfishly" meet your own needs, realize that it was in your parents' interests to have you think in this way. Turning you into a caretaker made their lives easier. By turning you into a caretaker, they didn't have to do the work to make their lives meaningful—it was so much easier to pass this responsibility onto you, to give you the job of fixing their empty lives.

Turning you into a caretaker was a crime against you. In so doing, they were depriving you of your right, as a human being, to look after your own interests and to make your own self happy. Having needs and wanting to satisfy them are components of being alive. Having needs and wanting to meet them is no different than feeling hungry and desiring food to satisfy your hunger. When you no longer have needs, you will literally be dead.

We all have needs. The question is, "Who is going to meet them?" If you meet them your self, you will have a happy life, filled with lots of people and prosperity. If you want your romantic partner to meet them, you will have a relationship filled with tension and stress for you will be obligated to try to control your partner's behaviour. Since no one likes to be controlled, you will be setting your self up for a life of conflict and unhappiness. To avoid conflict, and to ensure a happy life, develop your own ability to both meet your own needs and give to your self all the things you want.

The truth of the matter is this: <u>When you no longer need another person to supplement the gaps in your emotional profile and to take away your pain, you will match up with an emotionally whole, loving person who can give love to you, in the same way that you can give love to her/him. Your relationships will become more loving and fulfilling as you become more loving and fulfilled in your own right. There are no shortcuts.</u>

BEAU

7. WHAT YOUR BODY IS TELLING YOU

Your bodily symptoms will give you immediate clues as to what you are really feeling. If you get an inflammation—eye, ear, bladder, vaginal—realize that your body is trying to tell you that you are angry. The source of the inflammation will tell you what you are angry about. If your back seizes up, it's a message that you are feeling burdened by a huge emotional load. If you frequently get flus, it means your body is trying to clear out, through sneezing and coughing, the pent-up emotions you have been holding in.

TO WORK WITH: WHAT YOUR BODY IS TELLING YOU

Please refer to Chapter Nine, Your Body Is Talking But Are You Listening?

8. WHAT YOUR DREAMS ARE TELLING YOU

Your dreams will come to you in a language of symbols. Often they may not appear to make sense, but they are always trying to tell you something. Sometimes they are trying to reveal to you information concerning your buried feelings from your past, feelings that your conscious mind finds too difficult to face. Sometimes your dreams are trying to help you resolve a problem, and other times your dreams are trying to help you process the events that have occured in your day.

TO WORK WITH: WHAT YOUR DREAMS ARE TELLING YOU

Please refer to Chapter Ten, The World Of Dreams.

9. DO YOU OPERATE FROM A LOVE-BASE?

The main problem in your life may be related to the fact that you don't attract anything good into it. You may have a life devoid of happiness. You may be in a rut, career-wise, romantically, socially. Nothing has changed for years, and the only thing that's happening is that you're getting older.

If you aren't as happy as you would like to be, ask your self the questions, "Do I operate from a love-base?" "Do I love my self?" Your outer world will always reflect your inner world. If you don't truly love your self, the people around you will react accordingly.

Self-love can only result when you clear your self of all the negative beliefs and unreleased emotions that lie within your unconscious mind. Self-love can only result when you value your own intrinsic worth, believing that you <u>deserved</u> to be loved by your parents (even though they were incapable of giving love to you), believing that you <u>deserve</u> to be loved and treated with respect and admiration by all the important people in your life, believing that you have the same right to be happy as every other human being.

If you aren't as happy as you would like to be, it means that you don't love your self. Your unreleased emotions from your past, combined with your negative self-beliefs are preventing you from creating a happy, fulfilling, prosperous life.

Self-love is not an elusive goal. Every one of you is capable of creating a love-base if you do the work of releasing your buried emotions, and surfacing your negative beliefs. Going through the process of releasing your emotions may at times be both painful and draining. However, the results are definitely most rewarding—a lifetime of happiness.

HOW AM I DOING SO FAR?

THE FOLLOWING INDICATORS:

1. Your Emotional Operating System
2. Your Emotional Triggers
3. Who and What You Attract Into Your Life
4. How People Are Treating You
5. What You Want From Other People

6. Why You Are Attracted To Your Romantic Partner
7. What Your Body Is Telling You
8. What Your Dreams Are Telling You
9. Do You Operate From A Love-Base?

will let you know with 100% accuracy what you are really feeling and what you will need to do about your circumstances in order to improve your life. If you want to free your self to make choices, you now know what you must do to make this happen.

16 | FREE WILL STARTS HERE

This is your life. Throughout *Choices* you were told that your parents' treatment of you is the cause of the way you feel about your self today. If you think that you aren't good enough, it's because your parents didn't make you feel loved, cared for and respected; rather, they made you feel inadequate. If you feel that you have to prove to others that you are worthwhile, it's because your parents didn't make you feel that you were valuable, just for the person you are. If you feel that you can't live without an intimate partner loving you, it's because your parents didn't give you the love you needed to enable you to love your self.

So who caused the damage? Your parents did. Who can fix the damage? You can. Yes, your parents did dump their garbage on you, but the fact is, you are pinned under it now. If you want to get up and walk freely about, you are going to have to remove it. There's no point trying to pass the buck. You have it now.

If you owned a beautiful home, and one morning you woke up to find a ton of garbage on your front lawn, would you spend the rest of your life trying to find the culprit, or would you concentrate on clearing your lawn, and restoring it to its former beauty? You could choose to spend the rest of your life trying to find the culprit, but chances are, he's long gone, and you still have the problem of the garbage to deal with. The fact is, there's no way around it. You didn't put the garbage there, but if you want to have a happy life, you are going to have to be the one to clear it away.

So let's now look at some of the situations that might be currently troublesome for you, and figure out together what <u>you</u> can do to take charge.

YOU ARE FEELING LONELY

You are not lonely for other people. You are lonely for your inner self. You are not connecting up to your true feelings, and you are not releasing them. You are sitting on a whole lot of anger, sadness, fear and shame, and your pent-up emotions are acting as a barrier between you and your inner self. You have taken on the garbage that your parents have dumped on you, and you believe that you are both worthless and inadequate.

You must work on changing your beliefs about your self, and start seeing your self as you really are. You are not worthless. You believe you are worthless because your parents did not treat you with the respect, admiration, consideration, kindness, love and caring you deserved. Keep reminding your self, "You did not deserve the disrespectful, inconsiderate, neglectful, unkind, cruel treatment you received. You did not deserve to be frightened or made to do what you didn't want to do. No child deserves such treatment. You deserved to be loved, respected, considered, and valued."

In order to be free to value your self and realize just how good you are, you must release your pent-up emotions that you were forced to push down in order to survive. Once you release your emotions, you will begin to value your own worth and truly love your self. When you love your self, you will no longer feel lonely.

In addition, work on forgiving your self. Forgive your self for not being where you want to be, and having what you want to have. Forgive your self for being lonely. You are doing the best you can with the resources you currently have. It's not your fault that you are without caring friends, without emotional supports in your life. Your parents' treatment of you interfered with your natural ability to love your self and to take your own side.

If you don't accept your self, if you hate your self, if you believe you are inadequate or worthless, people will treat you and see you in like manner. You have the power to change the way people are treating you! As soon as you start forgiving your self for being human, as soon as you start realizing how great you really are, your new self-image will reflect outward. People will want to be with you. As you accept your self, people will accept you accordingly. And when this happens, you won't be lonely again.

In the meantime, ask your self why you are feeling lonely.

Ask your self who you would ideally want to be with, and what this person could do for you. Then do it for your self. Try not to call anyone when you are feeling lonely. Rather work on loving your self. Focus on your own ability to manufacture love. Work through the exercises in Chapter Twelve, Creating A Love-Base. When you feel ready to share your love, call a friend.

YOU ARE FEELING DEPRESSED

Depression is anger turned inward. Instead of connecting up with your feelings of anger toward your parent/s for ignoring you, humiliating you, abandoning you, not validating you, not loving you, not recognizing your worth, abusing you sexually or physically, frightening you into compliance, making you do what you didn't want to do, betraying your trust, criticizing you, controlling you, entrapping you, manipulating you, using you as a parent, taking your life away, not wanting you, not making you feel important, you are pushing these "unacceptable" feelings down, and you are turning them against your self.

Please recognize: <u>You are not worthless. The way your parents treated you made you feel worthless.</u> You must get in touch with your feelings of rage at the treatment you were forced to accept, your feelings of shame at having been made to feel worthless, your feelings of grief at not having been loved the way you wanted to be loved, and your feelings of fear resulting from your not having been able to stop the abusive treatment you were receiving. You must then release each of your feelings: anger, shame, sadness and fear.

There's no way around it: You must place the responsibility for the <u>damage</u> that was caused you on your parents. You were born believing that you were the most wonderful little being in the world.[6] Your parents' treatment of you made you believe that you were worthless. Only by ridding your self of your anger, shame, sadness and fear will you be able to love your self. Emotional release work with a professional therapist is advisable.

---

[6]If you, as an unborn child, were not wanted, you will most likely not have been born loving your self, for you will have picked up your mother's negativity while you were in the womb. Even in this worst-case scenario, releasing all four emotions: shame, anger, sadness and fear will free you up to love your self.

YOU ARE FEELING ANXIOUS

Anxiety is a coverup emotion. It's a feeling alright, but it masks your real feelings that you are afraid to face—anger, sadness, fear and shame. As a child, you had good reason to not want to feel and express your feelings: you may have been beaten if you had done so; you may have been emotionally cut off; you may have been so terrified for your own safety that you simply had to shut down and not feel anything at all. Anxiety is a sure sign that emotions are being blocked. The only way to free your self from your anxiety is to face your underlying feelings.

YOU CANNOT SURVIVE WITHOUT YOUR DEPENDENCY ITEM

You have learned to reach for your dependency item—alcohol, drugs, sex, a romantic partner, people, abusing others, work, physical activity, gambling, being busy—as a way to avoid facing your true feelings. There's no substitute for facing your feelings, for acknowledging your anger, your sadness, your fear and your shame. You must release your feelings at the source in order for you to feel both emotionally whole and worthwhile. Once you truly start to appreciate your own worth, the pull toward your dependency item will certainly diminish.

YOU ATTRACT PEOPLE WHO IGNORE YOUR NEEDS

If you find that you are usually encountering people who are pre-occupied with meeting their own needs (narcissists), people who seem disinterested in your issues or your feelings, people who don't seem to care about whether you are happy (win/win), you can be sure that you hold several of these beliefs: you aren't very important; you don't <u>deserve</u> to be either acknowledged or respected; your feelings don't count; you don't have the right to be happy.

If you were not treated with respect, love, compassion, understanding, consideration and adoration, you will have been obligated to compromise your integrity in order to get your needs met. In doing so, you would have concluded that you were just not as important or as valuable as other people. And so as an adult, you will continue to believe that your happiness is not as important as the happiness of significant others.

The fastest way to turn around this reality is to forgive your self. Forgive your self for any inadequacy you believe you have. Forgive your self for not having achieved all the things you want. Forgive your self for making mistakes. Forgive your self for not being as smart, attractive, successful, worldly as you would like to be.

When you forgive your self, you will free your self to start liking you. Once this happens, you will start valuing your own worth. And what you will begin to find is that you will start meeting people who <u>are interested</u> in you. The fact is, people will only treat you in the same way that you are treating your inner self. If you don't make it clear that you have needs, if you choose not to express your feelings and assert your needs, you are inviting people to ignore your needs. If you don't value your self, other people will not value you. You create your own reality.

YOU ATTRACT NEEDY PEOPLE

People who are needy are usually very demanding. If you believe that you're inadequate, that you aren't very important, or that you don't <u>deserve</u> to be respected and considered, you will get sucked into meeting the needs of your friends, family members and business associates. Their daily catastrophes will be thrust upon you, and even though their problems don't belong to you, you will feel obligated to solve them.

Solving the problems of needy people will prevent you from breaking free from your past. Solving other people's problems will deceive you into thinking that you are strong and powerful, because in being the "helper," you will be playing "god." But the reality is, you are avoiding facing your own issues. The fact that you are matching up with "helpless" people suggests that you are probably a sadness-based strong/distant matching up with your exact complementary match—a sadness-based needy person. This means that you are feeling the same degree of inadequacy as your needy counterpart, but that you are afraid to show your own inadequacy by revealing your needs. Thus you may feel most comfortable in taking on the role of the "helper." By focusing your energy and attention outward, rather than inward, you will be postponing resolving your own painful issues.

You must start addressing the needs of your inner self. You

have to work on releasing the emotions that are keeping you locked into feeling worthless and inadequate—the emotions that are preventing you from truly liking your self. Start taking care of your self. Work through the exercises in Chapter Twelve, Creating A Love-Base.

PEOPLE TAKE ADVANTAGE OF YOU

No one can do anything to you that you aren't doing to your self first. You just wouldn't tolerate it. If people are taking advantage of your kindness and generosity, it means that you are taking advantage of your inner self. You are ignoring your own needs and feelings, and you are denying your own worth.

If you allow people to take advantage of you, it's a sure sign that your parents used you to meet their own needs. In all likelihood, you were treated as an object of gratification: you were there to make your parents' lives easier and more pleasurable; your needs and feelings, and what was good for you were irrelevant.

You learned to care for your self the way your parents cared for you. It's time to stop being a slave, and to start valuing who you are. Let people know that you have needs too. Speak up when you're unhappy. Start expressing your feelings and asserting your needs.

For those of you who are sadness-based strong/distant, you must come to realize that you are not revealing your inadequacy when you want your needs to be considered. The truth is, you are not inadequate. You perceive that you are inadequate because your parents made you feel that there was something wrong with you for wanting your needs to be met. Everyone has needs. And everyone has a right to be treated with both respect and consideration—including you. Learn to say "no." You have the same right to be happy and satisfied as every other human being.

YOU HAVE DIFFICULTY RELEASING YOUR EMOTIONS

It's not as easy as it might seem to suddenly both connect up with and release your true inner feeling. You had good reason not to feel your true feelings. Now that you are suddenly giving your self permission to feel, your inner self might feel too scared to let loose. The following information can help you both bring to the surface and release your buried emotions.

ANGER

Anger is a key emotion for you to access. Sadness-based people have a difficult time both identifying their anger, and "having the nerve" to express it, because of the dangers inherent in openly expressing anger. When you express your anger, you are making it very clear who you are: you know your own worth; you won't tolerate either disrespect or a lack of recognition; you expect your counterpart to be accountable to you for the way s/he's treating you.

There's a great risk in becoming openly angry, and that is the risk of rejection, abandonment, and loss of love. If you have been living your entire life appeasing other people, making certain they are happy so that they will look after your interests, expressing your anger will appear self-destructive. In being angry, you will risk losing your emotional life supports (your spouse, lover, parent, child, friends, colleagues). And this is no small matter. Receiving love, affection, caring, recognition, attention, interest and kindess is crucial in giving each of us a reason for living.

Being prepared to get angry at your source of "apparent" love is a process. The process will begin when you start looking inside your self for your source of love, recognition and support. Until you build a base of inner strength, until you start truly valuing your own worth, until you start loving your self, you will be too frightened to risk losing your emotional life support. An analogy would be this: If you had a lung disease which required you to be on a life support machine, and you chose to cut that machine off before your lungs were strong enough to bring oxygen into your body, you would likely die. In the same way, if you were to cut your self off from your "apparent" source of love, caring and affection, your action would appear to be equally self-destructive.

Part and parcel of your deep-seated fear of losing love is your fear of abandonment. In all likelihood, you will have within your self the fear of a five-year-old child who wonders who will take care of her/him if her/his mom and dad stopped loving her/him. The fact is, if you were abused, neglected or overcontrolled, you were emotionally abandoned. And the little girl or boy within you still remembers all too well the sickening, horrifying, frightening feelings of being abandoned, left to fend for your self, and being terrified for your very survival. As a five-year-old child, you would have believed that without the love, caring and attention of your parents, you would have surely died. Even though as an adult, you will not die if your source of "apparent" love walks out on you, from an emotional perspective, you will believe that your death is imminent.

The first step then, in becoming angry, is to prepare your self to become angry, and this means doing the work to start loving your self. Once you start seeing your self as a source of support, comfort and love, you will be ready to face your buried anger. The fact is, you don't need anyone to tell you to be angry at your mom and dad. You have plenty of reasons to be angry, and these reasons are sitting within your unconscious mind, ready to be released.

Why should you be angry? If your life is not wonderful, exciting, dynamic, joyous and full of love and prosperity, you can conclude that the way your mom and dad treated you literally destroyed your ability to create a happy life. In one way or another, they made you feel so inadequate that you now lack the emotional capacity to realize your dreams.

As well, the "love" that many of you received was in all likelihood conditional, controlling and manipulative. This would have caused you to view love in the same way as a laboratory rat views cheese—you have to "do" something in order to be rewarded with the caring, affection, recognition, interest, attention and love that is so essential to all of us as human beings. Keep in mind that "real" love is when your source of love cares about how you feel, wants you to be happy and is as concerned about your happiness as her/his own (win/win).

It's time to face your pain. It's time to face your truth. For many of you, the truth is, you were abandoned; you were betrayed; you had no protection; you were sacrificed; you were made to suffer. A terrible crime was committed against you— the crime of being left as a vulnerable child to fend for your self.

You don't have to live out your past hell for the rest of your life. You can free your self from your past by acknowledging your truth and getting in touch with your very justifiable anger. If you were abused, neglected or overcontrolled, realize that your parents had no right to treat you as they did. You did not deserve this treatment. You had no choice but to accept what was dished out to you. There is no excuse for how you were treated.

Releasing your anger will free you from the past. Releasing your anger will free you to value your own worth. Releasing your anger will give you the power to tell the people in your world that they are accountable to you for their actions in relation to you. Releasing your anger will allow you to live as you choose—in the present!

SADNESS

You may not want to feel your grief because you don't want to feel helpless and vulnerable. Your belief may be that adults should be strong, and above feeling sorry for themselves. Crying might make you feel incredibly weak and powerless. Since you may have spent so much of your time trying to create a strong facade, you may not want to break it, even for your self.

The truth is, being strong is being able to feel your true feelings. Being strong is being in touch with your true feelings. Being strong is liking your self enough to be who you really are. Every one of us will have buried grief for not having been loved the way we wanted to be loved. Most of our parents will have fallen short of what we needed in terms of consideration, attention, affection and recognition.

Crying is a way to release the pain. Crying will enable you to release deep-seated pain and grief. Crying will free you from the state of waiting to be loved. When you face that very sad little boy or girl living inside of you, you will be able to comfort your own inner self, and give your self the love you always craved. By releasing your tears, you will no longer have to pretend to be strong. You will be strong.

FEAR

As a functioning adult, the last thing you would want to feel is terrified for your very survival. In surfacing your unconscious fear, however, you will feel just that—your life is in danger. In surfacing your fear, you will feel any combination of these emotions: terror, helplessness, vulnerability, powerlessness, danger, the feeling of being trapped, the feeling that there is no way out, the feeling of being unsafe—that there is no one to protect you.

Why the extreme emotions? As a child, you were totally dependent on your parents for your physical survival, as well as for your emotional wellbeing. For some of you, the risk that you would have lost the little love you had would have felt terrifying. For others of you, you would have perceived that your very life was in danger. If you were being sexually abused, you may have been threatened with, "I'm going to kill you if you tell anyone about this." If you were being abused in any way, verbally, sexually or physically, you may have truly felt that if you had said "no," your mom/dad would have killed you.

In preparing your self to face your unconscious fears, realize that working with your buried fear will be stressful. Fear is a very powerful emotion and will distort your present perceptions. If you were abused, verbally, physically or sexually, it is recommended that you work with a professional psychotherapist who will help you surface and release your frightening feelings. It's most important at this time to have a psychotherapist with whom you feel safe.

Why bother going through the pain and stress of facing your fear? Because your buried fear will prevent you from creating the life you want to live. Unless your past fear is released, it will prevent you from "Operating From A Love-Base": expressing your feelings, asserting your needs, trading equal value, saying "no," confronting denial, surfacing hostility and insisting on win/win relationships. The only way you will be able to stand up for your self, any time, any place, with any person, is if you clear your self of your past buried fear.

SHAME

Shame is an emotion that you may naturally feel, but in all likelihood, you may not even realize that you feel it. If you don't like your self, or if you believe that you are inadequate in some way, it's because you were made to feel worthless by your parents. If you were treated without respect, love and consideration, you will have concluded that there was something wrong with you: you were defective; you were a bad person; you deserved the disrespectful, inconsiderate, unkind, cruel, abusive, neglectful, overcontrolling treatment you received. You will then spend the rest of your life hiding your inadequacy from both your self and other people, not even realizing the origin of your negative self-image.

Shame can be viewed as a master emotion that you may need to release before you can get in touch with your other key emotions: anger, sadness and fear. If you feel worthless, you may not be able to feel anger toward your parents; rather, you may direct your anger against your self. If you feel worthless, you may feel that crying is a sign of weakness, making you feel even more despicable in your own eyes. If you feel worthless, you may believe that the reason you're feeling afraid is because you are an inadequate human being, and that you don't measure up to others.

The way to break free from your shame is to both work on accepting that you did not deserve the unkind, inconsiderate, disrespectful treatment you received, and that you forgive your self for any inadequacies you believe you have. Keep affirming, "I didn't deserve to be treated like an object. I didn't deserve to be bullied. I didn't deserve to be neglected, abused, overcontrolled. I deserved to be treated with respect, consideration, admiration, love and caring. I forgive my self for any inadequacies I believe I have."

Once you both forgive your self and recognize the truth— you did deserve good treatment, your parents were emotionally incapable of treating you with the respect you deserved—you will be able to free your self from your shame and your self-hatred. You will then be able to feel the emotions that your self-hatred and shame have been blocking: your anger, sadness and fear.

YOUR EMOTIONS SEEM OVERWHELMING

You may feel overwhelmed by the intensity of your emotions. Because many of you will have had to block out your true feelings in order to survive your childhood, it may come as a shock to you to have such intense feelings. If you find your self becoming frightened at the intensity of your feelings, or if you realize that you need help in both facing your feelings, and releasing them, it is recommended that you seek out a professional psychotherapist. This person can be a medical doctor, a psychologist, a psychiatrist, a social worker, a bodywork specialist.

The psychotherapist who will be most helpful is one who will encourage you to connect up with and release all the emotions you had to repress in order to survive your childhood, and one who is comfortable with the physical release of your emotions right in the therapeutic session. Remember, you cannot release your emotions intellectually; talking about your emotions will not enable you to free your self from them.

In terms of recommended therapies, my bias is towards any technique which will allow you to both connect up with and release your primary feelings towards your parents. In this regard, hypnosis can be a very effective therapy in enabling you to both identify and release the root cause of your pain. Another recommended therapy is bodywork where the goal is to help you both get in touch with and release your buried emotions.

The psychotherapist you choose should obviously be well-qualified to help you. But in a note of warning, do not be intimidated by professional qualifications. Realize that professional qualifications will not necessarily provide a psychotherapist with the practical skills required to free you from your past. To choose the right psychotherapist for you, always trust your gut instincts. If you feel that your psychotherapist is playing mind games with you, is causing you to feel inadequate, is putting her/his interests before your own, is unable to help you with your issues, is uncomfortable with the physical expression of emotions, this person is not for you. If you do not honestly believe that your psychotherapist truly has your best interests at heart, find one who does.

YOU FEEL TOO ANGRY OR TOO SAD

The intensity of your emotions will directly parallel the pain you felt as a child. Expect it to take some time to fully release your buried emotions. Realize that a mountain of pain is not going to be cleared away in a flash. It took a long time to build up that mountain of pain. It will take some time to clear it away.

It might however happen that you get stuck on one emotion—either sadness or anger. If this is the case, there's a strong likelihood that either your anger or your sadness is a coverup emotion that is blocking other feelings that are too painful or uncomfortable for you to face. Thus, the emotions that can be fuelling your anger are your shame, sadness and fear, and the emotions that can be fuelling your sadness are your shame, repressed anger and fear. To move through either your anger or your sadness, identify why you would have a difficult time feel-

ing the emotions that you wish to avoid, and then take the steps
to face them.

YOU FEEL TOO ANGRY

If you are an anger-based person, feeling your anger will make
you feel strong and powerful, while feeling your shame, fear or
sadness will make you feel weak. Being angry may enable you to
intimidate other people, and allow you to get your needs met.
You might worry that if you stop being angry, you will lose your
ability to get what you want in life. You might see your anger as
a protection, and fear that if you stop being angry, you will lose
your power (much as Sampson did when Delilah cut off his hair).

Your belief that you need your anger is just an illusion. The
fact is, you are a strong, resourceful person. No one can take that
away from you. Giving up your anger is a process, and it will
begin when you start acknowledging the source of your anger—
your rage towards your mom/dad for the way s/he treated you.
Remember, you deserved to be loved and you are loveable. You
don't have to keep fighting old battles for the rest of your life.
Open up your heart to love, and begin to love your self by releasing your painful emotions from the past.

YOU FEEL TOO SAD

If you're sadness-based, you may find that you can't move
beyond your sadness; you may find that you're stuck in a state of
powerlessness. If this is the case, realize that the way your parents treated you made you feel so inadequate and so helpless
that all you can do is feel sorry for your self.

To pry your self free from this powerless state, connect up
with your feelings of shame. Forgive your self for any inadequacy you believe you have; forgive your self for not having the
things you want; forgive your self for being alone. Once your
self-forgiveness registers in your unconscious mind, you will
start to feel angry at your parents for treating you unkindly.
Once you start feeling angry, you will start feeling your own
power and worth as a human being. You will start realizing
some basic truths: You didn't deserve the treatment you were
receiving; it was not your fault that you were ignored, used,
abused, humiliated, overcontrolled; your mom/dad did not have
the right to frighten you into compliance or force you to com-

promise your integrity and self-respect; you deserved to be loved, respected, admired, considered and valued.

In developing feelings of self-worth, you will be able to look at the origin of your fear. You will come to understand that you did have very good reasons to be terrified for your very life during your dependency years. When you discharge your fear, you will come to realize that as an adult, you don't have to live in fear. You now have the resources to protect your self. In this process, you will free your self to live a relaxed, happy and joyful life.

YOU ARE ATTRACTED TO PEOPLE WHO END UP DISAPPOINTING YOU

Whether it is a romantic partner, potential friend or business colleague, you may find that you repeatedly misjudge the true character of the people with whom you become involved. In misjudging the true personality, at that moment of truth, when you really expect the person to be there for you, you will be let down.

If this happens to you on a regular basis, it means that you are not consciously aware of the true reasons for your attraction to the people in question. In all probability, you will be attracted to appealing aspects of the external Operating Style, not realizing that on an emotional level, this person is emotionally empty inside, and truly has little to give, either to her/himself or to you.

By the Law Of Attraction, you will only be attracted to someone who is just like you (the same unresolved emotions); you can only attract someone who is just like you. Being the same as you emotionally, your counterpart will feel the same degree of emptiness as you do, the same lack of self-worth, the same inability to see beyond her/his own need satisfaction, the same inability to give love. This means that if you don't love your self, the people to whom you'll be attracted won't love themselves either, even though their external Operating Style may tell you otherwise.

Operating from a love-deficit position, you won't value and appreciate your own worth, and you won't be able to give your self the respect, recognition, attention, kindness, consideration, caring and support that self-love entails; your counterpart will have the same problems. This means that both of you will end up looking outward for love as opposed to inward. So in fact, as an empty person, you will be looking to another empty person to fill you up. It's not going to happen, and thus you will ultimately be disappointed by the people in your life.

YOUR ATTRACTION TO ANGER-BASED PEOPLE

You will be attracted to anger-based people because they "appear" to be full of life, energy, enthusiasm, and are fun to be with. They love talking about themselves, tell great stories, and are often quite entertaining. They express their anger easily and they "appear" to like themselves. This will be especially attractive if you aren't able to express your anger and if you feel dead inside.

What you must realize with anger-based people is that they are empty inside. They need external attention, recognition and validation in order to feel worthwhile. Their fight mentality prevents them from showing vulnerability and asking for love. As a result, they feel especially empty, and are desperate to be filled up even though they will never admit this is so. This means they will be doing a lot of taking without very much giving. And the fact is, anger-based people feel so empty inside that they find giving almost impossible. (They perceive giving as an emotional depletion.) They will have a very difficult time seeing beyond their own needs (recognizing your needs), because discharging their pent-up anger and satisfying their own needs is a full-time job. If you are expecting an anger-based person to be loving, giving, considerate and attentive of your needs, you are bound to be disappointed.

YOUR ATTRACTION TO STRONG/DISTANT PEOPLE

You will be attracted to sadness-based strong/distant people because they "appear" to be very supportive, kind, caring and giving. As well they "appear" to be very strong; they rarely have emotional upheavals and always seem to be very much in control of their lives. In addition, they are not demanding, and so they won't drain you. They may truly appear perfect on the outside—they give, and they don't expect very much in return.

What you must realize with strong/distants is that they are putting on a veneer of strength to mask their deep feelings of inadequacy. They "appear" to be there for you because they believe they must act strong and self-confident in order to preserve their own self-esteem.

In reality, strong/distants are simply going through the motions of appearing strong. They are as fragile as you are, although their Operating Style will appear to tell you otherwise. Their analytical approach to your issues will make them appear that they are problem-free. But don't be fooled. Most often they won't identify with your feelings, not because they don't have the very same unresolved emotional issues, but because they have chosen to block out their own pain. And so you may end up believing that you "really have problems," because your strong/distant counterpart will appear to be so problem-free by comparison.

Alternatively, you may find that your strong/distant counterpart is not there for you when you need her/him because, as with the anger-based person, giving is perceived as being emotionally depleting. That is why the strong/distant can be there for you one day and treat you like a stranger the next, or be very warm and then suddenly distant. Ultimately, your relationship with a strong/distant can leave you feeling very empty.

YOUR ATTRACTION TO NEEDY PEOPLE

You will be attracted to sadness-based needy people because they "need" you. You will feel valued and important to them because they need your advice, your help, your input, your support; they will make you feel wanted. In addition, needy people appear very warm and loving and are easy to get close to. If you were neglected, ignored, abused, not valued, not appreciated, needy people will make you feel that you are worthwhile. They will give you a reason for living. In the beginning of a romantic relationship, a needy person will give you the feeling that you are being loved.

The problem with sadness-based needy people is that they will drain the life right out of you. They are perennial takers and no matter how much you give them, it will never be enough; no matter how hard you try, you will never be able to fill up their emptiness. In addition, in being consumed with their own needs, they will have an impossible time considering your needs: your problems are not as serious as their problems; you are strong while they are weak. If you are a strong/distant, this may fit in well with your need to appear strong and perfect, but it will leave you feeling very empty because your needs will rarely be addressed. (Although on one level, the emotional distance will allow you to feel safe, on another level, you will often feel very lonely.)

An additional problem with needy people is that they can't allow you the freedom to live your own life, to enjoy your life away from them, because separation feels like a loss, and must be avoided. While needy people are usually very affectionate and loving, their loving behaviour is based on their need to fuse, to not be alone, to fill up their emptiness, as opposed to respecting you as a separate person with distinct needs. When you are with a needy person, you will truly feel that your soul isn't your own.

YOU CAN'T RUN AWAY FROM YOUR SELF

The only way that you can attract and be attracted to people who won't disappoint you is for you to create your own love-base. When you are able to give your own self the love, attention, kindness, consideration, support, caring, respect, recognition and validation you currently want from others, you will be able to attract love-based people who will freely give you this same love.

YOUR ROMANTIC RELATIONSHIPS ARE NOT LOVE-BASED

You may find that your romantic relationships deteriorate over time—that somehow you lose that "loving feeling." To create a love-based relationship, work on the following:

LOVE YOUR SELF

Love your self. Sorry, but there are no shortcuts. There is no way that you can match up with a loving partner if you don't love your self first. The fact is, the only person you'll be able to attract is someone who shares the same emotional profile as you do: the same unreleased emotions (anger, sadness, fear, shame); the same degree of denial; the same degree of pain; the same unresolved emotional issues (abandonment, trust, safety, self-worth, self-love). If you are sitting on a load of unreleased anger, fear, sadness, and shame, expect that your partner will be struggling with the same issues. Although your Operating Styles may be different, your underlying unresolved emotions will be the same.

In order to love your self, you must release all your buried emotions. When you do so, you will be freed up to realize how wonderful you truly are. When you know your own worth, you will match up with a partner who knows her/his own worth. Both of you will be able to give love as well as receive love. Thus, you will create the base of a loving relationship.

UNDERSTAND THE REASONS FOR YOUR ATTRACTION

Unless you are consciously aware of why you are attracted to your partner, you will not be able to love her/him for the person s/he is; you will not even be able to see her/him as the person s/he is. Rather, you will perceive her/him to be larger than life, having the capabilities of solving your problems, filling in the deficits from your past, taking away your pain, validating you, making you feel important, making you feel loved. In not understanding the nature of your attraction, you will perceive your partner as having a package of attributes, qualities and capabilities that this person does not actually possess. In wanting your partner to be the person you want her/him to be for you, as opposed to the person s/he actually is, you will be creating a conflict-based relationship; you will be trying to change your partner into the ideal mate who never was.

Let's look at an example in more detail. If you are a sadness-based needy person, you might find that you are attracted to an anger-based person because s/he appears so alive and happy, s/he is freely able to express that all important emotion that you cannot express—your anger—and s/he "appears" to have the capability of taking care of you and satisfying all of your unmet needs. On an unconscious level, what you really want is your own ability to feel alive and happy, your own ability to express your anger and your own ability to feel worthwhile.

If you bring your unconscious attraction to the surface, you will thank your partner for making you aware of what you must develop in your self to become the person you want to be. Becoming conscious of what you need to work on, you will no longer need your partner to be anything for you except to be the person s/he already is. You won't need to change your partner because you will not need her/him to be anyone but the person s/he wants to be.

If, on the other hand, you remain unconscious of the nature of your attraction, you will start expecting your partner to do things for you that s/he, as an anger-based person, has neither the desire nor the capability of doing—take care of you, protect you, fill you up, validate you, be giving to you, be loving to you. (Remember an anger-based person is just as empty as you are. You will not realize this because s/he "appears" to be strong. What you will not recognize is that an anger-based person has a very difficult time in giving; when s/he does give, s/he will tend to feel resentful of you because giving love is perceived as a personal loss.) ⤷ *ressentiment*

And so your expectations will not be based on who your partner really is (what s/he is capable of giving, what s/he is prepared to give, what s/he wants from you), but rather on what it "appeared" that your partner was capable of doing for you when you were first attracted to this person—satisfy your unmet needs from your past, make you feel important, make you feel special, make you feel loveable, make you feel worthwhile, make you feel loved and teach you to be as strong and powerful as s/he "appears" to be. But the reality is, expecting your partner to be the person you want her/him to be, as opposed to being the person s/he is, is like expecting milk to come out of your water tap—it's not going to happen, despite the fact that both milk and water are in the liquid category.

The only way you can create a love-based relationship is when you can both truly enjoy and appreciate your partner, and accept that what you see is what you get. It goes without saying that your partner should enjoy, appreciate and accept you as well. When you no longer need your partner to substitute as your unconditionally loving parent, to take away your pain, to fill up your emptiness, to make up for the deficits from your past, you will create a love-based relationship.

TAKE RESPONSIBILITY FOR YOUR EMOTIONAL ISSUES

No one can "make you" feel worthless if you don't already feel worthless deep inside. No one can "make you" feel powerless if you don't already feel powerless. All your partner can do is "trigger" emotions that are already sitting inside of you. In other words, all your partner can do is throw a lighted match onto a pile of wood soaked in gasoline. (The gasoline-soaked wood is the equivalent of your unconscious buried emotions that are inside you.)

When you are in an intimate relationship, there will be many times when you find your self being "triggered" by your partner. Refrain from blaming your partner for making you feel unhappy; refrain from expecting your partner to make you feel happy. The truth is, your partner is not responsible for your feelings being there; your partner is not responsible for fixing them. You are! Thank your partner for bringing up for you memories and feelings of which you were unaware (unconscious), and do the emotional release work as outlined in Chapters Eleven and Twelve.

Take responsibility for making your self feel emotionally whole. Take responsibility for loving your self. Remember, it's your mom/dad who first caused you to feel angry. It's your mom/dad who first abandoned you; who didn't love you in the way you wanted to be loved; who neglected you; who humiliated you; who abused you; who treated you as an object of gratification; who forced you to do what you didn't want to do; who frightened you, who bullied you; who became overinvolved with you; who deprived you of your freedom and your rights; who betrayed your trust. It's your mom/dad who first caused you to feel enraged, afraid, ashamed, hurt, powerless, helpless, trapped, worthless, hopeless, empty, lonely and isolated. It's your mom and dad who first contributed to the creation of the hole in your soul that you are trying so desperately to fill. Your partner's behaviour or actions are simply reminding you of your own buried feelings and your own buried pain. When you release your feelings at the source, you will be able to enjoy your partner for the person s/he is as opposed to the person you need her/him to be.

However, always keep in mind that the purpose of identifying your parents as the source of your pain is not to have a convenient excuse for why you are unhappy, or why you cannot move forward in your life. Remember, your parents were as emotionally deprived as you were; they couldn't give you love because they had no love to give; they felt as empty as you do now. Thus, the purpose of surfacing your buried emotions, in relation to your parents, is to enable you to release your pain so that you can be free to create a happy, love-filled life.

FREE WILL STARTS HERE

We all needed love as infants and growing children, and we all need love as adults. If, in order to receive love, you had to push down your rage while you were being verbally humiliated, sexually assaulted or physically abused—you had no choice. You had to survive. If, in order to receive love, you had to deny your anger at being controlled or manipulated by your parents—you had no choice. You had to survive. If, in order to receive love, you had to pretend that the crumbs of affection you were receiving were good enough—you had no choice. You had to survive. If, in order to get your needs met, you had to compromise your integrity and self-respect—you had no choice. You had to survive.

Whatever you had to do to get to where you are right now, forgive your self—you had no choice. As a human being, you were born with the instinct to survive. You did what you had to do to survive. You had no choice before, but you have a choice now!

You can choose to free your self from the damage that has been done to you. You can choose to clear away all the garbage that you are buried under: all the negative messages, all the abusive experiences, all your buried fears, all your shame, all your rage, all your loneliness and sadness. You can choose to love your self.

In all likelihood you are probably throwing a little tantrum right now, feeling that it just isn't fair. It isn't fair that the joy in your life was taken away by your abusive, neglecting or overinvolved parents. It isn't fair that you are now left to pick up the pieces. It isn't fair that you have to work so hard to bring people and opportunity into your life, whereas others have it so easy. It isn't fair that you have to work so hard to change the way you operate because your current Operating Style is preventing you from bringing happiness into your life.

While it's certainly unfortunate that for many of you, your childhood was a living hell, there's no getting around it: THERE'S NO WAY YOU CAN CHANGE YOUR PAST. But, you can change your future. You really can! You have free will, and you were born with the power to create the life you want.

However, your life won't change by wishing or hoping for better days. Your life will change as you open your self up to the process of discovering how truly wonderful you are. And this is no exaggeration. If you go through the process of releasing your painful emotions from your past, you will be amazed to discover how much you like your self. Living your life will become a lot of fun. For the first time in your life, you will delight in being you.

YOU CAN CHOOSE HAPPINESS

At the present moment, you may find it difficult to believe that you have the power to create happiness—and for good reason. Up to this moment, all you may have known is suffering, pain and sadness. Up to this moment, surviving on a day-to-day basis may have been your only goal. And now you are being told that you have this incredible power to make all your dreams come true. "Oh sure," you think. "Easy for you to say."

The fact is, the blueprint of both your present and future life is within your total control. Whether consciously or unconsciously, you are bringing your beliefs into reality through your own actions. Your outer world directly reflects your inner world. It follows then that to change your outer world, you must first change your inner world. And changing your inner world is within your control.

No one wants to suffer through pain, but everyone wants to enjoy that pot of gold and the pleasures of having it all. You don't have to wait to hit that illusive jackpot—you can excavate your own gold mine and access your own riches any time you so desire. It all starts with freeing your self to make choices—choices based on your own free will.

You have a choice, right now. You can choose to spend the rest of your life either complaining about your bad luck or accepting that happiness is not within your reach, or you can choose to free your self from those painful emotions and beliefs that are interfering with your happiness.

By choosing to accept your emotional pain, your addictions, your unhappy romantic relationships, and/or your lack of prosperity, you are choosing to remain enslaved to those patterns and negative beliefs which resulted from your parents' inability to give you the love you deserved. Thus by default, you are choosing to live your life from an anger-based perspective, believing you need to fight in order to get your needs met, a sadness-based needy perspective, believing you need to please others in order to get your needs met, or a sadness-based strong/ distant perspective, believing that you need to appear perfect in order to get your needs met. Each of these Operating Styles is preventing you from appreciating how good you really are, and realizing: <u>You can enjoy everything you want just as soon as you start appreciating your own worth and loving your self. You can make your life a dream come true just as soon as you start being your own true self.</u>

By choosing to free your self, you are choosing to end your emotional slavery. You are choosing to exercise your free will. You are choosing to create happiness. You are choosing to love your self. You have choices. Choose wisely!

Andrea J. Moses

| POWERBASE
| PERFORMANCE
| GROUP

Andrea J. Moses received her Master of Social Work degree from the University of British Columbia. She practised as a psychotherapist for 16 years in the areas of family therapy, marriage counselling, group psychotherapy, and individual counselling. In 1990 she started Powerbase Performance Group, a company dedicated to enhancing the real performance of both corporations and individuals.

Corporate Programs

Andrea consults to corporations in the area of performance enhancement, helping organizations become conscious of their own barriers to superior achievement. She provides professional training seminars, as well as keynote speeches, on topics related to *Creating and Selling Value, Conflict Resolution, Knowing What Prevents You From Achieving Excellence.*

Therapeutic Workshops

Andrea consults to individuals on barriers to personal growth and happiness, focusing on increasing the conscious awareness of unresolved emotional issues. She leads the intensive therapeutic workshops, *Creating Happiness By Breaking Free From Your Past* and *Creating Love-Based Relationships.*

You can contact Andrea J. Moses for information on any of these programs and services:

Powerbase Performance Group
2 Bloor Street West #100
Toronto, Ontario
M4W 3E2
Telephone—416/481-0635

GIVE THE GIFT OF *CHOICES* TO
YOUR FRIENDS AND FAMILY MEMBERS

Send a signed copy of *Choices-Creating Happiness By Breaking Free From Your Past* to the people you care about. Help those around you open up their lives.

Please complete the order form and include a cheque or money order for $17.50 plus 7% GST for Canadian residents. Add $3.50 for mailing costs on each book ordered.

Name _____

Address _____

_____

Postal Code _____

Telephone _____

Number of Copies Required _____

Amount Enclosed _____

Send Your Orders To:

Powerbase Communications
2 Bloor Street West,
Suite 100,
Toronto, Ontario
M4W 3E2

sture I had noticed the first day, as if the
er. He was sweating a little, and his eyes
ed. I noticed that he didn't look at me,
ace turned away, as if self-conscious or
ondered if he were being hag-ridden by
'smoke', and looked away, embarrassed.
his Gardens are dying.'
they're meant to.'
She doesn't know I came back?'

xpect you'd tell her, it's all right. I just
he said anything more about my cousin.'
d.'
p, and to the point. Well, he owed me
my escape. And far from preventing that,
er to get rid of me as I was to get out. He
f the main gate with me, and right to the
lateau, and stood there to watch me start
h. When I reached the ford I looked back,
still there, watching as if to make sure I

my back on Dar Ibrahim for the second
d carefully out over the stepping-stones.
e clear now, and already dry, but the water
ound them was higher than the last time I
and still ran iron red, blood red for the
. Twigs, leaves, scarlet flowers, had been
the stream and strewed in debris on the
f the goats browsed desultorily among the
could see no sign of the boy. As I gained
f the stream and picked my way up the

II

So free from danger, free from fear,
They crossed the court: right glad they were.
S. T. Coleridge: *Christabel*

I THOUGHT I wouldn't have slept well, but I went out
like a light for the five hours or so until my breakfast
came, and woke to a glorious morning, and the sunlit
peace of the Seraglio garden with the ripple of water
where a light breeze touched it, and the singing-birds.

All the same, I remembered that I came back to
consciousness not of the romantic peace of the place,
but of the incipience of something cloudy, the faintest
shadow of apprehension colouring the day ahead.
Even when I realised that this was probably only the
result of Charles's hints about John Lethman, whom I
would have to meet again this morning, and the rest of
the day would be shared with Charles himself, I still
found that the Seraglio Court, the whole palace locked
in its hot valley afflicted me with a sort of claustro-
phobia, and I got up quickly and swallowed my coffee,
restlessly eager now to get out of the place and back to
the hotel and the life and colour and vulgar bustle of
Beirut. And to Charles.

Hamid had been told to come for me at half-past nine, but it was barely half-past eight when I finished the coffee that Nasirulla had brought me, lingered for a few minutes for a last look at the garden with the sun on the pavilion's golden dome, then let myself – by the orthodox route – out of the Seraglio.

My first apprehension had been removed by Nasirulla's appearance with my breakfast. If he were here, the river must be passable this morning. I decided to go immediately, and walk up to the village to meet Hamid there. I had tried to indicate to Nasirulla by signs that I wanted to leave early, and though he had merely stared at me in his unsmiling way without a hint of understanding, he must have told John Lethman, for I met the latter coming to meet me in the second courtyard, where the anemones of the Adonis Gardens had already, in the one day's heat, withered and died.

I thought he looked the worse for wear this morning, and wondered if the same could be said of me.

'You're up early,' he said.

'I suppose I must have been worrying about the ford. I gather it's all right and I'll be able to get across?'

'Oh, yes. Did you sleep all right in the end after the alarums and excursions?'

'After the—? Oh the dogs. Yes, thanks. Did you shut the poor things up? I admit I was a bit scared at first, but they were rather pets, and it's just another romantic episode to think about later on. But they're not like that with everybody, are they?'

'By no means. You must have something special.' A smile that didn't reach his eyes. 'I wouldn't say they're

ever exactly sava
simply because th
anything out of th
may have been a

I didn't want to
he expected it, an
tion. At least the p
order, I asked: 'W

'I should have le
gate open. Anyone

'The side gate?

'There's one ope
What with that, a
aglio, Jassim seems
day.'

I said, as casua
break in? You don'
thing?'

'Oh, no. It's just
mine, particularly s
What time's your

'Nine,' I said, ly
take myself straight
the village. You've
me for so long. I kn
you can take it tod

'It's been a pleas

He didn't even try
Yesterday's calm
harassed and edgy.
court with quick, ne

face in that g
skin was tenc
looked inflan
but kept his
ashamed. I w
the need for

'Your Adc

'Yes, well,

'Of course

'No.'

'I didn't e
wondered if

'Not a wo
Short, sha
nothing but
he was as ea
walked out c
edge of the p
down the pa
and saw him
really went.

I turned
time, and tr

These we
that swirled
had crossed
dead Adoni
rushed dow
banks. Two
jetsam, but
the far side

stony bank I saw Hamid – this time unmistakably Hamid – coming down the path towards me.

We met in the shade of a fig tree where three more of the goats were sleeping in a dusty heap. When our greetings were over I asked him the question that had been simmering on the surface of my mind ever since Nasirulla had brought me my coffee.

'Have you seen my cousin this morning?'

'No.' He smiled. 'He is very like you, that one, is he not? I should have thought brother and sister.'

'We were always taken for twins. You didn't meet a white sports car on your way up from Beirut? Or see one parked?'

'This morning? I saw nothing on the road at all except one car – a black one with an Arab driver – and a Land-Rover with three Maronite fathers.' He eyed me curiously. 'I know your cousin's car, I saw it yesterday. You mean he has also been for the night at the palace?'

I nodded. 'This means he probably got away all right before he was seen. That's a relief . . . Hamid, you mustn't tell anyone, promise. Actually, my great-aunt doesn't even know he was there. She did see me on Sunday night – I'll tell you about it later – but she said she wouldn't receive my cousin Charles, and he needn't bother to come up to Dar Ibrahim. Well, you know how he drove up yesterday morning from Damascus, and came up to meet me, but the stream was flooded, so I had to stay another night anyway. It was partly because of that, that my cousin hatched up a plan to get inside the palace and take a look round for himself.' I went on to tell him rapidly the main facts: the meeting at the temple and the plans for the 'break-in'. 'So I let him in and we explored a bit. We didn't see my great-aunt again, and my cousin didn't think it right to force himself on her like that, so I went back to bed and he went to let himself out by the back entrance. I was just hoping he'd got his car away before anyone saw it.'

'I certainly didn't see it.' Hamid, though obviously intrigued by my story, contented himself with reassuring me. 'It's a Porsche, isn't it? I don't think you need worry. I know the quarry you mean, and I think I'd have noticed if the car was still there when I came by.'

We had been climbing as we talked. Now I saw what I had been looking for, a patch of shadow under a tree thirty feet away, where half a dozen goats stood or lay, chewing and eyeing us with supercilious boredom. Among them the faun, shock-headed, grinning, squatted cross-legged in the dust and chewed a leaf with the same kind of disenchanted thoroughness as the goats.

'There you are!' I said.

'I am always here.' It was said with a sort of cosmic simplicity that one could readily believe.

'It's all right,' I said to Hamid, who had looked slightly startled. 'It's only the goat-herd.'

'I never saw him.' He regarded the boy doubtfully. 'If he saw your cousin, Miss Mansel, the whole village will know by now that he spent the night at Dar Ibrahim.'

'I don't think so, I've a feeling this boy isn't exactly

an idle gossip. In any case if Nasirulla had known, you can bet Mr. Lethman would have had something to say this morning.' I called to the faun. 'Ahmad, did you see the Englishman leave Dar Ibrahim this morning?'

'Yes.'

'At what time?'

'Just after daylight.'

'About four o'clock, that would be,' said Hamid.

'He must have stayed on for a bit after we parted, then. I wonder what for? However . . .' I turned back to the boy. 'He went up this way to the village?'

'Yes. He went to get the white car which was in the quarry by the road.'

Hamid's eyes met mine. I laughed, and he shrugged, turning down his mouth.

'You heard him go?' I asked, and the boy nodded briefly, and waved a hand towards Beirut.

I was surprised at my own feeling of relief. 'Did he speak to you?'

'No. I was over there.' A jerk of the head seemed to indicate some inaccessible tumble of rocks a quarter of a mile away. 'He came from the gate at the back of the palace.'

There was no curiosity in his voice, but he was watching me intently. I regarded him thoughtfully. 'And this was very early? Before anyone else was about?'

A nod.

'No one else saw him?'

'No one, only me.'

'And I am sure that you have already forgotten that you saw him, Ahmad? Or that there was a car?'

A brief flash of the white teeth, clenched on the chewed green leaf. 'I have forgotten everything.'

I fished some notes out of my handbag, but though the black eyes watched me unwaveringly, the boy made no move. I hesitated, I had no wish to offend his dignity. I laid the notes on the rock beside me, and put a stone on them to hold them down, 'Thank you very much,' I said. 'May Allah be with you.'

Before I had got more than two steps away there was a flash of brown limbs and a swirl of dust, and the notes had disappeared into the dirty kaftan. Dignity, it seemed, took second place to common sense. 'The goats would eat it,' explained the boy carefully, and then, in a rush of Arabic which Hamid laughingly translated for me as we moved off up the path: 'And the blessing of Allah be upon you and your children and your children's children and upon your children's children's children and upon all the increase of your house . . .'

It was strange to find the hotel looking the same: I seemed to have been away for ever, like Sleeping Beauty, in a story-book world. It was even the same desk clerk on duty, and he smiled and lifted a hand and said something, but I said, 'Later, please,' and went straight past him to the lift with only two thoughts in my mind, to get out of these clothes and into a gorgeous hot bath before I spoke to a single soul, or even thought once about Charles.

It was heaven to be back in my airy, modern, characterless and superbly comfortable room, throw my horrible clothes on the bathroom floor and climb into the bath. The telephone rang twice while I was there, and once there was a knock at the outer door of the lobby, but I ignored the calls without effort, broiled myself happily for a dangerously long time in a concentrated solution of bath oils, then climbed languidly out, dried myself, and dressed carefully in the coolest frock I had – white and yellow and about as far-out as a daisy – then rang down for coffee, and put a call through to my cousin.

But here at last the desk clerk caught up with me, slightly aggrieved and perhaps in consequence just a little pleased that he could disappoint me. Mr Mansel was not there. Yes, he certainly had suite fifty, but he was not in the hotel. The clerk had tried to tell me; he had tried to give me Mr Mansel's letter, but I hadn't waited . . . Then he had telephoned twice, but had not been answered. A letter? Yes, Mr Mansel had left me a letter, he had left it this morning, to be delivered to me as soon as I arrived . . . Yes, of course, Miss Mansel, it had already been sent up to my room; when I had not answered the telephone, he himself had sent a page up with the letter. I hadn't answered the door, either, so the boy had pushed the letter underneath it . . .

It was lying out in the lobby, white on the blue carpet, startling as an alarm signal. I pounced on it and carried it back to the light.

I'm not sure what I had expected. Even after last night I couldn't see the situation *vis-à-vis* Great-Aunt Harriet as anything more than highly bizarre, but my disappointment at not seeing my cousin straight away

was such that I tore open the envelope in a fury of
irritation, and eyed the letter as if I expected it to be an
anonymous obscenity, or at least a forgery.

But it was, unmistakably, my cousin's hand. And
unequivocally ordinary, unexciting and infuriating. It
said:

Dear Coz,

I'm fearfully sorry about this, as there's nothing
I'd have liked better than to forgather this
morning once you'd got out of purdah, and hear
all about it. Am particularly interested to know if
J. L. let you see Aunt H again. Was nearly caught
just after I left you. Aunt H came down the
underground corridor with the girl, just as I was
letting myself out at the foot of the spiral stair. I
dodged back in time, but managed to get a
glimpse of her. As you say, a weirdie nowadays,
but she seemed active enough and was talking
nineteen to the dozen to the girl. I was very
tempted to pop out and have a word then and
there, but it might have scared the daylights out
of them, so I stayed where I was till they went in
through the Princes's door, then I let myself out.
No trouble. Picked up the car and got down here
without seeing a soul. Didn't want to walk into
the hotel at crack of dawn, so had breakfast at a
café and rang Aleppo to see if I could catch
Ben's father. Was told he'd left for Homs and is
due home today.

This is where you're going to be blazing mad

at me, especially after all my dark hints last night.
I may have been wrong about that – something I
heard her say to Halide explained quite a bit to
me. Tell you when I see you. But there's still a
bit of a problem, and the only person I can take
it to usefully is Ben's father, and I gather he'll be
leaving home again for Medina almost straight
away. So I've gone down to Damascus to catch
him. Sorry about this, I know you'll be mad at
me, but bear up, I'll be back as soon as I can,
tomorrow, possibly, or Thursday morning. Wait
for me till then, and sharpen your claws. But
don't, please don't do anything else, there's a
maiden – except extend your booking, and when
I get back we'll have fun. And I think – if my
idea works out – that I'll get to see Aunt H after
all.

Love and one kiss
C.

I read the letter twice, decided that my claws would do
perfectly well as they were, and Charles was lucky he
was half-way to Damascus right now, then poured out
my coffee, and sat down and reached for the telephone.
One was, of course, completely independent, and had
run one's own affairs for years. One was twenty-two,
and came of a family that declared itself indifferent.
One certainly didn't need help or advice, and one
didn't particularly like Great-Aunt Harriet . . .

But it would be very nice to tell Daddy all about it.
Just for a laugh, of course. I put a call through to

Christopher Mansel at Mansels of London, and then sat down to wait for it, drinking coffee and pretending to read Hachette's *Moyen-Orient* and watching the unchanging blue of the sky above the concrete sky-scrapers of the changing East.

Daddy's advice was short and to the point. 'Wait for Charles.'

'But, Daddy—'

'Well, what did you want to do?'

'I don't know. It's not that, I suppose, it's just that I'm furious with him; he *might* have waited for me! It's so exactly like him to play it the selfish way.'

'Certainly,' said my father. 'But if he was anxious to catch Ben's father he couldn't afford to wait for you, could he?'

'But why should he be? What's with Ben's father? I'd have thought if he wanted a useful contact he could get hold of some of our people in Beirut.'

There was a short pause. 'I've no doubt he has his reasons,' said my father. 'Do you know if he has actually made any contacts there yet?'

'Not unless he did some quick telephoning this morning. I suppose he could have talked to someone yesterday after his first trip to see me, but he never mentioned it.'

'I see.'

'Shall I get in touch with our people?'

'If you want to . . . But I'd leave family matters to Charles for the moment, I think.'

'Well, all right,' I said. 'For one thing, I haven't a clue

why he's gone rushing off like this, specially if his "dark hints" last night haven't come to anything.'

'Did you tell me all he'd said in his letter?'

'Yes.'

'Then I'd have said the sensible thing was to stop thinking about it. The boy seems to know what he's about, and he's certainly quite clear on one point.'

'Meaning?'

'Meaning, my child, don't go doing anything fat-headed just because Charles is getting on your wick,' said my parent frankly, 'Forget him, and get on with your sight-seeing, and telephone him tonight to find out what he's up to. Don't dream of going up to the palace again without him . . . Christy?'

'I'm still here.'

'Did you get that?'

I said: 'I got it. Blast you, Daddy, men are all the same, you're still in the Stone Age. I can look after myself perfectly well and you know it. In any case, what's *wrong*? Why shouldn't I go up again if I want to?'

'Do you want to?'

'Well, no.'

'Then try not to be more of an idiot than Nature made you,' said my father crisply. 'How are you for money?'

'Okay, thanks. But, Daddy, you don't really think—?'

The operator intervened, in that smooth mechanical voice. 'You time is up. Do you wish an extension?'

'Yes,' I said promptly.

'No,' said my father, across me. 'Now go and enjoy

yourself, my child, and wait for your cousin. Nothing's wrong as far as I can see, but I'd rather you were with Charles, that's all. He's got a lot of sense.'

'I thought he was spoiled rotten and lived for nothing but pleasure.'

'If that doesn't show sense I don't know what does.'

'And don't I?'

'Lord, no, you take after your mother,' said my father.

'Well, thank goodness for that,' I said acidly, and he laughed and rang off.

For some absurd reason relieved and immensely cheered, I put my own receiver down and turned to the serious business of doing my face and hair and thinking about lunch.

I had planned originally to see Beirut at leisure and alone, and it was indeed idiotic to be annoyed that I had been left alone to do so. In any case there was nothing else to do with the afternoon. I went out to explore.

The Beirut souks are dirty and crowded and about as dramatic as Woolworth's. Though my recent sojourn at Dar Ibrahim, and a lot that I had read about Beirut, had conditioned me to expect romance and excitement here, I have to report that nothing whatever happened except that I trod on a pile of rotten fish and ruined a sandal for good, and when I asked the name of some exotic blue powder in a sack, expecting it to be hashish or crude opium to say the least, I was told it was Omo. The Soul of the Goldsmiths was best and I fell heavily for a necklace of huge turquoises, and almost decided to start a bank account like Halide's – so lovely, and so cheap, were the thin gold bracelets tinkling and glittering in their hundreds along the rods that spanned the windows. But I resisted them, and eventually found myself emerging from the souk into Martyr's Square with nothing to show for the afternoon but a tube of hand cream and a gold-mounted turquoise bead that I had bought as a charm for Charles's Porsche before I remembered that I was furious with him and the sooner the Evil Eye got him the better I'd be pleased, and that if I never heard from him again it would not be a moment too soon.

It was dusk now, soon to be dark. Perhaps he had arrived in Damascus. Perhaps he had already telephoned . . . I got into one of the service taxis, and soon was set down within a few yards of my hotel.

The first person I saw was Hamid, leaning gracefully against the counter talking to the desk clerk. It was a different clerk this time, but Hamid smiled across the foyer at me and said something to the man, and before I had crossed to the desk the clerk had checked my pigeon-hole and was shaking his head. No messages.

I suppose my face must have given me away, for Hamid asked quickly: 'Were you expecting something important?'

'Only my cousin. I haven't seen him since last night.'

'Oh? He wasn't here when we got back this morning?'

'He'd already left for Damascus,' I said.

'For Damascus?'

I nodded. 'There was a letter waiting for me when I

checked back in this morning. He'd had to go early. I
thought he might have been there by now, and phoned
me . . . Yes?'

This to the clerk, who had been attending to some
query from a sad-faced Arab gentleman in a red
tarboosh, and who was now claiming my attention.

'I'm sorry, Miss Mansel, I heard what you were
saying, and I wonder if perhaps there has been a
mistake. There was a call from Damascus earlier. I
understood it was for Mr Mansel, but it might have
been "Miss Mansel".' He spread his hands. 'I am so
sorry.'

'Oh. Well, even if it was for me,' I said reasonably,
'I'd have missed it. I've only just come in. What time
was this?'

'Not long ago, perhaps an hour. I had just come on
duty.'

'I see. Well, thanks very much, that may have been
the one. Don't worry, it's not important – and if it is
he'll call again. I suppose he didn't leave a number?'

'I don't think so, but I can check.'

He reached a chit down from Charles's pigeon-hole
and handed it to me. It said merely that a call had
been made from Damascus at 5.05. No name. No
number.

I handed it back. 'Well, I shan't be going out of the
hotel again tonight, so if he does call again, you'll have
me paged, won't you?'

'Of course. I'll tell the switchboard right away.' He
picked up the telephone and began to talk into it in
Arabic.

'If you knew where he was staying,' said Hamid, 'you could ring him up yourself, now.'

'That's just it, I'm afraid I don't. He's gone to see a friend, and it's only just occurred to me, I've forgotten the surname completely – can't even remember if I ever heard it, but I suppose I must have done. I've even visited the house, but haven't a clue what the address is.' I laughed. 'I could find out easily enough if I rang around a bit . . . they've connections in Beirut, and there's a brother-in-law who's something in the Cabinet – Minister of the Interior, whatever that may be.'

'Among other things, the police,' said Hamid cheerfully, 'Which should make him very easy to trace. Do you wish me to ask—?'

'No, no, don't bother, really. I'd much rather not disturb them. My cousin will ring again.'

'Is he coming back to Beirut?'

'On Wednesday or Thursday, he wasn't sure.'

'Miss Mansel.' It was the clerk. 'Here is some luck. The call came again while I was talking to the switchboard. It is for Mr Mansel, but when the caller heard he was not here, he asked for you. He is on the line now.'

'Then it's not my cousin? All right, where do I take it?'

'In the booth just there, if you please.'

The booth was one of those open stalls which are supposed to be sound-proof if you lean far enough forward into them, but which in fact broadcast just about as well as the Whispering Gallery of St Paul's. Just beside it, two Englishwomen were discussing the

ruins of Byblos, a group of Americans were talking
about food, and a French youth twiddled the knobs of
a transistor, and in the booth next to mine the sad-
faced Arab was apparently failing in sullen Arabic to
get the connection he wanted. I put a hand over my
free ear, and tried to get on with it.

It was Ben who was on the line, and in the general
hubbub it was some time before we could sort ourselves out, and then he was decisive and a little surprised.

'Charles? Here? Not yet, at any rate. What time did
he leave?'

'I've no idea, but early. He didn't telephone?'

'No. Not that it won't be very nice to see him again.
He couldn't have waited and brought you along with
him?'

'It would have been lovely, but I gather there was
something fairly urgent he wanted to talk to your
father about, and he wanted to be sure of catching
him.'

'That's what I was calling him about. My father's
due home tomorrow from Homs. We expect him for
dinner. I promised I'd let Charles know.'

I said puzzled: 'But he said, he definitely said . . .
Oh, well, he must have got it wrong.'

'What's that?'

'Nothing, I'm sorry, I'm in the foyer of the hotel, and
there's a frightful row going on just behind me here. It's
just that Charles seems to have got his days mixed – he
thinks your father's due home today. Then he could
have waited, after all, instead of walking out on me!

Look, I wonder – I'm sorry to bother you, but could you please ask him to ring when he does arrive?'

'Of course I'll tell him. You're not worried, are you?'

'Not a bit,' I said, 'only mad as fire.'

He laughed. 'Well, look, I've had an idea. I've been longing to meet you myself, and I know my father would like to, so why don't you come down and join Charles here anyway – join the conference, whatever it is? Stay two or three days and I'll show you Damascus myself, and if Charles never does turn up, so much the better. How about that?'

'It sounds very tempting.'

'Well, why not? Temptation's no use if it's resistible. Do come. Have you got a car?'

'I – no I haven't. I've been using a hired one . . .' I hesitated. 'Do you know,' I added slowly, 'I think I'd like to, very much. If you're sure . . . ?'

'Of course I'm sure.' He certainly sounded it, he sounded warmly welcoming. 'It would be lovely to have you. I was sorry I missed you before, and I know my father will be pleased. That's settled, then! We'll expect you. Did you get to see the Lady of the Lebanon?'

'The –? Oh, I forgot you knew about that. Yes, I did, but Charles didn't. To tell you the truth, he's a bit needled about it, and there are one or two complications and I gather that's what he wants to talk to your father about. He's making a bit of a mystery about it all. We had quite a turn-up there, Charles and I, but I'd better not tell you over the telephone.'

'You intrigue me. I hope you don't mean there was trouble?'

'Oh, no, but he seemed to think there was something a bit off-key. He got all mysterious about it, and now he's belted off without telling me a word, and that's why I'm so mad with him.'

He laughed. 'I'll warn him.'

'As if he'd care!'

'Well, we'll get it out of him between us. I'd certainly like to hear all about Dar Ibrahim! Then I'll see you tomorrow? Have you got the address?'

'Lord, no, I haven't! What must you think of me? Half a minute. I've got a pencil here, if you could spell it out . . . ? Mr Who? Thank you . . . And the telephone number, just in case? Yes, I've got it. I'll read it back, shall I? . . . Okay? Fine, my driver will find it. It's really marvellous of you, I shall love it. Does it matter what time I arrive?'

'Not a bit. We'll look forward to seeing you, and we'll show you the real Damascus this time.'

The line – roaring and crackling and certainly bugged at the frontier – went dead. Behind me, the English ladies had switched to the ruins of Krak des Chevaliers, the Americans were still talking about food, and the Arab in the next booth, clinging to his receiver, regarded me with sour envy. I looked at him sympathetically, and emerged from my booth.

Hamid was still at the desk. The clerk looked up. 'It was not the right call?'

'In a way it was. It was the people my cousin was going to see in Damascus. They say he isn't there yet. He may ring later when he does arrive.'

'I'll have you called,' he promised.

'Thank you,' I turned to Hamid. 'Are you booked for tomorrow?'

'Not yet. You want me?'

'Will you take me to Damascus, please? I'm going to see them myself. The name's Sifara, and there's the address. You'll be able to find it?'

'Certainly.'

'I won't be coming back the same day, but of course I'll pay you for the return trip.'

'You have already paid me for a lot I haven't done. No, don't trouble yourself, I'll arrange to bring back another one-way fare from Damascus to Beirut. It's a perfectly normal arrangement and we do it every week. What hour shall I call for you in the morning?'

'Ten, please.'

'And if the cousin rings?'

'Let him ring,' I said. 'We still go to Damascus.'

But there was no telephone call from Charles that night.

12

But shall be overtaken unaware

E. Fitzgerald: *The Rubáiyát*
of Omar *Khayyám*

AND no telephone call in the morning.

Three times I picked up the paper where I had
scribbled the number, and three times put a hand to
the receiver. And three times dropped it. If he wanted
to ring me, he would ring me. If he didn't, then I
certainly wasn't going to bother him. The days of
trailing after my cousin Charles were over, but definitely over.

Besides, I was going to Damascus anyway.

I left the silent telephone and went down to the foyer.

The morning was hot and cloudless. The familiar
big car slid to the door at ten, and I slipped into the seat
beside the driver. Hamid, immaculate as usual in his
whiter-than-white shirt, gave me a cheerful greeting
and swung the car away from the kerb and up through
the traffic of Bab-Edriss and the narrow streets behind
the Great Mosque, to gain the long curve of the Route
de Damas and climb away from the coast and through
the summer gardens of the rich to the foothills of the

Lebanon. Just beyond Bar Elias the road divides, north for Baalbek, and south-east for the junction whose left fork takes you to Wadi el Harrir and the pass between Mount Hermon and the Djebel Ech Sheikh Mandour where the frontier lies.

I had crossed this frontier before in the reverse direction, travelling from Damascus to Beirut with the group, so I was prepared for the long wait, the crawl from point to point, the four tedious halts and the frenzy of suspicion that the almost domestic frontiers of the Arab countries demand. We were fourth in line at the Lebanese side, but two hundred yards away, across no-man's land, I could see quite a queue of north-bound vehicles, including a bus, waiting in the hot dust to be free of the Syrian border.

Hamid took the car's papers and my passport, and vanished into the concrete hutments which did duty as a frontier post. Time passed, crawling. The first car went through the barrier, stopped again for the car-check and the bribe to the gatekeeper, and crept across to repeat the performance on the other side. Fifteen minutes later the second car followed it. Only one in front of us now.

It was hot in the stationary car. I got out and climbed the roadside bank and found a boulder slightly less dusty than the rest, where I sat down. The hotel had provided a picnic, and I sat munching a sandwich, till I met the eyes of a thin dog which had crept to the edge of the road below me and was eyeing me wistfully, just out of stick distance. I held out the remains of the sandwich. He looked at it with his soul in his eyes, and came no nearer. I made to throw it down to him, but at the first movement of my hand he flinched violently away. I got up slowly, took two steps down to the road, leaned over and placed the bread and meat carefully in the dust, then retreated the few paces back towards the car. Watching me, the dog inched forward, every bone eloquent through his dirty skin, and took the food. The faintest movement of his tail thanked me.

'Was it nice?' I said gently, through my anger, and the dog's eyes rolled up whitely to me as the tail wagged again. It was so closely clamped to his body that only the tip of it moved, and I suspected it was the first time he had wagged it for years. The next sandwich, I saw, was chicken, a fresh roll full of luscious meat. I put it in the dust. He snatched it, more confidently this time, but even in the act of bolting it, turned and fled. I looked round. Hamid had left the frontier building and was approaching the car.

I had my door half open when I saw he was shaking his head. 'I'm afraid there's something wrong. They say we cannot pass.'

'Can't pass? Why on earth not?'

'Apparently your passport is not in order.'

'But that's nonsense! Of course it's in order! What's supposed to be wrong with it?'

He was apologetic and unhappy. 'There's no entry visa for the Lebanon . . . in fact he says that there isn't an exit from Syria, so you're not officially in the country at all, and he can't give you an exit now.'

I stared. I hadn't quite taken it in yet. 'Not officially

in the – well, how the blazes does he think I got here? Tunnelled?'

'I don't think he's worked that out. He realises there's some mistake, of course, but he can't do much about it here and now.'

I said angrily: 'Well, isn't that nice? Have you got the passport there? May I see? Damn it, I came through this very frontier on Friday, there *must* be a stamp . . . Hamid, why do you have such a terrible alphabet? Have you looked through this yourself?'

'Yes, I did, and I'm afraid he's right, Miss Mansel. There isn't a stamp.'

There weren't all that many stamps in my passport, so my hasty search didn't take long, and it did, indeed, seem as if he was right. I looked up, not prepared to admit even yet that the mistake, whatever it was, could actually prevent me from going to Damascus. 'But I tell you, I came through here on Friday. They must have stamped it then, surely? If they didn't stamp it, it's their mistake. I certainly handed the passport over, and they let me through . . . Did you tell the man I'd been through here on Friday?'

'I told him you'd come from Damascus recently. I was not sure which day.'

'I came with the group, five cars – twenty-two people and an English courier. It was Friday at about midday. If it's the same man on duty, he may remember passing us all through, and anyway, they'll have records, won't they? And the courier had a list; it would have my name on it. Would you please go back and tell him this?'

'Certainly I'll tell him. But you know, I think this

may be the trouble; if you came through with a group your name was no doubt on the group passport – the "list" your courier showed. They do not always stamp the individual passports of these groups unless you ask them specially. You did not ask them for a stamp, no?'

'Of course I didn't, I never thought of it. I suppose our courier should have realised – he knew I was supposed to be staying on in Lebanon . . . But look, Hamid, this is nonsense! They surely must *know* I couldn't be here illegally! Surely they know you and your car? You must come this way often.'

'Every week. Oh, yes, they know me . . . I can pass, and my car; our papers are in order. But not you, I'm afraid. The rules are very strict.'

Another car, it seemed mockingly, revved up and moved off through the barrier. From the other side the bus arrived, shaking and roaring and churning up dust, I moved back out of the cloud to the road's edge. People were staring, but not much interested. This must happen every day. The rules, as Hamid had said, were very strict.

I said angrily: 'It seems so stupid! It's like having this hooha between England and Scotland. It seems to me these days that the smaller the country the more silly fuss it makes . . . I'm sorry, Hamid, I didn't mean to be rude. It's just so *infuriating* . . . and it's beastly hot. I'm sorry.'

'You're welcome,' said Hamid, meaning it generously. His look was troubled and sympathetic. 'But he will be coming back tomorrow, no?'

'Who will?'

'The cousin.'

'I wasn't even thinking about the cousin,' I snapped. But I was of course, and Hamid had known I was before I did. I felt somehow vulnerable, a feeling which was new to me, and entirely unpleasant.

He was saying gently: 'I know these frontiers are annoying to foreigners, but we have problems here, I'm afraid, big problems. Among other things a good deal of smuggling goes on . . . Do not mistake me, I do not say that anyone thinks you are taking part in this, but the rules have to be made and kept, and unhappily you have fallen wrong of them.'

'Foul.'

'Pardon?'

'I have fallen foul of them. Fallen wrong means something different. Smuggling? What sort of smuggling, for pity's sake? Do we look as if we were loaded down with guns or brandy or whatever?'

'Not brandy, no, not here. But you could easily be carrying drugs.'

I raised my eyebrows. 'Drugs? I suppose I could. I was forgetting where I was. One of my cousin's books called it "the hashish run".'

He laughed. 'Is that the phrase? Yes, I'm afraid that Beirut has – shall we say it has certain reputations? And it isn't only hashish, I'm afraid – there's still opium grown in Turkey and Iran, and smuggled through to the sea. I told you the controls were tight now, and getting tighter. The National Assembly of the UAR has been making representations to the Governments

and the penalties are being made more severe, and as
you see, things are a little fierce at the frontiers.'

'I can see they have to be, I suppose. But surely they
needn't bother tourists about this?'

'A few tourists have even been guilty. Quite recently
two English students were arrested, and found guilty.
Didn't you see it in the papers?'

I shook my head. 'What happened to them? What's
the penalty?'

'For them, imprisonment. They're still in Beirut. It
used to be only about three years, but now it's a long
term of hard labour. For a Lebanese national, besides
the sentence, it would mean being deprived of his civil
rights and registered in the police files as a trafficker – is
that the word? – in drugs. And in other countries,
much worse penalties. In Turkey, for instance, the
penalty is death – and in Egypt now, and I think also in
Iran. You see how seriously it is taken.'

'But I thought you said the other day that it wasn't
taken seriously in the Middle East? At least, you
implied that nobody thought it very wrong to smoke
hashish.'

'Whenever a Government takes anything seriously
you will find that it is not a moral problem but an
economic one,' said Hamid cynically. 'In Egypt, for
instance, the problem is very serious – your addict is
pretty useless as a worker, you know – and the Government has been getting badly worried about its illegal
imports from the Lebanon, so it makes representations
to the National Assembly, and unhappily at present we
all have to take a lot of notice of what Egypt thinks and

wants.' He smiled. 'So you see why things are difficult? They are also, I may say, difficult for the Customs men. Do you see the bus?'

This had, mercifully, switched off its engine, and was immobilised at the Lebanese barrier. The passengers had alighted, and were standing about while their papers were checked. They all had the fatalistic air of people prepared to wait about all day, and one could see why, for on top of the bus, piled up like a refugee's cart or a poor man's removal van, were what looked like the household goods of every person on board. There even seemed to be overstuffed armchairs and mattresses, along with rugs, bundles of clothing, filthy canvas bags which had once been labelled Air France or BOAC, and a wicker cage full of unhappy-looking hens.

'They have to search all that,' explained Hamid.

'For a few packets of powder?' I exclaimed. 'Not really?'

He laughed. 'But yes. Sometimes more than a few packets. And there are hundreds of ways in which the hashish can be disguised and carried. Only last week a man was stopped, a cobbler he called himself, and with his cobbler's kit there was a large suitcase full of leather soles for shoes. But they were hashish, powdered very finely, and then stamped into this shape. Sometimes it looks like gum, or ham, or sheeps' droppings.'

'Well,' I said, 'I imagine that anyone caught carrying a suitcase full of sheeps' droppings through a frontier ought to be locked up anyway.'

'That is very true,' said Hamid gravely. 'Well, if you

like I will go and explain about the group passport. Will you wait here?'

'I'll come in with you if you don't mind, and talk to them myself. Does anyone speak English in there?'

'I doubt it, but I will translate for you.'

The room inside the hut was small and stiflingly hot, and rather too full of stout olive-coloured men all talking at once. The talk broke off as I went in with Hamid, and the uniformed man – stout and olive-coloured – behind the office counter raised his eyes despairingly and shook his head. I explained, and Hamid translated, and the official listened as well as he could, while other cars piled up outside and the drivers shoved their way to the counter with their dog-eared papers, and the flies droned in the heat, and the smell of sweat and ink and Turkish tobacco was almost visible in the air.

But it was no use. The official was civil but firm. He nodded understandingly when I explained, he even commiserated with me, but that was as far as he would go. And the matter was clear. There was no entry stamp; how then could he affix an exit? He was sorry, but it was not possible; he had his orders. He was very sorry, but a rule was a rule.

It was obvious enough that he wasn't being obstructive, and he had been patiently civil in the face of considerable odds. I gave up at last, before my own temper frayed in the sticky heat, thanked him, and fought my way back out of the shed.

After the sweaty crowded room the hot air outside seemed almost fresh. I walked over to the car, wondering crossly what to do now. Go back, of course, that was obligatory; all I could do was salvage the day somehow and get Hamid to take me somewhere for a run. Baalbek, I supposed . . . I had seen Baalbek already, with the group, but it had been a crowded sort of day; perhaps if we went up the Bk'aa valley, taking it slowly, saw Baalbek again, then went back into Beirut by the road through the mountains . . . I could telephone Ben when I got back, there was no hurry for that, and tell him what had happened. It was disappointing, even infuriating, but it really didn't matter.

But by the pricking of my thumbs, it did.

I met Hamid's eye. I said suddenly, abruptly: 'I know I'll probably be seeing him tomorrow, but I wanted to see him today, now, as soon as possible. I can't explain . . . Hamid, my cousin isn't just an ordinary cousin, we're almost twins. I know there's an awful lot of guff talked about twins, but there can be something a little bit odd about it. One tends to be rather – well, close. All I know is, I want to see Charles, today. I want to hear what he has to tell me. And I want to be with him. Oh, not in the sense you might think, not in any sense I can explain, but . . .' I lifted my shoulders, and spread my hands in a very un-English gesture, but one which must have been as familiar as every day to the Arab.

He said quickly: 'You mean you think he is in trouble?'

'Oh, no, no, nothing like that. How could he be? I told you I couldn't explain. Well, if we can't get through, we can't get through, and there's not much

point in staying here talking about it, is there? We'll just
have to go back, and I'll ring up Damascus when I get
to the hotel again. Thanks for being so patient with me,
Hamid – it's terribly good of you to take such a lot of
trouble for me. Oh Lord, wait a minute . . . I forgot!
Did you fix up a return job in Damascus? What'll
happen if you can't get there in time to pick them up?'

'It doesn't matter. I wasn't due to come back until
tomorrow in any case. I can telephone and someone
else can do it.' He opened the car door for me. 'Don't
give it a thought, today is yours. Where else can I take
you? You've seen Baalbek?'

I hesitated. 'I suppose it's too late in the day to start
now for Homs?'

'Not really, but there's a frontier there, too.'

'Hell's teeth, I suppose there is. We're nicely stuck,
aren't we? Well, if you're sure it's all right about your
Damascus job, I certainly wouldn't mind seeing Baalbek again on my own, with time to spare.' But in the act
of getting into the car another thought struck me, and I
paused. 'You know, I really think we'll have to call it a
day and go back to Beirut. I've just thought – what's
going to happen when I want to leave the country for
London? Will I have to get a new visa, or go to the
Consul and make inquiries about this wretched exit
stamp, or something? If there are going to be difficulties, it might take time. I'd better do it straight away.'

'I think you're right, but I don't think it will concern
your Consul, I think we'll have to go and see the Chef
de Sûreté in Beirut and get another visa. If you'll wait a
moment longer I'll go back and ask the official here

what we should do. And who knows, it may not take so very long. We might even be able to come back and get through to Damascus by night-fall.'

Even I was not expecting the surge of pleasure and relief that this gave me. I smiled at him. 'Oh, yes, that would be marvellous, and you could do your return job, too! Thanks a million, Hamid, you're very good!'

'For a smile like that,' said Hamid, 'I would be prepared to be very bad. The cousin is lucky.'

And he disappeared into the buildings.

The car was like an oven, so I waited outside in the road. The bus – it was labelled Baalbek – had been unloaded, and the dirty baggage was lying in the dust and being prodded over by sweaty, sullen-looking men. People hung around, staring, smoking, spitting. One or two youths lounged nearer, eyeing me.

I glanced across at the office buildings. Through the open door I could see the shoving, vociferous crowd round the counter. Hamid might be some time, I left the car and climbed the bank again above the road.

This time I went higher, out of the dust and the petrol fumes, but still keeping the car in sight and directly below me. The road here was in a shallow cutting, and almost immediately as I climbed I found myself in cooler air and treading on grass and flowers.

There wasn't the profusion of flowers that I had seen along the Afka road, but the hillside was green enough, with sparse grass moving in the breeze, and the grey whorls of thistles, and drifts of some small white flowers that looked from the distance like frost. Over this in violent contrast, blinding over grey stone, went the blazing, cascading gold of the broom; and everywhere, thrusting up boldly from the hoar-frost veils of the white flowers, were hollyhocks – the simple familiar hollyhock of the English cottage garden, red and yellow and white, crowding wild among the rocks of a mountainside in Lebanon.

And a quarter of a mile away, where the same hollyhocks and the same broom flowered above the same rocks, that was Syria.

I had climbed, I suppose, about a hundred feet, and from this height I could see away beyond the no-man's-land, beyond the Syrian frontier post, to where the road curved round underneath a rocky bluff and dropped down to cross the water at the bottom of the valley.

As always in this thirsty country, the green of the trees and cultivation followed the water, and the river wound its way south in a thick sash of trees and corn and vines which crowded along the valley bottom. Here and there, like green veins threading a dry leaf, the small tributary valleys ran down to join the main stream. I could see – perhaps a quarter of a mile beyond the Syrian frontier – one such tributary, curling down through the bare hillside with its ribbon of green, its few patches of growing corn, the bone-white stems of poplars with young leaves whitening in the breeze, and the dusty track where a donkey plodded with a woman beside it carrying a jar on her head. I was watching her idly, when I suddenly stiffened and stared, all attention now, at the point where that distant dusty track met the main road.

Just off the road was a small thicket of trees. And under those trees something white, metallic. A car. A familiar car, parked there in the shade, nose to the south.

I think I have mentioned before that I am very long-sighted. It did not take me more than a minute or two's staring to convince me that this was indeed Charles's Porsche. The screen of leaves prevented me from seeing if he was in the car, but soon I was almost sure I had caught a glimpse of movement beyond the bushes.

I turned and began to make my hasty way down to the road, arriving with a thump in the dust beside the car just as Hamid came out of the buildings.

He started without preliminary. 'I think it will be all right. It is the Sûreté we must go to, so if we go back now – Is something the matter?'

Excitement and the sharp scramble had made me breathless. 'I've just seen his car – Charles's – my cousin's! It's parked about a quarter of a mile past the other frontier. I went up there,' pointing, 'and you can see over that bluff down towards the river, and it's there, parked behind some trees. You don't suppose Ben's told him I'm coming, and he came to wait for me?'

'Perhaps, but it doesn't make much sense to me,' said Hamid. 'You're sure it's his car?'

'Pretty sure. At any rate it's a white Porsche, and they can't be all that common hereabouts. It must be his!'

'Which way is it facing?'

'South.' Near us the barrier shut with a bang behind a south-bound car, and the Arab guarding it squatted down by the roadside and lit another cigarette. Beyond the farther frontier the sun dazzled on the waiting windscreens. I frowned into the glare. 'But you're right it doesn't make sense. If he was all that eager to see me, he'd have waited for me yesterday, or else telephoned, not left it to a chancy pick-up. But then what *is* he doing here? If he did get to Damascus last night, he'd hardly come straight up again before Mr Sifara gets home, and Ben'll have told him I'm expected. Anyway he was facing south.'

Hamid said slowly: 'I've been thinking . . . he may be going south from Homs. Did you not say that this friend, this Mr Sifara, would be coming from Homs? It is possible that when your cousin telephoned Damascus he found this out, so he went to Homs instead.'

'And spent last night there? I suppose so . . . but then why didn't he come back to Beirut this morning? You'd have thought, even if he still had business in Damascus, he'd have come for me, or at least telephoned.'

'He probably did. If he rang up from Homs this morning and heard you had gone, he may have decided to drive down this way instead of the desert road, and catch you at the frontier. If they told him you hadn't yet passed here, then he would perhaps get himself through, and settle down to wait for you.'

'I suppose so . . . or it may be pure chance, and he's just come this way to avoid the desert road. And now this happens!' I glared at the dusty road in an agony of frustration. 'He may be gone at any moment, and I can't even get through to tell him!'

'No,' said Hamid, 'but I can.' He smiled reassuringly. 'Don't distress yourself, Miss Mansel, it's very simple. I will go through now and see your cousin.'

'You? Would you?'

'Well of course. I'll tell him you're here and can't get through the frontier. He may want to come back and take you to the Sûreté in Beirut himself, and if he does, I'll go straight on to Damascus and pick up my return job there. If not, I'll come back for you. You don't mind being left here?'

'Of course not. I'm terribly grateful. Yes, you're right, let's hurry in case he goes. I'll take the rest of my lunch packet up the hill and wait.'

'And your handbag – and the jacket in case you need it—' He was already fishing for them in the car. 'The coffee, yes? And fruit . . . so. If there is a crowd at the frontier, it may be a long wait.'

'Please don't worry about me. In any case I'll be able to see from up there.'

'Does he drive fast?'

'Sometimes,' I said. 'Why?'

'Only that if he doesn't know you're here, if it is just chance that he stopped there – he may be gone.'

'Would you try to catch him.'

'If it seemed possible. Now, can you carry these yourself? I think I should go straight away.'

'Of course I can. Don't wait for me, you go.'

He got into his car and started the engine. 'You said

he was parked behind trees? Can I see him from the road, do you think? Exactly where?'

'A quarter of a mile past the other frontier, some trees on the right, and just beyond them a humped-backed bridge. You can't miss it. There, the way's clear, you can get through. And thank you, Hamid, thank you—'

'Please . . . at your service . . .' A smile, a quick disclaiming wave of the hand, and he was off. I panted back to my perch above the road.

The Porsche was still there. I dumped my things among the flowers and shaded my eyes to watch. Since he had not already gone, my fear that this was just a brief 'comfort stop' must be unfounded. He must either have paused to eat, or in fact be waiting for me.

I peered down at the stretch of road immediately below me. The second Lebanese barrier was lifting to Hamid's bribe, and the big car sailed, windows flashing, through the stretch of no-man's-land. It checked at the Syrian barrier, and I saw Hamid jump out and hurry across to the buildings to show his papers. Since he was alone, and went this way frequently, they would surely let him go without more than a moment's checking.

I looked the other way at the Porsche.

Just in time to see the white car break out of the trees like a greyhound out of the slips, wheel right-handed in a swirl of dust, and shoot off down the road towards Damascus. Seconds later I heard the snarl of a racing change as he whipped over the bridge.

But by the time the sound reached me, the car was already out of sight.

13

As sure as heaven shall rescue me
I have no thought what men they be . . .
S. T. Coleridge: *Christabel*

I DON'T know how long I must have stood there on the
breezy hillside, staring at the empty stretch of road
where the white car had been. It was as if I had been
lifted up into the vacuum of its wake, and then
dropped, dazed, into its dust.

I pulled myself together, and looked to see how far
Hamid had got.

He was already at the second Syrian barrier, and
showing papers – the car's papers presumably – at the
car window. The man on duty took them, glanced, and
gave them back. A bribe passed. A few moments later
the barrier was pulled open, and the car was through
and had gathered speed down the road till it disappeared from my view behind the bluff.

I suppose he cannot have missed the Porsche by
much more than four minutes. In a matter of seconds
he had reappeared on the stretch of road leading to the
bridge, and I saw the dust mushroom up as he braked
and brought the big car in to the verge by the clump of

trees. He got out, must have seen straight away that the cover was not thick enough to hide the Porsche completely, and turned, hand to eyes, to stare south down the valley. He stood like that for only a second or two before he whipped back into the car, slammed the door, and was gone in his turn over the bridge and out of sight down the twisting road.

 It was a safe guess that he had glimpsed the white car on the road ahead. And it was anybody's guess how long it would take for him to catch it. I reflected that a professional driver who must know the road like the palm of his hand might well be able to cancel out Charles's start, and even the difference in performance between the town car and the Porsche. Four minutes is a long time on the road, but if Charles had really been in a hurry he would hardly have spent so much time in the grove. The racing start could only have been due to high spirits; by now Charles was probably idling happily along admiring the wild hollyhocks on the slopes of the Djebel Ech Sheikh Mandour.

I sat down beside a patch of broom that smelled of wild honey, and ate my lunch. They had given me (besides the rolls stuffed with meat) a paper of black olives and some creamy white cheese and some little ravioli-like pastry envelopes filled with a kind of sausage mixed with herbs. By the time I had eaten as much as I wanted and started on a peach, the road below me was clear of traffic except for another bus – southbound this time – and the gatekeeper was obviously well away on his afternoon snooze. I glanced at my watch. Half past one. And the road still empty either of Hamid or the returning Charles.

And at two o'clock it was still empty. And at half past two.

Nor was there any question, even on the flowery hillside, of a peaceful siesta for me. Two of the Arab youths who had been lounging idly at the corner of the customs buildings had decided at length, after a grinning, nudging conference which I had pretended not to notice, to come up and talk to me. It was probably nothing more than curiosity which drove them, but they had only three or four words of American English, and I had no Arabic at all, so they hung around grinning and staring till my nerve broke and in sheer irritation I got to my feet and began to pick up my things.

I thought I knew what must have happened. Hamid, misled by my outburst of exasperation at the delay, had construed it as acute anxiety for Charles, and imagined trouble where I only saw annoyance. Either he was still determinedly pursuing the Porsche, or there had been some sort of mishap delaying whichever car was on its way back to me. And if I waited much longer and neither of them came, there would be no possibility of my getting to Beirut in time to visit the Sûreté office about a visa, and that would be that.

So when one of the Arab youths, leering, sat down a yard from me on a dusty boulder and said for the dozenth time, 'New York? London? Miss?' and then made some remark in Arabic which sent his companion off into fits of mirth, and at the same moment a bus labelled Baalbek ground to a halt below me. I picked up the last of my things, said 'Goodbye' politely and finally, walked downhill to the road.

The thin dog was lying in the shadow of a parked car. He watched me with recognition, but (I thought) without much hope. I dropped the last of the meat rolls beside him as I passed, and saw him snatch it and bolt out of the way of the youths who were following me downhill. The crowd of passengers from the bus were standing about in the heat, apathetically watching as the customs men rifled the household goods of what looked like the entire Exodus. Someone was half-heartedly checking their papers. The gatekeeper let another car through, then relapsed into sleep. Nobody was bothering very much about anything. Even the two youths had abandoned the chase.

I went into the buildings, to be met by the slightly glazed and wholly unwelcoming stare of the olive-coloured gentleman behind the counter. It took a few minutes before I could find someone in the crowd with sufficient English to pass on what I wanted to ask, but I managed eventually.

'The bus,' I said, 'what time does it get to Baalbek?'

'Half past three.'

'Is there one that goes from here to Beirut?'

'Oh, yes.'

'At what time?'

'Five.' A shrug. 'Perhaps a little later. It gets there at six.'

I thought for a moment. Baalbek was well off the direct road home, but there would be a good chance of getting a car there, and taking the shorter route back to Beirut through the mountains. That way I should be there long before the problematic five o'clock bus. In any case I had no desire to sit here for another two hours or so. Even the bus would be preferable.

'Will there be a taxi to hire, or a self-drive car, in Baalbek?'

'Surely.' But he qualified it with a shrug. 'Well, you must understand, it is late in the day, but possibly . . .'

'Where do I find the taxis?'

'At the temples, or in the main street. Or ask at the Adonis Hotel, just where the bus stops.'

I remembered the Adonis Hotel. It was where the group had gone for lunch on Friday, and the manager, I remembered, had spoken reasonably good English.

I asked: 'Where is the Sûreté in Beirut?'

'In the Rue Badaro.'

'What time does it close?'

But here we stuck. 'One o'clock' was the first, dismaying answer. Then, from someone else, 'Five o'clock.' Then again, 'It opens again at five o'clock till eight.' 'No, no, till seven.' Then, with shrugs all round, 'Who knows?'

Since the last guess was obviously the most accurate of the lot, I abandoned the questions, to add my postscript. 'If my driver, or anyone else, comes back asking about me, tell him I've gone back to the Sûreté office in the Rue Badaro in Beirut, and then to my hotel, the Phoenicia. I'll wait there. *Compris.*'

They admitted it was *compris*, so I left them to it, said a thank you all round, and went out.

The bus's engine was roaring, and a cloud of black smoke poured from the exhaust. There was no time to do more than look quickly up the road for a white Porsche or a black taxi and to get in. Six seconds later, with a horrible shaking roar and a smell of soot, we were heading for Bar Elias and the Bk'aa road to Baalbek.

It was a horrible journey, and it ended perforce where the bus finished its run, in some dirty hot street within shouting distance of the ruined temples, and just in front of the portals of the Adonis Hotel.

I got out of the bus, shaking the creases from my skirt with a strong feeling that I was dislodging fleas from it in clouds. The bus went off to turn, the other passengers dispersed, and the filthy black fumes slowly cleared from the air. The street was empty except for a big, sleek black car parked at the kerb, and just beyond it, incongruously, a white camel with a ragged Arab holding the head-rope.

He bore down on me now, with a shrill stream of Arabic interspersed with a few English words, from which I gathered that I was being offered a ride on his camel for the paltry sum of five English pounds or more. I beat him off with some difficulty, parried off his offer to pose for a snapshot for only ten shillings, and ran up the steps into the hotel.

I was lucky to find the manager himself was still around, and not absent, as might have been expected, on siesta. I found him in the little gravelled court that did duty as a restaurant garden, sitting with a companion at one of the small tables under the pines, drinking beer. He was a smallish, round-faced Arab with a thin line of moustache and various chunks of Beiruti gold about his person. His companion, whom at first I barely noticed, looked English.

The manager rose and came hurrying to meet me. 'Madame – mademoiselle? You are back again? But I thought your party had left the Lebanon?'

'Good heavens, you recognised me?' I exclaimed. He was bowing over my hand with every appearance of joy. You'd have thought I'd spent a month in the hotel's best suite with all found, not merely bought a drink to take with the group's packed lunch a few days ago. 'What a memory you've got! I'd have thought you had so many tourists here that you wouldn't even see them any more!'

'How could I forget you, mademoiselle?' The bow, the gallant look, assured me without a hint of offence that he meant it. He added, frankly: 'As to that, I have only been here since the beginning of the season. So far, I remember all my guests. Please – will you sit down? Will you join us, it will be a pleasure?'

But I hung back. 'No, thank you very much – there was something I wanted to ask you. I'm here on my own today, and I wanted some help so I thought I would come to you.'

'Of course. Please tell me. Anything. Of course.'

He obviously meant it, but to my dismay, as soon as I began to explain my difficulty and mentioned a car, he made a moue of doubt, and spread his hands.

'I will do all I can, naturally . . . but at this time of day most of the local cars are already hired and gone. It is possible you may find one at the temples – do you speak Arabic?'

'No.'

'Then I will send someone with you to help you. There may be a car still there. If not – perhaps I can find one – perhaps one of my friends, even . . . It is urgent?'

'Well, I do rather want to get to Beirut as soon as possible.'

'Then please do not worry, mademoiselle. Of course I will do for you whatever I can. I am glad that you felt you could come here for help. I would offer to telephone for you now, but as it happens I had to get a car only ten minutes ago for one of my guests, and I had difficulty. But in another twenty minutes, perhaps, or half an hour, it will be worth trying again.'

'Forgive me.' It was his companion who spoke. I had forgotten all about him, and turned in surprise as he set down his beer glass and rose. 'I couldn't help overhearing. If you really are anxious to get to Beirut, and there's any difficulty at all, I'm going that way and would be delighted to offer you a lift.'

'Why, thank you—' I was slightly taken aback, but the manager intervened quickly, sounding relieved and pleased.

'Of course, that would be excellent! An excellent idea! May I perhaps introduce you? This is Mr Lovell, mademoiselle. I'm afraid I don't know your name.'

'Mansel. Miss Mansel. How do you do, Mr Lovell?'

'How do you do?' His voice was English and cultured. He was a man of rather less than middle height, somewhere in his forties, with a face made Arab-olive by the sun, and dark hair receding from a high fore-head. He was well-dressed in a lightweight grey suit and silk shirt, and wore heavy-rimmed dark glasses. Something about him was faintly familiar, and I thought I must have met him somewhere before.

Even as the thought crossed my mind he smiled and confirmed it. 'As a matter of fact we've met before, though without an introduction, and I don't suppose you remember it.'

'I'm afraid I don't, but I did have a feeling I'd met you. Where?'

'In Damascus, last week. Was it Wednesday – or perhaps Thursday? Yes, it was Thursday, in the morning in the Great Mosque. You were with a group then, weren't you? I'd been talking to your guide while you ladies were admiring the carpets, and then he had to intervene in some minor international incident, and we exchanged a word or two while it was going on. You wouldn't remember, why should you? But do tell me, did the stout lady allow herself to be parted from her shoes in the end?'

I laughed. 'Oh, that's what you meant by an "inter-national incident"! Yes, she did, and even admitted she wouldn't have wanted all that crowd walking on *her* carpets in outdoor shoes. There was a bit of a scene, wasn't there? I thought I knew your voice. That's it, then.'

'You're on your own today?'

'Yes. In fact, I won't make a story of it now, but that's the reason why I'm stranded here today looking for a car. Do you mean you're really going straight to Beirut?'

'Certainly.' He moved one square, well-kept hand to indicate the car parked at the edge of the road below the garden wall. I saw now that it was a black Renault with an Arab impassive at the wheel in native dress and white *kaffiyeh*. 'If I can be of any help to you, I'll be delighted. I was intending to leave within a few minutes anyway. Of course, if you want to stay and see the sights here first, then you might prefer to take a chance of getting a taxi later, and Mr Najjar will probably be able to help you.' He smiled. 'Any other day I'd have been delighted to show you the place myself, but as it happens I have an engagement in the city that I daren't cry off, so I'm driving straight down now.'

'It's terribly good of you, and I'd love to come with you,' I said. 'I've seen Baalbek before – I was here with the group on Friday – but in any case I'm anxious to get back to the city as soon as I can.'

'Then shall we go?'

The manager came with us to the car, the Arab driver whipped round to open the rear door, and Mr Lovell handed me in, spoke to the man in Arabic, and settled beside me. We said our goodbyes to the manager, and the car moved off.

We threaded the narrow streets quickly and skilfully, then gathered speed along the road to Beirut. In a few minutes we had passed the last of the houses crouching among their gardens, and on our right the great sweep of hill and valley stretched brilliant in the afternoon sun. The air through the open window was fresh and cool. I leaned back gratefully.

'Oh, this is heaven after that bus! Have you ever been in one of the local buses?'

He laughed. 'No, praise be to Allah, I have not.'

'I should have warned you to keep right away from me until I've had a bath.'

'I'll take the risk. Where are you staying in Beirut?'

'The Phoenicia. But don't you bother about that, I can get a taxi from anywhere it suits you to throw me out.'

'It's no trouble, we'll be passing it.'

'Thanks all the same, but as a matter of fact I've a call to make first in the Rue Badaro. I don't know where it is, but perhaps you do?'

'Yes, of course. Well, that's even simpler, it's practically on the way. The Rue Badaro joins this one just before the *place* where the National Museum is. If we cut through the side streets when we get to the city we can go in that way, and I'll drop you.'

'Thank you very much.'

His voice betrayed no curiosity. He had given me a brief glance – unreadable because of the dark glasses – when I had mentioned the Rue Badaro, and I thought he must surely know that the Sûreté Générale was there, but he was either too indifferent or too well-bred to question me about my affairs. He asked merely: 'What happened to your group?'

'Oh, I didn't break away from them today! I'm only stranded and thrown on your mercy because I hadn't a proper visa and my own car went on . . . that is, there were reasons why I had to send my driver on to Damascus, even if it meant my finding my own way home to Beirut. The group actually left on Saturday, and in a way, that's the cause of the trouble.' I explained briefly what had happened about the visa.

'I see. But how extraordinarily awkward. I suppose you have to get a new visa? Then do I gather it's the Sûreté you want in the Rue Badaro?'

'Yes,' In spite of myself I cast a worried glance at my watch. 'Have you any idea what their hours are?'

He didn't answer immediately, but I saw him give a quick glance at his own wrist, then he leaned forward and said something in Arabic to the driver. The big car surged forward smoothly at an increased pace. Mr Lovell smiled at me. 'You should be all right. In any case, I might be able to help you. Stop worrying.'

'You? You mean you know someone there?'

'You might say so. I can see how the mistake occurred, it's no one's fault, and I doubt if there will be any difficulty in getting you a new visa. You'll have to pay another half-crown, I'm afraid, and wait while they fill in a form or two in triplicate, but that's all it will take. So relax now till we get there. I promise you it'll be all right. And if you like, I'll come in with you and see you through it.'

'Oh – would you really? I mean – if you've time? It's terribly good of you!' I found myself stammering in a sort of confusion of relief.

'Think nothing of it,' he said calmly. 'Do you smoke?'

'No, well, sometimes I do. Thank you, I think I will. Oh, are they Turkish?'

'No, Latakia – it's the best Syrian tobacco. Go on, try it.'

I took one, and he lit it for me. The driver, who all this time had said nothing, was smoking already. Mr Lovell lit a cigarette for himself and leaned back beside me. His lighter I saw, was a gold Flaminia, and the cigarette-case had been gold, too. The cuff-links in the silk cuffs were of heavy gold with a beautiful, deliberately 'roughed' surface. A man of substance, and certainly a man of easy self-assurance. Someone of importance, perhaps? He had that air. I began to wonder if quite by chance I had found the 'useful contact' in Beirut that I had talked of to Daddy. It certainly seemed as if I could stop worrying about the Sûreté and the visa.

He was silent, half turned away to look out of his window. We sat for a while smoking in silence, while the big car sped silently south and west, then took the High Lebanon pass in its stride and began to nose downhill towards the distant sprawl of Beirut. I was content to sit back in silence and stop thinking. This was an interval, a gap in time, a moment to free-wheel before the next effort. And the next effort would be eased for me by the pleasant and competent Mr Lovell.

It was only then, as I found myself relaxing, brittle tension melting like toffee into a sweet goo of softened bone and nerve and sleepy muscle, that I realised how taut and tight-strung I must have been, how senselessly, uselessly keyed up to meet something which could have been no more than a challenge of my own imagination. Something I had let Hamid see and feel, and which, because he had over-interpreted me, I had been left to sort out on my own. Well, I seemed to be doing just that . . . and meanwhile the car sailed on at speed, and the sun beat warm and heavy through the window, and the breeze stirred the ash in grey dust from my cigarette and feathered the smoke away in veils of blue nylon, and I was content to lift a lazy hand to wave it away from my eyes, then drop the hand, palm up, into my lap while I leaned back, tranquil, without thought.

My companion, seemingly as relaxed as I, was turned away from me gazing out at the view on his side of the car. Here the steep hillside fell away from the road in an abrupt sweep of rock-strewn green to the dark sprawl of forest and the gleam of running water. Beyond the forested stream the land rose again through terraced fields of gold and green and dark-gold to more stony heights, and the grey seams of snow. The poplars along the road's edge flashed and winked past like telegraph posts, bare and lacy against the far snow and the hot blue sky.

'Good Lord!'

Mr Lovell, who had been gazing out almost dreamily, stiffened to attention, whipped off his dark glasses, craned his neck farther, and shaded his eyes to stare down the mountainside.

'What is it?'

'Nothing, really – rather a pretty sight, that's all. And not quite as out of place here as one might think.' He gave a short laugh. 'It still goes on, of course, the high romance – Haroun Al Raschid and the perfumes of Arabia and blood on the roses. It's an Arab riding down there with a pair of Persian greyhounds, you know them? – salukis, beautiful things. How very dramatic.'

I didn't for the moment take in what he was saying. I was fiddling with the ashtray in the back of the seat in front of me, trying to stub out my cigarette.

He added: 'He ought to have a hawk on his wrist, probably has, but it's too far away for me to see.'

I looked up quickly. 'Did you say a rider with two salukis? *Here*?'

It must be pure coincidence, of course. We must be miles on the wrong side of Beirut, and Dar Ibrahim was a long way away. It couldn't be John Lethman and the salukis. But it was enough of a strange coincidence to make me sit up straighter and say: 'Where? Can I see?'

I had to lean right across him to see down the hill. He sat back to let me do so, indicating a point well below us and some way off.

The car was sliding smoothly round the outside of a bend. The road was bounded by neither wall nor fence, its verge only a yard of dried clay where thistles grew between the poplars, and beyond this the steep mountainside. I peered down.

'I can't see anything. What's the colour of the horse?'

'Bright chestnut.' He pointed again. 'There, look, just going into the trees. Quick. The man's in white. See?'

I strained to see where his right hand pointed. As I leaned close across him his left arm came quietly round me and held me fast.

For a moment I thought he was supporting me against the swing of the car on the bend. Then – incredulously, as his arm tightened – that this was a heavy pass; and I stiffened against it and tried to pull away. He held me, the arm like iron, his hand now gripping my left arm and holding it helpless. With my body pressed to his my right arm was imprisoned against him.

'If you keep still you won't be hurt.'

The voice, whispering now, was recognisable. The eyes, too, uncovered and staring into mine. The long nose, the olive face that would look pale in lamplight . . .

But it was mad. If it was mad to suppose John Lethman was riding out here forty miles from Dar Ibrahim it was still madder to suppose that my Great-Aunt Harriet, disguised as a man of forty-odd was holding me with this ferocious strength with one hand, while the other came up holding something that gleamed . . .

I screamed. The Arab driver drove smoothly on without even turning his head. He took a hand off the wheel to tap ash into the tray under the fascia-board.

'What are you doing? Who are you?' Gasping and twisting in his grip, I fought as hard as I could, and the car rocked, swinging wide on the next bend. But there was nothing coming. There was nothing on the road.

The dizzy swoop of the car round the bends, cliff on one side, open sky on the other, like the flight of a fulmar through an empty bright afternoon; the flicking pulse of shadow as the poplars whipped by; the un-heeding silence of the Arab driver . . . all these com-bined in some curiously merciful way to insulate me from the nightmare of what could not – could not possibly – be happening.

He was grinning. From a few inches away, his teeth looked obscene, like something in a horror film. Great-Aunt Harriet's eyes blinked and glittered as he fought to hold me.

'*Who are you?*' It was a last gasp on the edge of hysteria, and I saw him recognise the fact. His voice was smooth. He had me still now, boneless, dumb.

'You remember now, of course. I told you we'd met before, but we weren't introduced properly. Henry Lovell Grafton, if you want it in full . . . Mean any-thing to you? Yes, I thought it might. And now hold still, or I'll hurt you.'

On the phrase his right hand flashed down at my bare arm. Something pricked, clung stinging, was with-drawn. He dropped the hypodermic into his pocket and smiled again, holding me tightly.

'Pentothal,' he said. 'Being a doctor has its uses. You have ten seconds, Miss Mansel.'

14

. . . Nor do I know how long it is
(For I have lain entranced I wis).

S. T. Coleridge: *Christabel*

I was to find that Dr Henry Grafton had a habit of
overestimating. It took about seven seconds to put me
under, and when I awoke it was to near-darkness, the
thick closeness of a shut and windowless room lit only
by the faint light from a small barred opening high in
the wall above the door.

At first, of course, the waking seemed normal. I
opened blurred eyes on a dark wall where shadows
moved slightly like rags in a draught. It was warm and
very quiet, a heavy airless quiet that slowly conveyed to
me the sense of being shut in. A small fluttering, like
that of a moth against a pane, pattered into my consciousness through the layers of drugged sleep. It
worried me. I must move and let the poor creature
out. I must open the window and let in the air . . .

But not yet; I wouldn't move just yet. My body felt
slack and heavy, my head was aching, and I was cold.
This last had its own compensations, for when I put a
hand to my throbbing forehead the hand was damply

cool, and comforting. I was, I found, lying on blankets. I scruffled a couple of these over myself, and turned on my face, cold hands against cheeks and forehead. The heavy lassitude of the drug still possessed me, and in a vague way – nothing was other than vague – I was thankful for it. I had an idea that something large, dark and terrifying loomed and gibbered just out of reach; but something in me refused to face it yet. I checked my groping mind, shut my eyes against the blankets, and thought of sleep . . .

I have no idea how long it was before I came back to consciousness the second time: I imagined it was no great while. This time the return was final, sharp, and altogether frightening. I was suddenly wide awake, and fully aware of all that had happened. I even knew where I was. I was back at Dar Ibrahim. The smell told me, seconds before my brain caught up with my senses – dead air and dust and lamp-oil, and the indefinable sharp smell of Great-Aunt Harriet's tobacco. I was in one of the storerooms under the Seraglio lake, behind one of those massively locked doors in the underground passage where Charles and I had gone exploring to find the Prince's Divan . . .

That was it. That was the gibbering thought that had lain in wait for my return from the dead; the thought I had been refusing to face.

The interview in the Prince's Divan. Great-Aunt Harriet. Henry Grafton . . . I could only think of one reason for Henry Grafton's grotesque masquerade to fob off my persistence, for the dusty abandonment of the Chinese treasures and the beloved books, even for the glimpse I had had of the ruby ring on Halide's hand. Something had happened to my Great-Aunt Harriet which this gang had been at pains to hide. Not just ill, or even crazy – they must have known they needn't fear her family when it came to Will-making, and wherever Lethman and Halide might stand, I didn't think this was Henry Grafton's concern. And surely the risks were too great for the rewards? Nor could she be a prisoner, like me; there had been no attempt to stop me wandering where I wished through the palace by daylight.

Well, then, she was dead. And for some reason the death had had to be concealed. At the moment, my skin crawling with cold in that warm airless dungeon, I could only think of one reason for that. But whatever it was that had necessitated the masquerade and the midnight prowling, and now the elaborate operation that had hauled me back into the net, I was soon going to find out – the hard way.

And Charles who had apparently, heaven knows how, suspected the truth – Charles was miles away, heading for Damascus with Hamid after him. Even if Hamid caught him up and persuaded him to come back for me, it would be some time before they would find my trail. No one would miss me at the Phoenicia; and Ben had said 'Come when you can . . .'

Christy Mansel, sunk without trace.

Like Great-Aunt Harriet and her little dog Samson. Or like the Gabriel Hounds, locked away in the dust of the rotting palace for ever . . .

This was sheer crying stupidity, the drug reducing

me when I could afford it least to a useless contraption of slack nerves and jellied bone. I slapped the nerves down hard, sat up, and tried to look about me.

Gradually, the place took shape. A few feet of dusty floor near the bed where the dim light fell, a low ceiling hung with webs, a stretch of rough stone wall where a tumble of leather and metal – harness, perhaps? – hung from a rusty hook. The tiny flickering sound came again from outside, the fluttering of a wick in an oil lamp. The weak light wavered through the tiny grating to drown within a yard or two in thick darkness where, faintly, could be seen stacked shapes of crates, boxes, tins like small petrol-cans . . .

I had certainly been right about where I was. The ventilator must look out on lamplight in the underground corridor, and the door below it could be one of those massively barred affairs with the uncompromising locks that Charles and I had seen. There would be no questioning that door. And there was, of course, no window.

The silence was intense, thick and suffocating like the stillness one finds in caves, the silence of underground. I held myself still, listening. My body felt stiff and sore here and there, as if there were bruises, but the headache was gone, to be followed by an awareness which at that moment was worse and more painful, a feeling of quickness, a light aliveness and nerve-end vulnerability, like a snail that has been torn from its shell and wants nothing better than to creep back inside.

The silence was complete. There was no way of

telling if anyone else was still about in the palace. You would think I had been buried alive.

The cliché slipped through my mind without thought, then struck home like a poisoned dart, as with it came the quick vision of the rock above me, the tons of rock and earth with the heavy sheet of water lying over it. Man-made; fallible; rotten, probably, as the rest of the place was rotten. The weight must be terrific. If there was the slightest flaw in the rock above me, the slightest movement of earth—

Then with the rush of cold prickling over my skin, I heard it through the dead silence, the tick of settling earth.

I was on my feet, rigid and sweating, before commonsense broke over me like a breath of sweet air. The ticking was merely my watch. I stretched up on tiptoe near the door, holding my wrist high towards the ventilator. I could just see it. The little familiar face was like a friend, the familiar tick brought sanity and the knowledge that it was a few minutes short of six o'clock. It had been just on four in the afternoon when I had accepted the lift from Henry Grafton. I had been unconscious for more than twelve hours.

I put a hand down to the door and, for what it was worth, tried it. The latch lifted silk-smooth, but the door never budged a millimetre. This was so much a foregone conclusion that I hardly registered it with any emotion at all. I was conscious all the time of the positive effort involved in keeping at bay the image of the tons of rock and water pressing down over my head.

The sound which a little while ago I had been dreading came now like the lifting of a nightmare. A key in the lock.

When the door opened smoothly, in that accustomed, well-oiled silence, I was sitting, I hoped composedly, on the bed, trying to conceal with a straight back and poker face that I couldn't have trusted my legs to let me stand. My lips were dry and my heart thumping. What I expected I have no idea. But I was afraid.

It was John Lethman, carrying a lamp, and behind him Halide, as ever with a tray. I smelled soup and coffee as soon as the door opened. If I had thought about it, I'd have expected to be ravenously hungry, but I wasn't. He put the lamp up in a wall-niche, and the girl came past him to set the tray down on a packing-case. She let her big kohl-rimmed eyes slide side sideways to look at me, I saw pleasure there. The smile reached the corners of her mouth in a malicious little curl. The silk of her dress shimmered, bordered with gold, and I was sharply reminded of what my own state must be, crumpled from the blankets and with my hair all anyhow. I ignored her stonily, and said abruptly to Lethman:

'What's happened to her?'

'To whom?'

'To Great-Aunt Harriet, of course. Don't try to keep the charade up, I know your beastly pal was masquerading. Where's my aunt?'

'She died.'

'Died?' I said sharply. 'Was murdered, do you mean?'

From the corner of my eye I saw Halide's silks shimmer as she started, and Lethman turned quickly to look down at me. His back was to the lamp, and I couldn't see him clearly, but his voice was edged with nerves. 'Don't be melodramatic. Naturally I meant no such thing. She died of natural causes.'

'Melodramatic! Look who's talking, what with your underground prisons and your sloe-eyed charmer there and your dear little pantomime dame upstairs with his White Slaver techniques. Natural causes my foot,' I said angrily, 'be precise. What did she die of and when?'

He said stiffly: 'I'm not going to answer questions. Dr Grafton was her doctor, he'll explain.'

'By God he will,' I said.

He had been moving towards the door, but my tone brought him round again to face me. The light was on him now. I saw in his face a sort of startled reappraisement, even a kind of alarm, and he opened his mouth to say something, then shut it again without speaking. I thought he looked as edgy as his voice, a down-drawn look, with pouched flesh under the eyes that betrayed lack of sleep, and lines which I had not noticed before and which had no business to be there. What had certainly not been there before was the swollen bruise at the corner of his mouth and a nasty-looking mark like a weal from the cheek-bone to the ear. I was just taking this in when Halide said, quickly and venomously:

'Don't let her talk to you like that. You are the master here.'

I laughed. 'It looks like it, doesn't it? For a start, who's been knocking you about? And you think I'm the one who's in trouble? Well, you'll learn. And I do assure you it'll pay you to listen to me and get me out of here. I should like to go now. At once, please.'

He drew a sharp little breath, either of anger or effort. His voice was deliberately braced. 'I'm sure you would. But you'll stay here just the same. Dr Grafton will see you later.'

'He'll see me now. After I've had a wash. And what's more, I should like my handbag back.'

'It's there by the bed. Now stop being stupid, you must see you've got to do as you're told. There's some food. We'll leave you now, and if you've got any sense you'll take it quietly. If you behave yourself you'll come to no harm. All right, Halide.'

'I don't want the blasted food!' I said angrily. 'Will you stop behaving like Oddjob and take me to the bathroom?'

'Later.' Halide was going, sliding out past him with a final gleam at me which made me want to slap her face. John Lethman was going too, closing the door.

I stood up and said sharply: 'Don't be such a clot, Mr Lethman. I want to go to the loo. You know – the loo, the lavatory, W.C. . . . do I really have to spell it out?'

'Oh.' He paused, and I saw with pleasure that he looked once more disconcerted. It seemed obvious that he had expected, possibily even braced himself for, a scene along set lines of outrage and perhaps fear, and that this intrusion of commonplace reality into his thriller-situation had thrown him completely. He said at length, lamely: 'Oh, well, you'd better come along, I suppose. But don't try anything. And it won't do any good—'

' "And it won't do you any good to scream for help, because I have a hundred Nubian guards within call"?' I finished the threat with a derision that got him right between the eyes, and sent my own morale rocketing. 'Come off it and take me to the lavatory, Commander of the Faithful.'

He made no reply. I laughed again, and went out past him. My exit was spoiled by the fact that I stumbled in the dim light over a broken flagstone, and my head swam dizzily with the aftermath of the drug. He took my arm, and I controlled the impulse to shake him off. For one thing, I needed the help; for another, he was probably determined to hang on to me, and I might as well go on turning the tables by treating the gesture as one of solicitude. So I thanked him and allowed him to escort me from the room. I don't know whether Halide followed: I didn't glance her way.

I had been right. This was the corridor under the lake, and my door one of the locked storerooms. There was the pile of tins still outside it. John Lethman led me up the stairs towards Great-Aunt Harriet's room. As we reached the heavy curtain and he drew it aside to disclose the bed, I gave an exclamation of surprise.

'Don't pretend you didn't know the way,' he said sourly.

'I'm not pretending anything,' I said. This was the truth; what had amazed me was the light. It was not morning, as I had expected, but golden afternoon, six o'clock of a blazing day. And it must be the same day on which I had set out for Damascus or my watch would have stopped by now. The pentothal had laid me out for barely two hours.

John Lethman stepped carefully through on to the dais, and handed me after him. I added: 'I'm just surprised it's daylight still. It feels like a month since I was out in the open air and in pleasant company. Tell me one thing, Mr Lethman, how did you get me here? Don't tell me you carried me over from the village in broad daylight.'

'The car didn't touch Beirut at all, or Sal'q. There's a road off past Zahle, and after that a quite negotiable track up behind the head of the valley. You only had to be brought down a couple of kilometers or so from the car.'

'Down the path behind the palace? I suppose that's why I'm as stiff as a board. What did you bring me on, a mule?'

Absurd though it may seem, I think I was angrier at that moment than I had been almost through the whole affair, angry and ashamed. There was humiliation in the knowledge of how these men had manhandled my unconscious and helpless body. So far, the thought made me want to run away and hide; but perhaps later on the anger would help.

He said: 'The bathroom's this way.'

It was the next door opening off the Prince's garden. I escaped into the labyrinth of the hammam like a rabbit scuttling down a safe burrow.

It had in its day been a grander hammam than the women's quarters had boasted. The walls were alabaster, and the light came from overhead in all the rooms from lozenges of stained glass which threw jewels of amber and jade and lapis on to the rosy floors. The sunshine, muted by this, glowed among the labyrinth of peach-coloured columns like light through a transparent shell, and the murmur of water trickling through the shallow channels and dripping into marble basins echoed like the sea in the corridors of a cave.

The cool touch of the water, the light, the blinding glimpse of the little garden as I had crossed to the hammam, dispelled immediately the claustrophobic nightmare of my prison. I threaded my way through the complex of rooms to the centre of the cool stone maze. Here water splashed and glittered into a blackened shell that had once been silver, and a stone faun leaned out with a cup of water-thin alabaster. I took it from him, filled it, and drank, then took off everything but pants and bra and washed deliciously in the cool water, drying myself on my slip. The sunlight swimming down in its shafts of amber and amethyst seemed to soak into my body like oil smoothing away the stiffness of the bruises. I shook my frock out and put it on, did my face and hair, and last of all dried my feet and put my sandals on again. I dropped the soaked slip in a corner, took another drink of water, rinsed the cup for the faun, then went out to meet John Lethman.

He was sitting on the edge of the dry fountain, I had only previously seen this garden at night, and now I got

no more than a brief impression of a maze of yellow
roses and a tumble of honeysuckle over broken pillars.
John Lethman got quickly to his feet and started to
speak but I cut across it abruptly.

'You needn't think you're going to get me back into
that foul little room again. If this Dr Grafton wants to
see me, he can see me here. What's more he can see me
now, in daylight. He needn't pretend any more that he
likes staying up half the night, so he can leave his
turban and his nightie off.' I marched past him into
Great-Aunt Harriet's bedroom, flinging over my
shoulder: 'and if you want me to eat anything you
can make the girl bring it in here.'

He hesitated, and I thought he was going to insist.
But he said merely: 'As long as you realise that this part
of the palace is locked right away. If you do try to bolt
you won't go far, and even if you hid, the dogs would
find you.'

I laughed. 'And tear me limb from limb? Big deal!'

I crossed to the red lacquer chair, and sat down with
as much of the grand manner as I could muster, while
Lethman, with a look of acute dislike at me, mounted
the dais to pull the bell.

The familiar jangling peal bounced and ricocheted
through the stillness, and, immediately, the clamour
from the hounds tore the afternoon to shreds. Somehow, the noise was comforting; they were on my side,
the 'Gabriel Hounds', Aunt H's dogs who had known
my voice and my cousin's step, and who (I saw it now
as the thought lit my mind like a sudden flare) perhaps
disliked 'the Dr' as much as Samson had done, and so

were kept shut away except when on guard at night to keep the nosy Miss Mansel within bounds.

Before the echoes of the bell had died the bed-curtains were pulled violently back and Henry Grafton came through the private door like a genie erupting from the lamp, and said furiously: 'What the hell's happened to that girl? The door's wide open, and if she gets as far as the main gate that idiot's probably forgotten his orders by now, and he'll see her on her way with an illuminated address.'

'It's all right,' said Lethman, 'she's here.'

Dr Grafton came up short like someone running into a wire, and swung round on me where I sat in the high-backed chair. For a nasty moment I thought he was going to come and grab, but he seemed to hold himself in with an effort, and gave me instead a long summing-up look that I by no means liked.

'What's she doing here?' He spoke to John Lethman without taking his eyes off me.

'She asked for the bathroom.'

'Oh.' The simple demand of Nature seemed to disconcert Henry Grafton as much as it had Lethman himself. He teetered there on the edge of the dais, seemingly at a loss, while I sat poker-spined on my chair, trying to look several degrees cooler than an ice cube, and preparing to fight every step of the way should they decide to force me back into my dungeon.

'You rang?' said Halide, at the garden door. At least I suppose that's what she said, it was in Arabic. She was wearing Great-Aunt Harriet's ring.

She was looking at Grafton, but I answered in

English. 'Yes, we rang. Not for you, but since you're here you might as well bring the tray in here for me. I don't want the soup, thank you, but I'll eat the bread and cheese, and I wouldn't mind a cup of coffee while I'm talking to him.'

She spat something at me – no pretences now – and whirled furiously on the men:

'You're not going to leave her out here? Why don't you put her back in the room and shut her up again? Why do you let her sit there like that and give orders? Who does she think she is? She is nobody, I tell you, nobody, and very soon she will know it! When we get her—'

'Look, Halide—' It was John Lethman, feebly, but she ignored him, blazing at Grafton.

'*You* are afraid of her too? Why? Dare you not leave her there? Then why not give her some more of the drug and put her in the other prison? Or tie her up? I would do it, me!'

'Oh, belt up,' I said wearily. 'Never mind about the tray, I can last out, just stop yelling and making me feel like an extra in *Kismet*, will you? And I'd still like the coffee. You can heat it up again before you bring it. I dislike lukewarm coffee.'

The look she gave me this time was pure bastinados and boiling oil, and I was glad to have deserved it. She swung back to Grafton, simmering like a kettle, but he cut her short. 'Shut up and do as you're told. John, for God's sake can't you clout some sense into her? It won't be long now.' He added something in Arabic to Halide, more conciliatory in tone, and there was a brief exchange which seemed to mollify her. After a while she went, scowling.

John Lethman gave a sigh, half of relief, half of exasperation. 'Sorry about that. She's been like a snake with the jitters for days. She'll come to heel when the time comes.' He dabbed at his face, winced, and dabbed again. 'Shall I take the Mansel girl back?'

'Not for the moment. You can get on. I'll talk to her here. And afterwards—' he finished the sentence in Arabic, and John Lethman nodded. His reply was wordless and quite horrible. He merely drew the edge of his hand across his throat in a murderous little gesture, and Henry Grafton laughed.

'If you can,' he said in English. 'All right, *ruh*.'

Lethman went out. I wanted to keep what miserable initiative I could, so I spoke immediately. My voice came out harsh and high with nerves, and surprisingly formidable.

'Well, supposing you start, Dr Grafton. You've got quite a bit of explaining to do, haven't you?'

15

So bury me by some sweet Garden-side.
E. FitzGerald: *The Rubáiyát*
of *Omar Khayyám*

He didn't answer for a moment. He stood there eyeing me under dropped lids, still with that appraising, almost clinical look. His eyes were dark and shiny as treacle, and in contrast the heavy lids looked thick and waxen. The skin all round the eyes was brownish, like overripe plums.

'Well?' I said curtly.

He smiled. 'You're a fighter, aren't you? I admire you for it.'

'You excite me beyond words. Sit down and get on with it.' He stepped down from the dais and crossed the room to get a chair which stood against the wall. He had changed his neat businessman's suit for dark trousers and a high-necked Russian shirt in olive green which made him look sallower, and did nothing to flatter his thick build. He looked very strong, with strength in the back of his neck, like a bull. My rudeness didn't even ruffle him. His manner was perfectly civil, pleasant even, as he brought the chair over and sat himself opposite me.

'Cigarette?'

'No, thank you.'

'It'll help compose your nerves.'

'Who said they needed composing?'

'Oh, come, Miss Mansel, I thought you were a realist.'

'I hope I am. All right. There, my hand's shaking. Please you?'

'Not at all.' He lit my cigarette, and waved out the match. 'I'm sorry I had to do what I did. Please be sure I don't mean you any harm. I just had to get you back here and talk to you.'

'You had to—?' I opened my eyes at him. 'Oh, come off it, Dr Grafton! You could have talked to me in the car. Or you could have talked to me before I left Dar Ibrahim, if you were going to drop the disguise anyway.' I leaned back, drawing on my cigarette. The gesture helped to give me the extra touch of confidence I needed, and I felt my nerves beginning to relax. 'I must say, I liked you a lot better in that neat little number you were wearing the other night. I quite see why you only interviewed guests at midnight. You and the room looked a whole lot better in the dark.'

As far as the room was concerned this was certainly true. What could have passed in the lamplight for romantic shabbiness was shown up by daylight as plain dirt and neglect. The bed hangings were tattered and filthy, and the table beside me was sordid in the extreme with used cups and plates and a saucer half-full of cigarette stubs. 'Well, all right,' I said, still aggressively, 'let's have it. And start at the beginning, please. What happened to Aunt Harriet?'

He looked at me frankly and showed an apologetic hand. 'Be sure I'm only too willing to tell you everything. I admit you've every ground for suspicion and anger, but believe me it's only on your own account, and I'll explain that in a moment. As far as your great-aunt is concerned there's nothing to worry you, nothing at all. She died quite peacefully. You know of course that I was her doctor: I was with her all the time, and so was John.'

'When did she die?'

'A fortnight ago.'

'What of?'

'Miss Mansel, she was over eighty.'

'I dare say she was, but there has to be a cause. What was it, heart? This asthma of hers? Plain neglect?'

I saw him compress his lips slightly, but he answered with the same pleasant appearance of frankness. 'The asthma was a fiction, Miss Mansel. The most difficult thing for me to disguise was my voice. When John told me how persistent you were, and we realised you might be impossible to fob off, we concocted a story that would allow me to speak in a whisper. And as you must realise now, the picture I had to give you of a forgetful and very strange old lady was far from the truth. Your aunt was very fully in possession of her faculties right up to the time of her death.'

'What was it, then?'

'Primarily her heart. She had a very slight coronary last autumn, and another in late February – after I had come to live with her here. Then, as you may know, she was difficult about food, and latterly had periodic sickness and stomach trouble which added to the strain. She had one of these gastric attacks three weeks ago, a bad one, and her heart wouldn't take it. That's the story, as simply as I can put it. She was, I repeat, over eighty. One would hardly have expected her to get through.'

I said nothing for a moment, drawing on my cigarette and staring at him. Then I said abruptly: 'Death certificates? Do you have them here?'

'Yes, I signed one, for the record. You can see it any time you wish.'

'I wouldn't believe a word of it. You concealed her death, you and John Lethman and the girl. One might even say you went to pretty fair lengths to conceal it. Why?'

He turned up a hand. 'Heaven knows I don't blame you, in the circumstances I wouldn't believe a word of it myself; but the plain fact is that, far from wanting your great-aunt out of the way, I'd have done a lot – in fact I did do a lot – to keep her alive. I don't ask you to believe me when I tell you that I liked her but you may believe me when I tell you that her death was damned inconvenient, coming when it did, and could have cost me a fortune. So I had a base motive for keeping her alive as well.' He tapped ash on the floor. 'Hence the mystery and the masquerade, which I'll explain in a moment. It didn't suit me to have lawyers or family invading the place, so I didn't report her death, and we've allowed the local people to think she's still alive.'

'And then my cousin and I turned up, just at the wrong moment. I see. But the wrong moment for what, Dr Grafton? You really had better start from the beginning, hadn't you?'

He leaned back in the chair. 'Very well. I was your great-aunt's doctor for about six years, and for the last three or four of them I came up here once a fortnight, sometimes oftener. She was very fit and active for her age, but she was something of a *malade imaginaire*, and besides, she was old, and I think, in spite of her fanatical independence, a bit lonely. And living alone as she did with the Arab servants I think she must have had some dread of illness or accident that would leave her completely at their – in their charge.'

I thought he had been going to say 'at their mercy'. I thought of Halide wearing the big ruby, of Nasirulla thick-set and tough and sullen, of idiotically mouthing Jassim. 'Yes?' I said.

'So I paid her a regular call, and this set her mind at rest – and besides, she enjoyed the company of a countryman. I may say I enjoyed the visits, too. She could be very entertaining when she was on form.'

'And John Lethman? He gave me a version of how he got taken on here, but I don't know if it was true.'

'Ah, yes, one of the few occasions where John managed a bit of lightning thinking. You may have guessed that he knows about as much as you do yourself about psychological medicine. He's an archae-ologist.'

'I . . . see. Hence my great-aunt's interest. Yes, I remember feeling a bit surprised when he talked about a "loony-bin" . . . They don't, if they know what they're talking about. But the Adonis Gardens?'

'They're genuine enough. You could say they were his premise. The paper he was working on was on the Adonis cult, and I suppose that's what suggested the exercise in morbid psychology – the "ecstatic religions" nonsense he gave you when he was cornered. Not bad, eh? Apart from that, I believe he told you the truth. He was travelling around doing research for his paper, and camping up near the little temple above the palace, and got caught by a storm one day – just as you were – and came to Dar Ibrahim. Your great-aunt took a fancy to him, and asked him to stay on while he did his work, and without anything much being said on either side he settled down and started looking after the place for her. I must say I was thankful when he decided to settle here. It made my job a lot easier.' There was a ghost of a smile I didn't quite like. He tapped ash off his cigarette again, delicately. 'A nice boy.'

'And useful?'

'Oh, certainly. He made a great deal of difference here. The lady thought the world of him.'

'I'm sure. But I meant to you. Useful to you.'

The heavy lids lifted. He gave a tiny shrug. 'Oh, yes, to me. I find him an excellent partner in my – business.'

'Yes, well, let's come to that now. Your business. You've been at Dar Ibrahim ever since you left Beirut? Yes, it figures. You were the "resident physician", not John Lethman. You were "the doctor" Jassim was talking about when Hamid and I came to the gate

. . . John Lethman certainly made a quick recovery from that one! But I was puzzled, because the Gab – the dogs liked him.'

'The dogs?'

'Oh, nothing to matter. She sent a letter home in February, did you know? She said her dog "couldn't abide the doctor".'

'Oh yes, that was the wretched little brute that I – that died . . . Yes, indeed. I was the "resident physician". That was part of the Stanhope legend, as you'll probably know; your great-aunt rather fancied having her own "Dr Meryon" in attendance.' He looked not unamused. 'It was a small price to pay. She was entitled to her own legend, even though I didn't quite see myself in the role of that unfortunate man ministering to that monstrous egoism day and night.'

'Don't tell me that poor Aunt Harriet made you minister to her monstrous egoism day and night? Even if she had it, which seems likely, since she was a Mansel, she had a sense of humour too.'

'Don't try and find motives for me, I told you I liked her.' He gave a little twist of a smile. 'Though I must admit that she was pushing it a bit the last year or two. On occasions the impersonation could get to be a little trying.'

I glanced above the bed to where the stick and the rifle hung.

'It'd be too much to hope that she really used them on Halide?'

He laughed, quite genuinely. 'She did occasionally throw things at Jassim, but that's about as far as it went.

And you mustn't be too hard on Halide. She's working very hard for what she wants.'

'John Lethman? Or Dar Ibrahim? Both sacred, I assure you.' I leaned forward to stub out my cigarette on the saucer. Then I regarded him for a moment. 'You know, I think I do believe you about my great-aunt . . . I mean, I doubt if you meant her any harm. For one thing you don't seem worried about what she may have written in her letters . . . unless you censored all her letters, and I doubt if you did, since I gather she was free to speak to the village people and to the carriers who brought supplies across. You obviously never saw her last letter inviting Charles to visit her, or Humphrey Ford's letter, either.'

I half expected him to ask what I was talking about, but he didn't. He was watching me steadily.

'And I'm inclined to pass John Lethman,' I said, 'but what about the servants? Are you quite sure that Halide didn't have a good reason for wanting the old lady out of the way?'

'No, no, that's nonsense, Your aunt used to be pretty fierce sometimes with the servants – they tend to do nothing at all unless one stands over them – but she liked the girl.'

'That wasn't quite what I suggested.'

'And Halide looked after her devotedly. I told you your aunt could be difficult, and the late-night sessions really were a fact. The girl was sometimes run off her feet.' He waved a hand. 'These rooms – they've only been neglected since her death, you must realise that. We cleared them a bit roughly of some of the worst clutter because we wanted to use them – they were naturally the best kept and most central rooms – but there simply wasn't time to clean them up properly before you saw them.' A look. 'We were glad of the darkness for more reasons than one. Oh, the place was always shabby, and she liked to live in a clutter, but the rooms were kept clean when she was alive . . . my God, they had to be! But to suggest that Halide hated your great-aunt enough to . . . No, Miss Mansel.'

He broke off as Halide came in with the tray. She set it down near me on the table with no more than a bit of a rattle, then, without looking at either of us or speaking a word, went straight out of the room. She had taken me at my word and just brought coffee. It was a bit weak, but it was hot and fresh. I poured a cup, and drank some, and felt better.

'What's more,' said Henry Grafton, 'the same applies to John and Halide as applied to me. They had more reasons to wish the Lady Harriet alive than dead.'

'Meaning that they're in your racket with you?'

'You could put it like that.'

'Did my great-aunt leave a Will?' I asked bluntly.

He grinned. 'She made them every week. Apart from crossword puzzles it was her favourite amusement.'

'I knew that. We sometimes got copies. What happened to them all?'

'They'll be somewhere about.' He sounded unconcerned. 'She used to hide them away in odd corners. I'm afraid this isn't exactly an easy place to search, but you're welcome to try.'

I must have looked surprised. 'You mean you'll let me look around?'

'Naturally. In fact it's possible that the property now belongs to you – or more probably to your cousin.'

'Or to John Lethman?'

He shot me a look. 'As you say. She was very fond of him.'

'Another of her eccentricities?'

'A very common one. But I'm afraid that there'll be little left of any value. There may be one or two personal souvenirs you may care to unearth from the general chaos, and as I say you're welcome to try.'

'Such as the ring that Halide's wearing?'

He looked surprised. 'The garnet? You would have that? It was certainly your aunt's favourite, she always wore it, but I understand she gave it to Halide . . . well, of course . . . probably Halide wouldn't mind . . .'

'Dr Grafton, please don't think I'm standing with one foot in my aunt's grave, but the ring has what they call "sentimental value", and I'm pretty sure that the family will fight to get it back. Besides, she meant me to have it. If she did give it to Halide then she must really have been round the bend, and no court would allot it to her.'

'Is it so very valuable?'

'I know nothing at all about the value of garnets,' I said, momentarily truthful, 'but you can take it from me it's not just a keepsake for the maid, however devoted. It belonged to my great-grandmother and I want it back.'

'Then you must certainly have it. I'll speak to Halide.'

'Tell her I'll get her something to take its place, or there may be something else left she'd like to have.'

I put down my cup. There was a pause. Some big insect, a beetle, hurtled in through the bright doorway, blundered around the room for a moment or two, and went out. I felt suddenly very tired, as if the conversation were slipping away from me. I believed him . . . and if I believed him surely the rest didn't make any sense?

'All right,' I said at length, 'so we come to what's happened since her death. But before we go on, will you show me where she is?'

He got to his feet. 'Of course. She's out here in the Prince's garden, as she wished to be.'

He led the way out into the little court, past the dry fountain, through diagonals of sun and shadow and between beds of baked earth where in early spring there would be irises and Persian tulips. Over the high outer wall fell a tangle of white jasmine, and beside it a cascade of yellow roses made a blinding curtain. The scene was wonderful. In the shade thrown by the flowers was a flat white stone, uncarved, and at its head stood the stone turban of the Moslem dead.

I looked at this in silence for a moment. 'Is this her grave?'

'Yes.'

'No name?'

'There hasn't been time.'

'You must know as well as I do that this is a man's grave.'

He made a sudden movement, quickly suppressed,

but I felt a jerk of apprehension as my body tightened back into wariness. This was still the man who had savaged me in the car, who was playing some nasty game or other where he had a lot at stake . . . Somewhere, not far below the surface – just under the sweating skin, behind the oil-black eyes – was something not as calm, as pleasant, as Dr Henry Grafton would like me to believe.

But he said with what sounded like gentle amusement: 'No, really, I can't have you suspecting me of anything else! You know – of course you do! – that she liked to dress as a man, and indeed behaved like one. I suppose it gave her a kind of freedom in Arab countries that a woman couldn't have normally. When she was younger the Arabs called her "the Prince" because of the way she rode, and the horses and state she liked to keep. She had this planned' – a gesture to the gravestone – 'some time before she died. It was surely part of the same conceit.'

I stared in silence at the slender column with its carved turban. Somehow of all that I had seen this was the most alien, the most foreign symbol. I thought of the leaning lichened stones in the old churchyard at home, the big elms, the yews by the lychgate, the rooks blown past the tower in the evening winds. A shower of yellow petals drifted down on the blank hot stones, and a lizard flashed out, palpitated for an instant there, watching us, then vanished.

'"I have purchased an excellent Tombstone locally".'

'What?' asked Henry Grafton.

'I'm sorry, I didn't realise I'd spoken aloud. You're right, this is what she wanted. And at least she's with friends.'

'Friends?'

'In the next garden. The dogs, I saw the graves.'

I turned away. The tired feeling persisted. The heavy scented heat, the sound of bees, perhaps still the effects of the injection and the strain of the day, were weighing on me.

'Come back in out of the sun.' His dark eyes were peering at me. They looked very intent. 'Are you all right?'

'Perfectly. Floating, rather, but it's not unpleasant. Was that only pentothal?'

'That's all. You weren't out for long, and it's quite harmless. Come along.'

The room seemed comparatively cool after the trapped heat of the garden. I sat down with relief in the lacquer chair and leaned back. The corners of the room were swimming in shadow. Henry Grafton picked up a glass from the table and poured water into it.

'Drink this. Better? Here, have another cigarette. It'll help you.'

I took it automatically, and he lit it for me and then moved away to hitch his chair out of the shaft of sunlight which slanted low now from a window, and sat down again.

I flattened my hands on the carved lacquer of the chair arms. Somehow the little, practised touch of solicitude had changed the tone of the interview, the doctor-patient gesture had put him back, subtly, on top. I made an effort, through the invading fatigue, to resume the cool accusing tone of attack.

'All right, Dr Grafton. That's the first part of the inquisition over. For the time being I'll accept that my great-aunt's death was a natural one, and that you did all you could. Now we come to why you had to conceal it, what you called the "mystery and the masquerade" . . . and what you've done to me. You've an awful lot of explaining still to do. Go on.'

He regarded his hands for a minute, clasped in his lap. Then he looked up.

'When you rang up my house and were told I was gone, did they tell you anything about me?'

'Not exactly, but they played hell with the silences. I gather you're in trouble.'

'True, I was in trouble, so I got out while the going was good. I can think of a lot of places I'd rather be in than a Lebanese prison.'

'As bad as that?'

'Oh quite. A little matter of getting and selling medical supplies illegally. You can get away with murder here more easily.'

'You wouldn't just have been deported?'

'That would hardly have helped. As it happens, I'm a Turkish national, and the penalties there are even worse. Take it from me, I had to get out, and fast, before they caught up with me. But I had assets in the country, and I was damned if I'd leave them without realising them. Naturally, I'd been afraid this might happen one day, so I'd made arrangements. Dar

Ibrahim had been my centre and – shall we call it
storeroom? – for some time, and over the past few
months I had managed to' – a flicker of the brown
eyelids and a tiny pause – 'engage John's interest. So
the actual getaway went smoothly enough. I was driven
to the airport and checked in, then someone else took
over my ticket and boarded the flight. If you know the
airport here you'll know it can be done. John was
waiting outside the airport and drove me up here by
the back road – the way I brought you today – and I
walked down to Dar Ibrahim. Your great-aunt
expected me. Naturally I hadn't told her the truth; I
spun her some story about an abortion and procuring
drugs without charge for certain poorer class patients.
Like the Stanhope woman, she had the highest dis-
regard for the laws of this country, so she took me in
and kept it secret. She was too delighted to have her
doctor here as a permanency to ask many questions,
and she talked too much herself to be over-curious
about other people. As for the servants – Halide had
her eye on John as a one-way ticket out of Sal'q, and
her brother was employed by me already. Jassim's
silence one hardly has to buy; it takes practice to
understand more than one word in twelve, and in
any case he's too stupid to know what's going on.
So here I was, sitting pretty, with a good base to work
from and John's help as outside agent to start cashing
in on my assets. It went like a dream, no suspicions,
winding up as smoothly as clockwork, cash due to
come in, myself due to check out finally at the end of
the summer . . .'

He paused. I leaned forward to flick ash into the saucer. It missed, and went on to the table to add to the patina of dust.

He went on: 'Then just a fortnight ago came your great-aunt's death. My God, for you to think I'd killed her! I spent nine hours solid at her bedside – right there – fighting for her life like a mother tiger . . .' He wiped his upper lip. 'Well, there you are. She died – and her death could have thrown the doors wide open, and me to the lions. In the end we decided to play it cool – I believe that's the expression nowadays? – and keep her death quiet. We thought we might just get away with it for the couple of weeks that were needed to complete the current operation. I couldn't hope to keep it quiet much longer than that, and the risks were too big. We had to cut our losses and plan a complete get-out in a big hurry – but we did it. What we didn't reckon with was you. Nothing your great-aunt had ever said led us to think we'd have a devoted family hammering at the door within a day or two. But – and just at the wrong moment – you came.'

The sun had almost gone, and its last light sloped in a low bright shaft across my feet. Dust motes swirled in it. I watched them half idly. Beyond their quick dazzle the man in the other chair seemed oddly remote.

'We thought at first you'd be easy to fob off,' he said, 'but you're a persistent young woman, and a tough one. You managed to put the wind up John, and we were afraid you were in a position, if you really got worried, to whistle up all sorts of help and come back armed with lawyers and writs of habeas corpus and

God knows what else; so we thought we hadn't much to lose by trying the masquerade, and if it seemed to satisfy you you might keep quiet for the few days' grace we needed. It was a desperate sort of idea, but I thought I might get away with it for a few minutes in semi-darkness, especially with the male clothes she used. In fact it was that habit of hers that gave me the idea in the first place. If we'd refused to let you see your aunt at all, you'd have been convinced she was ill, or that John was keeping you out for his own ends, and if you'd got suspicious enough to bring a doctor or a lawyer from Beirut, we'd have been sunk. So we tried it, and it worked.'

I nodded, thinking back over the interview; the hoarse whisper disguising the man's voice, the grotesque glimpses of the balding skull under the turban, the sunken mouth from which presumably he had removed his lower teeth, the alert black eyes. Halide's nervousness and John Lethman's watchful, edgy look had been for none of the reasons I had imagined.

'I get it now,' I said. 'All that chat of John Lethman's at supper – he was finding out all he could about the family so as to fill you in on things Aunt H didn't tell you. You knew I hadn't seen her since I was a kid, so you thought you'd probably fool me easily enough, but Charles had seen her recently, so naturally "Great-Aunt Harriet" wouldn't receive him. Oh, yes, clever enough, Dr Grafton.' I blew a long cloud of smoke into the air between us. 'And as a matter of fact you rather enjoyed it, didn't you? John Lethman tried to hurry me out, and heaven knows I'd have gone, but you wouldn't let me, you were enjoying yourself too much making a fool of me.'

He was grinning. Grotesquely, it was Great-Aunt Harriet's face as I had thought of her, vaguely seen through the smoke and the dusty shaft of sunlight, remote as something glimpsed down the wrong end of a telescope.

I said: 'Yes, all right, so it worked. You fooled me, and you fobbed Charles off quite successfully, and surely after I'd left the place you were in the clear, so why drag me back? I'd gone hadn't I, quite satisfied? Why drag me back here like this?'

'Because we hadn't fobbed your cousin off, and you know it. Oh, don't give me that great big innocent look, it doesn't suit you. Shall I tell you what happened? The first time you left here it wasn't your driver who met you, it was your cousin, and between you you hatched the plan to let him in on Monday night. He came, and you explored the place together. Yes, my dear, that stare's a bit more genuine.'

'How do you know all this?'

'Your precious cousin told me all about it himself.'

I don't think I spoke. I just stared. I couldn't quite take in what he was saying. The room seemed to be swirling round me, smoke and dusty sunlight dazzling like fog.

'After you'd gone back to your room that evening, he was to have left by the back gate – the mountain gate, wasn't he?' Grafton's voice was smooth as cream. 'Well, he didn't. John and I came across him in the passageway below here, trying to force one of the padlocked doors. It wasn't much use denying who he was – you're very like one another, aren't you? So we – er, we took him in. He's been safely locked away in the palace prison ever since. It won't surprise you to know the palace has its own gaol? Unhappily there was only one cell serviceable, so when we caught you as well, we had to use the storeroom for you.'

'Here? Charles here? I don't believe you. He can't be!' My brain seemed to be groping, like someone feeling through a roomful of smoke, not sure of the direction of the door or the distance to the window. I think I had a hand to my forehead, 'You're lying. You know you're lying. He wrote me a letter, and left it for me in Beirut. He went to Damascus to see Ben's father . . . no, to Aleppo. And we saw him – yes we saw him on the way . . .'

'He certainly wrote you a letter. He suggested doing that himself. If he hadn't done it to ensure you kept away from Dar Ibrahim and didn't start hunting for him when he failed to turn up at the Phoenicia, we couldn't have let you go in the morning.'

'Why did you?'

'Your driver,' he said shortly, 'and your hotel. Your cousin pointed out that it was easier to let you go than to risk someone starting to ask questions. Besides, as he told us, you thought you'd seen your great-aunt alive and well, and could spread the belief that all was normal.'

'So he wrote the letter – all those elaborate lies – he even pretended he'd seen her himself and recognised her . . . I've been wondering about that, I thought he

must have seen you and made the same mistake as I did
. . . You mean – that letter – it was all quite deliberate?
Just to keep me out?'

'Exactly that.'

I said nothing. The conversation no longer seemed
to have much to do with me. He was still smiling, and
as I stared at him, bemused, I saw the grin widen. The
top teeth were his own; the incisors were yellowish and
long. He was talking again, fragments of information
drifting like torn paper to lie in a crazy pattern: John
Lethman – no doubt the 'Englishman' seen in the
distance by the faun – had driven the Porsche down
to Beirut in the early morning, hidden it in someone's
backyard, woken the someone whose name seemed to
be Yusuf and given him the letter, then been driven
back by Yusuf, who later got the letter delivered to the
hotel and went himself to ride herd on me . . .

'But you, my dear, didn't stay out of the line of fire.
You made it fairly obvious that you were going to ask
some damned awkward questions and make some
damned awkward contacts. You even telephoned England. And from what our man heard of your telephone
conversation with Damascus, we decided to remove
you.'

'The Arab in the red tarboosh. He was in the next
booth.' I said it to myself, not to him.

'Certainly. Well, since you'd made your plans public, and that damned driver was already there with you,
and we didn't want any eyes turning to Dar Ibrahim,
we decided to get you the wrong side of the frontier and
then let you disappear. All very simple, no great harm

done – your car stopped, yourselves robbed, your papers taken and the car wrecked . . . somewhere beyond the Antilebanon, we thought, or even off towards Qatana. Yusef was confident he could immobilise you for long enough. So he got the Porsche out and drove it through to wait. It was the bait, of course. You'd have followed it—'

'Hamid! If you've harmed Hamid—!'

'Not if he's sensible. Most Arabs are, if you make it worth their while.' He laughed. 'I thought at first your being stopped at the frontier was going to bitch all our plans, but it worked out like a dream. You didn't see me, but I was there, and I saw what happened. My driver followed yours into the frontier buildings and heard the whole thing, so I sent him through to tell Yusuf to go south and get rid of your cousin's car, but as luck would have it you'd seen it yourself from above the road, and came running down to tell your driver to go through after it. My own car came straight back, and reported he'd crossed yours at the frontier. Since neither your driver nor the Porsche came back, one gathers Yusuf made him listen to reason, or else simply carried out the original plan and left him somewhere to cool off till tomorrow. We can't afford to let him near a telephone, you must see that.' A little grunt of amused satisfaction. 'After that it was so easy it was hardly true. You told everyone within hearing that you were going to the Adonis Hotel to get a car for Beirut, so I simply went there first and waited for you to come. The manager's new, so there was no fear of his recognising me, but I'm damned sure that by the time you turned up he was sure he'd known me all his life. You'd never have accepted a lift from someone picking you up on the road, but someone you met in the hotel, someone you were introduced to by name . . .' That smile again. 'I hope you appreciated the touch about the Great Mosque? You remember telling your "great-aunt" all about it?'

'Very clever. You're so very clever. Quite a little empire you've got, haven't you, with all your spies and drivers and cars. Something's paying pretty well. Don't grin at me like that, you snag-toothed little dago. What have you done with Charles?'

'I told you. He's in the lock-up.' The grin had vanished.

'Have you hurt him?'

'There was a bit of a rough-up last night.'

'You tried to rough Charles up? No wonder John looks the worse for wear. I thought his face was hurting him yesterday, and now I come to think of it, he kept that side turned away. It's come up lovely now, hasn't it? Good old Charles! And oh, my poor auntie! Did he hurt you much?'

The smile had certainly vanished. He had flushed darkly, and I saw the vein in his temple begin to beat. 'He didn't touch me. I had a gun. I admit John isn't much use, but then he drugs.'

'Drugs?' I don't think I managed to speak the question, I only looked it. He had gone far away from me again. The room was all shadows now. I found myself straining forward, peering to see where he had gone. Dimly, I knew I should be frantic with worry about Charles, with fear for myself. But I couldn't tie my brain down. It wouldn't work for me. It spun high and light. It floated, lifting me with it out of the chair, up towards the high dim corners of the room.

He was suddenly close, gigantic. He was out of his chair and standing over me. His voice was vicious. 'Yes, drugs, you silly spoiled little bitch. Drugs. I said "medical supplies", didn't I? There's a fortune in Indian hemp lying there in the cellars waiting for collection tonight, and another fortune growing in the fields above Laklouk if your great-aunt hadn't died, and I'd been able to hang on till harvest.' He drew in his breath. 'And not only hemp. They grow opium in Turkey and Iran, didn't you know? That's the real stuff. Opium, morphine, heroin – and I've a pipeline across Syria that's been working like a dream, and all it needs for the processing is a bit of time and the kind of privacy we get here at Dar Ibrahim . . .'

I'd been meaning to stub my cigarette out in the saucer, but the saucer was too far away, and the effort was too much. The stub fell through my fingers to the floor. It seemed to fall in slow motion, and I made no attempt to retrieve it, but just sat there, looking down at my own hand, which seemed a long way away and not attached to my body at all.

'. . . And that's just what we had, till you came. The room next to the storeroom where we put you, that's our lab. We've been working like slaves putting the stuff through since the last lot came down. Oh, we'd have had to pack it in this year, no doubt of that, and move our base – those bastards at the Narcotics Division of the

UN have been putting the screws on, and the National Assembly's promising to make it hotter than ever in this country next year . . . and of course since the old lady went Dar Ibrahim was due to shut down anyway. Phased withdrawal, don't they call it? The caravan comes through tonight . . .' His voice trailed off, and I heard him laugh again. He stooped and picked up the stub, and dropped it in the saucer. His face swam near mine. 'Feeling a bit far away, are you? Not exactly fit to cope? That was a reefer you had in the car, and you've just smoked two more, my pretty, and now you're going back to your nice little room to sleep them off . . . Till tonight's over.'

I wished I could care. I ought to care. Fragments of pictures were there in smoky darkness, like dreams edged with light. John Lethman's slack body and defeated young face with the sunken grey eyes. The Arab girl watching him fiercely. The patch of hemp with the label of the racing dog. The crates in the cellar. But they dislimned and the light beat in a steady echoing rhythm that was somehow my own heart beating, and someone's voice was coming and going in the throbbing air like the pulse of a drum, and I was out of it all, safe and high and floating as scatheless and beautiful and powerful as an angel among the cobwebs on the ceiling, while down there below in the dimming room sat a girl in a red lacquer chair, her body slack and drowsy in its plain expensive frock, her face pale, the cheekbones highlighted with a film of damp, her mouth vaguely smiling. Her hair was dark and smooth and fashionably cut. Her arms were sunburned, the hands long and slender, one wrist weighted down with a gold bracelet that had cost all of eighty pounds . . . A spoiled silly bitch, he had called her. She was blinking at him now. She had very big eyes, dark-fringed, made bigger by the make-up she affected, and now by the drug . . . Poor silly bitch, she was in danger, and I couldn't do a thing for her, not that I cared. And she didn't even look afraid . . .

Not even when John Lethman came quietly in, floating like another shadow in slow motion across the dim floor, to stand over her and ask of Henry Grafton, as if it hardly mattered.

'She's out, is she?'

'Two cigarettes. Well taken care of. And the boy?'

'Blocked. Cell blue with smoke and himself out cold. No trouble there.'

Henry Grafton laughed. 'No trouble anywhere. Safe under our hands till it's over. And you, young John, will stick to your ration and stay with it. You've just had your fix, by the look of you? Well, that's the last you'll get. Oh, you can smoke if you want to, but don't come asking me for more of the hard stuff because you won't get it till that cargo's safely through Beirut. D'you hear me? Right. Take her back.'

The younger man stooped over the chair. The girl moved her head dreamily and smiled at him, eyes misty. She seemed to be trying to speak, but couldn't manage it. Her head lolled back.

'I must say,' said John Lethman, 'I like her better this way.'

'Meaning she's too pretty to have a tongue like a

wasp's backside? I agree. My God, what a family! She reminds me of the old lady on her bad days. Well, she's asked for all she's getting. Take her away. I'm afraid you'll have to carry her.'

Lethman leaned over the lacquer chair. At his touch, some of the fumes of the drug must have lifted for a second. I came down from where I had been floating, into the body of the chair, as he pulled me forward to slide an arm round me and lift me. I managed to say slowly and with what I thought was immense dignity: 'Can manage qui' well, thank you.'

He said with impatience: 'Of course you can't. Come along, I won't hurt you. Don't be afraid.'

'Of you?' I said. 'Don't make me laugh.'

He bit his lip, yanked me out of the chair, and heaved me over his shoulder in the he-man lift. I'm ashamed to say I spoiled the heroic scene by laughing like an idiot upside down all the way back to my dungeon.

16

'Truly we have been at cost, yet we are
forbidden harvest.'

The Koran: Sura LVI

An empire I had called it, and I hadn't been far wrong.
Heaven knows the clues had been there if I had only
had the knowledge to work from; and heaven knows I
had all the pieces now.

It was hours later. My watch said eleven, within a
minute or two. The time had gone like a dream, literally
like a dream, passed like smoke from the cigarettes that
had sent me floating. I felt firmly enough based now –
too firmly. I was back on the bed in my prison, sitting
on top of the tumbled blankets holding an aching head,
no longer the slack-boned, don't-careish girl hopped
up with *bhang*, but a young woman with a crashing
hangover, still in reasonably full possession of her five
wits, and every one of them scared, with all the
evidence literally under her eyes.

They had left me a light this time. Up in its niche the
three-branched lamp held up its buds of flame. Beside
the bed was a jug of water and a glass. I drank, and my
mouth felt a little less as if someone had been cleaning

it out with an abrasive cleaner. I tried putting my legs down, and my feet to the floor. I could feel the floor, which was probably something. I didn't try anything violent, like standing up, but sat there, holding my head on to my body, and gently, as gently as possible, allowing my eyes to look here and there in the swimming light . . .

The room was far bigger than I had thought, stretching away back into the shadow. Behind the clutter of broken-down furniture and the piled rugs and harness that would be all one could see from the corridor, I now saw that the place was stacked, literally stacked with wooden boxes and cardboard cartons and small tins. Some of them, I thought, would probably be 'blinds' – genuine consignments of whatever article (like the cooking oil) was used to disguise the drugs – but if even a fraction of these held hashish or the opium derivatives, the room would have bought up Aladdin's cave four times over. I thought of Hamid's sheeps' droppings, but somehow it wasn't funny any more.

On the cartons nearest me the device of the running dog stood out clear and damning, with the grotesque warning carefully stencilled below: '*Best quality, beware immitations.*' It shook the last piece into place, and Henry Grafton's sketchy story, with all its gaps and evasions, became, with this gloss added, very clear indeed. The hashish, grown copiously in the high hills; John Lethman crop-watching, or bargaining with the growers, or arranging for the piecemeal ferrying of the stuff down by the peasants – perhaps one of them the very man whom Charles and I had seen approaching the back gate of the palace. Dar Ibrahim must have been used as the centre of the filthy trade for some time, might even have been so used long before the old lady moved in. It was the perfect clearing house, and also the perfect retreat for anyone in Henry Grafton's situation – the lonely hilltop fortress kept by the strong-minded old woman who refused to receive visitors, and who had (like her prototype Lady Hester) once or twice defied the law and would presumably defy it again on a friend's behalf. I couldn't believe that my great-aunt would have concealed Henry Grafton had she known what trade he was engaged in, but no doubt his story had been plausible enough, and equally plausible the account of whatever 'experiments' he and John Lethman were conducting in the under-ground storeroom. And John Lethman's own role in the business became pathetically clear. He had prob-ably started innocently enough, being persuaded by the unscrupulous Grafton that the occasional 'smoke' would do him no harm; then quietly, inevitably, hooked on the hard drugs that would ensure his dependence and continued help. It was not my Great-Aunt Harriet who was the victim of this affair – for every reason I was now convinced that Grafton would never have wished her out of the way – but John Lethman.

And I was very much afraid that there were going to be two more victims. Henry Grafton might keep in-sisting that he meant me and my cousin no real harm, but people have been murdered for a lot less than a fortune in drugs and a possible death sentence (since

Grafton was a Turkish national) if they went astray. He could hardly imagine that Charles or I would fail to report all we knew the moment we were able to, yet I – and probably my cousin as well – had been handed both information and evidence with a carelessness that terrified me. Whether he had got round to realising it yet or not, he would have to kill us both if he wanted to save his skin.

The door must have been very thick. I had heard no movement out in the passageway, but the door swung open suddenly to reveal Halide standing there with – as ever – a tray in her hands. There was nobody with her, and she managed the tray one-handed while she opened the door, so I supposed that my captors knew the condition their drugs would reduce me to. She now stood propping the door open with one shoulder, and eyeing me with her usual contempt and hostility.

'So, you are awake. Here is your food. And do not think that you can push past me and get away because the one way is only to the back gate, which is locked this time, and the key out of it and Jassim is in the outer court, and the men are in the Lady's room.'

I eyed her sourly, 'If you knew how funny that sounds in English.'

'*Quoi?*'

'Never mind.' Confronted with her shimmering grace – it was the green silk again – I felt terrible. And I didn't think the bathroom gambit would work again. I made no attempt to get to my feet, but watched her as she came gracefully away from the door and set the tray down on a box with a rap which made the crockery rattle.

'Halide—'

'Yes?'

'I suppose you know what they – the men – are doing, why they have locked me up, me and my cousin?'

'Oh, yes, John—' – she brought the name out with a kind of flourish – 'tells me everything.'

'You lucky girl. Did he tell you what the penalties were for running drugs in this neck of the woods?'

'*Quoi?*'

'Even in this dirty corner of the dirty world? Even in Beirut? Didn't John warn you what the police would do, to you and your brother as well, if they discovered what was happening here at Dar Ibrahim?'

'Oh, yes.' She smiled. 'Everybody knows this. Everybody does it, here in the Lebanon. For many years before the doctor came here, my brother used to bring the hashish down from the hills. It is only the brave men who are the carriers from the hills to the sea.'

I supposed it was too much to hope that the primitive mind would see it as anything other than a sort of Robin Hood gesture of bravery. To the peasant, the hashish brought pleasure, and money. If an unreasonable Government chose to forbid its growth for private purposes, why then the Government must be fooled. It was as simple as that. It was the same mentality which, in more sophisticated societies, assumes that the tax and speed laws are made to be broken.

'You need not be so afraid,' said Halide to me, with contempt, 'I think they do not mean to kill you.'

'I'm not afraid.' I met her derisive look as steadily as I could. 'But I think you had better be, Halide. No, listen, I don't think you quite realise what is happening here, and I'm not quite sure if John knows, either, just what he's got himself into. It isn't just a case of you and your friends having a quiet smoke now and then and your brother shooting it out with a few local police on his way to the sea. Not any more. It's big business, and the Governments of every responsible country are wild keen to stop it. Are you hoping to clear out with your John when this lot's been shifted and he's got his share of the money? Where d'you think you can go? Not into Syria – they'd catch you up in no time. Not into Turkey – there's a death penalty there. The same applies to Iran, Egypt, where you like. Believe me, Halide, there's no future in this for you or for John. Don't think he can take you to England, either, because you'll be picked up there as soon as I or my cousin open our mouths.'

'Perhaps you will not get out of here for a long time.'

'That's silly talk,' I said. 'You know as well as I do that any minute now the Damascus police will start looking for us, and where would the trail lead them first if not to Dar Ibrahim? Dr Grafton'll be lucky if he gets the stuff away at all.'

'He will get it away. I think you do not realise what time it is, or what day? It is nearly midnight, Wednesday. The caravan is already on its way here. The palace will be empty by daylight.'

'I . . . suppose it will,' I said slowly. I had lost count of time. I put a hand to my forehead, pressing the heel of it against my temple as if that would clear my thoughts. At least the headache had gone. 'Listen, Halide, listen to what I have to say. And take that look off your face, I'm not pleading for anything, I'm offering you something, you and John Lethman, because he's nothing much worse than weak and stupid, and you've no chance to know better. My family – my cousin's family – we're wealthy, what you'd call important people. I obviously can't offer you the kind of money you'll get by helping Grafton with this operation, but I can offer you some help which believe me you're going to need, and badly. I don't know your laws, but if you let me and my cousin go now, and if you and your John were to give evidence against Dr Grafton, and the police stopped the cargo of drugs, I think you'd find they wouldn't prosecute you or your brother, or even Lethman.'

I had been watching her as I spoke, but her face was turned away from the lamplight and I couldn't see if my words were having any effect. I hesitated. It would certainly be no use beginning to talk about rights and wrongs, or why I should have any interest not strictly personal in stopping the cargo from reaching the sea. I added, flatly: 'I don't know whether or not your Government would give a reward for information, but in any case I'd see that my family gave you money.'

'You!' The blazing contempt in her voice made it an expletive in its own right. 'I do not listen to you! All this talk of police and governments and laws. You are only a stupid woman, too stupid to get a man! Who are you?' And she spat on the floor at my feet.

It was all it needed. My head cleared miraculously, as the adrenalin came coursing out of the booster pumps. I laughed.

'As a matter of fact I have got a man. I've had one for twenty-two years. And as for who I am, I'm the great-niece and relative by blood of the Lady Harriet, your mistress. I'm also probably at the moment owner or part owner of this palace and its contents. So for a start, my nasty little Arab maiden – because in spite of your efforts I wouldn't back John Lethman ever to have got past first base – you can hand over my great-aunt's ring. And I may warn you that your precious Dr Grafton will make you give it up even if I can't. Hand it over, poppet.'

It was obvious that Grafton had already spoken to her. Her face darkened, and for a moment I saw her hand clench and hide itself in a fold of her silk robe. Then with a gesture she drew the ring off.

'Take it. Only because I wish. It is nothing. Take it, daughter of a bitch.'

And she threw it at me with the gesture of an empress flinging a groat to a beggar. It landed with an accuracy she could never voluntarily have achieved in a dozen years, slap in the bowl of soup.

'Well,' I said cheerfully, 'that should sterilise it. Or should it? I've never see the kitchens here, but when I was a guest I had to take them on trust. Now I'm only a prisoner I don't need to eat what I don't fancy, do I?'

I leaned over and picked up the fork from the tray, fished Great-Aunt Harriet's ruby out of the soup, dunked it in the glass of water, and dried it on the napkin provided. Then I noticed the silence. I looked up.

When she spoke I knew something had put her out considerably. 'You do not wish the meal?'

'Oh, I'm quite glad of something, and it's a wise gaolbird that let's nothing slip. I'll eat the bread and cheese. Thanks for the ring.' And I slipped it on to my finger.

'Not the soup? The ring was clean . . . it . . .'

'I'm sure it was. I wouldn't have been rude about it if you, my proud beauty, had not just called me the daughter of a bitch. Not that I mind, I like dogs, but Mummy might be a bit narked. No, Halide, not the soup.'

She had obviously not followed anything except the first and last statements. 'Then let me bring you more – please.'

I looked at her in surprise, then the surprise slid into a stare. To being with it had only seemed odd that she had offered to oblige me at all, but the last request had carried an urgent, almost pleading note.

'Of course I will bring more. It is no trouble. Any minute now they will come to start loading the boxes and you will be taken out of here and put with the man, so you must eat while you can. Please allow me!' There was an abject quality in the eagerness, the automatic bending of the shoulders and thrusting of the chin and opening of the hands, palms up, that suddenly spoke more clearly than any documentary could have done, of generations of slavery and the whip.

'It's good of you, but there's not the slightest need.'
My own reaction, I noticed with sour self-contempt,
was also predictable. While she was insolent I was
angry and unpleasant; as soon as she crept into her
place, I could afford a cold civility. I made an effort. 'I
don't want the soup, thank you. The bread and cheese
will do very well.'

'I will take it back, then, just in case—'

'No, no, don't bother. But I'd be glad if you'd go
straight to Dr Grafton—'

I never finished the sentence. We had both reached
forward together, she to lift the bowl from the tray, and
I to stop her, and for a moment, inches apart, our eyes
met.

Then I shot out a hand and took hold of her wrist
before she could take the bowl. Her expression, and the
tiny intake of breathe, told me that – incredibly – I had
been right.

'What's in it?' I demanded.

'Let me go!'

'What's in it?'

'Nothing! It is good soup, I made it myself . . .'

'I'm dead sure you did. What did you put in it? More
of your *cannabis indica* to keep me quiet, or something
worse?'

'I don't know what you're talking about! I put
nothing in it, I tell you! Chicken and herbs and vege-
tables and a little *zafaran* and—'

'And a drop or two of poison to top it up?'

She drew back sharply, and I let her go and stood up.
We were much of a height, but I felt inches the taller of

the two, and ice-cold with contemptuous rage. There is something infuriating, rather than frightening, about this kind of attack. That one is there to react to it at all means that the attempt has failed and the danger is over, and I suppose one's very relief at that failure explodes in contempt for the poisoner and blazing anger at the filthy method used.

'Well?' I said, quite softly.

'No, it was not! No! How can you be so foolish as to think so? Poison? Where would I find poison?'

The words were bitten off with a gasp as Henry Grafton said from the doorway behind her:

'What's this? Who's talking about poison?'

She swung round to face him, hands out as if to ward him off, her body still curved in that lovely windblown bow that one sees in the carved ivory ladies of Japan. Her mouth opened, and her tongue licked across her lips, but she said nothing. His eyes went past her to me.

'I was,' I said. 'The sweet creature seems to have put something in my soup that she doesn't care to talk about. Would this by any chance be by your orders?'

'Don't be a fool.'

I raised my eyebrows. 'Dope, yes, but poison, never? You and your Hypocritic Oath . . . Perhaps she'll tell you what it is, and why? Or would you like to take it away and analyse it in your little lab next door?'

He stared at me only briefly, then his eyes went to the tray.

'Did you take any of the soup?' he asked eventually.

'No, or I've no doubt I'd be writhing on the floor.'

'Then how do you know there's anything wrong with it?'

'I don't, it's an inspired guess. But she was too anxious by half for me to drink it, and she hasn't cared terribly for my welfare up till now. She threw the ring into it by mistake, and when I said I didn't want it after that she was upset. Then I knew. Don't ask me how, but I'd take a twenty to one bet on it now, and don't tell me you don't think the same. Look at her. And as for where she got it, hasn't she got a whole roomful at her disposal, all that stuff of Great-Aunt Harriet's? Ask her.' I nodded at the silent girl, 'ask little Miss Borgia here. Perhaps she'll admit it to you.'

Long before I had finished speaking his attention had switched back to Halide, the black eyes bright and deadly as an oil-slick. I had a moment's sharp relief that under this night's various pressures he should take time to handle this so seriously; it must only mean that he intended no real harm to Charles or myself. But the expression in his eyes as he looked at her, and the girl's obvious terror, surprised me. Her hands were tightly clasped at the base of her throat, clutching the lovely silk of the robe together as if for warmth.

'Is this true?'

She shook her head, then found her voice. 'It's all lies, lies. Why should I poison her? There is nothing in the soup – only the meat, and the herbs, and onions and *zafaran* . . .'

'Then,' said Henry Grafton, 'you wouldn't object to drinking it yourself?'

And before I knew what he was about, he had whipped the bowl up from the tray, and was advancing on the girl with it held up to the level of her mouth.

I think I gave a gasp, and then said weakly: 'Oh, no!' It was somehow too much, so absurdly the stock situation from a thousand and one Arabian Nights, an Eastern melodrama come ludicrously to life. 'For heaven's sake,' I said, 'why not just call in the dogs and try it on them? That's the form, isn't it? For pity's sake call the scene off, I withdraw the complaint!'

Then I stopped as I realised, not amused any more that the melodrama was taking Dr Grafton away from the door of the room as the girl backed in front of him . . . and there was a gun on the wall above the Prince's bed, if I could grab it before they got me . . .

Neither of them took the slightest notice of me. She had retreated until she was backed right up against a stack of crates beyond the bed, and her hands came up in front of her to push the bowl away. He drew back quickly to prevent its being spilled.

'Well, why don't you? Am I to believe this nonsense is true?'

'No, no, of course it isn't true! She only says this because she hates me! I swear it! I will swear it if you like on my father's head! Where would I get poison?'

'Considering my great-aunt's room is like remnant day at the chemist's,' I said dryly, 'I'd have thought one could lay hands on almost anything.'

He didn't look round when I spoke, all his attention was fixed on the girl, who stared back at him like a mesmerised rabbit which might at any minute burrow its way backwards through the stacked boxes. I edged a bit nearer the doorway.

'Why don't you call her bluff?' I asked.

I didn't see a movement, but she must have sensed that he was planning to do just that, for she gave in suddenly. 'All right, if you won't believe me! I did put something in it, and I did want her to drink it, but it is not a poison, it is only a purge, to give her pains and make her sick. She's a bitch and the daughter of a bitch, and you have made me give back the ring when she is rich already, and of course I do not try to kill her, but I hate her and I put the oil in the soup only to make her suffer a little . . . just a little . . .' Her voice faltered and seemed to strangle itself for a moment, defeated somehow by the heavy musty silence of the underground room.

'Charming, my God, charming!' I was within two jumps of the door now. 'Then you lock me in with Charles and leave me to it?'

Neither of them took the slightest notice of me. She finished in a rush: 'And if I must drink it I will, to prove to you that it is true . . . but tonight you will need me to help you, you and John so we will give it to a dog, or to Jassim, or to someone who does not matter, so that you will see . . .'

Grafton's face was suffused, and that ugly vein was beating again. Neither of them was concerned with me any more; whatever was between them shut me out completely, and I stood rooted there watching, afraid to move and direct that raging concentration back to myself.

'Where did you get it?' He spoke quite evenly.

'I forget. From her room, perhaps . . . I've had it a long time . . . all those bottles . . .'

'There were no purges in her room, I know that. Don't give me that, you never got it from there. I saw to it that there was nothing harmful lying about, and after she'd had her sick turns I checked to see if she'd been dosing herself. Come on, what was it? Did you get it from the village, or was it some filthy brew you made yourself?'

'No . . . I tell you it was nothing. It was something John had. I took it from his room.'

'From John? Why should he have that kind of thing? You said "oil". Do you mean castor oil?'

'No, no, no, I tell you I don't know what it was! It was a black bottle. Why don't you ask John? He will tell you it was harmless! He said it tasted strong, so I used to put in extra herbs, and pepper—'

'When did you see it first? The time I was away near Chiba?'

'Yes, yes, but why do you look like that? It was nothing, a drop or two, and then a little sickness – the pain was not bad – and afterwards she was always so quiet and good . . .'

I wouldn't have moved now for worlds, open door or not. The bowl had begun to shake in his hands, and his voice had that stretched, even thinness of a wire about to snap, but the girl didn't seem to recognise the signals. She had ceased to look alarmed, and had dropped her hands to twist them in the skirt of her dress, glowering back at him, sullen and defiant. I don't know just at what point through the swift, unemphatic exchange I had realised that they were no longer talking about me, but about Great-Aunt Harriet.

'Quiet and good!' He repeated the words with no expression at all. 'I see. My God, I wondered. Now I begin to see . . . Did this happen whenever I went away?'

'Not always. Sometimes when she'd been too diffi-cult. Oh, why the fuss, it did her no harm! You know how well I nursed her! You know how I had worked and cared for all those months, and how she would ring her bell night and day, and never must we be tired, always ready to run for this thing and that thing, and cook special food . . . But I wouldn't have harmed her, you know that! Only one or two drops I gave her, and then I would nurse her through it, and afterwards there would be peace for a few days.'

'And then she would be grateful. Yes, of course. Clever girl, Halide. Is that when she gave you the ring? Yes? What else did she give you?'

'Many things! And she meant me to have them! She said so! She gave me these things herself because I had cared for her! You shall not take them from me . . . indeed you dare not, because I gave them to my father and brother who will keep them! And then when I become an English lady—'

He spoke between his teeth. 'You killed the old woman. Do you not realise that even now, you stupid black bitch?'

'I did not!' Her voice was shrill with rage. 'How can you say this? It was only medicine, I tell you, and I took it from the chest that John keeps in his room – you know the old medicine box that the Lady's husband took on his expeditions—'

'That prehistoric collection? God knows what was in it! Do you mean to tell me John knew about this?'

'No, I tell you I took it! But I asked him what it was before I used it. I would not have used it unless I knew it was safe! It was not poison! He said it was a purge, made from the seed of some plant . . . yes, a spurge plant – I remember that because the words were the same, and—'

He had been sniffing at the bowl he held. Now he gave a great gasp as though he needed air. 'So that's it! Spurge plant, my God! It's croton oil, and I doubt if even old Boyd used the stuff in the last fifty years except for the camels! "One or two drops", indeed! Twenty drops and you'd kill a healthy horse! And you gave that stuff to an old woman, a sick woman—'

'It did her no harm! You know it did her no harm! Three times I gave it to her, and she got better—'

'And the last time,' said Henry Grafton very softly, with the wire in his voice beginning to shake, 'she'd had a coronary just three weeks before. And so she died . . . and if you'd kept your stupid fingers out of the pie she'd be alive today and we wouldn't have these damned people round our necks, and the whole job done as smoothly as kiss your hand and away with one fortune and time to collect another at harvest. But you – you—'

And he dashed the soup, bowl and all, in her face in an access of blinding rage.

The stuff was no longer hot, but it was greasy and it took her full across the eyes. And the bowl smashed. It must have been of fine china, because it didn't smash against the boxes behind her, but right across her cheek-bone. There was a still second before she screamed, and the scream choked because some of the slimy stuff went into her mouth and throat and gagged her, then she doubled up, retching and choking, and the blood came welling in a slabby stream on her cheek and mixed with the greensick slime of the soup.

Grafton swung his arm as if to strike her. I gave a cry of protest and jumped forward and grabbed it.

'That'll do! For pity's sake!'

He wrenched away to disengage himself. The movement was violent and – thrust by his shoulder – I went reeling back, sent the tray flying, and almost fell against the door. His face was that curious dark red, and his breath snorted in his throat. I don't know if he would have hit her again, but there was a flash in her hand, and she came away from the wall of crates like a leaping cat, claws and knife, and went for his face.

He was quick on his feet as many shortish men are, and I think it was purely reflex, too quick even for his thought, which made him leap back clear of those raking claws and the knife she had whipped from somewhere, Damascus-bright. She was on him. The knife flashed. He had no weapon – who would need it against me? – and he snatched up from the clutter the first thing that came to hand. I think even then what he snatched for was the whip that lay on the pile of camel harness, but his hand missed it by centimetres, and what he lifted and lashed down with was not the flexible whip, but the heavy, cruel goad.

It caught the girl full across the temple. She seemed to slacken in the middle, as if a spring had broken. She still lurched forward, but the claws slid loose and harmless down the man's neck, and the stabbing knife missed his throat by inches as her body pitched against him and slithered, joint by joint, into a slack and thudding collapse at his feet. The knife fell just before the final drop of the body, with a tinkling little sound on the floor. Then the upper part of her body slumped, and the head hit the stone with a small, and quite final little crack.

In the silence, I heard the lamp fluttering again like a caught moth.

My knees felt as if they didn't belong. I was back in the smoke, helpless, floating. I remember that I had to push myself away from the door, to go to Halide.

I had forgotten he was a doctor. Before I had done more than decide I must move, he was down beside her on one knee.

I took a step. I croaked somehow: 'Is she dead?'

What he was doing took not more than a moment, then he got to his feet. He didn't speak. He didn't need to. I'd never seen a dead body before, only people shamming dead on stage or screen, and I can tell you, no one could ever mistake death for anything but death, not once they'd seen it.

Whatever I was trying to say, choking on it through bile in my throat, never got said. Henry Grafton turned round on me now. He still had the goad in his hand.

Of course he had never meant to kill her. But she was dead, and I had seen it. And something else, I believe, got through to me – how, I don't know, except that just at that moment in the horrible little room reeking with soup and the oil lamp and something else that may have been death, all nerves were stripped raw and felt as if they were exposed like white roots all over the skin. He had never killed before, and maybe he didn't quite believe it even yet, or believe how simple it had been. Whatever soothing lies he had been telling himself about Charles and me, now he knew. Now the decision had made itself. He had taken the first step on a very easy slide . . . And behind those dilated black eyes, for all I knew, he could be smoked as high as an Assassin with the damned drug himself.

I shall never be sure if what I did then was the stupidest thing I could have done. Perhaps I should have stayed where I was and spoken calmly, till the dark-red look went from his face and the suffused eyes cleared.

But all I could see was that the doorway was clear and that I was nearer to it than he was.

I didn't stop to argue. I turned and ran.

17

The Stars are setting and the Caravan
Starts for the Dawn of Nothing – Oh,
    make haste!
          E. FitzGerald: *The Rubáiyát*
                of Omar Khayyám

The passage was well enough lighted; someone had put oil-lamps in one or two of the old torch-brackets – probably in preparation for the night's work – and these showed me the stairway to the Prince's Divan.

It was the only way to go. There was no point in making for the Seraglio, since I couldn't hope to get down from the window alone; the postern was locked, and Jassim was guarding the main door. Besides, there was Charles. My only hope was the Prince's Divan and the rifle.

I was about a third of the way up the stairs when the arras at the top was swept aside and John Lethman came through like a pea from a catapult, shouting, 'Grafton! Grafton!' and hurtled downstairs three at a time. Before I could stop myself, I had run straight into him.

He gave a grunt of surprise and held me fast. What

must have surprised him even more was that I made no attempt to get away. I suppose if I had been in a fit condition to think I might have expected Halide's murder to put him on my side against Grafton, but I wasn't thinking, and it was only instinct that made me see him almost as a rescuer, as corruptible rather than yet corrupt, a man who could surely not stand aside and watch me killed.

'How did you get out?' he snapped. Then – 'What's happened?'

I couldn't speak, but as I clung to him, pointing back at the storeroom door, Henry Grafton erupted into the corridor below us with the goad in his hand.

At the sight of us he stopped dead, and the goad slowly sank until its iron tip rested on the floor. There was a little pause, during which nobody said anything, then Lethman, gripping me by the arm, dragged me after him down the staircase and back towards the door.

I didn't look. I think I shut my eyes. Lethman didn't go in, he stopped just short of the doorway.

Henry Grafton cleared his throat and spoke. 'It was an accident. She went for me.' Then as no one said anything, suddenly savage, to me: 'Tell him it was an accident, you little fool! Tell him what happened!'

I didn't look at either of them. 'Oh, yes, it was an accident. He never meant to kill her, I'm sure of that. He threw the soup at her in a temper and she went for him and he grabbed for something – the whip, I think – and got hold of that thing. I don't suppose he noticed in the mad rush that it was made of iron.' I added in a tight voice that was unfamiliar even to me: 'And as a matter of fact I can't even pretend I'm sorry. I gather from what they were saying that she killed Great-Aunt Harriet.'

That brought him up sharply. He still kept his grip on my wrist, but he seemed to have forgotten about me. He swung on Grafton.

'She what? Halide killed the old lady? What's this?'

'It's true.' Grafton was staring down at the thing in his hand as if he'd never seen it before. 'She'd apparently been treating her off and on to doses of croton oil.'

'Doses of – Good grief, so *that* was it? I remember her asking about the stuff.' His hand went to his head. He looked sick and shaken. 'But why? I don't get it. That stuff – good God – what could she hope to gain?'

'A dowry,' said Grafton dryly. 'Oh, she didn't mean to kill her, that was ignorance. She was just clever enough to choose the times when I was away. I admit it never entered my head – it was one of those simple, stupid schemes one might expect from that mentality – she wanted the old lady periodically ill and helpless so that she could nurse her through it with the sort of devotion that sticks out a mile and gets its due reward. Which it did.'

He was watching the younger man as he spoke. Lethman said nothing. You can always tell when someone is thinking back, remembering. He was biting his lip, his face still shocked and sick-looking. Behind the slack lines and pin-pupilled eyes of the addict I thought I could see the ghost of the pleasant-faced boy who had been pulled into Henry Grafton's orbit. And I thought I saw, too, the ghost – hastily suppressed with shame – of a boy relieved of a burden.

Grafton saw it, too. 'Oh, yes, there were rewards. You know how lavish the Lady could be at times. I gather that most of her pickings are being kept for her by her family in the village. As I said, a dowry.'

'For heaven's sake,' I broke in, 'cover her face and let's get out of here before I'm sick.'

Grafton gave me a look, and then obeyed me, stooping over the thing on the floor to pull a greasy, merciful fold of the pretty silk across. John Lethman turned abruptly away, dragging me with him towards the stairs. I went, only too willingly. As we reached the top and he pulled the arras back. Grafton came out of the storeroom below, shutting the door behind him, then as an afterthought pushed it open again, and flung the goad back inside. I heard it go clattering down on the floor, then the door slammed again, finally, on the dreadful little room.

The Prince's Divan was brilliantly lit tonight. The usual lamp stood on the covered fountain which served as a table in the middle of the lower room, other lamps burned in niches by the door, and from a bracket high in the wall a double cresset gave a smoky red light. As Grafton followed us through and the arras swung shut behind him, the cresset blew and guttered in the draught, sending grotesque shadows reeling up the walls.

'For Christ's sake hang on to the girl.' His voice was harsh but controlled. It seemed he was back in charge.

'If you let her go we'll both be in the can. God knows
I'm sorry about what happened, John – it's perfectly
true that Halide killed the old woman and landed us
both in this, but do you seriously imagine I'd have hit
her if she hadn't gone for me with a knife? The way I
see it, we'd better get out of the jam we're in before we
start calling the odds over this. So snap out of it, and
let's get back on the job. One thing, I suppose you
know what'll happen if Nasirulla gets wind of it? We'll
have to shift the body now, and think up some way of
stalling him off if he asks where she is. Christ—' he
sounded suddenly, viciously irritable – 'Stop gawping
at me! What's done's done, and you can't pretend you
won't be damned grateful to me when you're free as air
and with money to burn and no dusky charmer wound
round your neck like a goddamned snake! And for a
start, you can get that girl under lock and key – and
hurry up, she looks as if she's going to pass out on us.
Shove her in the lock-up with the boy, there isn't long
to go.'

It was quite true that I wasn't feeling too good. Still
held by John Lethman, I had got as far as the red
lacquer chair, but as soon as he let go of my arm I felt
my knees give way, and collapsed into it, fighting back
the feeling of icy nausea that splashed over me again
and again, alternating with drenching heat. Through
the waves of goose-pimpling sickness I was aware of a
sharp and urgent exchange of words going on over my
head. I didn't catch what John Lethman said, but
Grafton's reaction was violent.

'*What?* What the devil do you mean?'

'I was coming to tell you. The boy's out.'

'That's not possible!'

'It's true. He's out. Gone. No sign.'

I surfaced for a moment. 'Bully for Charles,' I said.

'And,' said John Lethman, 'he'll be back here in an hour or two with every damned flic he can drum up.'

'Back here?' Grafton took him up like lightning. 'You mean *out* – he's right outside?'

'He must be. I found Jassim knocked out, and the main gate open. Of course he didn't know we had the girl here, or—'

'You bloody fool! And you've been wasting time!' This, it seemed, was how Halide's death could now be classed. 'How long has he been gone?'

'Not long, I guess. He'd knocked over his water-jug, and the footprints he'd left from treading in it were still wet when I came to find you.'

'Get the dogs out,' snapped Grafton. 'Go on, get them now. He'll be making for the village, he won't have got far. They'll catch him easily enough, and you can tell Nasirulla it doesn't matter how they pull him down as long as they do it.'

'They probably won't touch him. Don't you remember I told you—?'

'What the hell does that matter? Can't you see, the point is, kill two birds with one stone – get Nasirulla away from the place with the hounds, while we clear up down below. The dogs'll find the boy all right, and if Nasirulla takes a gun . . . He's to be stopped, do you hear me? I suppose Jassim's back on his feet again? Go on, man, hurry, leave this silly bitch, I'll deal with her.

And get back here as fast as you can and help me with the job below stairs.'

I made a grab at John Lethman's sleeve as he turned to go.

'Don't leave me with that little swine, for goodness' sake! Can't you see he's gone overboard? Halide, and now Charles . . . and you – can't you see you haven't a chance?' I gripped his arm, shaking it. It was like pleading with a zombie. 'Look, I know you've only been doing as he made you! You'd nothing to do with Halide's death! If you let Charles go, and get me out of here, I swear I'll stand up for you and tell them—'

'Get,' said Grafton, and John Lethman pulled himself free and went.

Grafton jerked his head at me. 'Come on. Get going.'

'Where to?'

'Back to your cage, my girl.'

I gripped the arms of my chair until the lacquer scored my palms. 'Not back in there with her?'

'By no means, we'll be busy there, didn't you hear? You can have the official dungeon this time, but don't think you'll get out of it, even if your cousin did.'

I began to get slowly to my feet, helping myself by the chair arms. The swimming nausea had cleared and I was steady enough, but I still can't have looked much to reckon with, for he had obviously dismissed me from a mind leaping ahead to the next – and major – move.

'Come on, don't waste my time. Get moving.'

I got moving. I shoved myself suddenly upright, and the heavy chair away from me with a jerk that sent it skating across the marble tiles between Grafton and myself. I ran the other way, towards the bed. Up the steps, across the dais, then I jumped on to the foot of the bed itself and yanked the rifle down from the wall.

I swung round, unsteady on the soft bed, bracing my shoulders against the wall, and had the thing levelled at his midriff before he had done more than take three strides after me.

I had no idea if the gun were loaded. I thought it probably wasn't, but Henry Grafton might not be sure. And you have to be very sure indeed to risk outfacing a gun. You only call a gun's bluff once.

He checked, as I had known he would, 'Put that damned thing down, it isn't loaded.'

'Are you sure?'

'Quite sure.'

Outside, suddenly, the hounds bayed wildly from the court where Nasirulla was presumably loosing them in the fond hope that they would pull Charles down. I laughed in Henry Grafton's face.

'Then come and get me,' I invited.

He didn't move. I laughed again, and keeping the rifle at the ready, put out a hand to the wall to steady myself as I stepped down from the bed.

And suddenly there it was again, the wave of heat, the choking nausea, the sweat and the stopped breathing. I groped for a fold of the arras and hung on, dimly aware of the rifle sinking forgotten to the trail, of Grafton hesitating momentarily before taking a step towards me, of the baying of the dogs wild and loud, of someone shouting.

I pulled myself upright. But it was too late. He was on me. He snatched the rifle from my slack hands, checked the empty magazine, kicked it under the bed, and with a vicious swing of the hand to the side of my head sent me sprawling across the bed just as the grey cat, spitting furiously, erupted from the blankets like a rocket on blast-off, and cleared me with a centimetre to spare and every hair on its body brushing my face.

I screamed. Grafton shouted something and I think he made a grab for me, but I had gone beyond fear or even thought of him. Caught up in my own private nightmare, fighting not the cat but my own terror, I struck out at him with feet and hands as I jack-knifed away towards the far side of the bed.

From the garden outside came a sudden volley of noise, a hoarse shout, a scrabble of racing paws, then the inhuman yell of a terrified cat, drowned in the wild exciting tumult of hounds sighting a kill. The cat shot back into the room, a hissing grey streak, and after it the salukis, full cry, with a broken leash trailing from one collar, and Nasirulla in loud pursuit.

The cat leaped for the bed hangings. The hounds saw it, and hurled themselves after it. The heavy chair went flying, crashed into the table, and toppled, smashing the lamp in a sprayed arc of oil. The flame ran along it like ball-lightning. Grafton yelled something, dragged a blanket from the bed, jumped clear down the dais steps, dodging the dogs, slipped in the burning oil and went down, striking his head hard on the stone edge of the table, Over my head the cat leaped like a silver bird for the high window sill, and was gone.

It all seemed to happen in seconds. The flames ran, clawed out, rippled, caught the bed hangings, and went licking up them in great lapping gulps of flame. I rolled off the bed, fighting clear of the curtains, and hurled myself into the quiet dimness of the corridor beyond. The last thing I saw as the arras swung back behind me was the Arab bending to drag Grafton clear towards the other door.

The hounds came with me. Sofi, whining with fear, scrambled through the arras and went tumbling anyhow down the steps. The dog was at the foot of the staircase already. I slammed the door and raced down after them.

'Here!' I called breathlessly. 'This way! Here!' And we ran on, down the curved corridor, past the room where poor Halide lay, through the still air already sharp with smoke – and there was the Prince's Door.

My hands were shaking, and twice the dogs, leaping in eager fear, shoved me aside before I could lift the heavy latch. Then I had it open, and we were through. It swung easily, massive and silent. It might make a lock on that dead air, and check the fire. I slammed it shut and drove the latch home. Then turned, to find that there was fire outside as well . . .

Or so I thought, for one heart-stopping moment, as I saw the outer passage lit and flickering before me. Then I saw why. This, too, had been illuminated for the night's work. The ancient brackets to either side of the Prince's Door held makeshift torches which flared suddenly, red and smoking. It must have been this smoke I had smelled in the corridor as I ran.

I hung there, irresolute, gasping, while the hounds whined and shivered and stayed close. The caravan was due soon, and presumably by the postern. But I had heard Halide say that the postern was locked and the key out of it. It would have to be the main gate, and chance it.

I ran up the passage to my right, and had stumbled perhaps some twenty yards on the rough and ill-lit cobbles when Sofi whined again and I heard, clearly ahead of me, a turmoil of shouts from the main court. I stopped dead. Of course they would all be there: Grafton, Lethman, Nasirulla, Jassim – go that way, and I would run into them all. What was more, if they had any hopes of salvaging their precious cargo, this was the way they would come at any moment now. And even with the whole rotten place going up like tinder round them I wouldn't have betted a pin on any of them doing other than throw me straight back into the flames.

I ran back to the door for the Seraglio stairs.

It opened, and we tumbled through. Darkness dropped over us like a velvet drape, stifling, silent, terrifying. I shut the door behind me and took two hesitating steps forward, then stumbled over the bottom stair and fell, hurting my shin. One of the dogs whimpered, pressing close. Under the silky coat the hot skin shivered. On my other side a narrow head nudged me, and I felt for the beast's collar and got to my feet. With one hand on the collar, and the other groping for the handrail on the outer wall of the staircase, I began to fumble my way up the spiral.

'Show me the way, mates,' I whispered.

The dogs thrust upwards so eagerly that I realised they could see even here. I wondered if they smelled water. I could almost smell it myself. The thought of that great sheet of water lying above our heads was no longer terrifying; it was the bright, cool promise of safety. With the big hound pulling me, and my left hand groping past the invisible minarets, the cypresses, the singing-birds, I stumbled and panted up the spiral stair. Then the bitch, leaping ahead, pushed open the painted doorway, and the three of us ran out into the night air, and the light.

But the night air smelled of smoke, and the light was red and gold and leaping. I ran with the dogs down the pavilion steps, and paused at the edge of the water.

Through all the buildings to the west of the lake, it seemed, ran the fire. The old rotten wood, crumbling dry, had caught like tinder in the night breeze, and as I stood there, afraid and dismayed, a stream of sparks like a comet's tail blew clear across the lake and scattered along the arcade to the east, near Charles's window, and began to burn.

18

'But not against the flame shall they shade or
help you.'

The Koran: Sura LXXVII

One thing the fire did; the place was as bright as day.
There was still a chance I could get into the junk-room
under the eastern arcade, find the rope, and sling it
down from the window before the flames took hold. As
for the dogs – as far as I could afford to think about
them at all – I certainly couldn't lower them from the
window, rope or no rope, but they were in the safest
place in the palace. They had only to take to the water.

I ran on to the bridge, the dogs pressing close to me –
so close indeed that when we got to the broken span
Sofi jumped first, and Star, pushing forward to follow,
shoved against my legs and threw me off balance. I
slipped, tried to recover, cried out as I trod on some
stone not quite secure, and went into the water.

I suppose it was about four feet deep. I went right in,
down under the lilies and the shiny lily-pads and the
floating weeds, before I struggled to the surface and
stood again, ankle deep in mud and breast deep in
water, with my hair streaming weed across my face,

and the hounds gazing at me, curious and excited, from the bridge.

Then Sofi, with a little yelp of excitement, plunged in beside me. Star, inevitably, followed. They swam round and round, with little whining barks, splashing and clawing, avid to be near me, and completely ignoring my distracted croaks of command as I tried to push them away among the creaking irises, and began myself to flap and struggle out through the clotted lily-leaves.

But not to the arcade. The few minutes I had lost through my accident had cost me access to the junk-room. Flakes of blazing stuff – straw or rags – had blown across the water and ignited the roof at several more points. Most of it was wooden shingles bleached dry for generations, and covered with creepers already brittle with coming summer heat. The honeysuckle went up like straw, and all along the arcade burning fragments fell or were blown like fire-arrows to start fresh buds of flame. A veil of smoke wavered across the junk-room door.

Even the garden was burning now. Here and there patches of the drier scrub smouldered, and at the tip of one young cypress, where some flying tinder had lodged, a brush of flame hovered like St Elmo's fire. The smoke was aromatic with blazing herbs.

The northern arcade was still clear, but without the rope I knew the window was useless to me. Useless, too, the gate out into the buildings. There was only one thing for me to do, what the dogs had already made me do, take to the water. But I didn't think I needed to do it yet. The island was safe enough for the time being, most of its plants too moist with the abundant water to catch fire easily. And I, thanks to the dogs, was in the same case. I reached the built-up shore and clambered out. The hounds, dripping, scrambled after me. They shook themselves over me straight away, of course, and the water flew from them like showers of liquid fire, so fierce now was the light.

I pushed my way up through the tangle of cool green bushes, and reached the pavilion steps. Smoke swirled in a sudden eddy, making me cough, but it fanned away and the air was clear. I ran up the last steps into the comparative shelter of the pavilion, then my legs gave way at last, and I sat down on the top step, with the dogs crouched close to me for comfort, and we had time to be afraid.

The hounds were really scared now, and huddled close, one on either side of me, shivering. I had an arm round each of them. Now and again some stream of sparks blew across the lake. The sky all around was ringed with fire, vivid tongues and spires and meteors of fire, so that the stars which swarmed thick and glittering overhead seemed cold and infinitely distant. Through the bright heart of the flames shot flashing pulses of blue and purple and green, and the noise they made was like the galloping of wild horses with the wind in their manes. There was very little smoke, and what there was streamed mercifully away in the light winds that fanned the blaze. The lake was a sheet of melted copper, so bright that it hurt the eye, with red and gold and silver flying through the stiff black spears of the irises, till the very water seemed alive, rippling and beating with flame like the sky.

I rubbed my stinging eyes to dispel the illusion. But when I looked again I saw that it was true. The water was moving, and not with the wind. This garden was a pocket of calm overleapt by the winds, but in it, the water was moving, alive with spearhead ripples as the creatures of the garden, driven by the fire, came arrowing towards the island.

The peacocks came first. The two hens flew, clumsily and in panic, from stone to stone of the broken bridge, but the cock, weighted by the magnificence of his springtime tail, came noisily yelling across the open lake, half paddling, half flying, his great useless wings flailing the golden water, his streaming train bedraggled with mud and damp and laying a wake like a VC 10; then the three big birds, oblivious of me and the hounds, raced with hunched and staring feathers up the rocky shore, and clucked to an uneasy roost near us on the marble steps.

The little rock partridges flew more easily. There were seven of them round my feet, fluffy with fear, their bright eyes winking like rubies as they stared at the flames that ringed the garden. In the flashing scarlet light their feathers shone like chased metal. One of them quivered warm against my ankle.

I didn't even see the squirrels till one slid up the steps beside me and sat bolt upright, chittering and bedraggled, within six inches of Star. Then I realised that the water was full of heads, little black arrow-tips heading for the island. I suppose there were voles and

shrews and housemice; I saw shadows galore, darting
and squeaking under the evergreens. Rats I certainly
saw, big beasts of every shade of grey and black and
brown, who eyed us askance with bright intelligent eyes
as they shimmied ashore and then streaked for the
safety of the shadows. Lizards darted and weaved up
the stones like something in an alcoholic's dream, and I
saw two snakes within a handspan of my shoes; they
lowered their beautiful deadly heads and went past like
smoke, and the dogs never moved, and nor did I. I
hadn't room for fear of them, or they of me; the only
thing that mattered was the fire. All of us, rats, birds,
snakes, dogs and girl, had a right to that island until the
danger was past. The hounds never even moved when
one rat went clean across my feet and brushed its way
through the silk of Sofi's tail.

A dove fell, out of the sky. The birds of the air were
safe enough, they had been blown away on the first hot
draught of air. But one grey dove fell, a wing damaged
or slightly singed, almost into my hands. It came down
like a badly made paper dart, sidelong and drifting, to
flutter between my feet, and I leaned forward between
the hounds and lifted it, then sat holding it gently.
Below my feet I thought that even the water nearest the
island boiled and bulged with fish, as the carp crowded
away from the bright edges of the lake towards the
quiet centre. I could see them just under the surface,
bright darts and gleams of gilt and glowing firecoal red.

And above the noise of the galloping flames was the
noise of the animals. The dogs whined, the peacocks
vented their harsh, scared cry, the partridges crooned

in panic, the rats and squirrels chittered and squealed,
and I said at distressingly frequent intervals, as I
hugged Sofi and Star close to me: 'Oh, Charles . . .
Oh, Charles . . . Oh, for heaven's sake, *Charles* . . .'

We hardly even noticed the heavy splash from the
north-east corner of the lake, or saw the violent run and
ripple of the melted-gold wake as the black head
speared straight for the island. I sat and rocked and
crooned comfort and held the grey dove and put my
cheek to Star's damp head and wondered how soon I
would have to crawl down to the water's edge and
plunge myself in again among the jostling fish.

The creature, whatever it was, had reached the
island. It broke from the water, tossed a black lock
of hair, and heaved itself ashore. Then it stood upright,
and resolved itself into my cousin, dripping and plas-
tered with weed, and dressed in the sodden drapes of
what could only be a pair of baggy Arab cotton trousers
girded up with a gilt belt, a pair of soggy Arab sandals,
and nothing else at all.

He advanced to the bottom of the steps, and
regarded me and the menagerie.

'Eve in the Garden of Eden. Hullo, love. But did you
have to set the bloody place on fire to fetch me back?'

'Charles.' It was all I could say. The dogs whined and
wriggled and stayed close to me, and Sofi waved her wet
tail. Half a dozen lizards whipped out of the way as he ran
up the steps, and when he stopped in front of us a quail
moved a couple of inches aside to get out of the drips. I
looked up at him. 'It wasn't me,' I said rather waveringly,
'the dogs did it. They knocked a lamp over. And I

thought you'd gone, they said you'd escaped. They – they had me locked up . . . oh, Charles, darling . . .'

'Christy.'

I don't remember his moving, but one moment he was standing there in front of me, with the firelight sliding in lovely slabs of rose and violet over his wet skin; the next he was down beside me on the marble floor, and Star was elbowed out of the way, and Charles's arms were round me and he was kissing me in an intense, starving, furious way that somehow seemed part of the fire, as I suppose it was. They say that this is how fear and relief can take you. I know I went down to him like wax.

We were thrust apart by the wet jealous head of Star, and then Charles, with a laughing curse, rolled aside from Sofi's eager paws and tongue.

'Hey, pax, that's enough – hell's teeth, will you call your beastly dogs off? Why do you have to hole up with a zoo? Oh, dear heaven, and that peacock's filthy, and I've rolled all over its tail . . . Shove over, mate, will you? I've only known the girl twenty-two years, you might give me a chance. When did I last kiss you, Christabel?'

'You'd be about ten. You've changed.'

'You must tell me sometime . . .'

It was a lizard, dropping from the dome, that shook us apart this time. He swore, swiped at it as it shot away unhurt, and sat up.

'Christy, I love you, and I could spend the rest of my life making love to you and probably will, but if we're going, the sooner we go the better, *nicht wahr*?'

'What? What did you say?'

'I said we ought to go.'

'Yes. I love you, too. Did I say?'

'You made it plain,' he said. 'Oh Christy, love . . . *Christy!*'

'What?'

His grip on me changed, as it were, and it was no longer my lover, but my cousin Charles who took me by the shoulders and shook me. 'Pull yourself together! Darling, are you doped, or what?'

'I'm all right.'

'We've got to get out of here while there's still a chance!'

'Oh . . . Yes, let's.' I sat up and blinked at the leaping flames. 'But how? Unless you can fly? Oh, the sadist you are, you've nearly squashed my dove . . . No, there it goes, thank goodness, it must only have been doped with smoke.' I started to get up. 'Mind the squirrel, won't you?'

He laughed. 'Is that what it is? Oh, and look at all the dear little rats. Come on!' He jumped up and pulled me to my feet and held me for a moment, steadying me. 'Don't look so scared. We'd be safe enough here, probably, if we had to stay, but it might get a bit hot and uncomfortable before it dies down, so we'll have a bash at getting out straight away. There's only one possible way out, and we'd best be quick about it.'

'What way? We'll never get down from the window now, because we'd never get at the rope, and I couldn't make it without one, I really couldn't—'

'It's all right, darling, I didn't mean the window. I meant the postern.'

'But the corridor'll be going like a torch! The fire started in the Prince's room, you know.'

'Even so, I doubt if it will. The shaft back there—' nodding at the painted door – 'would act as a chimney if the underground passage really were going up, and it shows no sign of it. Come and let's look.'

He pulled the door open cautiously. The smell of smoke was no stronger here than elsewhere, and the spiral shaft was pitch dark. Behind me, Sofi whined deep in her throat, and I made a comforting sound and touched her. 'You'll come too. Don't worry.'

My cousin turned his head. 'Was the big door shut, the bronze one to the Prince's corridor?'

'Yes, I shut it. I came that way. I thought it would seal off the draught.'

'You have your moments, don't you? And the air in there was so dead that it may only be burning slowly down from the Prince's room. We'll have to try it, anyway.'

'But even if the passage is all right, we can't get to the main court – the fire's there too by now – you can see it! And it's no good trying the postern, Charles, it's locked, and the key's out, they said so. And even you surely can't pick locks in the dark?'

'Not to worry, I've got the key.' He grinned at my look, fishing somewhere in the tatty off-white trousers, and producing a ring of keys that gleamed and rattled. 'What do you bet it's one of these? I snitched it off poor old Jassim when I made a break for it. They were no use for getting back in with, because they bolt the gates as well here, but if one of these fits the postern we'll get out.' He stopped short with his hand on the door. 'Look, before we go down you'd better dip a hankie or something in the lake to hold over your mouth if the smoke's bad. Come on, it won't take a moment.'

'Have you got something?'

'Half a trouser leg will do for me if I can tear the things.'

We ran down the steps. 'Where did you get that Carnaby Street rig anyway?' I asked.

'Oh, it's quite a saga, I'll tell you about it later. I suppose they're Jassim's, but never mind, they've had a dip now and only smell of weeds and water-mint and lovely mud. I only hope I can tear the beastly things, they're still damp and as tough as hell . . . There, that's it. What the well-dressed refugee is wearing. While you're about it I'd splash a bit more water over yourself, too . . .'

It was like kneeling by a lake of liquid fire, but the water was cool and sharply restorative. Its flickering reflection caught Charles's laughing face and brilliant eyes. I laughed back at him. It was impossible to be afraid. A light, almost wild exhilaration seemed to possess me, something sharp and positive and clear, the aftermath of a far more powerful drug than any Grafton had given me.

He jumped to his feet. 'That's better, shall we go?' We ran up the steps. Most of the small animals and birds seemed to have dispersed into the cool shadows of the bushes, or among the wet growth at the water's edge. 'This way, my lovely lady Christabel; give me your wet little hand. If anyone had told me when I had to share the bath with you twenty years ago . . .' A pause while we negotiated the threshold of the painted door. This was made no easier by the fact that he held me all the time, and I him . . . 'Though as a matter of fact I don't think I had any doubt even then. It's just been a case of taking the air here and there for a few years till the true north pulled, and here we are. D'you feel like that?'

'Always did. When I saw you in Straight Street, the bells went off like a burglar alarm and I thought "Well, really, here he is at last."'

'As easy as that. Are you all right? There is a bit of smoke after all.'

There was in fact a good deal. If it had been possible to feel fear any more, I might have felt it then. As we crept down the spiral stair – slowly because we had no light and even a twisted ankle might have meant disaster – the heat grew palpable, and smoke met us, the real thing, acrid and heavy and scraping the lungs like a hot file. The dogs whined at our heels. Nothing else had followed us.

'Will they be all right – the animals?' I asked, coughing.

'Should be. There's always the water if things get desperate, Once the fire's out and the place is cool again, the birds will be able to get out into the valley, and I'm afraid I'm not just terribly concerned about the rats and mice. Hold it, here's the door. Let's see what's cooking outside.'

He pulled it open cautiously. More smoke came wreathing in, and with it a red and sullen light, that flickered. He shut it quickly.

'Hell's delight! It looks as though we may have to try the window after all. We can—'

'Perhaps it's only the torches they lit for the fun and games tonight,' I said quickly. 'They frightened me to death when I came this way before. There's one just outside.'

He inched the door open again and craned through, and I heard his grunt of relief. 'You're right, praise be to Allah, that's all it is. Our luck's in. The smoke's seeping under the Prince's door like floodwater, but no fire.' He pulled me through and let the door swing shut after the dogs. 'Come on, darling, we'll run for it. Thank God to be able to see. Can you make it?'

'Of course. Let's just hope we don't run smack into the caravan.'

'The camels are coming, yoho, yoho . . . Don't worry about that, love, I tell you our luck's in – and it's going to hold.'

And it did. Two minutes later, after a terrifying run along a passageway hot and choking and blind with smoke, we reached the postern, and while Charles fumbled with the lock I felt for and dragged back the heavy bolts. Then the key clicked sweetly in the oiled wards, and he pulled the door open.

The hounds brushed past us. Ahead was clear air, and the cool rustle of trees. My cousin's arm came round me and more or less scooped me up the rocky ramp and on to the clean rock under the trees. The postern door clanged to behind us, and shut us out of Dar Ibrahim.

19

Only then did I notice the shouting. Not the noise from the direction of the *midan*, of which I had been vaguely conscious all the time, but a new uproar, as of an excited crowd, which came from beyond the west wall where the main gate stood.

With the hounds trotting, sober now, beside us, we picked our way through the dancing shadows of the trees and along under the rear wall. The shade it cast was inky black, the night sky above it fierce as a red dawn.

At the corner of the Seraglio, below Charles's window, we paused to reconnoitre. There seemed to be no one about. We ran across the path and into the belt of trees which overhung the Nahr el-Sal'q. High above us I could hear the cry of some wheeling birds, jackdaws, I think, flushed from the burning walls. Far down at the foot of the cliff I saw, through the stem of the trees, the red gleam of the river, this time dyed by the fire.

We paused in the darkness of the sycamore grove. There was smoke, thin and stinging, in the air, but it smelled fresh after the garden. Charles held me close.

'You're shivering. Are you cold?'

'Not a bit, not yet, there hasn't been time – and you must admit it was warm enough in there! Charles, the shouting. Ought we to go and help?'

'Not the slightest need,' he said shortly. 'Apart from the fact that I don't give a damn if Grafton and Lethman are both crisped to a cinder, half the village is there already by the sound of it, and with the place going up like a torch, any minute now they'll be running sight-seeing buses from Beirut. And there's the little fact that nobody came to look for you. Let them burn. But for heaven's sake, what were you doing back in there? You were supposed to be miles away and as innocent as the day. What happened?'

'They brought me back.' As briefly as I could I told him my story, cutting through his shocked comments with a quick: 'But you? What made you come back for me? How did you know I was there?'

'Darling, I heard you, screeching like a diesel train just before the place went up in smoke.'

'You'd have screeched if you'd been me, let me tell you! But never mind that now – how did you get in? They said you'd escaped by the main gate.'

'I had. They tried to dope me with their filthy pot, and I filled the place with smoke and pretended to be stoned, and poor old Jassim fell for it and I clobbered him and got out. The only trouble was that when they laid me out first and locked me up they took my clothes

. . . I can't imagine why Lethman thought that would stop me from getting out if I could find a way, but it seems he did.'

'He probably wanted them to wear. He went up to drive your car away, you know, and he'd want to look like you if anyone saw him.'

'I suppose so. He might in that case have left me with something more than an old blanket for the duration. And I rather cared for that shirt, blast him. Well, I took Jassim's keys off him and hurtled out of my little pad in a state of nature, and grabbed a few dreary-looking garments that were lying about in the gate-house. Don't you like them? I took what you might laughingly call the bare minimum, and ran for it. I knew if anyone followed me they'd go straight down by the ford, so I doubled round the back, this way, under the Seraglio windows. Big deal. There went our hero, stark naked, with his pants in his hand, and leaping like a grasshopper every time he trod on a thistle.'

'My poor lamb. Still, you wouldn't be the first.'

'What? Oh, storming the Seraglio. Sure . . . Well, I stopped under the trees to put the pants on. As a matter of fact there was a shirt and a *kaffiyeh* as well, if only I could find them . . . then I heard you scream. Did that so-and-so hurt you?'

'Not really. It was the cat I was screaming at, not him. Go on, I want to hear about you. How did you get back in?'

He had been casting about under the trees while we talked, and now pounced on something with a soft exclamation of satisfaction. 'Here they are . . . I sup-

pose I shall be thankful of this shirt, such as it is, before
the night's out . . . Where was I? Oh, under the
Seraglio windows – just about here, in fact – when I
heard you scream. I tore into the pants and shoes and
belted back to the main gate, but they'd barred it again.
While I was trying it, all hell broke loose inside the
palace, and then I smelled the smoke. I imagined that if
the fire was bad they'd open the gate, but even so I
didn't fancy our chances, so I ran round here again. I
knew the postern had been bolted again after they
caught me, so I didn't waste time trying it; I simply
ran round to that window and climbed in. It's not a bad
climb at all.'

'Not bad!' It was the first time I had seen it from
outside. I stared up at the sheer black wall. 'It looks
impossible!'

'Not for your big brave cousin. Anyway, I knew you
were in the garden, because when I was half-way up I
heard you swearing at the dogs, and as soon as I got in I
saw the Noah's Ark act on the island. That's all . . . I
wish Jassim's wardrobe ran to socks – there's nothing
more disgusting than wet sandals. Look, why don't you
put the head-cloth round your shoulders? It's not too
filthy, and at least it's dry. Let me tie it . . . What's this
round your neck?'

'Oh, I forgot I'd put it on. It's a charm I got for you
against the Evil Eye. You wanted one for your car, you
said.'

'For my love, I said. You'd better keep it, it seems to
work . . . There. Now you're almost up to my standards.'

'Flattery will get you nowhere.'

'I'm not flattering, you look wonderful. There's some weed in your hair, and that frock looks as if it had been poured over you out of a dirty jug, and your eyes are as big as mill-wheels and as black as outer space.'

'I've been smoking their filthy pot, that's why.'

'*Du vrai?*' he asked. 'I thought as much. Nice?'

'Hellish. You think it's rather pleasant and you stop worrying about things, and then suddenly you find your bones have sort of rotted from inside and your brain's made from old rags and you can't even think. Oh, Charles, it was so awful, they're dealing in the stuff . . . they've been planning for months—'

'Darling, I know. Lethman told me quite a lot, probably more than he realised. Did you know he was a junkie?'

'Grafton told me. I ought to have guessed from the way he looks sometimes, but I never thought about it. Did he tell you Great-Aunt H was dead?'

'I knew that.'

I stared. 'You mean you knew it all along? Was that what you were making all the mystery about?'

'I'm afraid so.'

'How did you find out?'

'Guessed, to begin with. Didn't you ever know that she had your cat phobia? Full blast and all the stops out?'

'*Did* she? I don't think I ever knew that. We never had a cat at home, of course, so when she stayed with us the subject wouldn't come up. Yes, I see now. I suppose as soon as I told you "she" had a cat in her room you knew there must be something wrong. But Grafton would know, surely?'

'He can't have realised the cat was in the room that night. More likely he never even thought about it. They may have always had stableyard cats – must have, now that I think of the rat population of the Seraglio – but in Aunt H's day they'd never have invaded that room.'

'Because of the dogs?'

'One imagines so. From the way these terrifying brutes behave with you and me' – he indicated Star and Sofi, who grinned amiably, feathering their tails – 'they were probably treated as pets with the run of the place, and I know Samson always slept on her bed, and he was death on cats. If "the doctor" was scared of the dogs and shut them up, then the inevitable would happen . . . Let's get somewhere where we can see, shall we?'

We began to pick our way along the stony cliff-top through the thickest part of the grove.

'Yes, go on.'

'Well, the cat business made me think there was something decidedly off-key somewhere, so I made up my mind to get in and look around and find out what, if anything, had happened to the real Aunt H. The fact that Lethman and Co. had let you wander around the place indicated that she wasn't hidden there. I thought she must be dead. Then when I got in and saw her things were left lying about derelict – the Koran and the Dogs of Fo – and that Samson had died and apparently not been buried properly with the benefit of clergy along with the other dogs, I was sure of it. So after you'd gone off to bed that night I went snooping back, and you know what happened; I got caught and knocked out and locked up and that was that. Here we are, steady, hang on to those dogs and don't let anyone see you. My God!'

We had reached the corner now, and we could see.

The scene was like something from a coloured film of epic proportions. The walls towered black and jagged against the leaping flames behind them, and one high roof, burning fiercely, was now nothing but a crumbling grid of beams, Windows pulsed with light. With every gust of the breeze great clouds of pale smoke, filled with sparks, rolled down and burst over the crowd which besieged the main gate, and the Arabs scattered, shouting and cursing and laughing with excitement, only to bunch again nearer the gate as the cloud dispersed. The gate was open; both the tall double leaves stood wide, and there was a coming and going of men through the general mêlée which indicated that some salvage work was going on – and also that Grafton would be lucky if he saw any of the salvaged goods again.

It was to be presumed that the remaining inmates of the palace were safe: the mules had certainly been got out; here and there among the crowd I saw the wicked heads tossing, the fire-light bright on teeth and eyeballs, as the loot piled up on the glossy backs, and yelling Arabs fought for the head-ropes. Then I saw the chestnut horse, its coat as bright as fire, and someone who could only be John Lethman at its head.

He was dragging something – some cloth or blanket – from the beast's head. He must have had to muffle its eyes and nostrils to get it out of the burning stable. It was fighting him, jibbing and terrified, as he tried to pull it clear of the crowd.

I clutched Charles's arm. 'Lethman's there! He's got the horse out. Charles, he's mounting! He'll get away!'

'Let him go. He can't do a thing. Grafton's the one – hullo, look, they're stopping him.'

Lethman, astride the chestnut, was fighting with knees, whip and head-rope to turn it for the corner where we stood hidden, and the track past the Seraglio wall to the open hillside and freedom. The animal, its ears laid flat back on its skull, whirled plunging in the dust, and the crowd scattered in front of it – all but one man, and he ran in under the vicious hooves and jumped for the head-rope and held it fast. He was shouting something at John Lethman. I saw the latter throw out an arm, pointing back to the blazing building, and he yelled something, his voice suddenly clear and powerful above the excited roar of the crowd. Faces turned to him like leaves when the wind blows through them. He brought his whip slashing down at the man below him, and drove the chestnut forward at full gallop towards the grove where we stood.

The Arab, struck by the beast's shoulder, was sent flying. As he rolled clean over, and came unhurt in one swift bunching movement to his feet, I saw that it was Nasirulla. Two or three other men had started, vainly, to run after John Lethman. One of them, yelling like a dervish, waved a shotgun. Nasirulla snatched it from him, whirled, levelled it, and shot.

But the chestnut was already out of range round the palace wall. It went by within a few feet of us. I never even saw John Lethman's face; he was just a crouching shadow against the bright mane, gone with a crash and sparkle of hoofs and the horse's snorting terror.

Nor did I notice at what moment Star and Sofi left us. I thought I saw two shadows, swifter than the horse and far more silent, whip through the trees to vanish in its dust, and when I looked round the hounds had gone.

The shot harmlessly chipped the masonry at the corner of the palace. The men who were running our way hesitated, saw it was no use, and milled aimlessly about, shouting.

'I think that's our cue to go, my love,' said Charles in my ear. 'Any minute now and they'll all be coming to look for a way round the back.'

'Wait . . . look!'

What happened next was almost too quick to understand, and certainly too quick to describe.

Nasirulla had hardly paused to see if his shot had gone home. While plaster still scaled from the bullet-marks on the wall he turned and shoved his way back towards the gate. The others crowded back with him.

Then we saw Henry Grafton. The knock on the head had obviously not incapacitated him for long, and apparently he had been organising the salvage oper-ations. As the crowd by the gate eddied and momen-tarily thinned I saw him, just emerging past the gatehouse, his arms full.

One or two men ran forward, presumably to help him. Another tugged one of the mules nearer. Then Nasirulla yelled something, high and clear, and I saw the crowd check again, and men turning. There must have been women there; I heard one screaming something that sounded like invective. Grafton paused, staggering a little as the man who had taken half his load abandoned it suddenly and left him. Nasirulla ran forward, still yelling, and as Grafton turned to face him, flung the gun up at a range of perhaps ten yards, and fired again.

Grafton fell. As he dropped the load and went slowly, how slowly, forward over it, the Arab swung the gun butt uppermost, and ran forward, and the crowd with him.

Charles pulled me back under the trees.

'No. No. There's nothing you can do. He's dead, quite certainly. We'll get the hell out of here, Christy my girl, before that bunch of J. Arthur Rank extras really gets going.'

I was shaking so much that for a moment I could only cling, and say through chattering teeth: 'It was Nasirulla. I suppose – was it because of Halide?'

'Sure to be. Nasirulla may have tried to salvage the stockpile before Grafton could stop him, and found the body. Or he may simply have been asking Lethman if she'd got out, and what we just saw was Lethman passing the buck. Hold up, sweetheart, I think we can get down to the ford this way. Can you make it? Let's get the hell out, shall we? Arab mobs are not exactly my thing at the best of times, and I doubt if this lot found us here if they'd stop to listen to my elegant literary Arabic. It's all right for you, they'd only rape you, but I don't want to be castrated the day I get engaged.'

'That's my big brave cousin.' The little spurt of laughter I gave was more than half hysterical, but it steadied me. He took my hand, and together, by the light of the now dwindling fire, we made our way down the cliff path, across the river still running scarlet for Adonis, and gained the safe shadows of the far valley side.

20

My dog brought by Kings from Saluq.
                    Ancient Arabian Poem

It was noon next day. The high hot sun poured into the village street. We sat on the low wall that bordered the graveyard, waiting for the car to take us to Beirut.

It was already difficult to remember clearly what had happened last night after we had left the scene of the fire. I had no recollection of the climb up the path to the village. I must have accomplished it on some emergency high-octane mixture of reaction, love, and residual hashish fumes. The only memory I retain to this day is some queer detached nightmare of staring eyes and neat hoofs pattering like rain and the smell of goat, as (Charles tells me) we disturbed the sleeping flock, and from some invisible corner the faun tore himself from a fascinated grandstand view of the fire to offer his entirely practical help as escort up to the village.

It was he who piloted us at length through the deserted streets to a house near the far end, set slightly apart behind a terrace of apple-trees. No light showed, but a woman was awake and peering half fearfully out of the door at the fire which still spurted among the smoking ruins across the valley.

The boy shouted a greeting, and then a flood of what must have been explanation. I was too dazed by now and too tired to care what was said or what happened, just so that I could get out of my damp and filthy clothes, and lie down somewhere and sleep.

Charles's arms lifted me up the steep rough steps of the terrace. He must have been as tired as I, because I seem to remember that he paused to collect himself before trying to speak to the woman in Arabic. Some minutes later, after an exchange helped out (from somewhere out of sight) by the faun, we were taken into the house; and there, behind the curtain which divided the single room, I undressed by the light of a small yellowish candle which spluttered as it burned, wrapped myself in some loose cotton garment which came from a box in the corner and which smelled clean, lay down on a bed of blankets which did not, and was almost immediately asleep. The last thing I remember was my cousin's voice, softly talking in his slow Arabic, and waiting – as I found out later – for the headman, the woman's husband, to come home from the fire.

So all the explanations had been made. Henry Grafton was dead – had died mercifully enough from the shot – and Lethman had vanished clear away into the High Lebanon. I never heard or cared overmuch what happened to him. He was gone, faceless and shadowy as the night-hunter with his horse and his Gabriel Hounds, as much a victim as poor Halide of Grafton's single-minded greed. The girl's body had been recovered. Some freak of breeze and fire had left the underground corridor more or less undamaged, and with it the contents of the storeroom, which the police, arriving with the dawn light, found mysteriously depleted but still well worth impounding and investigating.

Our turn came next. We had answered the first round of questions this morning, and now the police were down on the plateau where the palace ruins stuck up on their crag like a blackened tooth, still idly smoking. From the height where we sat we could just see the gleam of the lake, calm and jewel-like, with its unburned frame of green. The plateau and the charred ruins scurried with movement, like a corpse full of maggots, where – presumably dodging the police with some ease – looters prodded about the wreckage.

At length I stirred. 'I wonder if she'd have liked to know we were here?'

'From what I remember of the old dear,' said Charles crisply, 'she'd have been delighted to know she'd taken the whole place up with her – and laughed like a banshee to see you and me scurrying about in the lake with the rats and mice. Well, at least those hounds of hers put a nice flourish on the end of her legend. Talk about a funeral pyre. Nobody in the Lebanon will ever forget her now.'

'It certainly looks as if most of the local households will have a souvenir or two,' I said dryly. 'And your own "Gabriel Hounds", Charles? If the storerooms didn't burn they may still be there.'

'They'd hardly survive that.' He nodded at the scene below us. 'Anyway, I'm damned if I'll compete with those jackals and go raking among the ruins. Some day I'll find another pair, and buy them in memory of her. Ah, well . . .'

Some children, too small to be in the schoolroom or the looting party, came running by, kicking a tin, and stopped to play in the dirt under the graveyard wall. Two or three thin dogs skulked by, sniffing for scraps. A three-year-old boy threw a stone at the smallest of them, and it swerved automatically and dodged behind a rusty oil drum. A dirty white cockerel padded past, intent on a tattered brown hen.

'Love is everywhere,' said Charles. 'Which reminds me, Christy love—'

What it reminded him of I never knew, and have never asked him. With a gush of diesel smoke and a squeal of brakes, a tourist coach drew up not fifty yards from where we sat, and the driver turned in his seat to point across to the ruins of Dar Ibrahim before he killed the engine and dismounted to open the door. The passengers piled out, English, a party who knew one another and talked and laughed as they trod forward in twos and threes to the edge of the valley and stared down at the smoking ruins. Cameras clicked. I could hear the driver telling someone a version of last night's story. The legend was on its way.

Charles and I sat still. The children, retreating from the strangers, backed till they stood right beside us. The small dog, its long hair filthy and tousled like a wilting chrysanthemum, crept out from behind the oil-drum and watched with bright avid eyes a biscuit which one of the women was eating.

Her friend, a stout lady in a wide straw hat and sensible jersey suit, lowered her camera and looked about her.

'A pity it's not a more appetising village.' She had a splendidly carrying middle-class voice. 'The mosque's quite pretty, though. I wonder if they'd mind if I took a photograph?'

'Offer them something.'

'Oh, it's not worth it. You remember how horrible that man was in Baalbek, the old chap with the camel? *He* looks as if he could make himself quite unpleasant, too. Look at the way he's staring.'

'Layabouts, the lot of them. It's a wonder she isn't slaving in the fields to keep the children. Look at them all, and hardly a year between them. Rather revolting. He'd be quite good-looking, too, if he were clean.'

It was only then, as I felt Charles quiver beside me, that I realised who they were talking about. Actually he was as clean as cold water and a gourd full of Omo could make him; but he hadn't shaved for two days, and he still only wore the grubby cotton trousers girdled with a cheap and cracking gilt belt, and a shirt which exposed more than it covered of his brown chest. My frock had dried remarkably filthy, and my bare legs were scratched and bruised and hadn't answered terribly well to the Omo. The dip in the lake had done my sandals no good at all. The red checked *kaffiyeh* Charles had given me last night covered what was left of my very Western hair-do, and Great-Aunt

Harriet's ruby looked like Woolworth's last word on my hand.

I felt my mouth drop open, but Charles said under his breath, 'Don't spoil it,' and the women were already turning away.

'It's not worth it anyway,' the thin one was saying, 'there'll be better places. Oh, look, they're going. Well, what a stroke of luck seeing that! What did you say the place was called?'

She put the last of the biscuit into her mouth and wiped her fingers on a handkerchief. The children looked disappointed, and the small dog's ears sank, but she never noticed. The coach drove off. The children threw a few stones after it, then turned on the small dog again, till Charles clicked his fingers and said something to it in Arabic, and it came slinking to hide behind his legs.

'And they were dead right,' I said indignantly. 'Layabout's the word. Sitting there laughing! You might at least have *begged* or something! We could do with some cash! If the police don't give us a lift after all—'

'Then we'll walk, you trailing suitably in my wake with your children. Hullo, here's another car coming. More police, do you suppose? It can't be for us, it must be a top brass, a car like that.'

'It looks like a taxi. Do you suppose they'd take us on credit if we told them we were staying at the Phoenicia?'

'Not a chance. The way we look they wouldn't let us set foot in it.'

'Oh, I don't know, you'd be quite good-looking if you were clean.'

'My God.' Charles, who had been in the act of rising, sank back on the wall. At the far end of the village street the big glossy car had slid to a stop behind a gaggle of police vehicles. The driver dismounted to open the rear door, and a man got out, a tall man, unmistakably English as to tailoring, and unmistakably self-assured as to bearing.

'Father!' exclaimed Charles.

'Daddy!' I cried at the same moment.

'It's my father,' said my cousin, 'not yours. After I telephoned home from Damascus he must have decided—'

'It's not your father, it's mine. I telephoned from Beirut, and he must have caught last night's plane. D'you think I don't know my own father when I see him?'

'Want a bet? Hullo, Father!'

'Hullo, Daddy!'

The newcomer, for his part, had identified us even at that distance with unerring eye. He came our way, not hurrying. We stayed where we were.

He stopped in front of us, surveying us. 'My God.' The intonation was so exactly Charles's own that I was shaken, and screwed up my eyes against the sun to see him better.

'Give you twenty to one?' said Charles in my ear.

'N-no.' Whichever it was, he had come. It was absurd and un-adult to feel such a pleased rush of relief and pleasure.

He was still surveying us. If he felt the same way, he concealed it very well. 'My poor children. Well, I'm very glad to see you. I won't say it's a relief to see how well you've brushed through what's happened, because I have never seen you look worse, but I take it it's nothing that a bath won't put right? No?' His eyes went beyond us, to Dar Ibrahim across the valley. 'So that's the place?' He watched the distant scene for perhaps half a minute, without comment. Then he turned back to us. 'All right, you can tell me the whole thing later on, but I'll get you back to Beirut now, and into those baths, before I do anything else. I've squared the police; they say you can come, and they'll see you again later.'

'I suppose you know what's happened?' said Charles.

'Roughly. Nobody's talking about anything else in Beirut. I gather you two young idiots got into some nasty doings up to your necks. What the devil were you about to let Christy in for, Charles?'

'Unjust, unjust,' said Charles, without heat. 'The stupid girl got herself into a jam and I rescued her. Wait till her own father hears the story, I'm demanding a hero's welcome and his half of the kingdom. Incidentally, you might settle a bet for us, and tell her it's only you.'

'It's a wise child.' He smiled down at me, lifting an eyebrow. 'Actually, I don't think I particularly want to lay claim to either of you at the moment.'

My cousin uncurled from the wall. 'You're going to have to lay claim to both. One of us wants your consent and the other your welcome or blessing or whatever, you can take your pick which.'

'So? I'm very glad. Welcome, darling.' He put an arm round me and hugged me to him, reaching the other hand to my cousin. 'Congratulations, boy, we were beginning to think you'd never make it. Certainly far more than you deserve.' And he kissed us both in turn.

My cousin grinned at me. 'Well?'

'You win, of course. You always do. Oh, Uncle Chas, its wonderful to see you!' I hugged him again. 'Thank you for coming! Couldn't Daddy make it?'

'Afraid not. He sent me as deputy. You look a bit battered, child, are you sure you're all right?'

'Oh, yes, truly! And it's true Charles looked after me. Real hero stuff, too, wait till you hear!'

'This seems the right moment to tell you,' said Charles, 'that I lost the Porsche.'

'So I gather. It's at the Phoenicia.'

'Efficient devil you are,' said his son admiringly. 'How did you do that?'

'Christy's driver brought it back.'

'Hamid!' I cried. 'Oh, thank goodness! What happened to him?'

'The man who had stolen Charles's car was a bit too zealous with it, and ran it off the road at a bend. No, Charles, it's all right, a scratch or two, that's all; it simply went wide into the shale and bogged down. Hamid was right on its tail, and managed to lay the man out before he'd quite realised what had happened. You'll be able to thank him yourself – he's here, he drove me up.'

'Is that his taxi?' I asked. 'They all look alike, I didn't recognise it. Oh, that's marvellous! Do you think we could go now?'

'Why not?' He turned to look again, a longer look this time, at Dar Ibrahim. There was a pause. It was very quiet. The children had long since abandoned us to go and talk to Hamid, and now the little dog, perhaps encouraged by the silence, ventured out of hiding and crept across the space of dust to my uncle's feet. At length the latter turned. 'Well . . . that's the end of a long story. When you're both rested you can tell me all about it, and Charles can come back with me when the excitement's died down a bit. For the moment, you two had certainly better try to forget it. Leave it to me.' He stretched out a hand to me. 'Come along, child, you look tired out . . . What in the world—?' As he turned to go, he had almost tripped over the little dog, tangled and shapeless as a dirty mop, crouching flat at his feet in the dust. Through the filthy hair an eye shone out eagerly. An apology for a tail wagged furiously. 'Not yours, surely?'

'Good grief, no,' said Charles. 'It's one of these miserable village dogs.'

'Then do you mind discouraging the poor little beast? I'm afraid we can't – what is it?' This as Charles, who had stooped obediently to pull the dog aside, let out an exclamation.

'Believe it or not, it's got a collar on' – I peered over my cousin's shoulder as he disentangled the collar from the dirty hair – 'and a label. Yes, there's something printed. Its life hath had some smatch of honour in it

. . . If there's an address, then it's genuinely lost, poor little beast, and perhaps we can return it. Any dog in this country that achieves a collar must be one of the aristoc—' He stopped dead.

'One of the what?'

Then I saw the name printed on the collar. SAMSON.

Charles looked up. 'He knew our voices.' His voice was so dry that I knew he felt as I did, absurdly moved. 'He recognised us, me and Father. Some smatch of honour, by heck. He must have run away after she died, or more likely that little swine threw him out to starve.'

'Do you know the dog after all?' asked his father.

'Indeed, yes.' Charles had swung the little creature up, and now tucked him under one arm. 'And quarantine'll seem like the Phoenicia to him after this.'

'Quarantine? You're surely never thinking of taking that living mophead home?'

'Mophead nothing,' said my cousin. 'Don't you remember Samson? This is Great-Aunt Harriet's wedding present to me. Father, My personal Gabriel Hound. We can hardly leave him here to fend for himself; he's one of the family.'

Hamid, all smiles, was at the door of the car. I got into the back seat between the two men. Charles's arm held me close and my head went down on his shoulder.

The little dog and I were both fast asleep before the car had covered the first mile to Beirut.

Now read on for a taste of Mary Stewart's next tale
of adventure and suspense.

◆

TOUCH NOT THE CAT

I

It is my soul that calls upon my name.

Romeo and Juliet, II, ii

My lover came to me on the last night in April, with a message and a warning that sent me home to him. Put like that, it sounds strange, though it is exactly what happened. When I try to explain, it will no doubt sound stranger still. Let me put it all down in order.

I was working in Funchal, Madeira. Funchal is the main town of that lovely Atlantic island, and, in spite of its having been a port of call for almost every ship that has crossed the ocean since some time in the fourteenth century, the town is still small and charming, its steep alleys tumbling down the lava slopes of the island's mountain spine, its streets full of flowers and trees, its very pavements made of patterned mosaic which glistens in the sun. I was working as receptionist and tourist guide at one of the new hotels east of the town. This sounds an easy job, but isn't; in tourist time, which in Madeira is almost the whole year, it is hard indeed; but what had led me to apply for the job was that very few

qualifications seemed to be needed by a 'Young lady
of good appearance, willing to work long hours'.
Both these qualifications were mine; appearance was
just about all I'd got, and I would have worked any
hours to make some money. Whether I was the best
for the job I don't know, but it happened that the
people who owned the hotel had known my father,
so I was hired. The old-boy network they call it.
Well, it works, as often as not. You may not get the
brightest and the best, but you do get someone who
talks your own language, and who is usually someone
you can get back at the way it will hurt, if they let
you down.

It's barely a year since the things happened that I
am writing about, but I find that I am already thinking
of my father as if he were long gone, part of the past.
As he is now; but on that warm April night in Madeira
when my love told me to go and see him, Daddy was
alive, just.

I didn't sleep in the hotel. The friends who owned
it had a quinta, a country estate a few kilometres out
of Funchal, where the pine woods slope down the
mountains towards the sea. You reached the place by
a lane which led off the Machico road, a steep grey
ribbon of lava setts, bordered in summer with blue
and white agapanthus standing cool against the
pine woods, their stems vibrating in the draught of
the running water in the levada at the road's edge.
The house was big and rather ornate in the Portuguese
style, standing in wide grounds full of flowers and
carefully watered grass and every imaginable exotic

shrub and flowering tree, dramatically set against the cool background of mountain pines. The owners lived there all winter, but at the beginning of April, most years, went back to England to their house in Herefordshire which lay just across the Malvern Hills from ours. They were in England now, and the quinta was shuttered, but I lived in what they called the garden house. This was a plain, single-storey building at the foot of the garden. Its walls were pink-washed like those of the big house, and inside it was simple and bare – scrubbed floors and big echoing grey-walled rooms slatted all day against the sun, beautifully quiet and airy, and smelling of sunburned pines and lemon blossom. My bedroom window opened on one of the camellia avenues which led downhill towards the lily pools where frogs croaked and splashed all night. By the end of April the camellias are just about over, the browned blossoms swept away, almost as they drop, by the immaculate Portuguese gardeners; but the Judas trees are in flower, and the Angel's Trumpets, and the wisteria, all fighting their way up through a dreamer's mixture of cloudy blossom where every season's flowers flourish (it seems) all year. And the roses are out. Not roses such as we have at home; roses need their cold winter's rest, and here, forced as they are into perpetual flower by the climate, they grow pale and slack-petalled, on thin, over-supple stems. There were roses on the wall of the garden house, moonbursts of some white, loose-globed flower which showered half across my bedroom window. The breeze that blew the rainclouds from time to time across the moonlight tossed the shadows of the roses over wall and ceiling again and again, each time the same and yet each time different, as the roses moved and the petals loosened to the breeze.

I was still awake when he came. He had not been to me for so long that at first I hardly recognised what was happening. It was just my name, softly, moving and fading through the empty room as the rose shadows moved and faded.

Bryony. Bryony. Bryony Ashley.

'Yes?' I found I had said it aloud, as if words were needed. Then I came fully awake, and knew where I was and who was talking to me. I turned over on my back, staring up at the high ceiling of that empty room where the moonlit shadows, in a still pause, hung motionless and insubstantial. As insubstantial as the lover who filled the night-time room with his presence, and my mind with his voice.

Bryony. At last. Listen . . . Are you listening?

This is not how it came through, of course. That is hard to describe, if not downright impossible. It comes through neither in words nor in pictures, but – I can't put it any better – in sudden blocks of intelligence that are thrust into one's mind and slotted and locked there, the way a printer locks the lines into place, and there is the page with all its meanings for you to read. With these thought-patterns the whole page comes through at once; I suppose it may be like block-reading, though I have never tried that. They say it comes with practice. Well, he and I had had all our lives to practise; I had known him all my twenty-two years, and he (this much I could tell about him) was not much older.

I suppose that when we were children we must both have stumbled and made mistakes, as normal children do with reading, but I cannot remember a time when we couldn't confront each other, mind to mind, with ease. To begin with it seemed like sharing dreams, or having (as I believe is common among children) an imaginary companion who shared everything with me, and who was more real even than the cousins who lived near us, or than my friends at school. But, unlike most children, I never spoke about him. I don't think this was through fear of ridicule or disbelief; the experience was something I took very much for granted; but somehow, imposed over those thought-patterns, was a censor which wouldn't allow me to share him with anyone else, even my parents. And the same censor must have worked with him. Never by the smallest sign or faltering of the patterns did he let me know who he was, though, from the shared memories that we had, I knew he must be someone close to me, and it was a safe bet that he was one of my Ashley cousins, who had played with me at Ashley Court daily when I was a child, and who had later on shared almost every holiday. It's a gift that goes in families, and there were records that it ran in ours: ever since the Elizabeth Ashley who was burned at the stake in 1623, there had been a record, necessarily secret, of strange 'seeings' and thought-transference between members of the family. By the same token my lover knew me, since I was the only Ashley girl, and for the last year or so had addressed me flatly as 'Bryony'. There again, I only use the name for convenience; you might almost say he called me 'You', but in a manner which identified me fully. In return I called him 'Ashley', in an attempt to make him identify himself. He never did, but accepted the name as he had accepted 'Boy' and sometimes, in unwary moments, 'Love', with the same guarded and gentle amusement with which he parried every attempt I had lately made to force him to identify himself. All I could get from him was the assurance that when the time was right we would know each other openly; but until that time we must be close only in thought.

I know I haven't explained this well, but then it is a thing I have known all my life, and that I gather very few people know at all. When I was old enough to see the gift as something unique and secret, I tried to read about it, but all that could be found under headings like *Telepathy* or *Thought-transference* never seemed quite to tally with this easy private line of communication that we owned. In the end I gave up trying to analyse the experience, and went back to accepting it as I had done when a child. Though I gathered from my reading that gifts like this could be uncomfortable, and had been in times past downright dangerous, it had never worried me to possess it. Indeed, I could hardly imagine life without it. I don't even know when he became a lover as well as a companion; a change in the thought patterns, I suppose, as unmistakable as the changes in one's body. And if it seems absurd that one should need and offer love without knowing the body one offers it to, I suppose that unconsciously the body dictates a need which the mind supplies. With us the minds translated our need into vivid and holding patterns which were exchanged and accepted without question, and – since bodily responses were not involved – rather comfortably.

It was probable that when we met and knew one another physically it would be less simple, but at the moment there seemed to be no prospect of this. You can't, out of the blue, ask a second cousin who has given no hint of it: 'Are you the Ashley who talks to me privately?' I did once try to probe. I asked Francis, the youngest of my three cousins, if he ever had dreams of people so vivid that he confused them with reality. He shook his head, apparently without interest, and changed the subject. So I summoned up my courage to ask the twins, who were my seniors by almost four years. When I spoke to James, the younger of the two, he gave me a strange look, but said no, and he must have told Emory, his twin, because Emory started probing at me in his turn. Full of questions he was, and rather excited, but somehow in the wrong way, the way the psychical research people were when Rob Granger, the farmer's son at home, said he'd seen a ghostly priest walking through the walls of Ashley church, and everyone thought it might be Cardinal Wolsey who was there as a young man; but it turned out to be the Vicar going down in his dressing-gown to pick up the spectacles he'd left behind in the vestry.

My lover says – and he said it in clear only yesterday – that I have got so used to communicating in thought-blocks that I am not good with words any more. I never get to the point, he tells me, and if I did I couldn't stick there. But I shall have to try, if I am to write down the full story of the strange things that happened at Ashley Court a year ago. Write it I must, for reasons which will be made plain later, and to do that I suppose I ought to start by saying something about the family. What I have written so far makes us sound like something from a dubious old melodrama – which would not be far wrong, because the family is as old as Noah, and I suppose you could say it's as rotten as a water-logged Ark. Not a bad simile, because Ashley Court, our home, is a moated manor that was built piecemeal by a series of owners from the Saxons on, none of whom had heard of damp courses; but it is very beautiful, and brings in something over two thousand a year, not counting outgoings, from the twenty-five-penny tourists, God bless them.

The family goes back further even than the oldest bits of the house. There was an Ashley – tradition says he was called Almeric of the Spears, which in Anglo-Saxon is pronounced something like 'Asher' – who fled in front of the Danes when they came raiding up the Severn in the tenth century, and established his family in the densely forested land near the foot of the Malvern Hills. There had been settlers there before; it was said that when the British, earlier still, had fled in front of the Saxons, they had lived on like ghosts in the fragments of a Roman house built where a curve of the river let the sunlight in. Of this early settlement there was no trace except the remains of some tile kilns half a mile from the house. The Saxons dug a moat and led the river into it, and holed up safely until the Conquest. The Saxon Ashley was killed in the fighting, and the incoming Norman took his widow and the land, built a stone keep on the island and a drawbridge to serve it, then took the name as well, and settled down to rear Ashley children who were all, probably to his fury, fair and pale-skinned and tall, and Saxon to the bone. The Ashleys have always had a talent for retaining just what they wanted to retain, while adapting immediately and without effort to the winning side. The Vicar of Bray must have been a close relation. We were Catholics right up to Henry VIII, then when the Great Whore got him we built a priest's hole and kept it tenanted until we saw which side the wafer was buttered, and then somehow there we were under Elizabeth, staunch Protestants and bricking up the priest's hole, and learning the Thirty-nine Articles off by heart, probably aloud. None of us got chopped, right through Bloody Mary, but that's the Ashleys for you. Opportunists. Rotten turncoats. We bend with the wind of change – and we stay at Ashley. Even in the nineteen-seventies, with no coat left to turn, and with everything loaded against us, we stayed. The only difference was, we lived in the cottage instead of the Court.

Nothing is left now of the formal gardens, which had once been beautiful, but which I had never known as other than neglected, with the wild, tanglewood charm of a Sleeping Beauty backdrop. The lovely, crumbling old house on its moated island, and the wilderness surrounding, were all that was left of an estate which had once been half a county wide, but which by my father's time had shrunk to a strip of land along the river, the gardens themselves, the buildings of what had once been a prosperous home farm, and a churchyard. I think the church officially belonged as well, but Jonathan Ashley – my father – didn't insist on this. The church stood in its green graveyard just beside our main drive gates, and when I was a little girl I used to believe that the bells were ringing right in the tops of our lime trees. To this day the scent of lime blossom brings back to me the church bells ringing, and the sight of the rooks going up into the air like smuts blown from a bonfire.

This was all that was left of the grounds laid out by the Cavalier Ashley. He, incidentally, must have been the only Cavalier throughout England who did not melt the family silver down for Charles I. He wouldn't, of course. I suspect that the only reason his family didn't officially turn Roundhead was because of the clothes and the haircut. Anyway, they saved the Court twice over, because my father sent most of the silver to Christie's in 1950, and we lived on it, and kept the place up after a fashion until I was seven or eight years old. Then we moved into one wing of the house, and opened the rest up to the public. A few years later, after my mother died, Daddy and I moved out altogether, to live in the gardener's cottage, a pretty little place at the edge of the apple orchard, with a tiny garden fronting on the lake that drained the moat. Our wing of the Court was put in the hands of our lawyer to let if he could. We had been lucky in this, and our most recent lessee was an American businessman who, with his family, had been in residence for the past half year. We had not met the Underhills ourselves, because, eight months before the April night when my story starts, my father, who had a rheumatic heart, contracted a bad bronchitis, and after he recovered from this, his doctor urged him to go away for a spell in a drier climate. I was working in an antique shop in Ashbury at the time. We sold a bit more of the silver, shut the cottage up, and went to Bad Tölz, a little spa town in Bavaria, pleasantly situated on the River Isar. My father had often been there as a young man, visiting a friend of his, one Walther Gothard, who now had a considerable reputation as a *Kur-Doktor*, and had turned his house into a sanatorium. Daddy went there simply to rest, and to be cared for by Herr Gothard who, for old times' sake, took him cheaply. I stayed for a month, but he mended so rapidly in that air that it was impossible to worry any more, so, when the Madeira job was suggested, I was easily persuaded to go. Even my lover, when I asked him, said there was nothing to go home for. I only half liked this kind of reassurance, but it was true that none of my cousins was at Ashley, and the cottage in winter and the damps of early spring looked lonely and uninviting; so in the end I took the job, and went off happily enough to the sun and flowers of Funchal,

with no idea in the world that I would never see my
father alive again.

Bryony?

Yes. I'm awake. What is it? But the trouble was there
already, in the room. It settled over me in a formless
way, like a fog; no colour, neither dark nor light, no
smell, no sound; just a clenching tension of pain and
the fear of death. The sweat sprang hot on my skin,
and the sheet scraped under my nails. I sat up.

*I've got it, I think. It's Daddy . . . He must have been
taken ill again.*

*Yes. There's something wrong. I can't tell more than
that, but you ought to go.*

I didn't stop then to wonder how he knew. There
was only room for just the one thing, the distress
and urgency, soon to be transmuted into action; the
telephone, the airfield, the ghastly slow journey to
be faced . . . It only crossed my mind fleetingly then
to wonder if my father himself had the Ashley gift:
he had never given me a hint of it, but then neither
had I told him about myself. Had he been 'read' by
my lover, or even been in touch with him . . . ? But
there was denial stamped on the dark. With the
denial came over a kind of uncertainty, puzzlement
with an element of extra doubt running through it,
like a thread of the wrong colour through a piece of
weaving.

But it didn't matter how, and through whom it
had got to him. It had reached him, and now it had
reached me.

Can you read me, Bryony? You're a long way off.

Yes. I can read you. I'll go . . . I'll go straight away,
tomorrow – today? There was a flight at eight; they
would surely take me . . . Then urgently, projecting it
with everything I had: *Love?*

It was fading. *Yes?*

Will you be there?

Again denial printed on the dark; denial, regret,
fading . . .

Oh God, I said soundlessly. *When?*

Something else came through then, strongly
through the fading death cloud, shouldering it aside;
comfort and love, as old-fashioned as pot-pourri and
as sweet and sane and haunting. It was as if the rose
shadows on the ceiling were showering their scent
down into the empty room. Then there was nothing
left but the shadows. I was alone.

I threw the sheet off and knotted a robe round me,
and ran for the telephone.

As I put a hand on it, it began to ring.

Ashley, 1835.

He stood at the window, looking out into the darkness.
Would she come tonight? Perhaps, if she had heard
the news, she would think he could not be here,
waiting for her; and indeed, for very decency, he surely
ought not to have come . . .

He scowled, chewing his lip. What, after all, was a
little more scandal? And this was their last time – the
last time it would be like this. Tomorrow was for

the world, the angry voices, the laughter, the cold wind. Tonight was still their own.

He glanced across in the direction of the Court. The upper storeys showed, above the hedges, as a featureless bulk of shadow against a windy sky. No lights. No lights showing anywhere. His eye lingered on the south wing, where the old man lay behind a darkened window.

Something like a shudder shook him. He tugged at his neck-cloth, and found his hand shaking. She must come. Dear God, she had to come. He could not face the night without her. His longing, stronger even than desire, possessed him. He could almost feel the call going out, to bring her to him through the dark.